WHERE SHALL
WISDOM
BE FOUND?

SUSAN E. SCHREINER

WHERE SHALL WISDOM BE FOUND?

Calvin's Exegesis of Job from Medieval
and Modern Perspectives

THE UNIVERSITY OF CHICAGO PRESS
CHICAGO AND LONDON

Susan E. Schreiner is associate professor of church history and theology in the Divinity School at the University of Chicago

The University of Chicago Press, Chicago 60637
The University of Chicago Press, Ltd., London
© 1994 by The University of Chicago
All rights reserved. Published 1994
Printed in the United States of America

03 02 01 00 99 98 97 96 95 94   5 4 3 2 1

ISBN (cloth): 0-226-74043-9

Library of Congress Cataloging-in-Publication Data

Schreiner, Susan Elizabeth.
    Where shall wisdom be found? : Calvin's exigesis of Job from
medieval and modern perspectives / Susan E. Schreiner.
        p.   cm.
    Includes bibliographical references and index.
    ISBN 0-226-74043-9 (alk. paper)
    1. Bible. O.T. Job—Criticism, interpretation, etc.—History.
2. Calvin, Jean, 1509–1564. Sermons sur le livre de Job. 3. Bible.
O.T. Job—Sermons. I. Title.
BS1415.2.S335 1994
223′. 106′092—dc20   93-30301
                                                            CIP

This Book is Dedicated to

Nancy Tamulewicz

who
by her courage, wit, and intelligence
has always exemplified how to suffer well

CONTENTS

Acknowledgments
ix

Introduction
1

I
WHERE IS THE PLACE OF UNDERSTANDING?
The Coherence of Gregory's *Moralia in Iob*
22

II
THE EXULTING OF THE WICKED IS SHORT
Maimonides and Aquinas on Job
55

III
DOES GOD PERVERT JUSTICE?
Suffering and Justice in Calvin's *Sermons on Job*
91

IV
BEHOLD BEHEMOTH!
Nature and History in Calvin's *Sermons on Job*
121

V
MODERN READINGS OF JOB
156

Abbreviations
191

Notes
193

Index
259

ACKNOWLEDGMENTS

I am deeply indebted to the National Endowment for the Humanities for the award of a year-long grant for independent study and research, which made the writing of this book possible. Sections of the first, third, and fourth chapters appeared in somewhat different forms in *The American Benedictine Review*, *Church History*, *Calvin Theological Journal*, and *The Voice from the Whirlwind*. They are reprinted here by permission of the editors.

I also want to thank the following people for reading and commenting on all or part of the manuscript: Jerry Brauer, Clark Gilpin, Peter Homans, Bernard McGinn, Richard Muller, David Tracy, Kathleen Waller. Gregory Robbins read and helped edit the text with care and patience. As chair of the History of Exegesis section at the Society of Biblical Literature, he also helped shepherd this project through its earliest stages. I also would like to thank Curtis Bochanyin and Christina Bailey, librarians at Regenstein Library, who cheerfully helped me locate obscure and often difficult bibliographical data and texts. Lys Ann Shore, editor for the University of Chicago Press, deserves more appreciation than I can express. Her expertise in medieval studies, her editing skills, and her warm encouragement are ultimately responsible for bringing this book to publication. I owe a special note of thanks to David Steinmetz for his reading of the manuscript and for his own work on the history of exegesis, which has influenced many students in this field.

I also want to thank many of these same scholars as well as other friends for their personal help. Perhaps there was something about working on the Book of Job that sent me into one state of melancholia after another and called for the help of my friends while bringing this manuscript to completion. But unlike Job's friends, mine were true comforters with real advice. My parents were always present with encouragement. My sister Rebecca and her children, Manuel and Raquel, were a source of inspiration, aid, and laughter. In spite of their own illnesses and difficulties, my sister Deborah and her daughter, Karla, lent emotional support. And, finally, a second note of thanks to Clark Gilpin, David Tracy, David Steinmetz, Gregory Robbins, Jerry Brauer, Richard Muller, and Kathleen Waller for their endless patience, help, and humor. This book is dedicated to a childhood friend, Nancy Tamulewicz, who, despite great adversity and suffering, has always exemplified the highest wisdom found in the pages of this manuscript.

INTRODUCTION

Now I realized that not infrequently books speak of books: it is as if they spoke among themselves. In the light of this reflection, the library seemed all the more disturbing to me. It was then the place of a long, centuries-old murmuring, an imperceptible dialogue between one parchment and another, a living thing, a receptacle of powers not to be ruled by a human mind, a treasure of secrets emanated by many minds, surviving the death of those who had produced them or had been their conveyors.

Umberto Eco, *The Name of the Rose*

A PAWN IN a contest about which he knew nothing, the beneficiary of "friendly" advice he refused to accept, the target of suffering he could not understand, and a victim in a universe that threatened to overwhelm him, Job has been a man for all ages. Ever since the biblical era, the legend of Job has been part of the collective memory of the West and one of the defining myths of our civilization. The man on the dungheap repeatedly raised questions that would haunt the ages that followed him. The Hebrew Bible, the New Testament, and the Qur'an all testify to the powerful appeal of the Joban legend. Wherever we turn in the history of Western thought we find Job: The Talmud, ath-Tha'labi's "Discourse of the Prophet of God Ayyub and His Trials," and William Blake's illustrations demonstrate the enduring fascination with Job. From Gregory the Great to Franz Kafka the image of Job has challenged every attempt to explain suffering and to justify God's actions. Job belongs to the West; his story has captivated the human imagination and has forced its readers to wrestle with the most painful realities of human existence.

Undoubtedly, then, the Book of Job has attained the status of what Tracy calls a religious classic; in Job's tale the reader experiences a claim to truth that comes from the "power of the whole."[1] Even though Job's "truth" may be deeply disturbing, it has gripped the Western mind. The legend of Job bears the two marks that, according to Tracy, characterize all classics: permanence and the excess of meaning. This book explores that "excess of meaning" by turning to the world of precritical Joban exegesis.[2] As commentators probed the inner dimensions of the story and wrestled with the tensions in the text, Job became for them the personification of many fundamental dimensions of human life. In their commentaries Job symbolizes the layers and depths of suffering, the inexplicability of evil, the incompleteness of human existence, and the

1

noetic nightmare of history. But Job also exemplifies vindication, endurance, and survival, as well as transcendence, insight, and wisdom.

In his book, *The Legend of Job in the Middle Ages*, Besserman identifies three traditions in the history of the Job legend: the biblical, the apocryphal, and the ecclesiastical or liturgical and exegetical uses of Job.[3] In this study I examine the exegetical tradition by retrieving the interpretations of Calvin and his medieval predecessors. Before entering the labyrinthine world of precritical Joban commentaries, however, some preliminary remarks are necessary regarding structure, method, choice of texts, and purpose.

This study focuses on Calvin's *Sermons sur le livre de Job*. These sermons are analyzed against the background of the two trajectories that most influenced the Latin medieval tradition of Joban commentary: the allegorical interpretation of Gregory the Great and the more "literal" exegesis influenced by Maimonides and formulated by Thomas Aquinas. The texts examined in the core of this study, therefore, span the sixth to the sixteenth centuries. They were written in varying historical circumstances, for diverse audiences, by men with different theological and philosophical presuppositions. In chapter 5, which concludes this study, I direct my attention to a wide array of twentieth-century interpretations, including modern biblical commentaries, the work of Jung, and the literary transfigurations by Wells, MacLeish, Wiesel, and Kafka. I argue that the problem of perception is the thread of Ariadne that leads us through a maze of Joban interpretations, ancient and modern. This preoccupation with perception, adumbrated by Gregory in his interpretation of Job and brought to full expression with Calvin, reaches a chilling conclusion in the twentieth century as it wrestles with the same text. I suggest that the history of exegesis is not merely hermeneutical antiquarianism. When we learn how earlier thinkers read the Bible we learn something about how we read the Bible—and we also learn something about ourselves.

This book is intended for three audiences. The primary focus is on the Joban exegesis of John Calvin as found in his 159 *Sermons on Job*. The two central chapters of this book are devoted to Calvin. The first audience, then, is that of Calvin scholars. Nonetheless, this book is not only about Calvin, and the intended audience is wider than that of specialists on Calvin or Reformation studies. The second audience consists of scholars interested in the history of exegesis. Calvin's *Sermons* are best understood when compared to, and placed within, the wider interpretive background of Joban interpretation. The analysis of major commentaries preceding Calvin allows the reader to place his work in an exegetical tradition and to understand his interpretation by means of a comparative method. Furthermore, Calvin's treatment of the per-

ceptual themes in Job foreshadows issues that recur in modern interpretations. By attending to the modern readings of Job, I argue that
there are certain links to the past that shed light on these contemporary interpretations and also underline the importance of Calvin's
achievements and those of his predecessors. My third audience, then,
is one that shares the questions about suffering and human perception
that face modernity.

My study begins with the *Moralia in Iob*. Although Gregory the Great
was not the first thinker to comment on the Book of Job,[4] his *Moralia* became the most influential interpretation of Job's story through the early
and high Middle Ages. It held this place until the thirteenth century,
when Thomas Aquinas wrote his *Expositio super Iob ad litteram*. However,
neither later criticisms of Gregory's allegorization and moralization of
the text nor the influence of Aquinas's literal exegesis succeeded completely in supplanting Gregory's influence. Indeed, the extensive references to the *Moralia* by Denis the Carthusian (d. 1471) attest to the enduring popularity of this work in the later Middle Ages. Even though
Gregory's influence on the medieval exegetical tradition has not always
met with approval, either in his own era or in ours, there is no doubt
that, as de Lubac says, many scholars in the Middle Ages considered him
to be "Gregorius noster" and "sacrae Scripturae lucidissimus expositor."[5]

The *Moralia* was written in the late sixth century, a time characterized
by upheaval and the decline of Italian political and economic structures.[6] Theodoric's rule from 493 to 526 could not stem the deteriora-
tion of the economy. After Theodoric's death Justinian set out to recon-
quer the West in 535. For the next twenty years Italy was subjected to war,
starvation, population loss, the plague, and further economic recession.
The peace Justinian established in 554 was broken in 568 when the Lom-
bards crossed the Alps. Attacks by this fierce tribe were particularly destructive for the church as episcopal sees were repeatedly destroyed. As
T. S. Brown has demonstrated, the late sixth century was a period of social revolution.[7] To Gregory's eye, the world was tumultuous, disordered, and violent. Indeed, Gregory believed that he composed his commentary on Job in a time when the world was coming to an end.[8]

The *Moralia* began in 579–85 as a series of lectures for the monks who
accompanied Gregory to Constantinople. After serving in Constantinople as apocrisiarius for Pope Pelagius II, Gregory returned to Rome
in 586 and was elected abbot of St. Andrew's monastery. It was during
this period that he finished and edited these lectures on Job. In his
prefatory epistle to Leander, Gregory explained that his own illnesses
made him a particularly sympathetic interpreter of Job's story. Divine
providence, he said, had arranged circumstances so that "I as one who
has been stricken should set forth Job who was stricken and that by these

scourges I should more perfectly understand the feelings of one scourged."[9]

Gregory's *Moralia,* then, was intended for a monastic audience. Since he believed that the exposition of Scripture should be suited to the needs of the hearer, it is not surprising that he emphasized the moral and spiritual progress of the sufferer who strives for purification, detachment, and ascent toward God. In the *Moralia* we find a form of biblical interpretation that stresses the allegorical and moral levels of Scripture, searches out the deeper truths buried beneath the letter, discerns spiritual and moral lessons in almost every verse, and perceives exegesis as an instrument for spiritual edification. We also find discussions about suffering, providence, history, and perception, which in varying forms continue to find expression in the history of Joban commentary.

Following the examination of Gregory's *Moralia,* I turn to an analysis of the Joban interpretations by Maimonides and Aquinas. These two thinkers influenced all later Joban exegesis by establishing that the Book of Job was fundamentally about the nature of divine providence. As we shall see, Calvin appropriated several important exegetical arguments from Gregory but followed the Thomistic tradition by identifying the literal interpretation of Job with the doctrine of providence.

Maimonides's reading of Job is found in *The Guide of the Perplexed* and was written during the time he lived in Egypt. Maimonides was born in Córdoba, Spain, in 1135. In his early years he was educated by his father, Rabbi Moses ben Joseph. It is generally assumed that Maimonides and his family left Córdoba in 1148 because, like many Spanish refugees, they were fleeing the Almohad terror.[10] He settled in Fez but in 1165 had to leave Morocco. After a brief stay in Palestine, he finally settled in Fostat (near Cairo).

Life in Egypt was very different from the educated world of Muslim Spain.[11] Maimonides arrived in Egypt when Fatimid rule was disintegrating. In 1171 Saladin overthrew the Fatimid dynasty and restored Sunnite orthodoxy to Egypt. The Jewish population of Egypt was at an all-time high and included a large percentage of immigrants. As Cohen states, "the relatively unlearned middle-class mentality of most Egyptian Jewry stood in bold contrast to that of the refined aristocratic Jewish courtier society that the Maimon family had left behind on the Iberian peninsula."[12] Nonetheless, Maimonides took an active role in this new society. He served as the head of the Jews from 1174 to 1204. Shortly after his arrival in Egypt he received numerous religious questions, and his *responsa* shows that he acted as jurisconsult for the Jews of the country. He also established an academy of higher learning called the "yeshiva of Torah study" where students were expected to study his Mishneh Torah.[13]

By 1190 Maimonides had completed *The Guide of the Perplexed.*[14] This work was intended to instruct the educated Jew who had become troubled by the language and teachings of the sacred writings. As we will see in chapter 2, the intended audience of the *Guide* was individuals who were puzzled by the encounter of metaphysics and the traditional teachings of the Jewish religion. According to Maimonides, the belief in providence exemplified this troubling perplexity. When Maimonides most openly discusses the true nature of providence in book 3 of the *Guide*, he turns to the Book of Job. In Job's story he sees the conflict between the teaching of traditional religion with its emphasis on rewards and punishments and the true wisdom about providence that Job finally attained. Job, then, personifies someone who reaches wisdom by finding the metaphysical truths taught by the *Guide*.

With the *Expositio super Iob ad litteram*, the Latin Christian interpretation of Job moved from the cloister to the world of scholastic theology. Aquinas knew the interpretations of both Gregory and Maimonides. The original audience for his *Expositio* consisted of members of the Dominican priory of San Domenico in Orvieto. According to Weisheipl, Aquinas wrote this commentary at Orvieto between 1261 and 1264.[15] He had spent his earlier professional years in Paris and Naples. He was sententiary in Paris from 1252 to 1256 and regent master in theology at Paris from 1256 to 1259. Late in 1259 Aquinas went to Naples where he worked on his *Summa contra gentiles*. From 1261 to 1265 he was assigned to the cathedral city of Orvieto as lector for San Domenico. He was to lecture to the whole Dominican community on any book of Scripture. Tolomeo of Lucca reports that at this time Aquinas "expounded the Book of Job."[16] After these lectures, he committed his thoughts to writing, adding further source material and citations. The *Expositio* demonstrates the impact or challenge of Jewish and Moslem Aristotelianism but was composed before Aquinas's second regency in Paris (1269–72) when he fully confronted the Averroistic threat. Throughout his time at Naples and Orvieto Aquinas was intensely concerned with the mystery of evil. Book 3 of the *Summa contra gentiles* was written about the same time as the *Expositio super Iob*;[17] both texts address the questions of evil and providence.

As we shall see, the Thomistic Joban interpretation grew in importance, and Calvin, like many other sixteenth-century exegetes, read the story of Job as a book about providence. I have focused my study on Calvin, but the references in the notes to chapters 3 and 4 provide a running commentary by other sixteenth-century Joban exegetes represented by Brenz, Oecolampadius, and Cajetan.

Calvin preached his 159 *Sermons on Job* from February 1554 to March 1555. They were recorded by M. Dennis Raguenier and were published in 1563, the year before Calvin's death.[18] Unlike the *Moralia*, the *Guide*, and the *Expositio,* Calvin's *Sermons* were not composed for monastic or academic audiences. Rather, he intended them for the edification of laypersons in the church. Because Calvin lived and preached during a time of religious, social, and political upheaval, we inevitably ask whether these sermons can provide a glimpse of the religious and social changes of his age. Surely a biblical text about evil, suffering, injustice, and providence would naturally lead Calvin to comment on the events of his time.

Calvin undertook the *Sermons on Job* after having experienced the painful reality of religious persecution and exile.[19] The outbreak of persecution by Francis I led Calvin to Basel, where he arrived in 1535. Passing through Geneva in 1536 he yielded to Guillaume Farel's appeals to stay and organize the Reformation in that city. After his expulsion from Geneva, Calvin returned there in 1541. In following years the city endured illness as well as social and political disturbances. The plague intermittently struck the city between 1542 and 1545.[20] During this period Calvin became embroiled in the political and religious troubles of men such as Pierre Ameaux, Ami Perrin, Jacques Gruet, and, of course, Michael Servetus. He also had to address the tension caused by the increasing numbers of refugees to Geneva. Around 1550 the first great influx of religious refugees entered the city. Both the experience of exile and the internal assaults on the church lie in the background of Calvin's Job sermons. In his preface to the Psalms commentary (published in 1557), Calvin identified with David who also suffered internal attacks on the church. The suffering of David was, to Calvin's mind, repeated in the assaults by the Anabaptists, Jerome Bolsec, the Sacramentarians, and the "fury of the papists."[21]

Are these phenomena of exile, persecution, refugees, political turmoil, and religious dissent evident in the *Sermons on Job?* Certainly we find repeated polemics against Catholic doctrines, such as merit and free will.[22] More important, the *Sermons* reflect Calvin's view of the suffering church. Occasional references are made to those who are persecuting Christians "at the present time." Eliphaz's words in Job 5:15 ("He will save the afflicted from the sword, from the mouth and hand of those who are mightier") led Calvin to describe the members of the reformed church as "sheep among wolves." The enemies of God are of an "infinite number" and the "poor church" could not endure one day unless God delivered it.[23] The same description of the church can be found in Calvin's sermons on Job 14:5–6 and Job 35:4.[24] Moreover, Job 31:35–36 led Calvin to discuss briefly the martyrdom presently suffered at the stake (*posteau*) and the gallows (*potence*).[25] Calvin promised his congregation that God would sanctify these martyrs for the gospel. Commenting on Job 13:3 ("But I want to speak with God and dispute with him"),

Calvin warned his congregation that although they saw the church oppressed by the enemies of religion, they were *not* to dispute or contend with God.[26] In all these examples Calvin easily and irresistibly drew contemporary lessons from the Joban text for those whom he saw as suffering for the truth of the gospel.

Nonetheless, such applications to specific contemporary instances of persecution and unjust suffering are not a major theme in Calvin's Job sermons. Viguié was right when he wrote that in the Job sermons Calvin "rarely made allusion to the events of his day." Comparing Calvin's *Sermons on Job* to his *Quatre sermons traitant de matières fort utiles pour notre temps* (edited in 1552), Viguié concluded that the former offered consolation and courage to the faithful but did not chronicle or describe the "moment tragique de l'histoire de la Réforme," as did the latter.[27] Perhaps one of the reasons Calvin did not more explicitly recount the "tragic moment" of the Reformation had to do with the exegetical principles he applied to the Joban text. Expounding only the literal sense, Calvin did not practice typology and therefore did not make Job a prophet of Christ or a "type" of the suffering, martyred, or exiled church. Many of Calvin's descriptions of the persecuted church were based on the words of Eliphaz and Elihu, not Job. Explicitly portraying Job as the forerunner or type of the suffering endured by the sixteenth-century reformed church was clearly not the primary purpose governing Calvin's exegesis of the Joban text.

The *Sermons* may, however, grant us a deeper glimpse into Calvin's view of his time than is first apparent. As Viguié notes, these sermons express the cry of hope of an afflicted church and offer consolation in the midst of many evils.[28] The *Sermons on Job* was an extremely popular collection and was repeatedly translated and published. Viguié reports, for example, that Gaspard de Coligny read from these sermons every day. They were printed in 1563, again in 1569, and were reprinted in 1611. They were translated into English by Arthur Golding in 1574, and other English editions came out in 1579 and 1584.[29] The consolation offered by these sermons went beyond the interpretation or theological explanation of particular events. The sermons appealed to a suffering church because of their lessons about the divine governance of the world. Calvin explained repeatedly that the Book of Job was written for "our instruction." As the following chapters will show, Calvin's interpretation of Job centered on the inscrutability of divine providence.

For Calvin, Job's story demonstrated the spiritual temptation, anguish, and faith evident during those times when history appears disordered and God's rule cannot be discerned. On the basis of Job's story, Calvin directed his congregation to a God whom they could trust despite the deepest darkness and the most awful of divine silences. This was a message that his congregation surely welcomed. Calvin's task as a preacher and exegete was to create, in the terms of Bellah, a "community of memory."[30] He did so by representing the Joban story as a timeless model or lesson for his hearers. Calvin clearly saw the role of memory involved in his own exegesis and understood preaching as an aid to trust in providence. Therefore, he evoked the past by seeing the Book of Job as a historical work intended for present use or profit. He identified Job's situation as a vehicle for instruction and faith and summoned past sufferers to tell their tales. The stories of sufferers such as Job were not only historical but paradigmatic. It was precisely the paradigmatic nature of that history which gave Job's story its timeless and recurring significance for Calvin's audience.

Perspective of This Study

Having outlined the historical context of these Joban commentaries, I must state that this book is a study in intellectual history. Such an assertion is not easy to make, however, in the midst of present controversies about the nature of historical inquiry. Two such issues have a direct impact on the subject and method of this book: the question of influence and the recent challenges posed by literary critics.

The discipline of intellectual history immediately raises the problem of influence: Did former Joban exegetes play any direct role in Calvin's interpretation? The influence of medieval theology on the development of Calvin's thought has been a disputed point among Reformation historians. Wendel believed it possible that John Mair (d. 1550) taught Calvin to read Peter Lombard's *Sentences* through Ockhamist eyes.[31] Wendel also pointed to various strands in Calvin's theology that appeared to be influenced by Duns Scotus.[32] Reuter argued that Calvin learned a new conception of Scotist and anti-Pelagian theology as well as a renewed Augustinianism through his supposed contact with Mair.[33] Torrance has also argued for various similarities between the epistemologies of Mair and Calvin.[34] Stadtland-Neumann claimed the influence of Thomas Aquinas in his study of Calvin's interpretation of the Sermon on the Mount.[35] Ganoczy has countered some of these claims by showing that the young Calvin demonstrated no knowledge of major scholastic theologians; there is no textual evidence that he read Mair's *Commentary on the Sentences* before 1536. Moreover, Ganoczy maintains, in the 1536 *Institutes* Calvin identified scholastic theology with Gratian and Lombard, not with Thomistic, Scotist, or Ockhamist thought.[36] McGrath, however, has defended Calvin's continuity with certain trends in late medieval theology. Admitting that it is difficult to establish any personal contact between Calvin and John Mair, McGrath argues for the influence of a "general medieval current," which he identifies with Gregory of Rimini and the "schola augustiniana moderna."[37]

In most cases, these scholars have been concerned with the young Calvin and have attempted to establish the intellectual influences on his formative years in Paris. The *Sermons on Job,* however, date from Calvin's later years, by which time we can assume that Calvin had greater knowledge regarding medieval theology. Nonetheless, the question remains whether Calvin knew any of the medieval commentaries on Job. From the *Sermons* we cannot determine exactly whom Calvin had read. He does make references to other explanations that had been given for various words and verses, but he never cites anyone by name. A comparison of these passages to earlier commentaries in both the medieval and early sixteenth-century periods reveals only that Calvin's references are usually general and rather hurried paraphrases of either the Gregorian or Thomistic interpretations.[38]

As this book will show, Calvin did, indeed, know the *general* lines of both the Gregorian and Thomistic traditions. He explicitly rejected the allegorical meanings that stem from the *Moralia.* Like those who stood in the Thomistic tradition, Calvin expounded the literal sense of the text and believed that "literally" the Book of Job is about the doctrine of providence. We shall also see that Calvin appropriated the Thomistic interpretation by using the belief in immortality as a hermeneutical device to explain Job's teaching about providence. Still, Calvin may have known the *Moralia* and the *Expositio* in an indirect manner—that is, mediated through later works, such as the *Glossa ordinaria* or the commentaries by Nicholas of Lyra or Denis the Carthusian.[39] The critical point is that the present study is *not* concerned with questions of influence. I am not interested in charting a line-by-line indebtedness between Calvin and earlier commentators or in establishing Calvin's sources. Oberman's trenchant warnings regarding the pitfalls of *Ahnenforschung* in the *Initia Calvini* can profitably be extended to the present study:

There cannot be any doubt that it is essential to be committed to the close scrutiny of Calvin's late medieval *resources*. But without clear evidence these resources cannot be turned into *sources*. They are listening devices or hermeneutical tools to uncover Calvin's own profile by highlighting—always "zur Stelle" and ad hoc—both continuity and discontinuity. . . . In every such case the interest should be not to construct a pedigree, but rather in showing why and how the medieval backdrop is a pertinent and necessary tool for clarifying a particular passage or complex issue.[40]

The method employed in this study is comparative, not causal. Throughout the first three chapters I have alerted the reader to issues that resurface in Calvin's *Sermons,* but I have not done so with the question of influence in mind. I have analyzed the works by Gregory, Maimonides, and Aquinas independently of Calvin's *Sermons* in the attempt to read these earlier texts on their own terms rather than as conduits to Calvin. A thorough knowledge of the medieval backdrop makes us more keenly aware both of the issues Calvin shared with the medieval tradition as well as those places where Calvin makes a distinctive contribution to Joban interpretation. We will thereby be able to discern the twists and turns that reveal a fresh, if often disturbing, wrestling with the text in light of his own concerns. In short, I compare conclusions reached on the basis of the interpretations of these texts rather than alleged borrowings.

The concentration on texts raises another serious challenge to intellectual history: the "epistemological crisis" caused by developments in literary criticism and the philosophy of language.[41] These discussions affect the subject matter of this book because the history of exegesis is a field that involves us in the increasingly problematic world of interpretation. As Good observes, "reading has become problematic."[42] In recent years the relationship between reader and text has been dissected and found to be enormously ambiguous. The discussion has usually focused on the act of interpretation that takes place when a commentator studies a text. In the history of exegesis this relationship of commentator to text is doubly problematic because in this field we confront *two* hermeneutical levels: I am interpreting texts that are themselves interpretations of the Book of Job. We are, then, embedded in the question of interpretation, and the hermeneutical turn in the human sciences has important implications for the reading of past commentaries.

Novick has shown that the impact of literary criticism on the field of history has been to undermine any remaining allegiance to the ideal of objectivity.[43] The attempt to find fixed or determinate meanings in texts has been eroded by the hermeneutical or linguistic critique of the text, the author, and the reader. In all three instances, the result has been the abandonment of the search for authorial intention.

No one has done more to shake the confidence of historians in the old ideal of objectivity than Gadamer. As Gadamer explained, the goal of Romantic hermeneutics to find authorial intention presupposed the Enlightenment ideal of a mind free from prejudices.[44] Historians were to enter the mind of the author and to transpose themselves into the culture of an earlier age. To this presupposed ideal of objectivity and historical empathy, Gadamer opposed the historicity of understanding. Rejecting the "prejudice against prejudice" inherited from the Enlightenment, Gadamer argued that readers cannot free themselves from their prejudices and thereby recover the mind of the author. Such a shedding of presuppositions is neither possible nor desirable. Presup-

positions or prejudgments are the necessary preconditions for understanding. The language we use and the traditions in which we stand always influence us so that we approach a text from within the "history
of effects." The interaction between the text and this historically conditioned interpreter creates understanding and interpretation. Hence,
Gadamer says, "understanding is, essentially, a historically effected
event."[45]

The attack on objectivity extends both to the reader and to the text.
The reader is involved in the historicity of understanding, while the text
itself has lost the status of "object." The text has also been inserted into
the history of effects and can be encountered now only in terms of the
tradition of its interpretation.[46] The text has been passed down through
its interpretations, which now constitute the historical reality of its being. In Gadamer's view, therefore, a historically conditioned mind confronts a historically conditioned text. The interpretive process that en-
sues should ideally move back and forth like a "game of conversation."
The result is the "fusion of horizons" between the past and the present.[47]
According to Gadamer, "understanding is always the fusion of these horizons supposedly existing by themselves."[48] The truth perceived by this
"fusion" is always the truth seen from the historian's perspective, not an
unprejudiced, detached, or objective reading that captures the mind of
the author.

The understanding that emerges from the process of interpretation
is never identified as authorial intention. Nor is the inability to recover
authorial intention considered a great loss: "Every age has to understand a transmitted text in its own way, for the text belongs to the whole
tradition whose content interests the age and in which it seeks to understand itself. The real meaning of a text, as it speaks to an interpreter,
does not depend on the contingencies of the author and his original
audience . . . Not just occasionally but always the meaning of a text goes
beyond its author."[49]

The forsaking of authorial intention is one point of common consen-
sus in the widely varied contemporary hermeneutical discussions. Texts
have escaped the intention of the author as well as the understanding or
reception of the original audience. Answering the question of what is to
be understood and appropriated in a text, Ricoeur writes, "Not the intention of the author, which is supposed to be hidden behind the text;
not the historical situation common to the author and his original readers; not the expectations or feelings of these original readers; not even
their understanding of themselves as historical and cultural phenomena."[50] Although Ricoeur was not analyzing the nature of historical
methodology, such statements contradict what historians have traditionally considered themselves to be doing. The attempt to equate interpre-

tation with the re-creation of the historical setting or the original meaning of the author has been challenged by the inability of the interpreter
to "reach" the writer. In Ricoeur's analysis, there can be no direct dialogue between reader and writer because the text "eclipses" both parties:

> It does not suffice to say that reading is a dialogue with the author through his
> work, for the relation of the reader to the book is of a completely different na-
> ture. Dialogue is an exchange of questions and answers; there is no exchange
> of this sort between the writer and the reader. The writer does not respond to
> the reader. Rather, the book divides the act of writing and the act of reading into
> two sides, between which there is no communication. The reader is absent from
> the act of writing; the writer is absent from the act of reading. The text thus pro-
> duces a double eclipse of the reader and the writer.[51]

In place of authorial intention, the redactional setting, and the interpretations of the original audience, we are left with only the *text*. In most
cases, therefore, we are left with the phenomenon of the written word.
The "death of the author" has focused attention on the nature of language and writing. As structuralism gave way to poststructuralism, written language came to be seen increasingly as open, indeterminate, and
uncontrollable. Deconstructionists argued that the relationship between signifier and signified was arbitrary; there is no transcendent signifier that firmly anchors meaning.[52] Language is seen as prior to meaning and consequently as capable of both shaping and subverting the
intention of the author. The stability of "reference" is gone, only to be
replaced by the series of signs beyond the power of the author or reader
to control. Poststructuralists like Derrida and the later Barthes deny the
referential and representational capacity of language. Interest is focused rather on the inherent contradictions, indeterminacies, and dis-
continuities in written language so that the meaning in texts is endlessly
deferred. Thus we find what Umberto Eco characterizes as the "infinite
drift of deconstruction": "a semiosis of infinite play, of difference, of the
infinite whirl of interpretations."[53] According to Eco, the most radical
practices of deconstruction "privilege the initiative of the reader and reduce the text to an ambiguous bunch of still unshaped possibilities, thus
transforming texts into mere stimuli for the interpretive drift."[54]
Boundaries become increasingly fluid, and written texts are the intricate
and seemingly endless play of signifiers.
    For historians, particularly intellectual historians, claims about mean-
ing are at stake. Can scholars recover any intentionality or even any determinate meaning in the works they examine? Are texts impenetrable
because of the inherent nature of language or the role of presuppositions? The hermeneutical arguments emanating from literary criticism

have not gone unchallenged.[55] Some authors have simply ignored them. Nevertheless, the impact on historians has been unsettling, and those making authorial or objectivist claims are often defensive. Despite attempts to put a brake on these various interpretive trends, which seem to slide toward the abyss of total relativism, the attack on objectivity marches on and affects all domains of the human sciences. Anthropologist Clifford Geertz characterized the fear produced by these discussions when he mocked the defenders of objectivity who were "afraid that reality is going to go away unless we believe very hard in it."[56]

The analyses of language and texts caused many historians to debate the nature of the historical task. Three examples must suffice as evidence of this struggle to reconceive the nature of history after the linguistic turn: Foucault, White, and LaCapra. I consider these complex figures only insofar as their writings illustrate themes central to this study: perception, perspective, and the problematic nature of transcendence, knowledge, and meaning. These themes govern precritical Joban commentaries and resurface in the modern Joban interpretations examined in chapter 5.

When Foucault died in 1984, he left a corpus of writings that made him a troubling figure to interpret. O'Brien argues that Foucault's work is "an alternative model for writing the history of culture, a model that embodies a fundamental critique of Marxist and Annaliste analysis, of social history itself."[57] This judgment must be balanced by White's insight that Foucault is an "antihistorical historian" who "writes 'history' in order to destroy it, as a discipline, as a mode of consciousness, and a mode of (social) existence."[58] Foucault's analyses of discourse and history have called forth accusations that he is a nihilist, a fatalist, an irrationalist, and an exponent of epistemological relativism.[59] Even White admits that Foucault "not only finds little to lament in the passing of Western civilization but offers little hope of its replacement by anything better."[60] Debate has focused on Foucault's understanding of the generative role of discourse, his denial of the permanent and essential, his alleged dissolution of the subject, and his avoidance of any independent standpoint from which to assess the various conceptions of the self.

For our purposes the most important issues are Foucault's relationship to the epistemological tradition and his denial of a transcendent viewpoint. As White observes, "wherever he looks, Foucault finds nothing but discourse."[61] Foucault directly opposes the Cartesian use of language, which assumes that language is an accurate representation of an objective fixed reality.[62] In *The Order of Things,* Foucault identifies the major change in the history of Western culture as the assignment to language of the task of representation along with the conception of words as transparent signs of an external reality. For Foucault there is no preexistent "order of things" that can be properly and adequately represented in the "order of words." White argues that "far from believing that things have an intrinsic order, Foucault does not even honor the thing called order . . . Foucault views the mind's capacity to order the data of experience as a hindrance to a proper appreciation of the way things *really* are."[63] According to Foucault, language does not mediate between the mind and the world or the past; language constitutes both our mental categories and the perceptions ordered by these categories. The assumption that history is representational of an external order of things attributes to language a transparency that is simply not in the nature of words. Hence the history of the human sciences (including history) is predicated on the impossible ideal of linguistic transparency. Foucault writes, "I shall abandon any attempt, therefore, to see discourse as a phenomenon of expression . . . discourse is not the majestically unfolding manifestation of a thinking, knowing, speaking subject but, on the contrary, a totality in which the dispersion of the subject and his discontinuity with himself may be determined."[64]

Foucault rejects both the Cartesian and the Hegelian traditions, seeing the latter as a "self-deceptive continuation of the original Cartesian project."[65] Rorty has argued that Foucault sees the bond between the Cartesian and Hegelian traditions as the "conviction that there is a way of rising above the present and viewing it in relation to inquiry in general."[66] Like Nietzsche, Foucault denies the existence of a transcendental subject; his histories are a radical "decentering" that denies teleology, objectivism, and transcendence. Thus he states that "the essential task was to free the history of thought from its subjection to transcendence . . . to cleanse it of all transcendental narcissism."[67]

The attacks on transcendence and objectivity are further reflected in the works of White and LaCapra. Both thinkers recall historians to the essentially literary nature of history. In doing so, they also question the traditional Western epistemological and ontological assumptions of many contemporary historians. They challenge the nineteenth-century paradigm of history, the positivist, objectivist view of historical research.

White's examination of metahistory addresses several fundamental issues: the structure of historical consciousness, the epistemological status of historical explanations, and the possible forms of historical representation. Most important, metahistory asks, "What authority can historical accounts claim as contributions to a secured knowledge of reality in general and to the human sciences in particular?"[68] White argues that he is not denying a genuine historical knowledge. He is, however, attacking a "scientific" view of history modeled on the physical sciences.[69]

White contends that the nineteenth-century dream of making history an objective science and the consequent opposition of history to fiction is belied by the nature of language itself. Historians pursuing the objectivist ideal treat language "as a transparent vehicle of representation that brings no cognitive baggage of its own into the discourse."[70] Opposing this linguistic naivete, White analyzes the "linguistic determinism" embedded in the figures of speech that make discourse possible. According to White, historians prefigure a set of events or the conception of an age by means of certain literary tropes, such as metaphor, metonymy, synecdoche, and irony.[71] Historians transcend mere chroniclers because they gain their explanatory effect by "emplotment" or the "encodation of the facts contained in the chronicle as components of specific *kinds* of plot structures."[72] The analysis of these tropes or "pregeneric plot structures" allows one to perceive the figurative strategies and the "preconfiguration" of the "historical imagination."[73]

Equally important are the interrelated issues of objectivity, relativism, and perspectivism. White explains that a linguistic and rhetorical analysis demonstrates that history is not the objective reconstruction of the past; neither the text nor the context is a preexistent, prelinguistic reality that a transparent language faithfully reproduces. There is no "value neutral mode of emplotment."[74] The very "use of language itself implies or entails a specific posture before the world which is ethical, ideological, or more generally political."[75] Since all methodologies and forms are determined by language, "they are *all equally relativistic.*"[76]

But rather than leaving us with an epistemological relativism, White actually presents a perspectivism. Although there is no "nonrelativistic representation of historical reality," we gain a cumulative knowledge because "we can imagine ways of translating between different language codes."[77] Although we cannot achieve a "scientific" knowledge, we can attain "another kind of knowledge . . . the kind of knowledge which literature and art can give us. . . . We do not have to choose between art and science."[78]

LaCapra also challenges the illusion of "representational" history. Influenced by Derrida, he attacks the "documentary conception" of history and resists referential views of historical explanation. LaCapra advocates a "dialogical" approach to historical interpretation, an approach that makes the reader aware of both the creative nature of interpretation and the act of reception and recovery.[79] Moreover, this dialogical approach engages the historian in a deconstructive reading. The text is a scene of tensions, disconcerting and "contestatory" movements, networks of resistances, and inner struggles. The deconstructionist approach allows the reader to see that one tendency in the text is eventually privileged as the source of unity and order. Thus the dialogical, deconstructionist approach "problematizes" the text so that the historian can unmask this conventional privileging of order, coherence, and unity while examining the forces of resistance in the text. Above all else, the dialogical approach precludes closure or any determinate, final meaning. The text itself "resists the 'closure' of definitive and exhaustive interpretation."[80]

Despite their differences, these historians and theorists illustrate trends common to contemporary historiographical debates: the denial of objectivism, the emphasis on perspectivism, and the rejection of any possibility for a transcendent viewpoint. Like Foucault, both White and LaCapra resist what they consider to be the form of contemporary history, a form White calls Irony. The ironic perspective presupposes the possibility of a "realist" perspective on reality, a viewpoint from which a nonfigurative representation of the world can be provided. Historians employing the ironic mode signal the ascent of thought in a given area of inquiry to a level of self-consciousness in which a genuinely "enlightened" or self-critical conceptualization becomes possible.[81] LaCapra joins the attack on intellectual and social history as "excessively detached" historical perspectives that operate "in the air" and ignore the reality of language.[82] Thus LaCapra's attempts to neutralize the "privileging hierarchy" of notions of order and unity also signal a firm resistance to any claim for a transcendent viewpoint.[83]

Reading has, indeed, "become problematic." The history of exegesis cannot be immune from contemporary discussions about the nature of interpretation and historical inquiry. Historians of exegesis may, in fact, be able to contribute to debates about the nature of historical interpretation and authorial intention by addressing two issues: the question of ongoing interpretation that denies "closure," and the role of historical assumptions that limit the field of meanings in a text.

Certainly the history of interpretation is a discipline that further demonstrates Gadamer's claim that "not just occasionally but always, the meaning of a text goes beyond its author."[84] Without adopting a purely dialogical or deconstructionist reading, historians of exegesis must agree with LaCapra that texts "resist the 'closure' of definitive and exhaustive interpretation."[85] Moreover, there are no better texts than the Book of Job and its commentaries to demonstrate that historical interpretation is essentially literary and "ongoing." The present study illustrates that the Book of Job was interpreted in various ways throughout its history. There is not just one Job but a multitude of Jobs. Moreover, these observations about the multiplicity of meanings apply not only to the Book of Job itself but also to the commentaries that interpret the Joban story: The *Moralia,* the *Guide,* the *Expositio,* and Calvin's *Sermons* also transcend the original intentions of their authors and resist any attempt at definitive interpretations. The meanings of these commentaries confirm the truth inherent in discussions about perspectivism. These works yield different interpretations based on the various perspectives within the text of Job, the perspectives adopted by the commentators, and, of course, my perspective as interpreter. Although I commit the cardinal sin of seeking "coherency," I do not aim at the recovery of authorial intention. The historian cannot, in fact, speak with the author; therefore, phrases such as "according to Gregory" or "according to Calvin" mean according to the text under discussion. I am fully aware that in what follows I am engaged in an act of interpretation. Undoubtedly past readers have read these commentaries with different but valuable results. Future readers will find equally diverse and important meanings in these works and will thereby contribute to the history of their effects or the ongoing task of interpretation.

Still, the history of exegesis also teaches that texts do not have *infinite* meanings. We cannot simply attribute *any* meaning at all to these precritical Joban commentaries. In this study the reader will not encounter a deconstructionist reading of texts. Texts do have boundaries, and some interpretations are better than others. The following analysis presupposes, furthermore, that texts are to some extent rooted in their historical age. The historical vocabulary as well as the theological and philosophical presuppositions that constitute the text are important tools for understanding the work under discussion. A Neoplatonist uses spatial language differently from a twentieth-century reader, and it would simply be a misreading of the *Moralia* to overlook the value-laden, metaphysical importance of such language. Maimonides's cosmology and the role of the Active Intellect are indispensable for understanding his interpretation of Job. Identification of different attitudes toward suffering is important for interpreting the differences among various readings of Job's story. Knowledge of former interpretations of the whirlwind speech helps to explain Calvin's view of Behemoth and Leviathan. Differing views of the meaning of history determine all these texts. Historical works are not contemporary works, and historical knowledge enables the text to confront the modern reader with fuller force. As Gadamer has argued, appreciation for the historicity of texts and the historicity of understanding makes interpretation possible. Therefore, although interpretation no longer can naively aim at representational history or the intention of the author, it can seek what has been called the *intentio operis*.[86]

Perhaps the greatest contribution that the history of exegesis can make to current discussions of hermeneutics and historiography is the recovery of an ancient and medieval insight into scriptural interpretation: Texts have a field or range of meanings. Within the boundaries imposed by the text, the task of the historian is to make some of those meanings emerge. In his work on the history of interpretation, Steinmetz has best expressed this ancient insight: "A good literary text creates a field of meanings and associations not explicitly worked out in the mind of the author but implicitly contained in the text itself. In the interaction of reader and text, those implicit meanings are discerned and brought to expression. The meaning of a text is defined in part by the intention of the author as it is in part by the prior meanings of the words which he uses, but new experiences can cast new light on old texts."[87]

Not only do new experiences cast new light, but also differing epistemological assumptions determine interpretive results. I have surveyed briefly the discussions of Gadamer, Ricoeur, Foucault, White, and LaCapra in order to forewarn readers that we are about to turn to a world apart, a world far removed from the attacks on objectivism, transparency of language, and transcendence. For Gregory, Maimonides, Aquinas, and Calvin, there is a shared belief in the "order" of reality, a trust in language, and a yearning for transcendence. There is a kind of relative optimism about the ultimate ability of enlightened or redeemed noetic perception. Furthermore, these are exegetes who assume order and coherency in Job's story and who engage in exegesis as a means to truth and transcendence. In the final analysis, they believe that the proper understanding of scriptural words leads to a higher perception of reality and that exegesis will allow them access to this transcendent reality beyond the self.

This trust in perception, in words, and in transcendence finds its gradual entropy in the works of biblical scholarship and literary interpretations that constitute the last chapter of this book. In that final section we find ourselves once again in the world of assumptions expressed by contemporary theorists from Gadamer to LaCapra. The attacks on objectivity, language, and transcendence are reflected, in varying degrees, in the works of modern biblical scholarship as well as the interpretations by Jung, Wells, MacLeish, Wiesel, and Kafka. Therefore the Job of contemporary interpreters is as much a reflection of our current assumptions as is the Job who sought Neoplatonic ascent, union with the Active Intellect, faith in immortality, or hope in the hidden providence of God. Thus we will come full circle and return to these modern discussions about the problematic nature of perception, meaning, and transcendence when we encounter the twentieth-century Job who cannot escape the noetic nightmare of history and the meaninglessness of suffering.

The Theme of Perception

Discussions about the "clash of standpoints," the perspectival character of knowledge, the "infinite whirl" or "drift" of interpretations, the horror of "transcendental narcissism," and the fear that "reality is going to go away" connect these modern debates with the central theme of this book: the role of human perception. Rather than seeking to answer questions of influence or sources, this study asks whether there is a recurring issue that continually governs the interpretation of Job. We will find that there is. The commentaries analyzed in this book differ greatly from one another. Different exegetical methods and diverse philosophical and theological presuppositions make the world of precritical Joban interpretations seem labyrinthine. I will argue, however, that a unifying feature in all these works is the concern with human perception or understanding. This concern reaches its climax in Calvin's entertainment of the notion of double justice and his juxtaposition of nature and history. In the final chapter we will see that twentieth-century readings of Job are characterized by the gradual collapse of perception; in Kafka's world "Job" has entered into a perceptual nightmare from which he cannot awake. In short, these texts *work* perceptually; that is, their internal coherence is discovered by asking the question of what Job saw or understood. Fundamentally these interpretations of Job had to answer certain basic questions. Why did Job "speak rightly" before God? What did the friends, who defended God, misunderstand? Why did they not see things correctly? What did Job understand that explained his perceptual superiority over his friends?

In this study the word *perception* refers to insight or noetic perception. By using the term *perception*, however, I am not saying that epistemology drives exegesis. For Calvin and his predecessors, the issue of perception surfaces as a concomitant concern arising out of explicit subjects, such as suffering, justice, history, and providence. What can the sufferer who stands within history perceive about the self, God, and reality? Can suffering, particularly inexplicable suffering, elevate human understandings about God and the self? Can human beings truly perceive the workings of providence within their own personal lives or the tumult of history? Are evil and injustice really matters of perspective? Is there a darker side of God and of reality, which we must confront before wisdom can be found? The question that permeates these commentaries, therefore, is not *how* one knows but *what* one knows. Moreover, the question of what Job knew is continually expressed in visual allusions denoting insight, wisdom, or understanding. Thus I have drawn attention to the exegetical function of metaphors and discussions that feature words such as *sight, gaze, glimpse, experience, beholding, imagination, prophecy, hiddenness, insight, illumination, eyes, faith,* and *darkness,* as well as that which is "beguiling" and that which is true "apprehension" or "understanding." These commentaries are suffused with terminology referring to what the human mind can know through the imagery of sight, given a certain perspective, aided by revelation, and illumined by faith.

The issue of perception surfaces in a layered way with different meanings referring to understanding, points of view, levels of the text, revelation, faith, prophecy, and illumination. In the various commentaries, some meanings recede while others come to the fore. In all these works the perspectival structure inherent in the Joban text is central: Some speakers are perceptive while others are not.[88] Furthermore, the insights of the various speakers depend on where they "stand" within the story. Job speaks as the sufferer, while his friends speak as traditionalists and as those who are not suffering. God speaks from the elevated stance of the whirlwind. We will explore how the commentators explain the various degrees of perception or understanding in terms of their presuppositions about suffering, providence, spiritual growth, and the nature of God. Gregory, for example, accounts for the lack of insight by Job's friends in terms of their pride and their failure to turn inward. Job's wisdom comes through the ascent attained by suffering and interiority. Gregory's multilayered exegesis creates layers of perception matched by the levels he finds within the biblical text, so that we encounter the perspective afforded by allegory as well as the ever shifting position of the reader.

We will see that for Maimonides, Job's wisdom is due to his newly gained insight into the nature of the cosmos, the utter transcendence of God, and the true understanding of providence. Aquinas and Calvin both attempt a literal interpretation that remains true to the argumentative or perspectival opposition in the story. In these exegetes we will find the doctrine of immortality to be the source of Job's perceptual superiority. In Calvin's *Sermons*, however, we will be led more and more deeply into the ambiguous and sometimes frightening dimensions of the perceptual theme in Job as we see Job confront the terrifying hiddenness of God.

What is interesting about all these commentaries is that they immerse us in a world where empirical evidence is not ultimate. The senses, reflection, and experience often tell us less, not more, about the nature of human history. In this exegetical tradition the question of perception is intimately connected with the valuation or devaluation of *history*. For some thinkers, Job ascended to a higher perceptual level from which he could judge and transcend the historical realm. For Calvin, however, Job was trapped within history and had to rely on the perceptual power of faith. For all these thinkers, there is a depth dimension to reality that transcends purely sensory, historical, and experiential ways of knowing. Although they believed that some knowledge could be ascertained from historical experience and observation, they believed that this knowledge had to be supplemented by faith, illumination, and revelation. They all gave expression to a theme native to the Book of Job: Things are not what they seem.

The deceptive nature of appearances and the problematic character of human events have been a perennial theme in all discussions about suffering, theodicy, and providence. This book examines the concern with perception created by a problem inherent in Western religious traditions. These traditions bequeathed to Western thought a tension between the notion of revelation with its concomitant promise of God's providential rule over history and the reality of human experience within that history. In what follows, I seek to trace the history of that tension as articulated by certain authors on the basis of Job's story. We will follow a trajectory in which the possibility of revelation is gradually eclipsed. In the chapters dealing with Gregory, Maimonides, Aquinas, and Calvin, we will see the attempt to justify God's actions and to ascend to a higher understanding of both God and history. In chapter 5 we will make a jump that presupposes the Enlightenment and observe a concentration on the human existential situation as it is cut off from the deity. God becomes silent, and human perception or insight becomes increasingly narrow. This is a trajectory in Western culture that we cannot escape: In the end we will stand at the collapse of what Hans Jonas once called the "nobility of sight." We are left with the suspicion by Foucault and others regarding the problematic, suspicious, sinister, or "dark side" of ocularcentrism.[89]

I

WHERE IS THE PLACE OF UNDERSTANDING?

The Coherence of Gregory's *Moralia in Iob*

> Zeus, who into wisdom's way
> Guideth mortals, establishing
> This decree: "By suffering Truth."
> Woes' aching memories before the mind
> Ooze in sleep drop by drop
> So to men wisdom comes, without their will.
>
> Aeschylus

> Occasionally I feel an unhappiness which almost dismembers me, and at the same time am convinced of its necessity and of the existence of a goal to which one makes one's way by undergoing every kind of unhappiness.
>
> Kafka

IN THE DEDICATORY epistle to his *Moralia in Job,* Gregory the Great explains that his fellow monks and Leander begged him "to expound the Book of the blessed Job" and to "lay open for them the mysteries of such depth" in the literal, allegorical, and moral senses of the text. By the time he had completed this task, his exposition filled thirty-five books in six volumes. As a commentary on Job, however, the modern reader finds the *Moralia* a most difficult text to read. Many historians have dismissed it altogether as an exegetical work. Dudden writes that "the form of the book disgusts the modern reader. It is . . . the endless allegorizing, the twisting of every word and phrase into a symbol of hidden truth, that is so inexplicably wearisome."[1] Butler argues that "it would be a complete mistake to estimate the *Morals* as a commentary on Job. . . . They should be read without any thought of Job . . . and without any attention to the constant allegorizing."[2] Smalley admits that the method of the *Moralia* was well suited for educational purposes, but says of Gregory's exegetical method that "to us this is a most annoying system. Everything in St. Gregory's system is attached however loosely to the thread of the text, which precludes any attempt at coherence or logical arrangement."[3]

These reactions are understandable. Without question, the *Moralia* is diffuse, rambling, verbose, and filled with apparent digressions. Gregory would have been the first to admit this character of his work, since he believed that a good exposition of Scripture should flow and wind about like a river. If the interpreter finds any occasion "for suitable edification," he should digress and then return to his original subject.[4] The *Moralia* proceeds in this leisurely manner by providing instruction on a vast variety of topics which, to the modern reader, are completely unconnected with the Book of Job. In this unwieldy text we find discussions of everything from the virtues of marriage to the Council of Chalcedon. The multifaceted and meandering nature of the *Moralia* raises the question of its coherence and challenges its claim to be an "expositio in librum B. Iob." Yet in the midst of its seemingly desultory explanations one finds, according to Gregory, an exposition on the Book of Job. Consequently, historians of exegesis must ask whether Gregory had an understanding of the Book of Job as a whole or whether he used the text simply as a springboard for discussions about various theological and moral topics. We must further ask whether the expository or exegetical nature of the *Moralia* encompasses only the literal sense or whether it extends also to the "endless allegorizing" that finds deeper meanings in the "higher" levels of the text. In short, as an exposition of the Book of Job, does the *Moralia* serve at all as an exegetical treatise? I maintain that it does.

To understand Gregory's work as a commentary on Job, we must discern the presuppositions that most deeply influence his exegetical method and interpretive results. Gregory, of course, reads the Book of Job from the perspective of a sixth-century Christian. He views the Old Testament as a typological prophecy of the New Testament and finds in every verse his own convictions about the revelation and atonement of Christ. Such theological presuppositions are obvious even to casual readers and will emerge clearly throughout the following analysis. Our task is to identify the assumptions that are not so readily apparent as being "theological" or "Christian." We can only recover the coherence of this diffuse commentary by recognizing the hermeneutical function of two such assumptions that inform Gregory's entire interpretation of Job: his metaphysical presupposition that reality is hierarchical, and his assumption that the perception of the true nature of reality is gained only by an inward ascent made possible through suffering. The repetition of these assumptions about reality and suffering governs and unifies the *Moralia* both thematically and exegetically by defining Gregory's view of Scripture, driving his exegetical method, and determining his interpretive conclusions.

The first section of this chapter proceeds thematically, analyzing these issues as they recur throughout the text. The following sections document exegetically how these presuppositions give to Gregory's line-by-line exegesis of the Joban story a certain internal rationality and intelligibility on *all* levels of interpretation, an intelligibility that the history of scholarship has failed to appreciate. Most important, my analysis shows that Gregory's views about hierarchy, ascent, and suffering are expressed in terms of perception and perspective, terms that make the issue of perception a central heuristic key for understanding the *Moralia*. In later chapters we will see how the exegesis of Job changes because Gregory's assumptions about reality and suffering are not shared by later interpreters of Job's story. Nonetheless, in the later "literal" tradition the issue of perception remains central to the exegesis of the Book of Job. In varying ways, all our exegetes see that Job's tragic situation raised the agonizing problem of what the human mind can know in the midst of suffering.

NO ONE HAS ever accused Gregory of being an original metaphysical thinker. In fact, scholars frequently minimize his contribution to that field in favor of his work as a moralist or as a master of Christian spirituality. Nonetheless, we must not allow Gregory's shortcomings to blind us to the influence of his metaphysical assumptions on his exegesis. The works of Gillet, Courcelle, and Dagens confirm the importance of Augustine in Gregory's thought. Straw explains that, in addition to Augustine's works, Gregory knew in translation the works of important Greek thinkers and also the writings of Cassian and Ambrose.[5] Among the most significant themes inherited from this tradition is the ancient metaphysic of Being. Reality, divided between eternity and time, is described by Gregory in terms of the traditional, value-laden language of hierarchy, a vocabulary that opposes the higher to the lower, interiority to exteriority, the unchangeable to the changeable, and the eternal to the temporal.[6] This is not to say that the world is divided in any dualistic way. As Straw has demonstrated, "Gregory sees the universe as an ontological continuum flowing from pure spirituality to pure carnality." Gregory's universe is a hierarchical scale of Being with lower and higher levels connected in a fundamental unity.[7] The goal of the soul is to turn inward and ascend from the lower to the higher levels of reality. Transcending the "lower" external realm of change, the soul turns inward and seeks God who alone is immutable, eternal, and absolute Being. In traditional Neoplatonic language Gregory explains that to find this God the soul must turn inward.[8]

This turn inward is made possible through suffering. The soul disengages itself from the changeable, external world, confesses its sins,[9] and finally is free to rise through contemplation[10] to the eternal. At the lowest level of reality lies historical life, which Gregory does not define as evil but repeatedly depicts as the "dark night of present existence," the "chaff" that conceals inner truth, and the place of "exile."[11] This lower turbulent "sea" of historical life is characterized by mutability, exteriority, and temporality. Central to Gregory's exegesis is his view that the Fall was a fall into time. Originally the human being did not participate in the movement of time; like God, Adam "stood still [stare]" while time rushed forward.[12] Because of sin, however, humanity fell into involvement with the realm of change and external objects. Having fallen into the world of temporality and mutability, humans fell into full participation with history. Therefore, Gregory describes salvation as a turning inward of the soul as it ascends beyond the incessant passage of time toward the immutable "rest" of eternity.

A careful reading of the *Moralia* reveals that Gregory's view of Scripture corresponds to this hierarchical view of reality. As Catry argues, Gregory sees Scripture as a "letter" inspired by God. The Bible is the "voice" of God while the human authors are God's "pens" or "scribes."[13] But Gregory's view of Scripture also reflects his metaphysical assumptions. In Gregory's thought this strong doctrine of inspiration means that God has fashioned Scripture, like reality itself, in such a way that it too is hierarchical in nature. In his letter to Leander, Gregory explains that he will interpret the text of Job according to a threefold sense of Scripture: "First we lay the historical foundation [fundamenta historiae], next by means of the typical sense [significationem typicam] we build a fabric of the mind into a stronghold of faith, and finally, by the grace of moral instruction [moralitatis gratiam] we, as it were, clothe the edifice with an overcast of color."[14] As Gregory exegetically builds this interpretive fortress, he moves from the lower to the higher and "lays open" the dark mysteries "buried" in the "depths" of the scriptural building blocks. With the "historical foundation" he recounts the actual historical events narrated in the sacred text, events that by definition took place in the course of time. When he explains the "typical" or allegorical sense of Scripture, he "unravels" the inner meaning of these narrations as they relate to doctrine, a task that includes an interpretation of the typological or prophetic meaning of the text. Finally he provides the moral sense of the text, in which he gives ethical instruction regarding the turning inward of the soul, the confession of sin, the virtuous life, and the ascent toward God.[15]

This multilayered exegetical method has decisive implications for Gregory's view of history. We shall see, however, that the gradual rejection of his allegorical hermeneutic reflects changing attitudes toward the importance and perception of the historical realm. By the time we arrive at Calvin's *Sermons,* the hierarchical structure of Scripture and reality no longer governs Joban interpretation; for Calvin, there is only the literal or historical level of meaning. The Reformer, of course, also places the eternal over the temporal and assumes a depth dimension to reality. But having abandoned Gregory's hierarchical framework, Calvin places more emphasis on the perceptual ambiguity of temporal reality.

Gregory, however, operates within a Neoplatonic world view. The fundamental unity of the *Moralia* can only be discerned if we recognize the influence of this attitude toward history on his exegetical method. Gregory assumes that at the lowest level of *both* reality and Scripture lies history. This lower or outer layer of Scripture is the external "surface [superficies]" that both conceals and leads to an inner "depth [altum]."[16] Gregory's constant opposition between metaphors of surface and depth corresponds to his distinction between an inner and outer reality. The literal narration or "chaff" of history is the surface that covers an inner, deeper truth to which the reader must "penetrate" or "dig." This exegetical process of "digging" facilitates the renewal of the soul as it ascends, with Job, above temporality. "Sacred Scripture," Gregory writes, "bids to the heavenly country and changes the heart of the reader from earthly desires to the embracing of things above. By obscure sayings, Scripture exercises the strong and by humble words persuades the little ones; it is not so shut up as to be dreaded, nor so open as to become contemptible . . . in some way, it grows with the people reading."[17]

For Gregory, Scripture grows with the reader because the properly humble exegete ascends through the levels of the text passing from exterior (scientia exteriorum) to interior understanding (interna intelligentia).[18] This interconnectedness between the reader and the text is an engagement crucial to the process of inward ascent. Gregory's emphasis on interiority[19] is thus inseparable from his understanding of the exegetical task. Like Job, Gregory's reader is intended to turn inward to discover the inner truth buried beneath the surface of the letter. In so doing one moves from the lowest to the highest level of the text, from the visible to the invisible, from the exterior to the interior, from the face to the heart, from the surface to the depth, and from history to wisdom. Interpreting Job's lament in 3:21 ("Who long for death and it does not come, like men digging for treasure"), Gregory describes the searching for wisdom in a statement that helps unify this diffuse commentary and reveals the connection between his metaphysical presuppositions and exegetical results: "Wisdom," Gregory says, "lies not on the surface of things but lies hidden in the unseen."[20] Hence, just as Gregory portrays the historical person of Job piercing through temporality or history to find wisdom, so he also leads the reader beneath the surface of the scriptural text to those truths that lie hidden deep within the unseen.

These metaphysical assumptions alone, however, cannot explain fully Gregory's exegesis of Job's story. It is vital to realize that Gregory's view of suffering equally influences his interpretation. In the *Moralia* we encounter a preoccupation with suffering that will recur in various guises throughout the Joban interpretive tradition. We shall see how the notion of suffering undergoes a metamorphosis in later commentaries that has important hermeneutical implications. At present we must examine Gregory's particular attitude toward affliction. This will allow us to analyze his spirituality of suffering as an indispensable interpretive tool for uncovering the coherence of the *Moralia*. Only then can we understand the "progress" that Gregory's Job made "through suffering," a progress that made him "differ from that which he was before."[21]

In Gregory's view, the experience of suffering lies at the heart of the ambiguous nature of human existence. As Straw has shown, Gregory stresses the "paradoxical nature of God's blessings and punishments."[22] Fluctuations between adversity and prosperity characterize the fallen mutable world. Furthermore, both adversity and prosperity have an equivocal nature so that astute discernment is needed to interpret these states correctly. At times material and spiritual prosperity are divine gifts that aid Christians on their arduous journey to the homeland. But these conditions may also prove dangerous by diminishing discipline, hindering detachment, and leading to spiritual pride. Adversity also plays a dual role. While affliction may oppress the soul, it can also enlighten the mind of sufferers and free them from spiritual pride and immersion in temporal goods.[23] The subject of suffering, then, places us directly in the problematic world of perception.

Central to Gregory's exegesis of Job is the advantageous nature of affliction. In Gregory's mind the book coheres on a fundamental level because *both* Job and his friends understood the importance of suffering. The endurance of adversity recounted in Job's story does not pose the problem of theodicy that it does for later interpreters because, for Gregory, suffering is often *not* an evil. By the sixth century the beneficial nature of adversity was a commonplace.[24] But Gregory does more than repeat the traditional wisdom about the pedagogical purpose of affliction: He analyzes suffering in terms of interiority and then proceeds to use the sanative nature of affliction as a hermeneutical construct. In Gregory's spirituality, suffering and the hierarchical view of reality are intimately connected. Suffering turns the soul inward so that it can ascend toward God. The connection of interiority, suffering, and ascent reflects the parallel between Gregory's exegetical method and his hierarchical view of reality: Both suffering and exegesis lead to an interior ascent. The exegete seeks the inner meanings of the words, ascends to the higher levels of the text, and thereby renews the soul. The sufferer turns inward and ascends to the realm of the unchangeable. This emphasis on the interiority effected by suffering is not an attitude of masochism; Gregory advocates neither an *apatheia* nor a relishing of pain. As Straw has argued, he considers the *constantia mentis* to be the ideal state in both adversity and prosperity.[25] Nonetheless, this inner equilibrium or tranquillity must not be interpreted as passivity or indifference to suffering but rather as an ability to suffer well. Suffering well is the experience that takes full advantage of the benefits of affliction. Suffering well is the ability to have affliction enlarge and transform the soul. We can determine how Gregory's view of suffering informs his exegesis of Job if we take seriously his conviction that the endurance of affliction creates three spiritual realities: self-knowledge, freedom, and perception.

Suffering leads to a deeper knowledge of the self because it reveals one's spiritual strength as well as the intricacies of one's sin. According to Gregory, adversity tests the being of the sufferer and increases virtue and inner rectitude. Under the scourge individuals are "tested" or "proven" so that they learn what they truly are. Adversity creates self-perception because it "uncovers" the power of the virtues that lie concealed during times of peace. As Gregory says, "the gift which is received in tranquillity is revealed in tribulation."[26] In particular, suffering often manifests an inner strength or fortitude. Gregory does not advocate "patience" in any passive sense of the word.[27] Suffering is hard work and must be carried out or endured with all the resources of one's being. The idea of a painful struggle, fight, or contest is central to Gregory's view of spiritual growth. Thus in the midst of all his talk about Job's "patience," battle imagery is often in the foreground. "For no one at rest is conscious of his powers. For if there is no contest [bella], no opportunities arise for making trial of our virtues. He who boasts of his bravery in peace is but a short-sighted warrior . . . the quality of our strength is made known by the sufferings of the rod."[28]

Interpreting Job's adversities as a trial that revealed and strengthened his already considerable virtue,[29] Gregory portrays this "holy man" as the embodiment of a muscular view of suffering. But Job is not the only great sufferer in the Bible; Gregory stood in a long tradition of Christian interpretation in which Paul is the model sufferer. For Gregory, 2 Cor. 12:9 ("Strength is made perfect in weakness") shows that both Paul and Job understood the necessity for undergoing affliction.[30] In Gregory's reading, the elect "make progress in adversity" because "as the fight grows stronger" the very obstacles caused by suffering strengthen their mind and inflame their desire for God so that they are compelled "to hasten heavenward."[31]

Suffering also leads to a truer knowledge of the self by revealing the depth of one's sin. The soul that is afflicted is awakened from a mortal "self-security" so that "what escaped us in our insensibility is made known to us more exactly in tears."[32] On the moral level of interpretation, the concept of moral or spiritual "temptation" governs Gregory's discussions of the spiritual suffering that leads to self-knowledge. In Gregory's analysis, God drives spiritual pain deeper within the soul so that the soul learns the weakness of its inner self and thereby confesses its sin; by becoming humble the soul escapes spiritual pride. "But we lay down our 'greatness' and our exalted notions when we are compelled by the assaults of sin to consider what we are . . . because when humility makes progress through temptation, that very adversity is itself prosperous which secures the mind from self-exaltation. But yet this is not effected without great tribulation, the tranquil mind being assailed by the inroads of temptation as if by an unexpected enemy."[33]

We can fully appreciate Gregory's preoccupation with the necessity for suffering when we realize that earthly life is fraught with the dangers of tranquillity. For Gregory, peace, prosperity, self-security, and happiness can become perils that threaten to hinder or prohibit the soul from undertaking the arduous journey of inward ascent. The *Moralia* contains numerous warnings against the seductive life of "security" and "fatal tranquillity,"[34] a life that enslaves the soul to the "beguiling" nature of the world. This dread of tranquillity dominates Gregory's discussions about the endurance of affliction and leads him to associate suffering with freedom. The assumption underlying Gregory's view is his identification of freedom with detachment.[35] Embedded in Gregory's statements about the weariness of earthly life are images depicting the seductive and enticing nature of historical existence. We can only conclude, therefore, that the "weariness" of the present life is not immediately apparent and that the captivating character of the world can blind the mind.[36] Adversity awakens the soul, shakes it loose from its attachment to exterior and transient goods, and allows it to see the true nature of this place of "exile." The present life, Gregory argues, is only the "road" by which we journey home. God deliberately harasses us on this road so that we do not attach ourselves to temporal goods. "The Lord, then, makes the way of the world rugged to his elect who are traveling toward Him, in order that no one may enjoy the rest of the pleasant life."[37]

In Gregory's view, the "present life may aid us when pressing us" more than when it "flatters," because the world "shows liberty while it tortures."[38] Focusing on the numerous descriptions of pain and agony that constitute the Joban text, Gregory chooses to emphasize the *liberating* nature of affliction. Adversity "releases" or "delivers" one from the desires of the external world and brings the soul back to "interior joys."[39] He applies several verses to the speeches of Job and his friends to express this crucial relationship between suffering, interiority, and ultimately freedom: Gal. 5:17 ("For the desires of the flesh are against the Spirit and the desires of the Spirit are against the flesh"); 2 Cor. 4:16 ("Though our outer man perishes, our inward man is renewed day by day"); 2 Cor. 5:1 ("We know that if our earthly house of this tabernacle were dissolved, we have a building of God, a house not made with hands, eternal in the heavens"); and Deut. 32:39 ("I will kill and I will make alive; I will wound and I will heal").[40] Gregory interprets the dichotomies of these verses as a process that moves the sufferer from the exterior to the interior; pain drives the soul inward so that as the flesh is pressed or "dissolved" outwardly, the soul turns inward and seeks higher things. As God "abases the power of the flesh, he exalts the purpose of the Spirit."[41] God is said to "afflict his own outwardly in order that they may have life inwardly."[42] The "renewal" of the inner man is therefore dependent on the painful perishing of the outer man. Gregory presents no real alternative to suffering, no shortcut to interiority; the story of Job teaches that God *must* send afflictions in order to drive the soul inward and destroy its attachment to "perishable pursuits." The detached soul is the soul that is free from earthly desires, cares, and troubles. Suffering, therefore, leads to an inner, detached transcendence that is, in essence, a freedom from history, materiality, and exteriority.

The free soul gains a new and hard-won perception of reality and an ability to judge more wisely about the nature of earthly life. Primarily, the sufferer learns to resist what we have described as the "beguiling [blandus]" nature of the tranquil life.[43] Suffering turns us inward and redirects our love toward the unchangeable; it clears our mind so that we can *see* the seductive power of transient and perishable goods. The hierarchy of reality, the emphasis on interiority, and the necessity of suffering all function in Gregory's thought to cure the sight of the sufferer and to bring the individual to wisdom, a wisdom that perceives the oppressive nature of the "Egypt that is our present life." Sufferers, Gregory thinks, are "brought back to reason," and "returning back into themselves, they consider how empty are those things after which they were seeking. Immediately they weep for the foolishness of their desire and yearn more strongly for eternal things in proportion to the folly in which they grieve that they once pursued temporal things."[44] Suffering is indispensable to this new spiritual discernment, for "light approaches when the afflicted mind perceives the gloom of tribulation which it is enduring from perishable pursuits."[45]

If we recognize that suffering initiates interiority and produces a new self-knowledge, freedom, and perception, we can finally perceive how Gregory can conclude that the elect "rejoice in adversity." Whether it be illness, loss, pain, death, or dishonor, the elect experience the medicinal nature of affliction. Both physical and spiritual agony strengthen and free the soul by detaching it from the temporal and turning it inward to the eternal. From this vantage point we see why, in Gregory's theology, adversity is not to be avoided but rather to be embraced. The most dan-

gerous evil in life is not suffering but tranquillity; peace and prosperity
are conditions that often must be overcome. These discussions sound
like a deliberate misreading of Job unless we comprehend that, for Gregory, suffering actually is necessary to *cure* a deluding tranquillity. Rather
than asking why the righteous suffer and the wicked prosper, Gregory argues that divine providence is most *incomprehensible* when the good are
happy and the wicked suffer:

While the judgments of God are indeed hidden from sight, why is it that, in this
life it sometimes goes badly with the good and well with the wicked? Nonetheless, [those same judgments] are still more hidden when it both goes well with
the good here below and badly with the wicked. . . . Therefore, because in the
midst of divine judgments, the human mind is closed in by the great darkness
of its uncertainty, holy men, when they see the prosperity of this world to be
their lot, are apprehensive. For they fear that they are receiving the fruit of their
labors now. They fear that divine justice discerns in them something hidden
and, by showering them with external blessings, withholds them from the interior. . . . And so it is that holy men dread prosperity in this world more than adversity.[46]

Only by grasping how these assumptions about reality, perception,
and suffering provide the framework for Gregory's exegesis of Job's
story can we see the *Moralia* as anything but a series of loosely connected
topics. These presuppositions take concrete exegetical form in the three
main sections of the Joban text: the person of Job, the speeches by the
companions, and the whirlwind speech. In Gregory's reading, Job, his
friends, Elihu, and God all expressed different aspects of the truth depending on the perceptions afforded them by their respective abilities
to perceive the inner truth of reality.

Job Laments His Lot

On the historical level Job was a holy man scourged by God. In the
course of his adversities this historical Job personified how one should
suffer well. Turning inward and despising transient pursuits, Job
yearned for the eternal. Gregory explores this theme of exemplary suffering on both the moral and literal layers of the text. In fact, Gregory's
distinctions between the two levels are often obscure. In the case of Job
this lack of distinction occurs because the figure of Job repeatedly collapses the historical and moral levels into one: Job was the temporal embodiment of moral truth. The central themes treated on these two levels
of meaning are the proper discernment regarding the cause of suffering
and the perceptual advantages of affliction.

In the allegorical interpretation of the book, Job typifies Christ and the church. The sufferings of a "simple and upright" man positively begged Job's story to signify the passion of Christ and the persecution of the church. Here again the correct perception of the cause for suffering becomes important. Furthermore, as Gregory moves Job from the historical to the allegorical level, the issue of perception is heightened because on the allegorical plane Job functions as a prophet. In the end, the perception of reality granted to the prophet bestows new meaning on portions of the lower historical realm.

The historical and moral figure of Job raises a series of questions for Gregory, all of which continued to trouble later commentators.[47] These problems arise from difficulties primarily within the *literal* level of the text and concern the relationship among sin, suffering, and divine justice. Why would a just God permit Satan to afflict a "simple and upright" man "without cause [frustra]"? Was Job truly innocent of all sin? Did he claim to be innocent? Did Job fall into sin during his debates with his friends by blaspheming about God? If Job did not sin before or during his scourges, why did he repent in 39:34–35 and 42:5–6?

The question of Job's sinfulness preoccupied later exegetes as well, especially Aquinas and Calvin. These later commentators inherited many problems with which Gregory had wrestled. They also adopted many of the solutions Gregory had originally worked out. This preoccupation with Job's sin or sinlessness stems from several factors: the difficulties posed by the text itself, the theological presuppositions about original sin, and the defense of divine justice made by the friends. By tracing Gregory's repeated struggles to make the story cohere, it appears that for him the text itself created the problem because Job made statements that seem contradictory. In 6:2–3 Job argued, "I wish that my sins by which I have deserved anger and the calamity which I am suffering were being weighed in a scale. As the sand of the sea, the latter would appear graver." But in 9:20 he said, "If I desire to justify myself, my own mouth would condemn me. If I show that I am innocent, He will also prove me perverse." Gregory and his successors encounter such inconsistencies throughout the text: Job 7:21; 9:13–15, 20; 13:18, 14:16–17; 17:2; 27:5–6; 42:6–7.[48]

Gregory concludes that Job was not sinless, and he does not think Job ever made such a claim. As Job himself said in 14:4, "Who can make clean one born of an unclean seed?" This verse proves to Gregory that the "historical" Job knew himself to be subject to the curse of original sin.[49] Job's own confessions of sin uttered throughout the story further demonstrate that he was conscious of his own sinfulness.[50] Nonetheless, Gregory insists that Job was not guilty of any grave sins and hence was correct in verses such as 27:6, when he declared that his heart "did not reproach" him.[51]

Nor will Gregory admit that Job fell into sin or blasphemy during his debates with his friends. We can detect that throughout this massive commentary Gregory allows two verses to govern his interpretation of Job's laments: 2:5 and 42:7. In 2:5 Satan said to God, "But send forth your hand and touch his bone and flesh and you will see that he has blessed [cursed] you to your face." For Gregory, this challenge places the story of Job's sufferings within the wider context of God's power and honor: "The enemy applied his strength against the blessed Job. In doing so, however, he entered the contest against God, and in this way the blessed Job was in the middle of the contest between God and the devil. Whoever then maintains that the holy man, when in the midst of the scourges, committed sin by his words, what else does he do than to reproach God, who had pledged Himself for him, with being the loser?"[52] To prove that Job never cursed God during his afflictions, Gregory uses verse 42:7: "But after the Lord had spoken these words to Job, he said to Eliphaz the Themanite, 'My anger is aroused against you and your two friends because you have not spoken what is right before Me as has my servant Job.'"[53] By framing the question of Job's behavior in terms of these two verses, which occur at the beginning and the end of the text, Gregory can defend his portrayal of Job as the model sufferer.

But if Job had not committed any grave sins before or during his scourges, why did God permit Satan to afflict him? In the preface Gregory lists the various causes of suffering.[54] God sends scourges sometimes only as chastisement and sometimes as correction for sins. At other times he sends afflictions for the prevention of future sins. None of these reasons, however, can apply to Job because the Prologue precludes any possibility of attributing Job's tragedies to past sins. Like all later Joban interpreters, Gregory confronts in Job's story the problem of nonretributive suffering—that is, suffering *not* due to punishment for past or future sins. To interpret Job's situation, therefore, Gregory draws on the theology of suffering, a view of affliction that encompasses more than retribution. The beneficial nature of adversity applies even to men like Job who are not in need of correction. On the basis of 1:8 and 2:3, Gregory concludes that God may send adversity to reveal the power of divine deliverance and to increase the merit of suffering.

Because of the contest between God and Satan the power of divine deliverance can be said to form the proscenium of Gregory's interpretation. In Job's situation Gregory sees a parallel with the fate of the blind man described in John 9:2–3. When asked whose sin accounted for the blind man's fate, the Lord answered, "Neither has this man sinned nor his parents but so that the works of God should be made clear in him."[55] By comparing Job to the blind man, Gregory continues to place Job's plight within the larger question of God's honor and power. Just as the blind

man suffered so that "the works of God should be made clear in him," Job
endured affliction "so that when unexpected deliverance follows the
stroke, the power of the Deliverer is made known and therefore more ar-
dently loved."[56] In Gregory's reading, Job's endurance of suffering
proved to defeat Satan in his contest with God.

But the reader must wait for the whirlwind speech to witness this
power of divine deliverance. After the Prologue, Gregory follows the
Book of Job—and changes perspective. In his exegesis of the Dialogues,
Gregory interprets the reality of suffering from the human rather than
the divine viewpoint. What advantage does he achieve by focusing on
the human perspective? By shifting to Job's experience, Gregory can explore the advantageous nature of "undeserved" suffering, a suffering
that did not punish Job but did increase his merits. In his reading of
Job's speeches, Gregory expresses a truism later reaffirmed in Calvin's
commentary on Job: The suffering of the just is the biblical norm. God
always afflicts those whom he loves. Picturing Job on his dunghill, Gregory asks: "How is it that the almighty God, as though unconcerned, afflicts so harshly those whom he looks upon as dear to him from all eternity?" The suffering Job now calls to Gregory's mind not the blind man
but John the Baptist, about whom it was said that "none has arisen
greater among those born of women." Still, John the Baptist was cast
into prison and beheaded. When, Gregory asks, could he have sinned,
"for how could he transgress who never went out from the desert?" Reflecting on the adversities of saintly men such as Job and John the Baptist, Gregory concludes that God strikes those whom he loves because
"he knows how to reward them. . . . He casts them down outwardly to
something despicable in order to lead them on inwardly to the height of
things incomprehensible."[57]

This rhythm of being "cast down" and then "led on inwardly to the
height of things incomprehensible" fascinates Gregory and explains his
belief in the beneficial power of nonretributive suffering. Gregory
makes an inseparable connection between oppositions of interiority and
exteriority and of adversity and prosperity. These structural motifs are
inseparable because they are causally related: Suffering turns people inward and leads them upward toward God. Suffering, then, leads to interiority, and interiority leads to a higher perception. Through adversity
even the just sufferer learns "who he is" and benefits from the liberating
and perceptual effects of affliction.

Gregory's Job made progress through his suffering. His endurance of
affliction brought self-illumination and made Job a model for future
generations. According to Gregory, Job's suffering made his inner virtue
known both to himself and to others. Job, who "knew how to serve God
when surrounded by blessings," was subjected to "a most searching se-

verity," which put him to the test so that his rectitude and fortitude would be "made clear."[58] Job proved his love of God, his constancy of mind, and the strength of his patience. Gregory reflects on Job's virtuous suffering by explaining that "strength is never shown except in adversity and therefore patience immediately leads to strength."[59] Through his patient endurance of adversity, Job gained mastery of himself, for "he who has patience possesses his soul, since from the strength with which he conquered all adversities, he has conquered himself and is made master of himself."[60] Such "possession of his soul" enabled Job to battle against Satan. In his "trial of probation" Job fought against his wife, his friends, temptation, and the devil. He proved himself a "mighty warrior" against the accusations of his companions[61] and stood unconquered against the machinations of Satan.[62] He fought both external and internal wars, but his "fortifications" remained unshaken.[63] In his interpretation of Job, Gregory combines a militant spirituality, a muscular view of suffering, and the perceptual theme of self-knowledge.

This robust suffering produced not anger or rebellion but *detachment*. Gregory's primary purpose is to portray Job as the exemplary sufferer whose main virtue was detachment from temporal realities, including adversity and prosperity. To do so he must read Job's speeches as the words of a patient sufferer. In this he differs from Maimonides, Aquinas, and Calvin, all of whom more fully acknowledge Job's anger and bitterness. Gregory, however, belonged to a different exegetical tradition. Since Job was said to have "spoken what is right" before God, Gregory denies that his laments were curses, complaints, or accusations against the deity. In a way that was to make Calvin very uneasy, Gregory resolutely defends the reverence and piety of *all* Job's words. Job's cry, "Nor will I contradict the words of the Holy one," proves to Gregory that throughout his many speeches Job never "murmured" against divine justice.[64] To reconcile Job's words with the divine vindication in 42:7, Gregory insists that Job always spoke as one "full of humility."[65] Nonetheless, Gregory is aware that Job's statements "sound harshly" to readers of little experience.[66] He warns that we must understand Job's words according to their "interior meaning" and not remain tied to the "mere outside" of the text.[67] This exegetical principle allows Job's laments to become expressions of a wise man who transcended the allurements of time, change, and exteriority. Gregory, therefore, reads passages such as the following to be true insights into the vain and transitory nature of fallen human existence, an existence from which Job desired to escape:

After this Job opened his mouth and cursed his day. . . . Perish the day on which I was born. . . . Why was light given to a miserable man and life to the bitter in soul who long for death but it does not come? (Job 3:1–2, 20–21)

The life of man upon earth is warfare. And like the day of the hireling is his day. Just as a slave earnestly desires the shade and as a hireling waits for the end of his work, so, too, I have endured worthless months and I have counted wearisome nights. . . . My days have passed more swiftly than a web is cut off by the weaver and they have been consumed without any hope. Remember that my life is wind. (Job 7:1–7)

I have despaired. . . . I will not live any longer. Spare me, for my days are nothing. (Job 7:16)

For the modern reader, these verses are expressions of Job's despair and defiance. For Gregory they are the opposite. In Gregory's view, these passages demonstrate Job's detached transcendence and internal constancy of mind; Job's words describe the vanity of temporal life, the advantage of suffering, the turning inward from exterior goods, and the longing for eternity. Furthermore, these themes are not found simply in the allegorical and moral meanings of the text; they are the *literal* intent of Gregory's Job.[68] To understand the *Moralia* exegetically we have to step through the looking glass into an inverted world. What for the biblical Job was the realm of ultimate reality becomes for Gregory's Job only the lowest level of existence. What the biblical Job considered valuable about earthly life is seen as a temptation by Gregory's Job. Gregory, then, transvalues Job's words, judging the nature of the temporal world contrary to our normal expectations. In short, he turns Job's speeches upside down.

At this juncture we can see how Gregory's interpretation is informed by the combination of his spirituality of suffering, his appeal to interiority, and his hierarchical view of reality. For Gregory, these verses are expressions of a perspective on reality gained through the experience of suffering. Affliction turned Job inward and allowed him to ascend to a higher level of being. Job's laments, then, describe the lowest level of reality in the Neoplatonic hierarchy. This lower historical existence often seduces its inhabitants, thereby entrapping them in the fallen world of time. But Job's inner detachment prevented him from being enticed by the beguiling nature of history. In these discussions Gregory articulates a principle that became crucial to Maimonides, Aquinas, and Calvin: Job alone perceived history honestly. All of our commentators seek to explain Job's perceptual superiority over his friends. Gregory attributes Job's perceptual advantage to the perspective on history provided by detachment, a perspective gained only by one who, turning inward, suffers well.

Gregory's transvaluation of the text is clear from his interpretation of chapters 3 and 7. Job's wish that the day of his birth would perish cannot be taken literally because, like all temporal realities, the day of his birth has passed. One cannot curse that which "has no existence."[69] References to time give rise in Gregory's exegesis to descriptions of humanity's tragic involvement in the mutability of temporal life. When cursing the day of his birth, Job was really condemning "the whole period of our mortal state"—that is, the "time of guilt" in which humanity must now live.[70] In this passage Gregory's Job wished "the day of change would perish and the light of eternity burst forth."[71] Thus in chapter 7 Gregory reads Job as bewailing the harshness and frailty of human life, since that life is now entangled in change and exterior things.[72] Life is "warfare [militia]" because through sin human beings have fallen from a state of interiority into the world of exteriority.[73] Job's comparison of himself to a hireling is not a sign of despair but of hope for eternity; like a hireling, he waits for his days to pass so that he may attain the reward of his toil: "and so the days of man enlightened with a knowledge of the truth of the things of eternity, are rightly compared to the days of a hireling because he considers the present life to be his road and not his country, a warfare, not the palm of victory, and he sees that the further he is from the reward the more slowly he is drawing near to his end."[74] Because the reward is eternal life, Gregory's Job dreads that the moments of life will pass by *without* "labor" because, like all of the elect, "he rejoices in adversity, he is restored by suffering, he is comforted by mourning, because he sees himself to be the more abundantly repaid with the rewards of the life to come, the more thoroughly he devotes himself by the love of that life through daily deaths."[75]

Gregory's Neoplatonic view of history influences not only his reading of Job's laments about the harshness and brevity of life but also Job's protests about divine injustice. Gregory's Job clearly saw the prosperity of the wicked. He simply did not interpret that prosperity as a sign of God's injustice. In the following passages, Gregory again finds expressions of Job's inner detached transcendence. Viewing the happiness of the wicked, Job rose above the fatal enticements of the temporal life and renounced all desire to wealth and earthly security:

Why do the wicked live, are raised up and comforted by riches? Their seed remains before their eyes and a crowd of relatives and grandchildren are in their sight. Their houses are secure and peaceful, and God's rod is not upon them. Their ox has conceived and has not aborted. . . . They spend their days in wealth and in an instant [puncto] they go down to the underworld. (Job 21:7–9, 13)

The interpretive assumptions that lead Gregory to read these verses as literal condemnations of the prosperity enjoyed by the wicked are clear when read in conjunction with his preface to chapter 5 (the passage cited above that warns against the dangers of tranquillity).[76] Gregory inverts the meaning of these texts by reading them as warnings about the dangers of peace and happiness. Gregory is not denying the empirical evidence of what Calvin later called the "confusion" or "disorder" of history. The wicked really do live a life of ease. But that fact only demonstrates further the depth dimension of reality and the problematic nature of human perception. Once again, the perceptual issue functions as a decisive exegetical device. When it concerns divine judgments, "the human mind is closed in by the great darkness of its uncertainty."[77]

For one who has transcended the earthly realm, the ambiguity of historical events is clear. This means that the secure and pleasant life may be a divine punishment and sign of God's abandonment because it leaves human beings without the necessary "rod of discipline," which can release them from the enticing attractions of the temporal life. The very real prosperity and tranquillity of the wicked are dangerous because their perishable and seductive nature goes unseen. Only interiority, suffering, and death clarify the illusory character of this earthly joy. Hence Gregory's Job knows that the judgments of divine providence are "still more hidden when it both goes well with the good here below and badly with the wicked."[78] In these verses Gregory's Job did *not* envy the life of the wicked or impugn God's justice, but rather reflected on the fleeting and ultimately deceptive nature of the happiness enjoyed by the impious. All the riches of the wicked disappear "in a point of time" or an "instant" because "all the length of time of the present life is known to be only a 'point' when it is cut short by an end."[79]

These examples demonstrate how the perceptual implications in the ancient hierarchy of Being transform Job's words into statements about the vanity of historical existence. By turning inward, Gregory's Job rose above both adversity and prosperity and thereby exemplified the virtue of detachment. Job's perception of reality manifested his wisdom and ability to evaluate properly the adversities of temporal existence. Visual or perspectival imagery dominates Gregory's explanations of why holy men such as Job rejoice over the brevity of life. According to Gregory, the wise man gains a true perception about the nature of the transient world. Commenting on Job 7:7 ("Oh remember that my life is wind"), Gregory writes:

But holy men insofar as they lift their hearts toward the eternal world, consider life's end and its brevity. All that is transient becomes worthless to their senses; the eternal pours in its light through the rays of intelligence which, once received, never departs. As soon as they contemplate the infinite reach of eternity, they cease to desire as comparable anything which has limitation. The mind, when lifted up, is carried beyond the limits of time. Even when such a mind is constrained in time by the flesh, it nevertheless scorns [despicit] from this greater height all that is to have an end, and more truly understands the things that are without end.[80]

Repeatedly Gregory argues that external circumstances left Job's interior nature untouched, "for no bad fortune throws down the man whom no good fortune corrupts."[81] Change cannot reach the "citadel of the interior."[82] Job's continual arguments about the justice of his case, the innocence of his life, and his desire to argue with God are assertions that his soul remained fixed and had not been swept along by the movement of temporality. "For as times pass by," Gregory insists, "they are unable to draw along the just man . . . a man completely subject to God knows how to stand fixed [stare] among transient things."[83] In Job's words in 31:24 ("If I thought that gold was my strength or have said to bullion 'Thou art my security'") Gregory again finds proof of Job's inward detachment. One who places his hope in temporal goods such as gold or bullion "lays his foundation in running waters."[84] Therefore, Gregory argues, "he who adheres to things that are slipping away [labentibus] is surely drawn along with those things onto which he is holding . . . being united to objects which are running downwards [decurrentibus], the soul soon loses its immovability [statum]."[85] Not so Job: Throughout the *Moralia*, Gregory depicts Job's virtue in terms of his turning inward and rising above all changeable things so that he might remain fixed on the unchangeable. In 31:34 Job said that he "kept silent" and did not fear "the contempt of neighbors" because his mind was firmly fixed on the heavenly country. Such a mind is truly free from all external commotions and, by retreating inward, attaches itself to the Immutable so that "ascending above all changeable things, by the sheer calmness of its rest, is henceforth in the world but also without the world."[86] Although the infirmity of his flesh suffered pain and disquietude from lower things, Job rested in the "security of a holy mind."[87]

When Gregory turns to the allegorical level of the text, the modern reader of the *Moralia* is often left with a sense of disjunction and incoherency. However, a patient reading shows that the theme of the perception granted to one who ascends above history again unifies all levels of the text. While the "historical" Job inwardly transcended the vicissitudes of time, the "allegorical" Job rose above the immediate historical present and in so doing both prophesied Christ and the church and recounted God's salvific acts in history. A certain rhythm recurs throughout the *Moralia:* As Job ascends, the reader descends to the deeper meanings buried beneath the historical surface of the text. These deeper meanings finally lift both Job and the reader to a higher perceptual level that allows them to bestow value on a portion of the historical realm.

That the centrality of suffering resurfaces in the allegorical interpretations shows that Gregory finds the depictions of suffering in the Joban text to characterize the essence of Christian existence. According to Gregory, the elect of the Old Testament were all forerunners of Christ and prophesied his life in both their deeds and their words. Job was no exception, and his life of sorrow was only too suitable for the Christocentric interpretation bestowed on it by Gregory. In Gregory's view, it was fitting that Job "should signify by his words the One whom he proclaimed by voice and by all that he endured should show forth what were to be the Lord's sufferings and should foretell the mysteries of his passion as he prophesied not only by speaking but also with his sufferings."[88]

Gregory can make this exegetical claim because, unlike our other commentators, he identifies Job as a prophet. To interpret Job as a prophet of Christ, Gregory reads the events recounted in the Prologue as descriptions of Christ's suffering; just as Job suffered "without cause," so too Christ suffered "without sin."[89] When God said to Satan, "Behold he is in your hand," he was declaring that Christ would give himself up to Satan's members for the salvation of sinners.[90] Thus Gregory interprets many of Job's laments as descriptions of the adversities sustained by Christ. Job 19:15 ("And I have been like a foreigner in their eyes") refers allegorically to the rejection of Christ by the synagogue.[91] Job's wish for death in 9:23 refers to his prophetic desire for the death by the Mediator.[92] When Job lamented in 9:24 that the "earth is given into the hands of the wicked [one]," he predicted the crucifixion of Christ.[93]

Employing the exegetical rule regarding the interchangeability of head and body, Gregory reemphasizes the centrality of suffering by interpreting Job's "afflictions and groanings" as the sufferings experienced by the body of Christ. Gregory defines the adversities of the church as the suffering inflicted on the church by persecutors, by the wicked, and by heretics (represented by the friends).[94] Verses such as Job 16:8 ("But now my pain has crushed me and all my limbs have been reduced to nothing") and 16:12 ("God has shut me up with the ungodly one and turned me over into the hands of the wicked") are only two of the many passages Gregory reads as prophetic descriptions of the afflictions endured by the church in battles with internal and external enemies.[95]

Many scholars find this turn exegetically egregious. On the contrary, if we analyze Gregory's theory of prophecy—a theory that has important implications for his view of time and history—we can understand how this allegorical style of exegesis actually forms a coherent interpretation of the Book of Job. Gregory argues that as a type of Christ and the church, Job was filled with the "spirit of prophecy" so that he was capable of "looking down" and surveying past, present, and future at once.[96] Passages such as the following recur throughout the *Moralia* and illustrate Gregory's view of the perceptual abilities granted to Job by the "Spirit of Eternity":

The holy man, then, full of the Spirit of Eternity, binds to his memory by the hand of his heart, all things that are passing away [cuncta labentia] . . . he views both what shall be [hoc quod erit] and what has been [hoc quod praeteriit]; turning the eye of the mind both below and above, regarding things that are coming or are past, he burns in the core of his heart toward eternal being.[97]

In his *Homilies on Ezekiel*, Gregory shaped into a more coherent view of prophecy many of the insights scattered throughout the *Moralia*. Most significant is his statement in the first homily on Ezekiel that "prophecy is so called not because it predicts the future but because it reveals what is hidden."[98] Prophecy "reveals what is hidden" by drawing events and their meaning out from the depths of the past or the hidden future. By dispelling the limits of time, the prophet "lays bare" that which lies concealed.[99] Gregory presupposes such a view of prophecy when he argues that Job viewed "both what shall be" and "what has been" because on the prophetic or allegorical level of the text he transcended the limitations of time. Thus he remarks that "sometimes it is not enough that the Spirit of Prophecy foresees future events unless at the same time it presents to the view of the prophet the ancient and past events. Thus the holy man opens his eyes both below and above [infra supraque oculos aperit] and not only fixes them on the future but also recalls the past."[100] In 13:1 Gregory seizes on the phrase "Behold, all!" and interprets it to mean that all things were "made present" to Job's mind by the spirit of prophecy: "For those things which were to follow, [Job] saw as present in Him who neither things future come to nor things past go from, but all things are present at once and together [simul] before his eyes."[101] Moreover, because the spirit of prophecy lifted him to see things "in God," Gregory's Job understood all his own prophetic significance and viewed the entire scope of history: "Therefore, in order that the blessed Job might testify that he had the spirit of prophecy, he declares not only that he had 'seen and heard,' but also that he had 'understood' all these things."[102]

When Job ascended, time collapsed; looking "both above and below," he could perceive all God's mighty acts in history. Thus, Gregory portrays Job as recounting the life and virtues of the prophets and patriarchs, the hope for a future Mediator, the incarnation, Passion, and resurrection of Christ, the work of the apostles and martyrs, and the growth of the church. When Job cried, "Or as a hidden miscarriage I would not exist," Gregory thinks he was recalling all the elect from the

beginning of the world to the time of the incarnation who had lived as
though "dead" to the world.[103] When Gregory's Job "shaved his head,"
he prefigured Christ who also "shaved his head" by taking the sacra-
ments from the Jewish priesthood and thereby cut off the glory of Israel.[104] When Job cried, "Naked I came from the womb of my mother,"
he prophesied Christ who left the synagogue (his mother) and manifested himself to the Gentiles.[105] Job's question in 21:31 ("Who shall
criticize his way in his presence. . . ?") foretold that God alone would
rebuke the Antichrist.[106]

This theory of prophecy bears major significance for the perceptual
implications of the hierarchy of Being that permeate Gregory's interpretation. In particular, the perceptual dimension of prophecy transforms
his hierarchical evaluation of the temporal sphere and reclaims as salvific at least part of history. Gregory is not doing anything new here; he is
simply employing typology on the allegorical level of the text. However,
this traditional Christian insertion of typology into allegory serves an
exegetically perceptual function for Job in the *Moralia*. Seeing past and
future salvific events "at once," Job was able to "look down" and bestow
value on the stream of redemptive acts that wound its way through the
historical realm. The reader can begin to see the ambiguity in Gregory's
many references to the vanity of historical existence. Like Job, the
church suffers from its entanglement with time and change. The church
also "counts wearisome nights" and "endures worthless months" because of suffering the weaknesses of members and enduring the "tribulations of the present life."[107] The "flesh" of the church is "clothed in
corruption and with the filth of dust" because she still leads a life of cor-
ruptibility and never ceases to bewail "her condition of mutability."[108]
Nonetheless, Gregory also recognizes that the church makes progress in
and through the passage of time. Thus Job's words in 9:8 ("And [He]
walks upon the waves of the sea") are interpreted by Gregory as the
church's advancement within history:

The sea rages and is lifted up in the waves of its madness. Nonetheless, because
it is trodden upon by the manifestation of interior power, Holy Church makes
progress [proficit] and, by the passage of time [temporum incrementa], rises to
her own rank. . . . For with the end of the world pressing upon us, the knowledge from above advances [proficit] and becomes greater with the progress of
time [tempore excrescit].[109]

From his transcendent viewpoint, gained on the allegorical level of
the text, Job could perceive the salvific nature of the historical events
that were a part of that world he yearned to leave behind. In the midst
of this "wearisome" and "turbulent" realm of history, change, and exteriority, Gregory's Job glimpsed and traced God's entrance into time.

Speeches of Job's Friends

For one who seeks to read the *Moralia* exegetically, Gregory's interpretation of Job's friends is one of the most frustrating and confusing aspects of the text. The fundamental reason for this confusion is that in the speeches of Job's companions, Gregory confronts a problem that many later commentators also had to face: how to rescue the moral wisdom of the friends and yet still account for the divine reproof in the end. Why didn't Job's friends "speak what is right" before God? Gregory cannot deny that God "does great and inscrutable things," that God "does not pervert justice," that the creature "cannot be more pure than his Maker," and that the "innocent man shall be saved."

Gregory manages to reclaim what he thinks are the incontrovertible truths of such verses by making several arguments that grant a certain polyvalence to the speeches of the friends. On the historical level of the text, Job's companions were simply men who said many true things but misapplied them to Job's situation, the true cause of which they could not understand. The friends, Gregory argues, could not see that Job's suffering was intended to increase his merit and reveal the power of divine deliverance. Assuming that affliction was only due to the chastisement for sin, the friends concluded wrongly that Job must have been guilty of past crimes.[110] He proceeds to transform this concept of causes for suffering into a perceptual issue with important exegetical consequences.

On the allegorical and moral levels of interpretation, Gregory invests Job's companions with the same multidimensional texture. In his reading, Eliphaz, Bildad, and Zophar represent heretics who wrongly condemned Job and the church for their adversities and further inflicted them with deceptive teaching. Their teaching was deceptive because, like all heretics, they "mix truth with error" to mislead their hearers.[111] The case of Elihu differs somewhat from the other friends. Gregory argues that since in 42:7 God rebuked only Eliphaz and his *two* friends, Elihu signified not heretics but "a class of teachers who are faithful but arrogant."[112] In some ways, Gregory has created an interpretive nightmare. Is what the friends say true or false? Are the teachings of these heretics right or wrong? How does one discern the correct teaching? While Gregory's readers seek the interior meaning of Job's words, they must also scrutinize and screen carefully the outer and inner meanings of the words of Job's friends. Gregory, of course, acts as their guide. There is a purpose, however, behind this apparent exegetical chaos. Although he is not always successful, Gregory is trying to attain a certain theological consistency that allows the *entire* Book of Job to serve as a source of moral and theological edification. Unlike modern interpreters, Gregory does not admit that the Book of Job intends to make the reader choose between conflicting viewpoints. As a result, Gregory's attempt at harmonizing the book creates a constant and shifting density in the text that is often disorienting.

Gregory's exegetical principles allow him to affirm many teachings of Job's companions. Although not applicable to Job, their speeches retain an "intrinsic worth" for the reader. Gregory justifies this point by observing that St. Paul quoted Eliphaz in 1 Cor. 3:19. Concluding from Paul's citation that the reader is supposed to benefit from the wisdom of the friends, Gregory asks, "How can we reject as evil what Paul established by authority?"[113] In some passages, however, his defense of these chapters creates a seemingly monotonous continuity between the speeches by Job and those by the friends. This continuity obscures or ignores the debate going on between the parties. In the words of the friends, for example, Gregory finds many of the same truths expressed by Job: the transcendent and immutable being of God, the nature of contemplation, the priority of the eternal over the temporal, the fall into time, the need for interiority, and the ascent above temporality.

In part, this continuity between Job and his friends extends even to their theology of suffering. One would expect the friends alone to be the exponents of retributive suffering. But the importance Gregory attaches to the connection between adversity and sin is clear when he attributes even to Job a knowledge of the benefits of penitential affliction. For example, Job knew the importance of affliction for self-knowledge of sin. Commenting on 30:6 ("They dwelt in the desert places of the torrents"), Gregory remarks that as soon as people fall into sin, they are further removed from the knowledge of the self. Transgression becomes a perceptual obstacle "before the eye of reason."[114] Thus Gregory's Job knew that the elect need adversity because of their sinfulness. In 6:10 ("And let this be my consolation, that He not spare me, afflicting me with pain"), Job knew that the elect expect suffering for sin and fear "unless safe from the punishment for evil, grace should have forsaken them forever." The elect, then are always eager to be corrected by God.[115]

These affirmations of retributive suffering are consistent with Gregory's view that Job himself confessed to sin. In Gregory's mind, therefore, there is a shared theology of suffering between Job and his friends. The difference is that Job's friends had too narrow a view and so did not recognize that "many are the afflictions of the righteous" (Ps. 34:90) and that "God scourges every son whom he receives."[116] Job differed from his companions in his insistence that his present adversities served a purpose *other* than correction or punishment. Here we see a certain uneasiness on Gregory's part regarding the figure of Job, an uneasiness that became much more pronounced in Calvin's *Sermons*. Gregory knows that Job's situation is not the commonest reason God sends adversity. By finding the retributive theology of suffering in his words and by making the moral sense of the text always apply to the reader, Gregory is insisting that if the reader suffers adversity, he or she should attribute it to sin. In other words, one should not assume too quickly that one's own situation is that of Job.

The situation of the reader is most likely that described by Job's friends. Suffering will still lead to self-knowledge, contemplation, a new perspective on reality, and detachment. Nonetheless, for most people the benefit of suffering will begin with the recognition of sin, for this is the overriding purpose of most affliction. Not surprisingly, most of the passages explaining the necessity for penitential suffering are found in the speeches of the friends. Thus, in his discussion of the words of the companions we find Gregory's most extended analyses of sin, the role of temptation, the nature of particular vices, the necessity for humility, and the dangers of pride. Eliphaz's words in 5:6 ("Nothing happens on earth without a cause, and pain will not come forth from the ground") naturally give rise to a discussion of sin as the cause of suffering. Pain does not come forth from the ground because the scourges of God are chastisement for sin.[117]

In the retributive theology preached by the friends, Gregory often defends the medicinal function of chastisement, a function always expressed in the perceptual terms of self-knowledge. Sufferers gain an awareness of vices and spiritual sins of which they were unaware in times of peace and prosperity. As punishment, affliction awakens the mind from "self-security," reveals the healing power of confession, and drives the soul to humility. Speaking of the "terror" of God's voice, Gregory's Elihu describes how the divine scourge brings to mind the strict judgment of God and opens the eye to sin.[118] The classic text depicting the perceptual advantage of chastisement is Eliphaz's statement in 5:l7: "Blessed is the man who is corrected by the Lord; do not reprove the rebuke of the Lord." Noting that other biblical verses teach this same truth, Gregory cites Eph. 5:13, Heb. 12:ll, Eccles. 10:4, and Prov. 3:2 to explain the validity of Eliphaz's insight. Eliphaz wrongly applied these words to the "holy man" because he believed that Job's was a trial of "purification" rather than "probation."[119] Nonetheless, Gregory insists, trials of purification are real and beneficial, and on the moral level of the text such verses apply to the reader:

And the mind of the sinner is enveloped in deeper darkness so that it does not see the harm of its own blindness. Hence it is often the case, by the greatness of

God's gift, that punishment follows guilt, and scourges open the eyes of the transgressor, who was blind, caught up in the vice of self-security. For a sluggish soul is touched by the rod . . . and thus the very harshness of correction becomes a source of light.[120]

This exegetical strategy is appealing to Gregory because it allows him to defend the pedagogical and punitive character of suffering and permits him to make the moral sense of the story equally applicable to the speeches of Job and to those of the friends. But Gregory does not affirm the friends in an unqualified manner, occasionally criticizing even their "true" teachings. Heretics, for example, cannot truly understand the mystery of the incarnation.[121] Moreover, the friends were hypocrites and pretenders. They falsely accused the church of sin because of her adversities.[122] His explanation of their reproof again reveals his concern with the problematic nature of *perception,* a concern governed by his assumptions about interiority and exteriority. On the historical level, Job's friends sinned out of ignorance rather than out of wickedness, so they could not discern the true cause of Job's adversities. As hypocrites and heretics, however, they "outwardly feigned" good deeds and appeared to teach sound doctrine when "in reality" they spoke deceitfully and preached heresy. On all levels they lacked humility. Even on the literal level, Job's companions were of a "high mind."[123] This emphasis on humility is not due simply to Gregory's praise of obedience as a virtue; for him, one's inner spiritual disposition determines the depth of one's insight. Gregory summarizes the perceptual failure of the prideful, exemplified by Elihu:

Blessed Job said rightly that he had been scourged without any fault. . . . But Elihu did not believe . . . he [Job] could be scourged as a matter of grace. . . . For it is a quality of the arrogant to be more eager to convict than to console. . . . They do not know how to inquire deeply into the secret judgments of God and to investigate with humility that which they cannot understand. . . . Even when these persons seem to acquire knowledge, they feed, as it were, on the husks [cortice] of things and not on the marrow of their innermost sweetness [et non de secretae dulcedinis medulla]. And with their biting skill, they frequently reach only to outward things [exteriora], but do not know the savor of inward taste [interni gustum]. Indeed though they are sharpsighted outwardly [foris], inwardly [intus] they are blind. Nor do they form a notion of God which tastes secretly within, theirs are like utterances without meaning, a "sound" but no more. . . . But the mind of arrogant men does not penetrate the meaning of its own words; because by a righteous judgment [their mind] is driven away from the inward taste of things.[124]

Whether due to hypocrisy, ignorance, the love of temporal goods, or spiritual pride, their lack of humility prevented the friends from seeing

all that was discerned by Job. The perceptual failure of the friends creates an exegetical disjunction in the text that is crucial for interpreting
the *Moralia*. Gregory's exegesis of the dialogues causes him to find a dizzying array of levels in the Book of Job. There are, of course, the historical, moral, and allegorical meanings of the biblical text. But Gregory's
interpretation of the friends creates even more layers by introducing
new distinctions among the words, the object of these words (Job), and
the speakers.

Gregory's procedure gains a certain intelligibility if we recognize that
his arguments validate the friends by perceptually shifting the position
of the reader. While Gregory's readers are expected to be receptive to
the teachings of Job, they must exercise critical judgment with reference
to Job's companions. Unlike the friends, readers can discern the proper
cause of Job's adversities. This perceptual advantage enables them to distinguish properly in the speeches of the companions between the truth
and its misapplication. By distinguishing what was true for Job and what
applies to the readers, Gregory and his readers make a distinction between the original intent of the biblical words and their universal application. Although wrongly applied to the "historical" Job, the words of
the friends do pertain to others.

Gregory makes a similar exegetical maneuver on the allegorical level
of interpretation. Since heretics include right teaching with false doctrine, the task of Gregory's readers is to "sift" and "distinguish" between
their words and to "penetrate" their inward meanings, thereby choosing
the true and rejecting the false.[125] Gregory thus places himself and his
readers at a critical distance from the friends so that they can discern
truth from falsity in the theological or doctrinal statements of Job's companions.

By making the perceptual abilities of the friends more problematic
than those of Job, the *Moralia* places the reader on a higher moral and
perceptual level than the speaker. In so doing Gregory grants to his readers a discriminating capacity that exceeds that of the friends. He thus
makes the *whole* biblical Book of Job available for theological and moral
reflection. For example, after criticizing Elihu's lack of inward perception in 33:12, Gregory validates his vision in 33:15.[126] He is then able to
discover in Elihu's words profound descriptions of contemplation, as
well as prophecies of Christ and the church. So, too, after condemning
the pride, hypocrisy, and heresy of Job's friends, Gregory confirms the
truth of their teachings about creaturely impurity, divine justice, the relationship between suffering and sin, the judgment of the wicked, and
the pedagogical and perceptual power of affliction.[127]

The Whirlwind Speech

At first reading, the exegesis of the whirlwind speech swirls with myriad Gregorian themes, apparently ignoring the fact that chapters 38–41 are supposed to answer the questions posed by the Book of Job. This section compounds the difficulty of discerning any exegetical coherence in the *Moralia*. Moreover, any attempt to find Gregory's interpretation intelligible is further complicated by our modern expectations of the whirlwind speech. For many contemporary commentators the divine response is problematic since it does not seem to resolve Job's questions about the injustice of his suffering. In the face of Job's unjust afflictions, God responds with a demonstration of overwhelming power. As Tsevat says, "The problem of the innocent sufferer is everywhere in the book. Where is the answer?"[128] Girard calls the God of the whirlwind a charlatan and argues that "like the Prologue and the conclusion, the only purpose of the speeches of God is to eliminate the essential and to make the Dialogues unreadable, to transform the Book of Job into a ludicrous antidote mechanically cited by everyone."[129]

This judgment would surprise Gregory (and his successors), for whom the whirlwind speech is not particularly troublesome. Is this because he does not see that the question of justice has been answered only by an appeal to power? To understand how Gregory perceives the divine response as an answer to Job, we must first recognize that he does not see chapters 38–41 as answering primarily the question of justice. Gregory does address the issue of divine justice in this section, but only because certain texts compel him to do so. His defense of God's actions remains a minor theme in the *Moralia* because he does not see theodicy as the main issue raised by inexplicable suffering.

If Gregory's assumptions about the beneficial nature of affliction mitigate the problem of justice, what can he understand as the purpose of the whirlwind speech? Gregory's exegesis of chapters 38–41 becomes comprehensible only if we understand that to his mind they answer the "problem" posed by the Book of Job by quite rightly revealing the power of the Creator. For Gregory, God's power is symbolized by his mastery of Behemoth and Leviathan who are identified with Satan. This identification of the great beasts with Satan was repeated by Aquinas but derisively repudiated by Calvin. The interpretation of Behemoth and Leviathan as Satan, however, is important because it alters how the exegete considers the function of the whirlwind speech in the book as a whole. We must appreciate, then, the question *Gregory* thinks the whirlwind speech had to answer: By what power does one overcome the attacks and temptations of the devil? In Gregory's view, what Job needed was not justice but a God powerful enough to protect him from the assaults of Satan.

The revelation of divine power takes its initial form in all the seemingly disparate subjects Gregory finds in chapters 38–39. Those subjects crystallize into a twofold demonstration of God's power: the creation and history of the church, and the work of God in the soul. When God asked, "Where were you when I was setting the foundations of the earth?" Job heard of the prophets, apostles, and preachers upon whom the church was founded.[130] On the moral level of instruction Job was told that God gives the human being faith, which is the "foundation" of divine work in the soul.[131] So too when God asked, "Who shut up the sea with doors?" Job understood that God protected the church against the "sea" of the world or the wrath of persecutors by setting up "bars and doors"—namely, Christ.[132] On the moral level of the speech, Job saw that God restrains the "storms of temptation" in the heart through the "door" of divine grace.[133] Throughout these first two chapters of the divine speeches, Gregory's Job learned about the virtues of past saints; the suffering, protection, and growth of the church; the mystery of predestination; and the power of grace in the soul.

This demonstration of God's power reaches its zenith in chapters 40–41 with the appearance of Behemoth and Leviathan, whom Gregory identifies as Satan and the Antichrist. We can isolate several verses that prove central to Gregory's interpretation of these chapters as descriptions of the fall and damnation of the devil: 40:10 ("Behold Behemoth, whom I made along with you"), 40:14 ("[Behemoth] is the beginning of God's ways"), 41:16 ("When [Leviathan] has been taken away, the angels will fear and being frightened, they will be purified"), and 41:25 ("[Leviathan] is king over all the sons of pride"). Verse 40:10 refers to the creation of Satan as an angel when God "made all things at once."[134] Behemoth is called the "beginning of the ways of God," because when first created, Satan was preeminent among the angels. The angels were "purified" when Leviathan was "taken away" because when the devil fell, they were given a special gift that prevented their defection from God.[135] Leviathan is "king over all the sons of pride" because as Eccles. 10:13 states, "Pride is the beginning of all sins."[136] God's call, "Behold Behemoth," therefore, warned Job that since a rational angelic nature could fall, he too should beware lest Satan overthrow him through the same original sin of pride.[137]

We see, then, that with Behemoth and Leviathan the "Ancient Enemy" reappears in Gregory's rendering of the Joban story. Through detailed allegorical analyses, Gregory finds descriptions of the slyness, fury, and power of the devil. The fact that Leviathan "will consider iron as straw" shows that the virtues and strength of the elect are as "straw" before the power of Satan.[138] Behemoth "will swallow a river and will not wonder and has confidence that he can pour the Jordan into his mouth," because the devil has drawn to himself "like a river, the human race flowing downward from the beginning of the world."[139] Job 41:24 teaches that "no power on earth can be compared to [Leviathan's]" since Satan's angelic nature still surpasses all human strength.[140]

But where humans fail, God succeeds. The defeat of Satan is finally described through the references to a "hook" in 40:19–20 ("In his eyes he will catch [Behemoth] as with a hook. . . . Or will you be able to draw out Leviathan with a hook?"). For Gregory, these verses demand an account of the atonement whereby Christ overcame the devil by tricking him with the "hook of his incarnation," because "while [the devil] sought in Him the bait of his body, he was pierced with the sharp point of His divinity."[141]

If we search for the text that gives Gregory's interpretation of chapters 38–41 an internal interpretive rationality, we discover that 40:27 serves as the hermeneutical key to the whirlwind speech as a whole: "Will you lay your hand upon [Behemoth]? Remember the battle and speak no more." At this point Job saw how powerful was the adversary arrayed against him. He also understood how useful were his many adversities because "if our flesh is not afflicted with pain before it is strengthened with the incorruption of resurrection, then it is unchecked in temptation."[142] By scourging Job, God strengthened and protected him against the cunning temptations of Satan, temptations that human virtue cannot withstand:

For every weight would be as nothing to our minds if we considered the assaults which the secret adversary might level against us. What if Almighty God were to lighten the burdens we suffer and yet withdraw from us his assistance, abandoning us amidst the trials of this Leviathan? Where shall we flee from the rages of such a furious enemy who is raging against us if we are left defenseless by our Creator? . . . Lest [Job] should exceed in the sin of murmuring, let him be reminded what to fear and let it be said to him, "Remember the battle and speak no more." As if it were plainly said to him, "If you consider the warfare of the secret enemy against you, you would not blame whatever you suffer from me. If you would behold the sword of the adversary assailing you, you would not at all dread the scourge of a Father. For you see with what scourge I strike you, but you fail to recognize from how great an enemy I keep you free by my scourging."[143]

In this passage we can see clearly why, to Gregory's mind, the divine answer to Job was rightly about God's "dreadful power." Since he interprets Behemoth and Leviathan as Satan, Gregory must have understood God's speeches as addressing not the issues recounted in the Dialogues but rather the celestial contest recounted in the Prologue. In Gregory's hands the end of the book refers the reader back to the beginning, and Job's story becomes only one more example of the celestial warfare that has raged since the devil's fall. Thus the overarching theme of God's honor reappears at the conclusion of the book in Gregory's description of God's victory over Satan. At the end of his ordeal, Job finally learned the craftiness and power of his real enemy, the devil, an enemy before whom his virtue and humility were no match. Thus Gregory recalls us not only to the Prologue of the Book of Job but to his own preface in the *Moralia* where he has explained that Job was afflicted to increase his merit and "show the power of the Deliverer when deliverance follows the scourge."[144] In God's defeat of Satan, Job finally witnessed the power of God's deliverance.

Before this vast demonstration of God's majestic power, Job confessed twice, once in 39:34–35 and again in 42:3. On the basis of these verses Gregory expresses his rare criticisms of Job. According to Gregory, Job confessed that he was "far from patient under the rod," that he was both "wicked before the scourges and stubborn after them," and that he knew himself to be "justly accused."[145] These statements jar the reader who has become accustomed to Gregory's unrelenting defense of Job's patience and humility. However, we gain some empathy with Gregory's criticism of Job if we read his remarks in terms of his constant preoccupation with the subtle dangers of spiritual pride. Throughout the *Moralia* Gregory analyzes the danger that a person may become elated by real progress in virtue.[146] Here a new element emerges as he applies the threat of such spiritual pride to the figure of Job. In Job, Gregory sees an untested propensity for pride at having endured suffering so virtuously. Thus he thinks that God responded to Job to protect him "unless his victory should lay him low with the sword of pride." Having "stood firm in his virtues," Job "needed to be humbled unless the weapons of pride should pierce that most sturdy breast, which plainly even the wounds that had been inflicted had not conquered."[147]

In these two confessions, therefore, Gregory's Job bowed before the transcendence of God. Recognizing his need for divine protection, Job was humbled by comparing his human righteousness to the righteousness of God. Job's confessions and such texts as 40:3 finally lead Gregory to articulate most completely his defense of God's justice. He makes two points that found decisive expression in Calvin's exegesis of Job: that God's will is the rule of justice and that all human virtue is nothing before the purity of God.[148] When God asked, "Will you make my judgment invalid?" (40:3) Job recognized that all God's acts are necessarily just, "for the righteous will of our Maker is a great satisfaction for the blow. For since God's will does nothing unjust, it is acknowledged to be just, even though hidden."[149] Gregory reconciles God's approval in 42:7 with Job's confession in 42:3 that he had indeed "spoken foolishly" or "unwisely" by arguing that Job admitted that "all human deeds which are just and beautiful are, when compared to the justice and beauty of God, neither just nor beautiful nor have any existence at all."[150] By holding him to a higher "standard of uprightness" God made Job "known to himself" and thereby preserved him from the temptation of pride.[151] Job's second confession testified to the "progress" he had made both from suffering and from listening to the divine speeches. Having experienced the beneficial power of affliction and having seen God's "huge strength," the "power and craft of the devil," and the transcendent wisdom and justice of God, Job resisted the sin of pride by realizing that "he was nothing or next to nothing."[152] Recall that Leviathan is the "king over all the sons of pride." By reproaching himself and doing "penance in dust and ashes," Gregory's Job escaped becoming one of Leviathan's sons.

IN SPITE OF the often desultory nature of the *Moralia*, Gregory does formulate a coherent interpretation of Job that is unified by his underlying assumptions and finds expression on all levels of the text. In both method and interpretive results, Gregory's exegesis reflects his presuppositions about hierarchy, interiority, suffering, and perception. By combining the hierarchical metaphysic of Being with his views about the purifying, enlightening, and liberating nature of suffering, Gregory reads Job as a description of the arduous interior ascent toward God undertaken by the elect. He assumes that this ascent requires an inward perception of reality—that is, a search for wisdom that lies hidden in the "unseen." For Gregory, the words of the text, the "chaff" of history, and the events of Job's life all concealed within themselves a deeper truth that is perceptible only through the double movement of turning inward and rising to a higher level of reality. This double movement is effected through the revelatory and liberating power of affliction. Therefore, when expounding the literal and moral levels of the text Gregory explains how suffering alters and elevates perception. By embracing suffering, Gregory's Job escaped the dreaded dangers of tranquillity and attained an inward transcendence that allowed him insight into the true nature of the self and the world.

It is precisely the perspectival structure inherent in the Joban text that allows Gregory to bring together the themes of suffering and perception. In his view, the story of Job is fraught with perspectives, layers, and depths of meaning; all the speeches of the various interlocutors are interpreted on the different levels of the text according to whether the speaker had an inner or outer, higher or lower, temporal or eternal perspective. Depending both on the level of interpretation and the relative validity he grants to the speaker's words, Gregory moves the reader in and out of, and up and down in, the text. Because of this constant "movement" the *Moralia* takes on a definite vertiginous quality, but one that reflects the perceptual implications in Gregory's assumptions about suffering, interiority, and hierarchy.

Gregory's praise of Job's virtue is based on his conviction that for one standing within time, the historical realm must be renounced in order to ascend to a higher spiritual reality. His identification of Job's upright-ness with detachment shows that the realm of time, change, and exteriority is indeed the "Egypt" of the present life. Having fallen into involvement with the quiet horror of time, the human being lives an earthly life that is truly an exile. Gregory's view of history as the "dark night of present existence," however, is more complex than may appear at first glance. His theory of prophecy and his allegorical interpretations of the text turn the mind not upward but downward toward the realm of time. It is true that as the historical and moral Job ascended, he expressed his contempt for the vain and fleeting nature of the temporal world. But as the prophetic or allegorical Job ascended, he looked down upon history and recounted or foretold God's redemptive acts, all of which took place in the realm of time. The whirlwind speech provides the clearest example of this downward perspective attained from the eternal viewpoint. In Gregory's analysis of chapters 38–41 the figure of Job either remained on the historical level or typified the church; in both cases God addressed not the prophet but the Job who was struggling through the realm of time. Speaking to this Job from out of the whirlwind, God proclaimed his mighty acts throughout history and foretold Christ's victory over Satan as well as the defeat of the Antichrist. From the higher perceptual viewpoint attained through the revelation of God's response, Job and the reader see that history is not utterly rejected.

Gregory's exegesis of the Epilogue upholds this limited affirmation of history. Because he has emphasized Job's detachment from temporal and external goods, Gregory faces a particularly difficult interpretive challenge in Job's final restoration. It is hard to explain why the man who formerly possessed these goods "without regard" should care whether they were recovered. Gregory's uneasiness with God's twofold recompense to Job is clear from the way in which he hastily both affirms and dismisses the historical sense of the passage. Repeatedly Gregory tells the reader that while the historical sense of the passage must be believed, the allegorical meaning is most important.[153] According to Gregory, the "rational being" will put aside the "chaff of history" evident in the story of Job's material rewards and feed on the "grain of mysteries" provided by the deeper truths of the text.[154] The "mystery of allegory" hidden in the Epilogue is not concerned with Job's material restoration. Rather, it is a prophecy about the fulfillment of history. The Epilogue, then, completes the allegorical narration of the whirlwind speech by remaining true to the perspectival viewpoint of the prophetic mode. In Gregory's reading, the sacrifice made on behalf of Job's friends and the restoration of Job's family and possessions prophesied the future conversion of the heretics and the Jews, the reparation of Adam's disobedience through the obedience of Christ, and the multiplication of the number of believers in the final age of the church's history.[155] While the historical sense of the Epilogue is only perfunctorily affirmed, the fulfillment of God's historical work again becomes the object of the book.

In all these sections of the *Moralia* we can see that in a limited way Gregory appropriates the ancient theory of sacred history articulated, among others, by Augustine. This view of history acknowledges that throughout the sphere of time, change, and exteriority winds the history of the church.[156] Redemptive history, recognized only from the nontemporal standpoint, forms a philosophy of history that both affirms a part of the historical realm and relegates temporality to the lowest level of Being. In Gregory's hands, this theory of sacred history becomes an exegetical device that casts the Joban story in terms of perception, perspective, and the limitations imposed by time. By seeing sacred history as part of the message of the Book of Job, Gregory's allegorical interpretation of the text reclaims a portion of historical existence as redemptive. That Christian allegory reveals sacred history means that, for all his talk of "fleeing" or renouncing the earthly historical life, Gregory's Job understood that the historical world was still the arena of God's redemptive acts. Therefore, as Gregory's readers "penetrate" the text, they rise with Job toward the eternal and bow before the truths buried deeply within the realm they left behind.

THE EXULTING OF THE WICKED IS SHORT

Maimonides and Aquinas on Job

Who among mortals, beholding these things, would thereafter stand in dread of the Immortals, and what spirit will be his when the man who is unjust and wicked, fearing the wrath neither of man nor of gods, vaunts himself adorned with opulence, while the righteous are afflicted with distress and suffer poverty?

Theognis

CALVIN INHERITED NOT only the interpretive tradition launched by Gregory the Great but also a second exegetical trajectory initiated in the West by the works of Moses Maimonides and Thomas Aquinas.[1] With these two thinkers, we move away from an allegorical reading toward parabolic and literal interpretations of Job. Moreover, with Maimonides and Aquinas there is a shift away from the therapeutic notion of suffering and the perception of typological and redemptive history to questions about providence and the apparent disorder of everyday historical events. Both men see Job as illustrating the true belief in providence, a belief that raised Job above the seeming confusion of history. To understand why Job becomes emblematic of divine providence, we should recall the intellectual climates of Maimonides's *Guide of the Perplexed* and Aquinas's *Expositio super Iob ad litteram.*

Maimonides was born in Córdoba, Spain, but settled eventually in Fostat, Egypt. Throughout his life he was immersed in the cultures of Moorish Spain as well as his own tradition of Judaism. In the twelfth century Spain was the center of Greek and Arabic thought. The dominant philosophy of the age was a Neoplatonized Aristotelianism, with features derived from Plotinus and Proclus but mistakenly attributed to Aristotle.[2] The twelfth-century reading of Aristotle was also influenced by Greek and Arabic commentaries on Aristotle's works. This Greek and Arabic culture had a significant impact on scholars in Spain and elsewhere, including Maimonides.

Maimonides wrote treatises that represented both his religious and philosophical traditions. In various works he interpreted the Jewish faith and addressed himself to the Jews of his new homeland in Egypt. The *Book of Illumination (Commentary on the Mishnah)* was completed in 1168. Written in Arabic and later translated into Hebrew, the *Book of Illumina-*

tion is a rabbinic commentary on parts of the Talmud. The *Book of the Commandments* classifies many Jewish commandments and prohibitions. The *Mishneh Torah* is his fourteen-book codification of Jewish Law. These books are his two main ethical works and, to a large extent, are a response to the situation of the Jewish community, which was in a state of internal crisis. The law governing Jews in remote places was itself in a state of confusion, and thus Maimonides dedicated himself to clarifying and providing a clear structure to Jewish law.[3] As Maimonides stated, he wrote the *Mishneh Torah* because "in our days, severe vicissitudes prevail and all feel the pressure of hard times. The wisdom of our wise men has disappeared; the understanding of our prudent men is hidden."[4]

The work that most notably reflects the two traditions behind Maimonides's thought is his magnum opus, *The Guide of the Perplexed,* completed sometime before 1190.[5] The dedicatory epistle to Rabbi Joseph explains both the purpose and the audience of the *Guide* and provides the context for the interpretation of Job in book 3.

The *Guide* is explicitly addressed to educated Jews who have become puzzled about certain aspects of their religion. In the opening letter Maimonides explains his views on the study of metaphysics and the relationship between metaphysics and religion. Fearing that Joseph's desire for knowledge might exceed his ability, Maimonides insists on the proper method of study. He argues that logic, mathematics, and the natural sciences should precede metaphysics. Because Joseph left before reaching the study of metaphysics, Maimonides wrote the *Guide* for those, like his former pupil, who had studied the sciences and some philosophy and who were also believers in the Jewish faith. Such people were often bewildered about many issues, such as the status of religious knowledge, the use of equivocal language, the divine attributes, prophecy, creation, the existence of God, the reason for Jewish laws, and the nature of human happiness. Thus, Maimonides's intended audience was the group of individuals perplexed by the encounter of metaphysics and the traditional teaching of the Jewish religion. According to Maimonides, the doctrine of providence exemplified this perplexity. He chose the Book of Job for his text in order to oppose the traditional rabbinic views of providence. For Maimonides, Job's tragic story could lead the perceptive reader to the truth about providence—namely, to an understanding that conformed to his own (revised) Aristotelianism. The story of Job, then, raised questions for Maimonides that were central to his thought: questions about divine knowledge, human knowledge of God, the nature and extent of providence, the problems of suffering and evil, and the appropriate attitude toward the vicissitudes of human events.

The *Guide* was translated into Hebrew by both Samuel ibn Tibbon

(c. 1160–c.1230) and by Judah al-Ḥaziri (1170–1235). Both Hebrew versions were translated into Latin. Although Aquinas does not always agree with Maimonides, his interpretation of Job clearly reflects his reading of the *Guide*. The Latin text known by Aquinas follows the Hebrew version of Judah al-Ḥaziri and circulated under the title of *Dux neutrorum, Dux dubiorum,* or *Dux dubitantium*.[6] Aquinas also refers to Gregory's *Moralia* and, at crucial junctures, adopts the Gregorian interpretation. When explaining his intention to expound the literal sense of the Book of Job, Aquinas says that "Blessed Gregory has already disclosed to us its mysteries so subtly and so clearly that there seems no need to add anything further to them."[7]

In Aquinas's commentary, written between 1261 and 1265, Aristotle or "the Philosopher" is a major influence, even though the *Expositio super Iob* was written before Aquinas's many expositions on Aristotle. During this time in Italy Aquinas was a master in theology, deeply involved in theological issues. In particular, he was preoccupied with the problems of evil and divine providence. At about the same time that Aquinas was working on Job, he was also writing books 2 and 3 of the *Summa contra gentiles*. Both the *Expositio super Iob* and the *Summa contra gentiles* III.4–15 and 64–113 deal with the questions of evil and divine governance, topics he treated again in the *Summa theologiae*.[8]

Throughout his works, Aquinas is concerned to develop a view of the universe that defines providence in terms of order. Wright demonstrates that Aquinas's concern with the order of the universe is apparent as early as his *Scriptum super libros Sententiarum* and is more fully developed in his later writings.[9] According to Aquinas, the goodness of the universe is precisely its order; divine wisdom or providence is the source of order in the world.[10] The world is composed of grades of being so that all irrational and corporeal creatures were created for the sake of intellectual creatures.[11] Therefore, rational creatures or intellectual substances are providentially governed for their own sakes, while others are governed in subordination to them. For Aquinas, providence consists of a twofold order: the internal order of things or creatures to one another and the order of the whole universe to God.[12]

This understanding of providence is stated in the seventh chapter of the *Expositio super Iob* where Aquinas explains that "all the particular goods in the universe seem to be ordered [ordinari] toward the common good of the universe as the part is ordered to the whole and the imperfect to the perfect. In this way some things are disposed according to divine providence according as they have an ordered relationship [ordinem] to the universe."[13] Throughout his works, Aquinas uses Aristotle's words in the *Metaphysics* XII.1075a.13 as the locus classicus for the discussion of order in the world.[14] In that passage Aristotle compares the order of the universe to the order in an army, with each part ordered to another part and the whole army ordered to its leader. In the *Summa contra gentiles* the comparison is also based on the analogy with the human body, where all parts of the body are "ordered to the perfection of the whole, inasmuch as one is made to serve another."[15] Elsewhere Aquinas argues, "So, things are not ordered to God as to an end for which something may be obtained, but rather so that they may attain Himself from Himself, according to their measure, since He is their end."[16]

This identification of providence with order makes evil difficult to explain. Aquinas insists that the occurrence of evil must fall within the total exercise of divine government. He often discusses evil in terms of privation; evil is not an essence or first principle. Aquinas argues that evil is never a cause of anything. Rather, evil is caused only by the good, and it can never destroy the good.[17] Sometimes physical evil is understood according to the grades of being in the universe; to manifest divine perfection completely, both the corruptible and the incorruptible must exist. Moreover, Aquinas explains, God permits evil because he governs creatures according to their proper natures and because he can order evil to the good. God wills physical evil *per accidens* because he wills the generation of one thing, which in turn requires the corruption of something else. Furthermore, God wills the order of justice, which demands punishment for sin. For Aquinas, God orders evil to good when he wills the order of justice or when the suffering of the just produces patience and sin leads to humility. But despite his "use" or "permission" of evil, Aquinas's God never directly wills moral evil.[18]

Perhaps Aquinas's concern with providence, order, and the existence of evil within order made the Book of Job an irresistible choice in the years 1261–64. The story of Job presents in graphic detail the full challenge of *disorder,* or at least the apparent disorder of human events. Why would God allow Satan to strike a "simple and straightforward" man "in vain" or "without cause"? Why did Job, who lamented the disorder of injustice, speak "what is right" before God? The commentary on Job is very important for Aquinas's doctrine of providence because it is Job's story of inexplicable suffering that most forcefully compels Aquinas to confront the seeming disorder of everyday historical events.

Both Maimonides and Aquinas understood the Book of Job to be about divine providence, and each formulated a view of providence that was informed by Aristotelianism. For both men, the Book of Job raised issues central to their thought as a whole. For Maimonides, Job's story taught that human conceptions of providence fall abysmally short of God's true nature. For Aquinas, the Book of Job imparted the true teaching about the Christian doctrine of divine governance. On the basis of the Book of Job, these two thinkers developed very different understandings of providence and, consequently, very different interpretations of the Joban story.

In the following pages, Maimonides and Aquinas are justly paired because they shift the interpretive focus of Joban exegesis to questions about providence and the apparent disorder of everyday historical events. Interpreting the Book of Job as a debate about providence, Maimonides and Aquinas raised four issues that continued to govern Joban interpretation and established the thematic framework later utilized by Calvin. These issues concerned the nature and perception of providence, the immortality of the soul, the extent and limitations of human knowledge, and the relationship between divine and human justice.

Maimonides's Interpretation of Job

Maimonides did not write a separate commentary on Job; his interpretation is found in book 3 of the *Guide* (III.22–23). He opens this section by stating that the Book of Job is a "parable." He adds that Job's story is "not a parable like all others, but one to which extraordinary notions *and things that are the mystery of the universe* are attached. Through it great enigmas are solved, and truths than which none is higher become clear."[19] In his brief exegesis of the Joban parable, Maimonides condenses his views on such "extraordinary notions" as providence, divine knowledge, human knowledge about God, and the hierarchical structure of the universe. But his interpretation is not just a summary: When we penetrate to the heart of Maimonides's exposition, we perceive that his real concern is to discuss the nature of wisdom and particularly the relationship between wisdom and suffering.

Maimonides's description of the text of Job as a "parable" goes beyond his belief that the story is not literally true. To understand why he introduces his interpretation in this way, we must briefly examine his view of Scripture. According to Maimonides, Scripture was written largely as a parable containing both an external or exoteric sense and an internal or esoteric meaning.[20] Drawing on Prov. 25:11 ("A word fitly spoken is like apples of gold in settings of silver"), Maimonides describes the twofold nature of Scripture in terms of a quest for inner meanings, which are perceived by looking beyond the external sense of the words. The "settings of silver," he argues, are "filigree-traceries" with very small holes: "When looked at from a distance or with imperfect attention, it is deemed to be an apple of silver; but when a keen-sighted observer looks at it with full attention, its interior becomes clear to him and he knows that it is of gold."[21] The parables, Maimonides concludes, are similar to these "apples of gold" because "their external meaning contains wisdom that is useful in many respects, among which is the welfare of human societies . . . Their internal meaning, on the other hand, contains wisdom that is useful for beliefs concerned with the truth as it is."[22]

Maimonides's belief in the twofold nature of Scripture is rooted in his conviction that people should not be taught knowledge they are incapable of understanding. The external sense of the Torah, Maimonides explains, "speaketh in the language of the sons of man," so that "the young, the women, and all the people begin with it and learn it."[23] Such groups, he says, can only "accept tradition" but are not yet capable of understanding the "secrets and mysteries of the Torah" as they really are.[24] This outer level of Scripture conforms to the religion of the masses but still serves an important purpose. According to Maimonides, the exoteric sense is related to the esoteric sense as silver is to gold, in that it promotes the well-being of society by ensuring public order and ethical instruction. Ideally this community, governed by the Law, will move the individual toward the contemplative love of God by nourishing a moral life, by restraining the wicked, and by communicating (at an elementary level) correct doctrines about God's existence, unity, incorporeality, and eternity.[25] The reader trained in metaphysics and the sciences, however, is capable of perceiving the esoteric sense of Scripture and thereby attaining a higher knowledge and love of God.[26]

When examining Maimonides's interpretation of Job, it is critical to remember that he wrote the *Guide* in a style that imitates his understanding of Scripture. He states explicitly that he has composed the *Guide* in such a way that truth may "be glimpsed and then again be concealed."[27] Like Scripture, the *Guide* is not written "to make its totality understandable to the vulgar or to beginners in speculation."[28] By writing the *Guide* in this way, Maimonides is trying to reveal the different levels of knowledge his various readers are capable of receiving. The necessity to conceal knowledge from the multitude was reinforced by the legal prohibition against teaching "the secrets of the Law" to the public. Since Maimonides states that his purpose in the *Guide* is to explain the "science of the Law in its true sense," he must do so in a guarded and cryptic way.[29] The esoteric teaching of the *Guide* was intended for the observant Jew who was able to comprehend the teachings of metaphysics and the sciences. For this person, the literal sense of Scripture seemed to conflict with the conclusions of philosophy. In this esoteric sense, then, Maimonides defends the truths of Judaism by reconciling them with the teachings of philosophy (a Neoplatonized Aristotelianism). In the figure of Job we will see the relationship between Maimonides's modified Aristotelianism and the teachings of authority or tradition.

When we remember the secretive nature of the *Guide*, we recognize that Maimonides's exposition of Job confronts us with a hidden teaching camouflaged in a twofold way. The Book of Job is a parable and therefore, according to medieval notions about that genre, contains an inner and outer meaning. Its interpretation is found in the *Guide*, which is itself written so that its message can be perceived only by the trained reader. The interpreter of Maimonides, therefore, must proceed like a detective to "glimpse" the true meaning of the Joban text. To decipher Maimonides's careful construction of chapters 22–23, we must understand the "hints," "contradictions," and secret identifications he has smuggled into earlier sections of the *Guide;* in this way only do the "great enigmas" and "mystery of the universe" taught by the Joban parable become clear.

Maimonides explains that the parable of Job is "intended to set forth the opinions of people concerning providence," a doctrine we know from I.35 to be one of the "secrets of the Law" whose meaning cannot be divulged to the masses.[30] The suffering of people such as Job, Maimonides says, raises the issue of "God's knowledge and His providence" and throws people into doubt about whether there is any order in human affairs.[31] The esoteric meaning of the Book of Job, therefore, conveys Maimonides's own teaching about the closely related subjects of divine omniscience, divine attributes, the afterlife, and providence.

The reference to God's knowledge refers the reader to Maimonides's earlier discussions about divine knowledge and the divine attributes. Does God know the course of human events and govern individual human affairs, or is God too transcendent for the knowledge of particulars? Can God "govern" that which he does not know? Maimonides is aware that the anthropomorphisms in Scripture and passages such as III.17 can be interpreted in the traditional personalized understanding of providence, in which God specifically knows all singulars and wills actions toward particular individuals according to their deserts. The reader, however, finds contradictory views about divine knowledge stated in the *Guide*. These views include the affirmation that God knows particulars, the belief that God knows only species, and the conviction that it is simply impossible to formulate any coherent statement about the reality and nature of divine knowledge.[32]

Some scholars, such as Reines, have argued that Maimonides's esoteric teaching is that God is totally transcendent and enters into neither a cognitive nor volitional relationship with the human race. Raffel maintains that Maimonides's purpose is not to prove directly that God knows human events but "to portray a possible model in which God knows everything and thereby knows human circumstances as a part of his creation." Rudavsky insists that Maimonides's God knows both concrete and unactualized particulars, of course without any change occurring in the divine nature. Ivry's argument appears to me the most reasoned account of Maimonides's esoteric position. Placing the question of divine omni-

science and providence within Maimonides's theory of emanation and
the distinction between form and matter, Ivry concludes that the ideal
or pure forms only are "the objects of God's knowledge and constitute
his being and that of the essential being of the universe. The two beings
are one and the same in God, though not in the universe, through the
mystery of emanation." Ivry's essential point is that, according to Maimonides, the material cause itself is beyond direct divine knowledge and
ministration. God's knowledge is confined to the form of things in general: God has chosen to create a substance (matter) "over which he has
no immediate control, the concrete individual instances of which he is
ignorant."[33]

The most crucial point for the interpretation of Job is that Maimonides's God does not exercise a direct personal providence in the traditional sense of the term. In Maimonides's reading of Job we must recognize some important principles. The first is the equivocal nature of
language about divine attributes. In his discussions of the divine attributes, Maimonides again reminds his readers that the Torah "speaketh in
the language of the sons of men" and therefore uses terms drawn from
human experience. When applied to God, however, all essential attributes are of a purely equivocal nature; there is no common meaning in
such terms when applied to God and to creatures.[34] Although Maimonides affirms the omniscience of God, he insists on the equivocal nature of terms such as *knowledge, providence,* and *purpose.*[35] Biblical proof
for this transcendent view of God becomes the hermeneutical introduction and framework for Maimonides's interpretation of Job. He finds
the proof in Isa. 55:8–9: "'For My thoughts are not your thoughts, neither are your ways My ways,' saith the Lord. 'For as the heavens are
higher than the earth, so are My ways higher than your ways and My
thoughts than your thoughts.'"[36] Through a very subtle exegesis, Maimonides argues that the esoteric meaning of the Joban parable teaches
this transcendent view of God and the equivocal nature of the term
providence.

The second important principle is that Maimonides understands
providence in terms of emanation, as consequent upon the divine overflow. The Joban parable becomes the demonstration for Maimonides's
opinion that "providence is consequent upon the intellect." Maimonides presents these views through a series of critical identifications
and in his use of Job's confession as the heuristic key for understanding
the book.

In the different speakers of the story, Maimonides sees the various positions that characterize the debate about providence. At the beginning
of the story, he explains, both Job and his friends believed "everything
that had befallen *Job* was known to Him, may He be exalted, and that

God had caused these misfortunes to befall him."[37] Maimonides sees, however, that the speakers differed in their opinions as to why the "heaviest misfortunes befall the most perfect individual." Eliphaz believed that Job had committed sins for which he deserved his adversities, even if those sins might be unknown to him. Bildad argued that Job's undeserved suffering would increase his reward. Zophar believed that all things proceeded from God's will alone and that "no reason should be sought for his actions."[38]

Most important, of course, was Job's opinion. In the midst of his afflictions, Maimonides's Job came to believe that "the righteous man and the wicked are regarded as equal by Him, may He be exalted, because of His contempt for the human species and abandonment of it."[39] Maimonides cites 9:22–23, 21:6–8, and 21:23–26 as proof of Job's belief: "It is all one, therefore, I say: He destroyeth the innocent and the wicked. If the flood slay suddenly, He will mock at the calamity of the guiltless. . . . One dieth in his full strength, being wholly at ease and quiet . . . And another dieth in bitterness of soul and hath never tasted of good. They lie down alike in the dust, and the worm covereth them. . . . Wherefore do the wicked live, become old, yea wax mighty in power? Their seed is established in their sight."[40]

Readers should note that Maimonides takes Job's complaints at face value; they are not expressions of virtuous detachment from worldly goods but rather literal statements of despair about God's disregard for human events. This literal interpretation of Job's laments was recapitulated by Aquinas and later by Calvin. Maimonides identifies Job's opinion with the teaching of Aristotle.[41] To understand this critical identification, we must recognize that, according to Maimonides, Aristotle believed providence extended only to the celestial spheres and ensured only the "durability and permanence of the species" in the sublunar realm. In Maimonides's view, Aristotle denied that providence applies to individuals on earth.[42]

It is equally important to realize that Maimonides equates Job's opinion with a lack of wisdom by pointing out that only "moral virtue and righteousness in action" were attributed to Job. "For if he had been *wise*," Maimonides says, "his situation would not have been obscure for him."[43] What did Maimonides seek to gain by describing Job in this way? He is alerting his readers that the esoteric meaning of the parable, which is identical with Job's newly obtained wisdom, is somehow significantly different from the teaching of Aristotle. As Maimonides moves on, he adds yet another suggestive comment about the character of Job: that *before* his misfortunes Job knew the deity only by "his acceptance of authority, just as the multitude adhering to a Law know it."[44] Here Job is portrayed as a member of that group of "the young, the women, and all the people" who are confined to "accepting tradition" because they cannot yet understand metaphysical truth.[45] At this point, Maimonides explains, Job knew the deity only "through the traditional stories and not by the way of speculation."[46] We now arrive at a significant question: What "authority" or "traditional stories" would have taught "Aristotelianism"? To understand these statements, two further identifications are necessary to allow us to follow Maimonides as he traces Job's progress from "authority" to "wisdom."

The two identifications are the meaning of Satan and of Elihu's angel. Several statements help us to identify Satan. According to Maimonides, Satan, not God, was the sole cause of Job's suffering. Commenting on Job 1:6, Maimonides states that although Satan is said to roam over the earth, he is forbidden to gain dominion over the soul.[47] And, most revealing, Maimonides equates Satan with the "evil inclination" and the "angel of death" who "turns people away from the ways of truth and makes them perish in the ways of error."[48]

Among these statements the main clue is the reference to the "evil inclination." As Kravitz has rightly noted, this term sends the reader back to II.12, where Maimonides equates the "evil inclination" with the imagination, a term with negative implications in Maimonides's epistemology.[49] In II.12 Maimonides is explaining the nature of incorporeal causation or the "overflow" of God to the lower intellects and spheres that constitute the universe. The human intellect, he argues, cannot fully understand this idea because it concerns incorporeal reality, while the human mind is limited by its association with matter. Whenever the intellect fails to comprehend some abstract concept, the imagination enters the epistemological process and tries to make up for the mind's inadequacy. Having a corporeal nature, however, the imagination cannot function properly in the attempt to grasp incorporeal realities. The result is error: "For every deficiency of reason or character is due to the action of the imagination or consequent upon its action."[50] By saying that Satan was the cause of Job's calamities, Maimonides is arguing that Job's suffering was due to the force of "imagination," which leads a person away from truth into error. Therefore, as Maimonides probes the esoteric meaning of the Prologue we can see that the real contest depicted in the Book of Job is the struggle between "God" and the human imagination.

The deluding power of "imagination" or the "evil inclination" is broken by Elihu's angel, referred to in Job 33:23, 29: "If there be for him an angel, an intercessor. . . . Lo, all these things doth God work twice, yea thrice, with a man."[51] Kravitz is correct in referring readers to II.6, where Maimonides defines angels as "natural forces." He also explains that the

Active Intellect is called "the *angel* and *prince of this world*" who is the giver of forms to the material world.[52]

Maimonides's interpretation of both Elihu's angel and the whirlwind speech is based on his cosmology.[53] To Maimonides the universe is a vast and hierarchical system, consisting of three parts: the ten separate Intelligences, the bodies of the spheres, and first matter. The spheres and Intelligences are the result of emanation. This process of emanation continues down to the formation of the ninth sphere and the Tenth Intelligence, at which point the heavens are complete. The Tenth Intelligence is the Active Intellect who, with the spheres, creates and conserves the sublunar world. The human being is the "most noble" of those things that are subject to generation, which makes humanity subject to the changes and corruptions inherent in matter.[54] As Ivry has shown, however, God is remote and removed from this lower material realm, separated by a series of intermediary Intelligences and spheres. The divine "will" of which Maimonides speaks, then, is not a personal force in history in the traditional sense of the term.[55] Does this mean that Job was right when he said that God had forsaken the human race? If Job was correct, why did he repent in 42:6?

Maimonides begins to resolve the issues raised by Job's story through the following description of Elihu's angel, the reference to which is in 33:23 ("If there be for him an angel, a mediator"):

For he says that it is an attested and well-known thing that when a man is ill to the point of death and when he is despaired of, if an angel intercedes for him— regardless of what angel—his intercession is accepted and he is raised from his fall. . . . However, this does not continue always, there being no continuous intercession going on forever, for it only takes place two or three times.[56]

Here Maimonides drops an important clue. This description parallels his earlier portrayal of the action by the Active Intellect on the human intellect or "soul." The human intellects that have studied metaphysics and science become capable of intermittent union with the Active Intellect. In these felicitous moments, the Active Intellect exercises what Maimonides calls "providence" over those individual human beings. Thus the Book of Job confirms Maimonides's belief that providence is "consequent upon the intellect":

But I believe that providence is consequent upon the intellect and attached to it. . . . Accordingly everyone with whom something of this overflow is united will be reached by providence to the extent to which he is reached by the intellect . . . when any human individual has obtained, because of the disposition of his matter and his training, a greater portion of this overflow than others, providence will of necessity watch more carefully over him than over others . . . divine providence does not watch in an equal manner over all the individuals of the human species, but providence is graded as their human perfection is graded.[57]

The identity and function of Elihu's angel becomes clearer when we note that Maimonides ends his interpretation of Job with a discussion of the prophecy in both Elihu's "vision" and the whirlwind speech. By citing Job 33:14–15 ("For God speaketh once, yea twice, yet [man] perceiveth it not. In a dream, in a vision of the night, when deep sleep falleth upon men"), Maimonides finds language reminiscent of the biblical texts cited in II.42 and thereby refers the reader to his former discussions of prophecy.[58] He opens II.42 by saying, "We have explained that wherever it is mentioned that an *angel* was seen or had spoken, this has happened only *in a vision of prophecy* or *in a dream*." If we read closely, we can see that the comment interpreting this statement, Elihu's angel, and the voice from the whirlwind is found in II.36: "Know that the true reality and quiddity of prophecy consist in its being an overflow overflowing from God, may He be cherished and honored, through the intermediation of the Active Intellect, toward the rational faculty in the first place and thereafter toward the imaginative faculty."[59] It is important to remember, however, that "God" is only the very remote cause of prophecy; revelation takes place through the mediation of the Tenth Intelligence, and thus the phenomenon of prophecy does not indicate that God has a direct relationship with the individual in history.[60] The "angel" who is the *immediate* cause of prophecy is the Active Intellect; by working in conjunction with the natural cognitive powers of the human intellect, the Active Intellect bestows and realizes the prophetic capacity of the prophet.[61]

Maimonides further pursues the idea of prophecy by referring to Job's "prophetic revelation . . . through which his error in everything that he had imagined became clear to him."[62] By reading this section with Maimonides's former analysis of prophecy in mind, we can conclude that the Active Intellect is both Elihu's angel and the voice from the whirlwind. The hidden path of Maimonides's reasoning becomes evident if we note the content of these prophetic revelations. Maimonides observes that both Elihu's vision and the whirlwind speech do not go "beyond the description of natural matters."[63] The purpose of these prophecies is to show that human intellects cannot transcend the natural realm so as to understand God's governance. The whirlwind speech taught Job the equivocal nature of terms about God, especially terms about God's providence:

This is the object of the *Book of Job* as a whole: I refer to the establishing of this foundation for the belief and the drawing attention to the inference to be drawn from natural matters, so that you should not fall into error and seek to affirm in your imagination that His knowledge is like our knowledge or that His purpose and His providence and His governance are like our purpose and our providence and our governance. If man knows this, every misfortune will be borne lightly by him. And misfortunes will not add to his doubts regarding the deity and whether He does or does not know and whether He exercises providence or manifests neglect, but will, on the contrary, add to his love as is said in the conclusion of the prophetic revelation in question, *"Wherefore I abhor myself and repent of dust and ashes."* [64] As the [Sages], *may their memory be blessed*, have said: *Those who do out of love and are joyful in sufferings.*[65]

What did Maimonides's Job learn from the divine response? Did his perception change? What role did suffering play in his progress toward wisdom? In attempting to answer these questions, we should begin with what Maimonides does *not* grant to Job. In Maimonides's view, Job did not find reward for virtuous action or innocent suffering in a life after death. Union with the Active Intellect did not bestow personal immortality. As he makes clear in I.74, there can be "no thought of multiplicity" in the things that are separate from matter—namely, intellects. This means that since matter is the form of all particularization, all individuality dies with the body. When Maimonides refers to the "soul" as that which remains after death and over which Satan has "no dominion,"[66] he is describing only the disembodied intellect, which is absorbed into the object of its contemplation. Maimonides's resolution to Job's situation precludes the problem of justice in the sense of reward and punishment.[67]

Maimonides does, however, grant Job a deeper perception into the nature of God and the structure of reality. Like our other Joban commentators, he develops the perceptual implications and composition of the book. The *Guide* as a whole is permeated with visual and perceptual imagery. Maimonides begins by telling his readers that the "great secrets" contained in the biblical parable and the books of the prophets are never fully understood. "But sometimes truth flashes out to us so that we think that it is day, and then matter and habit in their various forms conceal it so that we find ourselves again in an obscure night. . . . We are like someone in a very dark night over whom lightning flashes time and time again."[68] We recall that the *Guide* is written so that these truths or secrets "may be glimpsed and then again be concealed."[69] Maimonides stresses the issue of perspective and explains that the perception of truth depends on the perspective presently attained through the advance of the human intellect. Repeatedly he refers to the perception of the "multitude" as opposed to that of the learned elite capable of glimpsing coruscations of truth, or to the message of the external sense as opposed to the meaning of the concealed or inner sense.

In his explanations of the hidden matters in Scripture, Maimonides distinguishes between levels of perception or knowledge in terms of opinions, beliefs, and demonstrations. The famous parable of the palace in III.51 is a description of the varying levels of perception that have been recounted and analyzed throughout the *Guide*.[70] Those who have "achieved demonstration" and ascertained in divine matters everything that is possible are those who have "come close to certainty." The highest level belongs to those who have passed beyond "imagination" to "intellectual apprehensions" and finally to "love."[71] Thus, the possibilities and limits of human perception are the subject matter of the *Guide* as Maimonides moves the reader from the lower to the higher perspectives, inward and outward through the text.

Job is the classic example in the *Guide* of one whom Maimonides moves from the lower to the highest level of the sublunar realm; the reader observes Job's progress from virtuous action to knowledge, and from authority, traditional stories, and imagination to wisdom. Having reached union with the Active Intellect, Job's perspective on his condition changes. The "great enigmas" solved by the Joban parable are precisely Job's new insights on providence and the knowledge of God. Maimonides's Job came to understand that the highest level of reality accessible to the human mind was the Tenth Intelligence, an Intellect that exercised only a limited providence over certain human beings. Job perceived the vastness of reality and the utter transcendence of the deity. He learned that even the Active Intellect did not exercise providence in the way taught by "imaginative" religion or normative rabbinic Judaism. From this higher perspective, Job renounced his former error: his belief that everything that had happened to him was known to God "and that God had caused these misfortunes to befall him."[72]

Job's new perception allowed him detachment from the material realities he had once mistaken for happiness. As we watch how Maimonides moves Job from "imagination" to wisdom, we see that Job's *confession* becomes the hermeneutical key to the book. Previously Job had imagined that happiness consisted of health, wealth, and children. These goods belonged to the material world and thus were subject to generation, decay, and loss.[73] Having been struck by afflictions that were not punishments for sins, Job realized that his earlier beliefs could not explain why a just God would inflict "unjust" suffering. This failure made Job have "doubts regarding the deity, and whether He does or does not know, and whether He exercises providence or manifests neglect."[74] Such doubts caused Job to fall into the error of "Aristotelianism": the complete denial of providence. In 42:6, however, Job said, "Wherefore, I abhor myself and repent of dust and ashes."[75] Maimonides interprets this verse as meaning, "Wherefore I abhor all that I used to desire and repent of my being in dust and ashes," and identifies it with "correct apprehension."[76] At this point Job realized, through union with the Active Intellect, that the things he had imagined to constitute happiness were not the ultimate goal of human beings. Furthermore, the Job who moved beyond traditional stories and reached union with the Active Intellect believed in Maimonides's revised Aristotelianism as he learned that providence does extend to some individuals in proportion to the "measure of their perfection." At this point Job finally came to see that providence is to be understood not as an activity of God but rather as a perception of the human being about the nature of the relationship between the divine and the human world.

It is vital to realize that Maimonides consistently portrays Job's deepening insight not so much in terms of "ascent" and "interiority" as in terms of restriction, limitation, and incomprehensibility. His literal or naturalistic reading of the whirlwind speech allows him to argue that human knowledge cannot pass beyond the sphere of "nature."[77] Thus, Maimonides's Job always remained in the natural realm and grew increasingly aware of the limitations of his comprehension. Job's highest point of understanding was to confess what he could *not* know. This interpretation of the whirlwind speech and the limitations of Job's knowledge were again expressed, this time in Christian guise, by Calvin. The limitation of human perception means that Job learned the equivocal nature of language about God. To admit the equivocal character of terms such as *knowledge* and *providence* was to acknowledge the incomprehensibility of the deity and the confinement of the human mind to the sublunar realm.

Maimonides's exposition still leaves us with the question of justice. Does he ever address the issue of divine justice? It is clear that he thinks Job suffered justly because by overestimating the value of earthly goods, he suffered inordinately when he lost them. The detachment afforded him by his new knowledge allowed Job to see the true nature of the material world, knowledge that allowed him to bear misfortune "lightly." Hence Job repented "of dust and ashes"—that is, he repented of his former sorrow over loss of material goods. Why did Maimonides not include the term *justice* when explaining that the Book of Job taught the error of believing that human notions of "providence," "purpose," and "knowledge" applied to God? Fundamentally, Maimonides is saying that the question of justice was improperly asked by Job. To grasp the principle underlying Maimonides's reasoning, we must understand that the equivocal nature of terms about God made irrelevant the question about God's justice that Job's suffering had previously caused him to pose to the deity of imaginative or traditional religion. Just as the meaning of terms such as *knowledge* and *providence* was unknown to the human mind when applied to God, so too the term *justice* would be equally incomprehensible.

We are now in a position to evaluate the function of suffering in Maimonides's interpretation of Job's story. Maimonides depicts the "early"
Job as virtuous but not wise. The meaning of the parable attempts to
solve the ancient question about why a righteous man should suffer.
Maimonides does this by relating suffering not to righteousness but finally to wisdom. In so doing, he subordinates justice to knowledge.
With Maimonides we see a very different attitude toward affliction than
we saw in the *Moralia*. Although Maimonides's Job attained detachment and wisdom, he did not do so through the process of suffering. In
the exposition of Maimonides, we do not encounter any descriptions of the growth in strength or the perceptual progress made possible through the endurance of adversity. Maimonides does not portray
Job as making an arduous interior ascent through suffering. The perfection of Job's intellect is not attained through any moral action, including actions based on the virtues of patience, endurance, or suffering well.[78] It is true that the experience of pain and sorrow may have
provided the starting point for Job's journey toward wisdom, since it offered an opportunity to begin to question his old beliefs and the value
of temporal goods; in this sense, suffering can be said to have played
an initial pedagogical role. For Maimonides, however, suffering essentially belongs to the realm of error, matter, Satan, or the "imagination."
Since suffering belongs to the realm of ignorance or error, it is an impediment rather than an avenue to wisdom.

For Maimonides, then, wisdom *frees from* suffering.[79] When he states
that the person over whom providence watches "can never be inflicted
with evil of any kind," Maimonides does not mean that this person is exempt from bodily realities or misfortunes.[80] He is saying, rather, that to
the degree one has attained union with the Active Intellect, one transcends the effects of matter and material realities. Matter is that which
necessitates the experiences of change, suffering, pain, and death. Matter also prevents apprehension.[81] Providence, or conjunction with the
Active Intellect, lifts one from the material world and allows for a new understanding. That understanding frees the individual from the illusions
or misperceptions that cause sorrow. In short, the liberating power of
Job's new knowledge gave him a different perspective or wisdom, which
detached him from the errors that had originally caused his suffering.

Thomas Aquinas on Job

Aquinas's *Expositio super Iob ad litteram* reflects the insights of both the
Moralia and the *Guide*. In his appropriation of elements from Gregory
and Maimonides, Aquinas creates his own unique interpretation of the
story, determined by his underlying assumptions about suffering, per-

ception, and history. Aquinas, of course, shares with Gregory a common Christian framework within which he interprets the Book of Job. He adopts some of Gregory's exegetical solutions regarding the celestial contest, the explanation for Job's afflictions, and the meaning of Behemoth and Leviathan. But Aquinas's hermeneutical method and his presuppositions about suffering make his commentary significantly different from the *Moralia*. He agrees with Maimonides that the Book of Job is about the nature of providence. Unlike Maimonides, however, he uses the doctrine of personal immortality as a hermeneutical tool with which to interpret the book. This doctrine of immortality is what causes the issue of perception to emerge as a definitive element in Aquinas's interpretation. This perceptual dimension, made possible by a belief in the afterlife, most decisively separates Aquinas's understanding of history and divine justice from that of Maimonides; it was later restated by Calvin.

An examination of Aquinas's hermeneutical method will give us a vantage point from which to judge, in a preliminary manner, how the *Expositio* differs from both the *Moralia* and the *Guide*. In the prologue to his commentary, Aquinas writes, "For we intend briefly, as far as we are able, having trust in divine help, to expound according to the literal sense, that book which is entitled *Blessed Job*."[82] The meaning of the word *literal* evolved in Aquinas's thinking from his earlier statements in the *Scriptum super libros Sententiarum* (1252–56) to his mature view in the *Summa theologiae* (1266–73).[83] If we agree with Weisheipl that the *Expositio* was written between 1261 and 1264, we can safely restrict our discussion to the latter definition:

That God is the author of Holy Scripture should be acknowledged, and He has the power, not only of adapting words to convey meanings (which man is also able to do), but also of adapting things themselves. And, therefore, as in every branch of knowledge, words have meaning, but what is special here is that the things meant by the words also themselves mean something. That first meaning whereby the words signify things belongs to the first sense; namely, the historical or literal. That meaning, however, whereby the things signified by the words also signify other things is called the spiritual sense; it is based on and presupposes the literal sense.[84]

Aquinas goes on to explain that "the literal sense is that which the author intends, and, moreover, the author of Holy Scripture is God."[85] In Aquinas's various discussions of the literal sense, the term *author* is somewhat more ambiguous than this statement indicates. On the one hand, the "literal sense" or "sensus historicus vel litteralis" is the meaning intended by the human author. The literal sense, however, also possesses a theological dimension since God is the principal author of Scripture while the human writers are only God's instruments. In any event, the "literal sense" is the meaning that Calvin later called the "plain" or "natural" meaning of the text, determined by a knowledge of language and grammar. To understand Aquinas's exegesis of the whirlwind speech, we must note further that he includes the parabolic within the literal sense. He argues that when words are used figuratively, their literal signification is precisely the metaphorical or figurative meaning of the term.[86]

In comparison to the interpretations by Gregory and Maimonides, Aquinas's literal style seems like a flat and simple paraphrase of the text. This impression, however, is misleading. If we can see how Aquinas very gradually constructs his interpretation and fully develops the perspectival structure of the book, we find the *Expositio* to be much more complex than it first appears. We discover, for example, that Aquinas's literal method actually serves both to heighten the perceptual issues in the book and to accentuate the problematic nature of providence and history.

The perceptual implications of Aquinas's commentary begin to emerge if we compare his exegetical method to the allegorical and "parabolic" interpretations of Gregory and Maimonides. In Aquinas's interpretation there is, at least until chapter 40, only one level of meaning.[87] With Aquinas, therefore, we leave behind Gregory's hierarchy of senses and Maimonides's esoteric meanings. Aquinas's exegesis allows for no ascent to higher perceptual levels of interpretation or more elevated perspectives from which one can "look down" on the vast providential plan of history. The reader cannot dive into the mysteries of allegory or find deeper meanings in the text. Like Maimonides, Aquinas locates Job and his friends firmly within the perspective of the sublunar, temporal realm. Unlike Maimonides, however, he does not see either the Book of Job or his own interpretation as concealing hidden knowledge from the uneducated masses. In this regard, Aquinas's identification of the parabolic with the literal sense illustrates his divergence from Maimonides. For Aquinas, the Book of Job is not a parable but a historical work.[88] The parabolic dimensions of the story are equated with a metaphorical style, not with an esoteric sense hidden from the multitude. Nonetheless, even though Aquinas does not develop the themes of ascent and hiddenness in the ways his predecessors did, he by no means presents the teaching of the Book of Job in a one-dimensional manner. Rather, he construes it as a *debate,* which the reader must follow carefully to come to a fuller understanding of the truth.[89]

This notion of a debate lies at the center of Aquinas's interpretation and intensifies the issue of perception or perspective that permeates the *Expositio.* He explains that the Book of Job recounts a debate in order to show "through probable reasons that human affairs are ruled by divine providence."[90] Aquinas begins by listing the various erroneous opinions about providence held by earlier and later philosophers.[91] The later thinkers, he argues, knew more about the nature of providence because "just as in the case of things which are generated naturally, there is a gradual development from the imperfect to the perfect state, so it happens with the case of men with respect to the knowledge of truth; for in the beginning what they attained to of the truth was slight but afterwards, step by step, as it were, they came to some fuller measure of the truth."[92]

Aquinas places this theory at the beginning of his commentary because it prepares the reader for the style of the book. Coming to a "fuller measure of the truth" is the exegetical program of the *Expositio* as Aquinas makes this gradual apprehension the goal of the debate recounted in the story. While Gregory's explanations of the multiple meanings of the text tended to obscure the disputatious nature of the Book of Job, Aquinas's reading emphasizes the disagreements among the various interlocutors. Throughout his commentary, Aquinas explains which statements a speaker is challenging so that the reader sees the cross-references, arguments, misunderstandings, and points of controversy. For example, Job's words in chapter 7 refute Eliphaz's statements in 5:17–27, while Bildad's arguments in 8:3–7 challenge Job's complaints in 7:6.[93] Aquinas stresses the controversy between the speakers because he assumes that "truth may shine forth from arguing back and forth [mutua disputatione]."[94] With his literal method of exegesis, Aquinas replaces the multilayered hierarchy of meanings with the give-and-take of debate. In so doing he develops the perceptual dimensions of the book in terms of a process of learning through argumentation.

Aquinas identifies the main point of disagreement in the debate between Job and his friends not as the existence of providence but rather as the doctrine of personal immortality. According to Aquinas, both Job and his accusers believed in the reality of divine providence. God rebuked Eliphaz, Zophar, and Bildad not because they denied the reality of providence but because they rejected any belief in the afterlife.[95] Aquinas supports this interpretation of the friends by reading their statements about temporal rewards and punishments as a lack of faith in the spiritual life to come.[96]

We can discern how Aquinas understands the structure of the story if we briefly analyze how he portrays Job as only gradually asserting the truth of his doctrine. In Aquinas's view, Job did not clearly articulate his belief in the future life until chapter 19; up to this point Job argued either by adopting the position of his adversaries or by merely alluding to his hope in the life after death. We can identify several verses that, for Aquinas, are turning points in the debate. In 13:3–4 ("But yet I would speak with the Almighty and I desire to debate with God, first showing that you are fabricators of a lie and worshippers of perverse dogmas"), Aquinas's Job became less equivocal and identified his purpose as the destruction of "perverse dogmas."[97] Throughout the rest of Job's speeches, Aquinas charts the progress of the debate by noting that "from now on [ex nunc]" or "now for the first time [ubi primo]," Job asserted new points more clearly against his opponents.[98] Not surprisingly, 19:25–26 becomes the hermeneutical key to the book. At this juncture Job explicitly disclosed his argument by declaring his belief in the afterlife when he cried, "For I know that my Redeemer lives and on the last day I will rise from the earth. And I will be covered by my own skin again and in my flesh I will see God." Aquinas explains that from this point on, Job argued more openly with the greater insight afforded him by his belief in immortality.[99]

Regardless of his forceful arguments, Job could only partially convince his opponents. Nonetheless, Aquinas does detect some movement on the part of Job's friends. In 20:18 Zophar said of the wicked man that "he will atone for all he has done and yet he will not be consumed." In Aquinas's view, Zophar began to believe that there might be a future life where God meted out justice.[100] In 22:30 ("The innocent man will be saved, but he will be saved by the cleanness of his hands"), Eliphaz began to recognize the importance of spiritual goods.[101] When Aquinas arrives at chapter 32 he makes a distinction between Elihu and Job's other friends. Unlike Zophar, Bildad, and Eliphaz, Elihu clearly shared Job's belief in the resurrection and the conviction that there would be retribution in the life after death. Still, Elihu also believed that the adversities of this life were due to sin and, consequently, accused Job of suffering because of divine punishment.[102] At the end of the Dialogues, therefore, none of Job's interlocutors came to a complete understanding of the truth, a situation that necessitated God's response from the whirlwind.

Although the doctrine of immortality was, at one level, the subject of the debate between Job and his friends, a careful analysis of the *Expositio* reveals that the perception of order was really at the heart of the controversy. Aquinas sees the presence of order in nature and in history as evidence for the reality of providence. He makes a preliminary distinction between nature and history, a distinction Calvin later made central to his interpretation. Placing the Book of Job in the context of ancient debates about providence, Aquinas argues that the majority of thinkers agreed that "natural things were not driven by chance but by providence because of the order which clearly appears in them."[103] Agreeing with Maimonides, he goes on to explain that doubts about divine providence arose regarding human events because in history "no certain order" appears.[104]

Aquinas sees, however, that this latter point is the source of disagreement: Do human events exhibit order, or is injustice evident in human events? Aquinas believes that because Job's friends denied the immortality of the soul, they had to restrict providence to the earthly life. To defend the justice of this earthly providence, they had to maintain that present adversities were punishments for past sins and that prosperity was reward for virtue. Bildad's words in 8:3–6 ("Does God overturn judgment and does the Almighty subvert what is just? . . . if you will walk clean and straight, at once He will wake up to you and He will put the dwelling place of your justice at peace") describe what he believed to be God's earthly and visible justice.[105] Commenting on 5:9–16 ("who gives rain upon the face of the earth and irrigates everything with waters; who sets humble men on high and raises up mourners by salvation? Who dissipates the thoughts of the wicked?"), Aquinas focuses on how Eliphaz moved his discussion from nature to history by assuming that order was equally discernible in both spheres.[106] Having explained that natural things were governed by providence, Eliphaz wrongly argued that human events displayed the same order. He then concluded that all misfortunes, including Job's, were just retribution for past sins.[107]

In the speeches of Job's friends, Aquinas sees what modern scholars call the Deuteronomic view of history, which portrays history as justly ordered, intelligible, and predictable. In this view, God always punishes and rewards according to the Law. Cause and effect are clear and knowable to the human mind. This Deuteronomic theory is not one that Aquinas wants to reject completely. He also believes that God knows human sins and justly governs human affairs. Moreover, he admits that at times the wicked do suffer adversities in this life.[108] And like previous Joban commentators, he greatly admires the descriptions of God's wisdom and righteousness found in the speeches of the friends. Nonetheless, Aquinas faces the age-old problem of 42:7, which states that Job alone spoke "what is right before" God. To reclaim the truths preached by the friends, Aquinas makes a somewhat different argument than did Gregory. Gregory maintained that the words of the friends were wrongly applied to Job but often true in themselves, an argument found again in Calvin. Aquinas, however, relies on the fact that Job often agreed with his detractors. In 9:2 ("Truly I know that it is so and that a man is not justified placed next to God"), Aquinas's Job concurred with Eliphaz's statement in 4:17 that a man cannot be justified in comparison with God. Thus Job claimed that he too could extol the power, justice, and counsel of God.[109] The divine reproof of the friends, therefore, did not apply to their words about God's justice, goodness, and wisdom; on all these crucial issues, Job agreed with his detractors.

Nevertheless, Aquinas believes that Job's friends were fundamentally

wrong and that their error was a perceptual one: their claim to perceive
within history a justice and an order that were not discernible to the human eye. To grasp the principle underlying Aquinas's interpretation of
the book as a whole, we must recall that for him the subject of the argument between Job and his friends is not the reality of providence but
rather the perception of providence. Aquinas does not want to re-
nounce the Deuteronomic theory; he simply wants to say that the causal
law of reward and punishment is not always discernible to the human
mind. Therefore, in the words of Job's companions he sees a constant
misperception of the causality and order present in history. The justice
they professed to observe in the course of human events was often a justice reserved to the afterlife.[110] In Aquinas's view, Job "spoke what is
right before" God because of his faith in the future life of reward and
punishment.[111]

It becomes clear in the course of the commentary that Job's vindication encompassed more than this correct doctrine. Job argued correctly
because his belief in immortality provided him with a perceptual superiority over his friends, a truer insight into the nature of history and
providence. To understand how Aquinas explains Job's perceptual advantage, we must appreciate the link in his mind between the doctrine
of personal immortality and an ordered view of history. In his interpretation, the existence of the afterlife functions as an extension of history
so that God can exercise justice after death. In his criticism of Eliphaz,
Zophar, and Bildad, Aquinas is not interested in simply defending the
correct belief in immortality. His real concern is to show that a belief in
providence without the supporting doctrine of immortality results in a
false perception about the true nature of human history. Without a belief in the afterlife, one must conclude that either there is no just providence or history appears justly ordered. By making the debate between
Job and his friends center on the question of immortality, Aquinas actually focuses the Book of Job on the nature of history.

By examining Aquinas's attempt to confront the nature of human history as presented in Job's story, we reach the heart of his concern with
the Book of Job. To discern how he wrestles with the text, we should first
analyze the important ways in which he differs from Gregory. Unlike
Gregory, Aquinas is not talking about a redemptive history that is typologically perceived. Instead, he is discussing the realm of everyday,
temporal events. Moreover, Aquinas is aware that in the story of Job, the
problematic nature of history is exemplified by the unjust and inexplicable character of Job's afflictions. Thus Aquinas must approach the nature of history through the reality of suffering.

Here the reader detects an unmistakable tension in Aquinas's attempt to provide a consistent literal reading of the book. The issue of

suffering presents him with certain problems. Did Job understand the reason for his afflictions? Did his suffering serve any purpose? Like Gregory, Aquinas explains that Job's adversities were not punishments for past sins.[112] Aquinas admits that Job had committed venial sins, but since he bore no mortal guilt, his afflictions were not intended as corrections or penalties.[113] Following Gregory, Aquinas argues that Job's afflictions were a test by which his virtue would be "made manifest [conspicuam reddit]" to others.[114] Again following Gregory, Aquinas places Job's ordeal within the wider context of God's celestial contest with Satan. By remaining patient and faithful, Job was to prove Satan wrong by showing that he "feared God from the right intention and not because of temporal goods."[115]

Yet these exegetical decisions, adopted from Gregory, cause a disjunction within the *Expositio*. On the one hand, Aquinas portrays Job as knowing that the devil was testing him. Commenting on chapter 16:9 and 16:12 ("and a liar rises up before my face, contradicting me. . . . God has shut me up with the ungodly one"), Aquinas explains that "it can be said that Job understood through the Holy Spirit that his adversity had been brought about by the devil with God's permission."[116] Although he stops short of attributing to Job a knowledge of the celestial battle and the Satanic challenge, he does say that Job "understood that his afflictions had been inflicted upon him by the devil" and that "his distress proceeded from divine providence."[117] Furthermore, according to Aquinas, verse 23:10 ("Nevertheless, He knows my way and He will test me like gold that passes through fire") shows that Job knew he was being tested. Like Gregory, Aquinas explains that "here for the first time Job clearly explained the reason for his adversity which was brought upon him so that he might appear to men to have been proved as a result of it, just as gold which can withstand the fire is proved." Thus, Aquinas continues, "just as gold does not become true gold but its real nature [veritas] is manifested to men as a result of the fire, so Job has been tested through adversity not so that his virtue might appear before God but so that it might be manifested to men."[118]

On the other hand, Aquinas wants to give Job's laments a strictly literal reading so that he may depict Job as one who perceives the ambiguous and problematic nature of history. To achieve this, he must portray Job as one who complains about the inexplicability and the injustice of his afflictions. Aquinas's Job can do this because he rightly claims that he is not being punished for past sins, which makes his suffering truly problematic. Job must speak according to "the persona of an afflicted man" who cries that God multiplies his wounds "without cause"—that is, "without a cause that is manifest and perceptible by the afflicted man."[119] Job's words must describe the misery of human life and the injustice of innocent suffering. Job must declare his innocence, hate his pain, point to the prosperity of the wicked, and express the sadness of his soul.

For Aquinas, this tension is inherent in the Joban text; in his view, Job both knew the reason for his afflictions and bewailed the inexplicability of his suffering. To stay true to the book as a whole, he relies not on a hierarchy of meanings but rather on the notion of the debate in which Job is involved and on the idea of the tripartite nature of the human soul. Like a debater, Aquinas's Job revealed the true nature of his ordeal only gradually. As we have seen, Aquinas thinks that in 33:10 Job clearly explained "for the first time" that he was being tested. Equally important is Aquinas's theory that Job spoke "three ways" in the course of his trial: according to his sensual nature, according to human reason, and according to divine inspiration.[120] In passages such as chapter 3, Job's bitter complaints were statements uttered according to the "lower part of his soul," or the "sensual side" of his nature.[121] Although Job's "reason" was never overcome by sadness, "reason cannot remove the condition of nature."[122] Aquinas goes on to explain that "it is natural to the sensual nature that it be delighted in fitting things and be pained and saddened over harmful things."[123]

This interpretation of Job's laments signals a deeper difference between Gregory and Aquinas. If we read closely, it becomes apparent that Aquinas's appropriation of Gregory's explanation for Job's suffering is very superficial, even though he also repeats Gregory's understanding of the many reasons God may send suffering. Like Gregory, he argues that God inflicts adversity to restrain malice, to test a person, to punish sinners, and to appear virtuous before men.[124] He even repeats the traditional view that trials contribute to one's salvation.[125] Despite these statements, however, we can discern an essential difference between the attitudes toward suffering articulated by Gregory and by Aquinas. This difference emerges most clearly in Aquinas's comments on those verses about Job's "inexplicable" or nonretributive suffering, that is, the passages that clearly state that his afflictions were not sent by God for punishment, restraint, or correction. In these sections we can see that Aquinas's Job did not embrace suffering; he was not more suspicious of prosperity than of adversity.[126]

Several passages in the *Expositio* illustrate the marked divergence between our two exegetes. Repeatedly, Aquinas argues that Job was "impeded by pain." Commenting on chapter 17:11 ("My thoughts have been scattered"), Aquinas says that Job's reflections were "impeded [impeditae] from the quiet contemplation of wisdom because of the sharpness of bodily pain," and that his thoughts had been "led away from the sweet consideration of truth by the bitterness by which his heart was being tormented."[127] Interpreting 16:8 ("Now, however, my pain has crushed me"), Aquinas writes that Job's pain "impeded [impedivit] " him from being able to use his reason as freely and easily as he did before.[128] "For when there is vehement pain in the senses," Aquinas says, "it is necessary that the attention of the soul be distracted [avocetur] or impeded [impediatur] from the consideration of intellectual matters."[129] Aquinas does not restrict his remarks to Job's physical pain. Speaking in conformity with his "sensual nature," Aquinas's Job admitted in 30:16–20 ("Now, however, in me languishes my soul. . . . I will cry out to You") that his soul did indeed languish because of sadness and that he did seek to be freed from his adversity.[130] When Job cursed the day of his birth, he "repudiated a life under adversity" because "both good and evil men abhor adversity."[131] Crying that the day of his birth should be turned into darkness, Aquinas's Job remarked that "even if life itself is desirable, nonetheless a life subject to miseries is not."[132] So, too, in chapters 3, 7, and 10, Job wished not for "death to the world" but for a corporeal death, saying that "if I had been consumed in my mother's womb, I would have had the dignity of being without the misery which befell me."[133]

This largely negative attitude toward suffering informs Aquinas's exegesis of Job's laments. What is the appeal of this exegetical turn, and how does it function in the *Expositio*? Clearly, Aquinas is simply interpreting Job's speeches in harmony with his own presuppositions about the effect of suffering on the mind. The critical point, however, is that he wants to use Job as a personification for the ambivalent character of human events. To do so, he cannot portray suffering as an advantage to the spiritual progress of the soul; suffering must be the indisputable sign that human affairs are seemingly disordered. Job's perceptual superiority derived not from the beneficial and medicinal nature of suffering but rather from his belief in the afterlife. In Aquinas's view, Job's hope in immortality freed him to be honest about the real ambiguity of history, an ambiguity exemplified by the problematic nature of "unjust" suffering. By arguing correctly that he was not being punished for past sins, Job denied the visibility of the causal law of reward and retribution. Job alone, then, recognized that "no certain order" appeared in history. Aquinas exegetically expresses Job's view of history in three ways: by his appeal to the afterlife, by his thoroughly literal reading of Job's laments, and by his defense of divine justice. With these exegetical maneuvers, Aquinas manages both to vindicate the justice of God's providence and to insist on the empirical disorder of human history.

For Maimonides, the verses that depict Job's denial of providence are 9:22–23, 21:6–8, and 21:23–26. Aquinas also explains these passages. By comparing the interpretations of these verses provided by Maimonides and Aquinas, we can discern how Aquinas's belief in immortality clearly determined his exegesis of Job's laments.

He [God] consumes the innocent and the guilty. If he scourges, let Him kill at the same time and let Him not smile over the punishments of the innocent (9:22–23).

Even I, when I have thought it over, am stricken with awe and trembling pierces my flesh. Why, then, do the wicked live? Why have they been lifted up and comforted with riches? Their seed remains before their eyes, a crowd of relatives and grandchildren in their sight (21:6–8).

One man dies mighty and healthy, rich and happy. . . . But another man dies in the bitterness of his soul, without any resources. And yet they will sleep together in the dust and the worms will cover them (21:23–26).

Aquinas gives these verses the same literal interpretation Maimonides gave them. In these statements, Job was simply bewailing God's apparent abandonment of human history, an abandonment evidenced by the injustices and inequalities that characterize human affairs.[134] Yet he qualifies his interpretation by reminding the reader that Job is engaged in a "debate." "In the manner of a debater [more disputatoris]," Job assumed the viewpoint of his opponents—that is, that there was no afterlife.[135] By adopting their viewpoint, Aquinas's Job then argued that the opinion of his friends really resulted in a denial of providence. According to Aquinas, Job alone took a hard look at human events and discovered there not the order claimed by his friends but the disorder and injustices expressed throughout his laments. Job's speeches, then, were his honest and experiential observations about the nature of history—if that history is judged without a doctrine of immortality. When one is limited to what Aquinas calls the "evidence of experience,"[136] the facts are indisputable: The innocent and the guilty both die. The wicked prosper and the good suffer. Looking directly at human events, one is left not with a justly ordered history but with Job's vision of the world.

The line-by-line nature of his commentary means that Aquinas's very close reasoning is spread over thirty chapters. The reader must follow him chapter by chapter to see how he is going to overturn the arguments of Job's companions, particularly their claims to be defending and praising the justice of God. The key to reversing the claims of the friends is the doctrine of the afterlife.[137] By adopting the denial of immortality espoused by the friends, Aquinas's Job made the dispute center on the true nature of history. Aquinas is arguing that if divine providence is restricted to the earthly life, then injustice is the true character of that history over which God allegedly rules. As Aquinas says, if one looks to the "temporal state only" or judges "according to external appearances," then God does indeed seem to be unjust.[138] Aquinas's Job was thus able to accuse his friends of charging God with injustice. A realistic view of human events leaves Job's friends with the dilemma that an unjust God determines history.

This dilemma disappears if there is an afterlife. Aquinas is assuming the doctrine of immortality mainly to argue for the reality and justice of providence in history and not to prove immortality directly. Throughout the commentary, Aquinas insists that the friends were using "a lie" to defend God's providence. That lie was their claim that history visibly demonstrated divine justice. Job's purpose, then, was to prove that God's righteousness did not need their lie.[139] According to Aquinas, Job insisted that he was trying to refute their "perverse dogmas" by asserting the truth of the resurrection.[140] By pointing to the inequalities within history, Job forced a choice upon his detractors: Either God's rule is unjust, or there is an afterlife that guarantees the justice of divine governance.

Aquinas's argument becomes clear at the end of chapter 10 where he explains that "Job pursues all these points in order to persuade his opponents necessarily to posit another life in which just men are rewarded and evil men are punished, since, if that belief is not posited, no reason can be given for the trials of just men who, it is certain, are sometimes troubled in this world."[141] Aquinas is making a very shrewd move by arguing that without a doctrine of immortality, it was Job's friends who actually accused God of injustice. Job, then, turned the charge of blasphemy against his accusers. With a doctrine of immortality, however, one can trust that God "had time," so to speak, to remedy the injustices of history. Aquinas can conclude, therefore, that because Job was armed with a belief in the afterlife, he could squarely confront the true nature of history and rightly argue that "it was not incompatible with divine providence if wicked men prosper in this life."[142]

Through these various arguments Aquinas has layered the text in such a way that he can grant Job superior insight without denying the full reality of his desire to be free from adversity. Nonetheless, since he maintains that Job argued his "correct doctrine" from the beginning to the end of his ordeal, Aquinas is left with difficult questions: What did Job learn from the whirlwind speech, and why did he repent in 39:35 and 42:6? Recall that Maimonides made these confessions the hermeneutical key to the meaning of the book because Job's repentance signaled his path to "wisdom." There is a fundamental difference, however, in the way that Maimonides and Aquinas identify the central point of the story. While Maimonides follows the intellectual progress made by Job, Aquinas's main interest, until chapter 38, is in the intellectual development of Job's debate with his friends.

With Aquinas we see the continuation of the Christian tradition of interpretation, which portrays Job as largely unchanged in the course of his ordeal; for both Gregory and Aquinas, Job's beliefs and faith remained constant throughout the story. In this tradition, the fact that Job is said to have spoken what is right before God is allowed to govern the interpretation of Job's speeches in the Dialogues. (This tradition, however, does not hold true for Calvin.) But because Aquinas's Job remained essentially unchanged in the debate with his friends, the whirlwind speech presents a problem, for at this point Job is the one being instructed. At this juncture, therefore, the perspective has to shift so that Job's limitations are identified. Aquinas finds a way to explain the change that took place in Job by combining the themes found in the interpretations of Maimonides and Gregory. He stresses the limitations of human knowledge and interprets the final chapters in terms of the battle over salvation. By combining these two interpretations, he joins the theme of intellectual hubris with the danger of spiritual pride.

Aquinas introduces chapters 38–41 by saying that because Job "seemed to have spoken presumptuously [praesumptuose] when he challenged God to debate," God responded to him from the whirlwind.[143] Aquinas is eager to explain that Job had never wanted to "contend [contendere]" with the Deity or to impugn divine justice; he wanted only to "debate" with God as one who desired to "learn [ad addiscendum], as it were, like a student with a teacher."[144] And yet Job spoke in such a way that he "seemed" to his friends to talk pridefully or contentiously. Aquinas interprets the divine response as a way of ending the debate between Job and his friends and finally settling the question about the nature of providence. Commenting on 38:1 ("Now the Lord responding to Job from the whirlwind said"), Aquinas writes:

> But since human wisdom is not sufficient for comprehending the truth of divine providence, it was necessary that the debate [disputatio] just mentioned be determined by divine authority. Since Job had thought correctly about divine providence but had been so excessive in his manner of speaking that scandal was produced from it in the hearts of others when they thought that he was not displaying due reverence to God; therefore, the Lord, as an arbitrator of the question, reproved Job's friends concerning what they thought incorrectly and Job himself for his inordinate manner of speaking, and Elihu for his unsuitable conclusions.[145]

In recent years scholars have disagreed in their interpretations of the way in which Maimonides and Aquinas explain the divine rebuke. Yaffe argues that while Maimonides thought Job was perfectly just but unwise, Aquinas believed Job to be perfectly wise but unjust. Yaffe concludes that because of his overemphasis on "theoretical reasoning," Aquinas's Job failed to understand the limitations involved in teaching the truth to others in society. Job repented, therefore, because he "sinned, not from pride or from impurity of motive, but from 'levity' or superficiality of thought—presumably in thinking that he could accomplish the practical conversion of his friends to Christian wisdom merely by intellectualizing to them."[146] Despite his thorough and suggestive analysis of the *Expositio,* Yaffe in his conclusion does, I think, overlook several important features of Aquinas's interpretaton. Most crucial is the central role of the element of spiritual pride in Aquinas's exegesis of the divine rebuke.

Dobbs-Weinstein appears to be closer to Aquinas's meaning when she says that "although Job held a correct opinion about divine providence, his disordered speech reflects not only the limitations of human reason, but also a lack of understanding and of acknowledgment of such a limitation. Job's opinion may have been correct, but it was an unexamined opinion, and thus neither was it assented to rationally, nor could it realize the limitations of human reason."[147] In her analysis, Dobbs-Weinstein correctly maintains that we cannot conclude that Aquinas believed Job to be perfectly wise, especially since the whirlwind speech aimed at demonstrating the extent of Job's ignorance. She also rightly argues that both Maimonides and Aquinas emphasize Job's sin of intellectual pride or the unacknowledged limitations of human reason. Neither of these interpretations, however, can fully explain Aquinas's meaning, which becomes clear only when the conclusion of the *Expositio* is read in comparison to both Maimonides and Gregory.

From 38:1 to 40:10 (where Behemoth and Leviathan appear), Aquinas gives the text a strictly literal reading. In his view, these chapters describe "God's effects" in nature, effects that he explains with the help of Aristotle as well as Albert the Great, Thomas of Cantimpré, Isidore, Pliny, and others.[148] Recounting the majestic nature of creation, God spoke in order to convince Job of "his ignorance."[149] Throughout the *Expositio,* Aquinas explains that although the contemplation of nature allows us to know something about God, the power and wisdom of God far transcend all that is revealed in the cosmos.[150] The interrogative form of the whirlwind speech intensifies this theme. As Aquinas says, God "questions Job about His effects [de suis effectibus] which are available to the human senses, and when he is shown not to know them, he is much more convinced of having no knowledge of more sublime matters."[151]

Yet it is crucial to realize that Aquinas understands the questions spoken from the whirlwind as demonstrating both human ignorance and human powerlessness. For example, God showed up Job's lack of knowledge by such questions as "Where were you when I was setting the foundations of the earth? Declare to me if you have understanding," and "Who has explained the plan of the heavens and who will make the harmony of heaven sleep?"[152] However, God demonstrated Job's weakness by asking, "Who shut up the sea with doors . . . ?" and "Have you held the ends of the earth, shaking them, and have you shaken the wicked out of it?"[153] Aquinas's concluding comment on 38:35 illustrates his understanding of the twofold nature of the divine response: "Now all of these questions are introduced to show that man is not able to reach either divine wisdom or divine power."[154]

The importance of this distinction becomes clear when we compare Aquinas's exegesis of Job's two confessions. The first confession (39:34–35) reads: "What can I respond who have spoken lightly [leviter]? I will put my hand upon my mouth" (39:34). "I have spoken one thing which I wish I had not said and a second to which I will not add further" (39:35). In his interpretation, Aquinas introduces elements of both pride and the insufficiency of human reason. Commenting on verse 34, he states that Job repented in his desire to "debate" with God, a wish uttered in 13:3. The "second" thing of which Job repented was that he had "put his justice first when it was a matter of divine judgments."[155] Immediately following this twofold explanation, however, Aquinas chooses to emphasize again the insufficiency of human reason. Summarizing the meaning of these confessions, Aquinas explains that Job was repenting of the words he had spoken in conformity with the "deliberation of human reason." According to Aquinas, "since human reason ought to be directed according to divine inspiration, after the Lord's words [Job] reproves the words which he had said according to human reason."[156] This latter emphasis confirms that Aquinas saw the first part of the whirlwind speech as condemning primarily Job's intellectual hubris and thus as demonstrating the limitations of human knowledge. In Aquinas's reading, however, Job's second confession refers not to the insufficiency of human reason but rather to human powerlessnes and the sin of pride.

The critical point is that an emphasis on divine power increases in the course of Aquinas's discussion until it culminates in 40:7–41:23. In 40:7–9 God said to Job, "Look upon all proud men and confound them and tread down the wicked in their place. . . . You will hide them in the dust together and plunge their faces into the pit. [Do this] and I will admit that your own right hand can save you." At this juncture in the text, Aquinas separates the issue of power from the world of nature and applies it instead to the problem of salvation. Interpreting this passage, he portrays God as having said to Job, "If you can do the works just mentioned, which are God's alone, you can reasonably attribute to yourself that you do not need divine help for salvation. But just as you cannot do the former, so neither can you do the latter. Therefore, you ought not to glory in your justice."[157]

In Aquinas's view, the references to "proud men" and to salvation prepare the reader for God's battle against the great beasts. With the appearance of Behemoth and Leviathan, Aquinas shifts the meaning of the divine response completely toward a discussion of divine power and human weakness. Following Gregory instead of Maimonides, he interprets the great beasts as Satan and refers the reader to the celestial contest recounted in the Prologue:

And suitably enough Job's debate, which concerns his adversity, ends in a description of the devil since it is also recounted above that Satan was the beginning of his adversity. Thus while Job's friends were trying hard to refer the cause of his adversity to himself, thinking he had been punished because of his sins, the Lord, after he had rebuked Job for his inordinate speech [inordinata locutione], as if offering a final decision to the debate, deals with the malice of Satan which was the beginning of Job's adversity and is the beginning of human damnation, according to Wisdom 2:24, "The envy of the devil introduced death into the world."[158]

By comparing the *Expositio* to the *Moralia*, we can determine that the same verses that proved crucial to Gregory's interpretation of Behemoth and Leviathan also demonstrate to Aquinas that the text "figuratively" or "metaphorically" describes the devil "under the figure of the elephant and the whale."[159] Aquinas reads 40:10 ("Behold Behemoth, whom I made along with you") in conjunction with 40:14 ("He [Behemoth] is the beginning of God's ways"). Appropriating Gregory's exegesis, Aquinas states that these verses show that Satan was created among the first works of creation. In harmony with his emphasis on providence, Aquinas adds that by the "ways" of God we should also understand the works of divine providence because Satan is one of the "ways" God uses for benefiting and punishing human beings.[160] Verse 41:16 ("When [Leviathan] has been taken away the angels will fear, and frightened, they will be purified") cannot mean that the angels would be "amazed over the killing of any corporeal whale."[161] Rather, Aquinas insists, this verse refers to the "spiritual Leviathan," namely, the devil "who was removed by divine power when he fell from heaven through sin." The angels, then, "amazed at divine majesty, were purified by separation from [Satan's] company."[162] Most important, this "spiritual Leviathan" is referred to in 41:24 as the "king over all the sons of pride." Thus Aquinas comments that God "concludes His narrative on the subject of proud men in order to show that Job particularly had to fear lest the devil, who had tried to tempt him, might try especially to lead him into pride so that in this way Job might be transferred into his kingdom. Therefore, he ought to have been cautious of an attitude and words that smacked of pride."[163]

Aquinas also appropriates Gregory's portrayal of Christ's victory over the devil, depicted in 40:19–20: "In his eyes He will capture [Behemoth] as with a hook. . . . Or will you be able to draw out Leviathan with a hook?"[164] Recall that Gregory read this verse as a description of Christ's defeat of the devil. In his interpretation, Aquinas retains both the strictly literal and the the "principal" senses of these verses. On the first literal level, the passage depicts the details of how one hunts for an elephant (Behemoth) and a whale (Leviathan). "Principally," however, the text refers to the work of Christ as he overcame Satan through the "hook" of his seemingly mortal nature.[165] Witnessing the slyness, power, and ferocity of the devil, Aquinas's Job recognized that he could not hope to win this demonic contest through human power. As in the *Moralia*, therefore, chapters 40–41 become a description of that ancient power struggle narrated in Gen. 1–3 and enacted in the person of Job. And once again, adopting Gregory's explanation, Aquinas makes 40:27 ("Put your hand upon [Leviathan], Remember the battle and speak no more") the interpretive key for unlocking the meaning of the whirlwind speech:

Having shown, then, that man cannot in any way by his own power overcome the devil, God concludes, as it were, from all that He has said before, adding, "Put your hand upon him," meaning, "if you can," as if to say: In no way by your own power can you put your hand upon him to subject him to you. But although he cannot be overcome by man, he is, nevertheless, overcome by divine power. Thus God adds, "Remember the battle"; namely, in which I fight against him, "and speak no more"; i.e., against Me, when you see one being overcome by My power whom you cannot overcome by your power.[166]

We can now see how Aquinas's exegesis combines themes we have observed in the interpretations of both Maimonides and Gregory. Like Maimonides, Aquinas sees chapters 38–41 as teaching the limitations of human reason; unable to "comprehend" the wonders of nature, human reason cannot hope to penetrate the secrets of divine judgments. The reader can only conclude, then, that Job's correct doctrine of immortality did not mean that he completely understood the mysteries of God's providence, mysteries that were only partially revealed in creation.

The emphasis on the insufficiency of human knowledge, however, is replaced in chapter 40 with a discussion about the inadequacy of human power. Like Gregory, Aquinas intricately connects the subject of divine power with the temptation of spiritual pride. Although he insists that Job had not really spoken pridefully during his debate with his friends,[167] Aquinas makes clear that Job's claims to innocence pale in comparison to the power of the devil in the great battle for salvation. At the end of his ordeal, therefore, Aquinas's Job confronted the same test as did Gregory's Job: the propensity for spiritual pride. Aquinas's exegesis of Job's second confession in 42:3 ("Therefore, I have spoken fool-

ishly and things that exceed my knowledge beyond measure. . . . I heard
You with the hearing of my ear but now my eye sees You") differs significantly from that of Maimonides. At this point, Aquinas's Job acknowledged that God "could remove the adversity brought about by the
devil." Moreover, Job "reproaches" himself and "does penance in dust
and ashes," not because of the limitations of his reason but because he
recognized "that he had been driven inwardly by some proud thought"
and knew that he had not "shown due reverence for divine excellence."[168] Bowing before the transcendent wisdom and power of the
Creator, Aquinas's Job came to see that he needed not only vindication
before his opponents but also a defender powerful enough to protect
him from Satan. Consequently, Aquinas explains God's rebuke of Job by
combining intellectual with spiritual pride. Confessing his guilt before
this more powerful God, Aquinas's Job also escaped becoming one of
Leviathan's children.

WE HAVE SEEN that while Aquinas appropriates crucial elements from
both the *Moralia* and the *Guide,* his interpretation of Job differs significantly from those of his predecessors. Having examined the way he
adopts and rejects features from Gregory and Maimonides, we are now
in a position to analyze how Aquinas envisions the Book of Job as addressing the interrelated issues of suffering, perception, and history.
    Although his attitude toward suffering is somewhat more ambivalent
than that of Maimonides, Aquinas essentially agrees that suffering is not
an avenue to wisdom. He portrays Job's sorrow as "natural" to his "sensual nature." Still, that sorrow is not the element that expresses or leads
to Job's wisdom. Aquinas's Job sought to be freed from adversity and was
"impeded" by his sadness. These statements, scattered throughout the
Expositio, indicate a decisive difference from Gregory's spirituality of suffering. The *Expositio* reflects the understanding of affliction that Aquinas
expressed more fully in the *Summa theologiae* (I.II.35–39). In this section
of the *Summa,* Aquinas explains that pain and sorrow weigh down one's
spirits and inhibit one's ability to learn. "By being weighed down," Aquinas says, "the soul is not free to take an interest in things outside itself;
it shrinks into itself and contracts."[169] In the *Summa,* the most Aquinas
will grant is that the contemplation of truth can assuage pain and grief;
however, pain and grief do not lead to the contemplation of truth.[170]
    Aquinas's statements about pain follow his analysis of Aristotle as ex-
pressed in the *Ethics.* In his commentary on the *Ethics,* Aquinas explains
that pain (including sadness) is naturally shunned and considered to be
bad by all people.[171] He writes that "one kind of sadness is evil simply,
e.g., sadness about good; the other kind is evil in a limited way, as a hindrance to the good, since even sadness about evil impedes the soul from

doing good readily and quickly."[172] Commenting on book 7, Aquinas defines pleasure as an "unimpeded activity of a habit that is natural, which harmonizes with the nature of the one having it."[173] Having defined the highest pleasure as the contemplation of rational truth, Aquinas makes clear that contemplation is an intellectual pleasure opposed by no pain "because [contemplation] is not an imperfect but a perfect state."[174] Clearly, Aquinas sees pain as an impediment to the act of contemplation.

Although Maimonides was willing to suggest that suffering was an impetus for Job's path to wisdom, neither Maimonides nor Aquinas portray Job as ascending through suffering. The experience of affliction did not turn Job's soul inward, direct him to the eternal realm, or grant him new knowledge. Neither Maimonides nor Aquinas sees suffering as playing an instrumental role in Job's understanding of the truth.

For Aquinas, Job's perceptual priority over his friends was due not to the manifestation of his virtue or to the liberating effect of suffering but to his belief in personal immortality. In Aquinas's rendering of the story, Job held this belief before his ordeal began and therefore did not attain it through suffering. It is this doctrine of the afterlife that definitively separates Aquinas's interpretation from that of Maimonides. Following Gregory, Aquinas reads chapter 19 as an affirmation of the resurrection. He defends divine providence by extending God's justice to the life after death. The belief in immortality, however, points to a deeper difference between Maimonides and Aquinas, a difference detected only by understanding the implications of the belief of immortality for the perception of history and justice.

If we compare the *Expositio* to the *Guide,* we can see that Aquinas's view of history is fundamentally antithetical to that of Maimonides. True, both men read Job's laments as literal descriptions of the apparent confusion of historical events, in which the wicked prosper and the good suffer. For Aquinas, however, Job's hope in the afterlife provided him with a different perception of history than that expressed by Maimonides. Providence may, for Maimonides, be termed historical in the limited sense that it is exercised over select people who still exist within the historical realm. Yet Maimonides explains that during those moments of the intellectual overflow, providence brings about deliverance from history, or what he calls the "sea of chance."[175] In the *Guide,* therefore, the historical sphere remains the realm of chance (and matter) for those incapable of contemplative union with the Active Intellect.

In Aquinas's theology, history is never the "sea of chance." God exercises providence (often through lower agents) over all individuals and events.[176] The different understandings of history emerge most clearly if we look at Aquinas's comments on chapters 22–24. In chapter 22,

Aquinas portrays Eliphaz as accusing Job of holding the Aristotelian or Averroistic position that God does not know singulars and that earthly events are not ruled by divine providence.[177] In chapter 24, Aquinas's Job replied by saying that God "knows the course of the times" and "judges temporal matters."[178] In Aquinas's theology, God's providence extends to more than the preservation of the species; God regulates human lives and knows individual sins.

Because Aquinas makes the indiscernibility of providence a major theme in the *Expositio*, he runs into difficulty with the Epilogue. As we are learning to recognize, these precritical exegetes see the Epilogue, not the whirlwind speech, as the most problematic part of the text. Gregory's emphasis on Job's detachment from all external and temporal goods caused him to minimize the historical or literal meaning of chapter 42. For Aquinas, it is the emphasis on the ambiguity of history that makes the Epilogue particularly difficult. If one's vindication is in the afterlife, how does one account for the visibility of providence recounted in the Epilogue? Aquinas wrestles with chapter 42 by citing Matt. 6:33 ("First seek the kingdom of God and His justice and all these things will be added to you"). According to Aquinas, although Job did not base his hope on recovering temporal prosperity, God rewarded him because he first sought God's kingdom and justice. Moreover, Aquinas adds, this restoration was consistent with the "state of the Old Testament in which temporal goods were promised," so that through his recovered prosperity Job might become an example for others in order that they might also turn back to God.[179] Unlike Gregory, Aquinas does not hastily dismiss the historical level of the Epilogue. Nevertheless, his interpretation creates a certain awkward tension in relation to the rest of the *Expositio*, an awkwardness evident in his refusal to allow the Epilogue to govern his interpretation of the Dialogues. Throughout his commentary, Aquinas's main purpose is to argue that Job's literal and realistic depiction of history is true but not ultimate; history does often look disordered but there is a higher, though indiscernible, order and purpose by which God is governing human events. In comparison to the Job of Maimonides, Aquinas's Job found no deliverance *from* history but rather faith in the ultimate order *of* history.

Until chapter 40, that faith is not seen as a perception of God's providential plan, which winds its way through the realm of earthly events. As noted earlier, Aquinas does not understand the Book of Job to be about a sacred or typologically perceived history; there is no allegorical level upon which either Job or the reader stands in order to survey God's creation and formation of the church throughout history. Nor is Aquinas's Job a prophet who possesses prophetic insight and the ability to see all things "at once."

Nonetheless, the interpretation of Behemoth and Leviathan as Satan grants to Aquinas's Job a perception of the purposeful nature of history that could never be available to the Job of Maimonides. By reading chapters 40–41 as a recitation of God's victory over Satan through Christ, Aquinas concludes his exegesis of the Book of Job by casting Job's story within the wider redemptive and historical plan that began at creation. Job—and the reader—are made a part of the historically fought battle for salvation. Human life is involved in a history redeemed by the "hook" of Christ's mortal nature. In the end, therefore, Aquinas's Job is granted a higher perception into both the reason for his ordeal (the celestial contest) and the redemptive purpose of God's action in human history.

Finally, by extending the resolution of earthly events to the afterlife, Aquinas affirms not the equivocal but the analogous nature of the term *justice*. Throughout the *Expositio* we find passages that assert the profound transcendence of God's wisdom, purity, and justice. As Aquinas writes, "divine justice exceeds human justice since the latter is finite and the former is infinite."[180] Nonetheless, God's justice is not completely incomprehensible. The use of the doctrine of immortality as a heuristic device functions only to delay God's justice, not to make it completely unknowable. The idea that God will reward or punish in the afterlife, therefore, serves to assure Job of the essential analogy or continuity between human and divine notions of justice and retribution.[181]

III

DOES GOD PERVERT JUSTICE?

Suffering and Justice in Calvin's *Sermons on Job*

The Almighty has His own purposes.

Abraham Lincoln

THE FOREGOING RECAPITULATION of medieval commentaries has prepared us to hear Calvin's 159 *Sermons on Job* with greater acuity. With those voices fresh in our ears, we quickly discern in these *Sermons* now familiar themes and exegetical problems, along with new ones. In many ways Calvin's treatment harmonizes with the earlier tradition, but his interpretation often develops in new directions.

Many of Gregory's exegetical concerns found their way into later commentaries, both literal and allegorical. His attempt to understand the pedagogical purpose of suffering, his effort to validate the words of the friends, his interpretation of the whirlwind speech, and his interest in Job's noetic and virtuous superiority all find expression in the medieval exegetical tradition. Despite his rejection of some of Gregory's explanations, Calvin does repeat several of these Gregorian themes. It was the literal tradition of Joban exegesis that had grown most in importance, a tradition that read Job as a debate about the nature of divine providence.[1] Calvin, too, insists on pursuing the "natural" sense of the text. Repeatedly he scorns all allegories, seeks to follow the thread of the text, tries to note the context of a verse, and attempts to explain the "clear," "simple," or "natural" sense of the passage.[2] In short, Calvin tries to find what Aquinas called the historical or literal sense of the text: the meaning that allows the "things signified by the words" to become clear.

Using this exegetical procedure Calvin preaches on the Book of Job within what is basically the Thomistic framework. Like Aquinas and the later Thomistic tradition, Calvin uses the belief in immortality to explain the meaning of Job's story. According to Calvin, Job's friends reserved no judgment for the last day and therefore concluded wrongly that Job was punished for past sins.[3] Calvin also adopts the Thomistic argument that Job was vindicated because he defended the true doctrine of providence; that is, Job knew that God did not restrict his judgments to the earthly life and did not always inflict suffering because of sin.[4] The *Sermons on Job,* therefore, should be read within the context of Calvin's theology of providence.[5] Scholars have long recognized the importance of provi-

dence in Calvin's thought. The crucial issues of suffering, history, creation, predestination, the church, and the nature of God are all intimately
connected to Calvin's doctrine of divine governance. Considering the
universal and all-pervasive action of providence on every aspect of human life, Calvin wrote that the "ignorance of providence is the ultimate
of all miseries; the highest blessedness lies in the knowledge of it."[6]

It is not surprising, therefore, that in the various editions of the *Institutes,* in his sermons and commentaries (particularly those on the Old
Testament), and in his debates with groups such as the Libertines Calvin
repeatedly tried to explain the true meaning of divine providence. No
biblical book elicited a longer, more thorough, and more nuanced exploration of providence than did the Book of Job. In the *Sermons on Job*
we quickly become aware that Calvin approached Job's ancient story
armed with all the major arguments, assumptions, and themes that are
central to his understanding of God's rule. In the Job sermons Calvin
continually preaches on the sovereignty of God, the restraint of evil, the
denial of fortune and chance, the governance of history and nature, the
revelation of creation, the restoration of order, and the justice of God's
will. Ideas that are discussed seriatim in the *Institutes* are explored in a
less organized way, verse by verse, in the *Sermons on Job.* These sermons,
then, can be placed in the wider framework of Calvin's theology by recalling that they are the exegetical expression of topics that found their
definitive form in the 1559 *Institutes.*

In Calvin's understanding of providence, a fragile and often endan-
gered world of nature and history stands in radical dependence on the
will of a powerful and sovereign God. The transcendence and sovereignty of God play a major role in both the *Institutes* and the *Sermons on
Job.* The Prologue, the whirlwind speech, and many verses of the Dialogues prove to Calvin that God's omnipotence is "not the empty, idle,
and almost unconscious sort that the Sophists imagine, but a watchful,
effective, active sort engaged in ceaseless activity." In the tragic story of
Job's life, Calvin sees evidence that God regulates, governs, and controls
every event. The exchange between God and Satan in the Prologue
demonstrates that there is no permission, fortune, or chance in God's
will. As Calvin wrote in the *Institutes,* "But let them recall that the devil
and the whole cohort of the wicked are completely restrained by God's
hand as by a bridle, so that they are unable either to hatch any plot
against us or, having hatched it, to make preparations or, if they have
fully planned it, to stir a finger toward carrying it out, except insofar as
he has permitted, even commanded."[7] In a new chapter added to the
1559 *Institutes,* Calvin used the Prologue of Job to prove that there is no
mere permission in God: "From the first chapter of Job we know that Satan, no less than the angels, who willingly obey, presents himself before

God [Job 1:6, 2:1] to receive his commands. . . . However, even though a bare permission to afflict the holy man then seems to be added, yet we gather that God was the author of that trial of which Satan and his wicked thieves were the ministers."[8]

Therefore, although the biblical portrayal of Job raises the specter of a history abandoned by God or a God who torments human beings, Calvin finds in this story an affirmation that God justly and providentially decrees every event in nature and in history. Moreover, because of God's constant providential care, the cosmos is a manifestation of his glory. The order, beauty, and stability of nature are revelatory of God's goodness and wisdom. In Elihu and the whirlwind speech, Calvin finds ample testimony to the ideas expressed in book I of the *Institutes*. The stars, the waters, the earth, and the animals illustrate that "God daily discloses himself in the whole workmanship of the universe."[9] As Psalm 104 makes clear, ever since the creation of the world, God has "brought forth those insignia whereby he reveals his glory to us, whenever and wherever we cast our gaze." And, as Heb. 11:3 shows, "this skillful ordering of the universe is for us a sort of mirror in which we can contemplate God, who is otherwise invisible."[10]

Calvin's discussions of providence are filled with this imagery of mirrors, theaters, insignia, and reflections of divine glory. The *Sermons on Job* are no exception. Yet there is another side to Calvin's doctrine of providence: the darkness, obscurity, confusion, and hiddenness of God's rule. As Gerrish aptly notes, "Calvin's doctrine of providence, so far from being inferred from the visible tokens of God's presence, is in fact developed despite God's hiddenness."[11] Calvin's statements about the hiddenness of divine providence primarily, though not exclusively, concern history: how the justice and purpose of human affairs often seem inscrutable, chaotic, unjust, and obscure to the human mind. In the *Institutes,* Calvin readily admits that the causes of events are often hidden, and consequently human history often seems to be fortuitous, disordered, and confused. Indeed, it often seems as if "God were making sport of men by throwing them about like balls."[12] Hence Calvin says that God has "another hidden will [aliam voluntatem absconditam]," which is incomprehensible and a "deep abyss."[13] When the order, reason, and end of events lie hidden in the divine purpose, everything "seems to us to be confused and mixed up."[14] But Calvin insists that God "cannot put off the office of judge."[15] Therefore, despite the seemingly chaotic character of earthly life, "God, out of the pure light of his justice and wisdom tempers and directs these very movements in the best conceived order to the right end."[16]

All these themes find exegetical and homiletic expression in the *Sermons on Job*. This concern with God's hiddenness and this dialectic between revelation and darkness make Calvin share with the medieval tradition a preoccupation with the perceptual aspects of the Joban story. I have argued that all our medieval exegetes fully mined the perspectival structure of the Book of Job, and Calvin is no exception. Like his predecessors, Calvin develops the perceptual elements inherent in the biblical text of Job in order to draw out the perspectival structure of the story. Like Gregory, he seeks to understand the perceptual dimension of suffering and the purpose of different types of affliction. Again like Gregory, he tries to defend the perspectives of both Job and the friends. Like Maimonides and Aquinas, he discusses the ambiguity of history, the problematic discernment of providence, and the limitations of human knowledge. Like all these thinkers, Calvin attempts to determine what Job perceived about himself, God, and history in the midst of inexplicable suffering.

Calvin does not simply reiterate earlier medieval themes or repeat former exegetical solutions. With Calvin the perceptual issues are more pronounced and, frankly, take a more disquieting turn. Calvin stretches the perceptual dimensions of the book to their limit. His reading of Job is characterized by a recurring tension between divine revelation and divine hiddenness, a tension that permeates his interpretation of passages about creation, providence, God's justice, and human suffering. In Job's story, Calvin sees a God who holds sovereign sway over nature, history, and Satan. He revels in descriptions of creation and exhorts his congregation to contemplate the divine glory evident everywhere in the cosmos. But he also finds confessions that the wisdom, providence, goodness, and justice of God are often inscrutable and far beyond the distorted perception of fallen human beings. In Job's story, Calvin finds a God who "hides his face." Unlike Gregory, Calvin is not speaking of a wisdom that "lies hidden in the unseen" but rather of a hiddenness that darkens history, threatens faith, and tempts one to despair. As he progresses through his line-by-line exposition of the text, Calvin struggles more and more intensely with the hidden and darker side of the divine nature. In so doing, he becomes increasingly aware of Job's noetic agony.

In this chapter and the next we will examine Calvin's concern with Job's perceptual dilemma and analyze his attempt to account for God's hiddenness. We will analyze how Calvin's interpretation of Job's story strives to hold together the competing strains of divine visibility and divine hiddenness so that the God of history does not recede into utter inscrutability. We begin with Calvin's struggle to follow Job's tortured and labyrinthine quest for divine justice in a world where the wicked often triumph and the good suffer. The nature of Job's tragedy demanded that Calvin articulate the proper relationship between God's justice and power, and inexplicable human suffering. As Calvin tries to understand the justice and power of God, he comes to probe the frightening reality of spiritual suffering: the anguish caused by the fear that God has turned away and "hidden his face." In his reading of Job's laments, Calvin seeks a knowable God in unexplainable suffering. He finds that the Book of Job tests his presuppositions about human nature, the rationality of history, the proper cause of suffering, and the nature of divine justice.

Job and David: Calvin's View of Suffering

Calvin did not have to read very far into the text before confronting Job's age-old cry: Why do the righteous suffer? This question immediately raises for the Reformer that host of interrelated questions about the purposes of suffering that we have seen in our earlier commentators, especially Gregory. What is the relationship between suffering and sin? Is there really any "innocent" suffering? Is there only one explanation for suffering? Is suffering beneficial? How is one best to endure adversity? Calvin also asks the ancient question that leads to wisdom: How does one suffer well? To understand fully how Calvin answers these questions on the basis of the Book of Job requires analysis of his presuppositions about the nature of suffering.

Like earlier exegetes, Calvin assumes that suffering is definitive of the faithful life and must be interpreted in a wider biblical and Christological context. Calvin thinks in a thoroughly traditional way by explaining affliction in terms of the life of Christ; Christ's suffering is the fundamental reality that lies at the heart of faithful and obedient existence. Calvin makes clear that God's scourging of those whom he loves was personified in Christ so that the life of the faithful is the history of suffering. It is not simply suffering for the sake of Christ or the gospel that is so important; suffering in itself is definitive of the spiritual life.[17] The following passage clearly illustrates how Calvin repeats a theme common in the history of Christian thought, namely, that "beginning with Christ" the Christian life is, by definition, one of affliction:

For whomever the Lord has adopted and deemed worthy of his fellowship ought to prepare themselves for a hard, toilsome, and unquiet life, crammed with very many and various kinds of evil. It is the heavenly Father's will thus to exercise them so as to put his own children to a definite test. Beginning with Christ, his first born, he follows this plan with all his children. . . . Why should we exempt ourselves, therefore, from the condition to which Christ our Head had to submit, especially since he submitted to it for our sake to show us an example of patience in himself?[18]

Throughout his writings, Calvin defends the traditional insight that the suffering of the faithful is the biblical norm; like Christ, all the patriarchs, heroes, and saints were exercised, tried, and tested by God. When defending the view that Old Testament figures must have longed for the celestial life, Calvin recounts the continual miseries of God's people.[19] Adam "meagerly sustained his need with anxious toil" and recoiled from his only surviving son, who had murdered Abel. Noah spent "a good part of his life in great weariness building an ark" and was later derided by his own son.[20] Abraham, according to Calvin, was not only the champion of faith but also the great sufferer. He was taken from his country, parents, and friends, driven from the land by famine, and forced to prostitute his wife. He wandered about for many years and found himself childless in old age. And as his final test he was commanded to sacrifice Isaac. "In short," Calvin concludes, "throughout his life, he was so tossed and troubled that if anyone wanted to paint a picture of a calamitous life, he could find no model more appropriate than Abraham's."[21] Similarly, the "short and evil" life of Jacob was filled with calamities. He fled from his parents, endured twenty years of affliction by his father-in-law, lost his beloved Rachel, and grieved over his son's death, his daughter's rape, and Reuben's act of incest with his own wife. "Who," Calvin asks, "can imagine that in such a flood of misfortunes he would have a single moment to breath in peace?"[22]

Calvin brings this image of the faithful but calamitous life to bear on the story of Job and explains repeatedly that Job's adversities are no exception in the Bible. Abraham, Jacob, Ezekiel, Paul, and Christ are further examples that the faithful have always suffered.[23] But when he seeks to place Job's story in the wider biblical context, he turns primarily not to Abraham or to Christ but to David. In the last years of his life, Calvin devoted a considerable amount of time to the biblical books that recounted the stories of Job and David: the Psalms, the Book of Job, and 1 and 2 Samuel.[24] In these biblical texts he found two men, Job and David, both of whom were loved and afflicted by God. As Calvin states in his *Sermons on Job,* Job and David led parallel lives; God both elevated and afflicted them.[25] Just as Job was upright and withdrew from evil, so too David was a faithful servant who delighted in the Law.[26] The lives of both men, however, were filled with tragedy. Job lost all his possessions, his children, and his health. David was pursued by Saul and endured the death of his son, the rape of his women, the threats from his enemies, and the conspiracy of his son Absalom. In the lives of Job and David, Calvin sees the preeminent proof that God afflicts those whom he loves.[27] On the basis of Job and David, Calvin tries to articulate what he understands to be the biblical teaching about the proper endurance of suffering. Between the tragic figures of Job and David, Calvin sees an existential connection, which he transforms into a hermeneutical device.

Calvin was not the first commentator to use the parallelism between

Job and David as an exegetical tool. To appreciate Calvin's use of these two figures, we must interrupt our chronological progression and turn back to the fourth century. The exegetical decision to join Job and David was made at least as early as Ambrose's series of four sermons delivered between 387 and 389, entitled "On the Prayer of Job and David."[28] For our purposes, these sermons are important because they stand as an excellent counterpoint for comparison with Calvin and because they typify the spirituality of suffering we have already seen in the *Moralia*.

According to Ambrose, the Book of Job and the Psalms address the same fundamental issue: the doubt about divine providence caused by the prosperity of the wicked and the inexplicable and seemingly unjust suffering of the good. Interpreting Psalms 41 (42) and 72 (73) in conjunction with the story of Job, Ambrose finds David's confession representative of the temptation that haunts all the faithful: "My feet were almost moved, my steps had nearly slipped, for I was envious when I saw in the case of sinners, the peace of sinners."[29] In the afflictions of Job and David, Ambrose depicts the often unexplainable physical and spiritual affliction experienced by believers, a type of suffering Job and David shared with Abraham, Moses, Elijah, Peter, and Paul.[30] As models or moral exemplars for future generations, Job and David are, to Ambrose's mind, models of how one ought to endure suffering faithfully.

In his exposition of Job and David, Ambrose explains the meaning of suffering within the context of sin and redemption. Job 7:1–5 ("Man's life on earth is a state of trial") depicts the wretchedness of human existence in the "shadow of this world."[31] In Job and David, Ambrose says, "the nature of human life is described."[32] Within this fallen life, the affliction of the righteous is preparatory for the life of immortality. Rom. 8:18 ("The sufferings of the present time are not worthy to be compared with the glory to come") allows Ambrose to use Paul as a model for suffering and provides him with the overarching framework of immortality within which he interprets the suffering of the just.[33] According to Ambrose, both Job and David shared Paul's belief in resurrection and came to understand their own hardships as a purifying process that granted entrance to eternity.

Ambrose employs two themes to explain the scourging of the faithful. As Gregory later argued, Ambrose explains that suffering produces strength. Repeatedly Ambrose uses the image of athleticism to explain that suffering enables one to gain spiritual fortitude. To describe the muscular benefit of suffering, he also draws on 2 Cor. 12:9 to explain that strength is made perfect in weakness.[34] Ambrose says of Job that "even though he felt that the arrows of the Lord were in his body and said that he was pierced by them, yet like the good athlete who does not give in to pain or refuse the hardships of the contest, he said, 'Let the

Lord, having begun, wound me but not destroy me in the end.'"[35] In Ambrose's view, Job was "as an athlete of Christ [ut athleta Christi], in order that he might be fashioned by temptations and attain to the crown of a greater glory."[36] Comparing Job's speeches to those of his friends, he observes that "the discourses of the sick man were stronger than the discussions of those who were not sick. . . . For Job was stronger when sick than he had been when healthy." This was because "strength is made perfect in weakness [virtus in infirmitatibus consummatur]."[37] This "athletic" interpretation of suffering recurs in Ambrose's descriptions of David. Commenting on Psalm 73, he argues that "the man who has not struggled or been tried in the combat of various contests will not be able to hope for future rewards."[38] Because Job and David were scourged in their lives, Ambrose insists, "they had strength in their afflictions."[39]

Ambrose also expresses the traditional theme that was later articulated most fully in Gregory's *Moralia:* that suffering leads to wisdom. Visual metaphors denoting insight and knowledge describe the sufferings borne by Job and David. Job's friends are said to have suffered from "feeble insight," while the afflicted Job, as a "brave athlete," "spoke in mysteries," made "distinction in the spirit," and uttered truths according to a knowledge of God's judgments.[40] The "insight," "discernment," or "knowledge" gained by both Job and David led to a "wisdom" that allowed them a deeper perception and enabled them to see the vanity and illusory nature of earthly power, prosperity, possessions, and happiness. In answer to Job's cry, "Why do the wicked live?" Ambrose notes that not only do they live, but also they are filled with riches, they have their children, and their houses are abundant. By this description of the prosperity of the wicked Ambrose understands that the life of the wicked is "at first glance clearly a good, but in a deeper and more profound sense, you will discover that what is considered good is not good and what is considered evil [the just] reckon preferable."[41] David overcame his temptations about providence by seeing that God's plan "is not to be weighed by the appearance of things present but by the advantage of things to come."[42] Unlike the wicked, Job and David were not "drunk" with the abundance of "worldly possessions" but were wise in the knowledge that "abiding things cannot follow unless earthly things have failed."[43] Repeatedly Ambrose interprets the insights gained by Job and David in terms of Paul's exemplary suffering, by citing or paraphrasing 1 Cor. 2:14–15, 9:11, 12:14, and 13:12; Rom. 11:33; and Phil. 1:21.[44]

Ambrose makes clear that Job and David attained this spiritual wisdom about the self and the world only through affliction; the endurance of suffering allowed both men to rise above the temporal realm and to gain wisdom. Not surprisingly, Ambrose argues that faithful men like Job and David *desire* suffering because "the Father scourges the Son whom he receives."[45] In Ambrose's interpretation, the adversities endured by Job and David enabled them to transcend the "waves" or "sea" of this temporal, ever fluctuating world.[46] Therefore, in his discussions of this "flight from the world,"[47] Ambrose also articulates that ancient association between suffering and freedom. Only suffering can lead to a true perception of reality, a perception that frees the sufferer from earthly entanglements and from enslavement to that which is illusory, vain, and fleeting.

This brief analysis of Ambrose's sermons on Job and David recalls our analysis of the *Moralia.* Ambrose's spirituality of suffering shares certain elements with that of Gregory; most important of these are the connection between suffering and strength and the belief that the endurance of adversity can lead to freedom and wisdom. We can now consider Calvin's view of suffering against the background of this Ambrosian-Gregorian tradition and analyze how he uses the heuristic device of interpreting Job in conjunction with David.

Calvin is keenly aware that in the stories of Job and David two types of affliction coexist: retributive and nonretributive suffering. Retributive suffering, espoused by Job's friends, is adversity inflicted as chastisement for sin. Inexplicable suffering is affliction sent by God for reasons unknown to the sufferer. Like Gregory, Calvin tries to justify God's action in both types of suffering. Throughout the *Sermons* he tenaciously defends the retributive theology of suffering espoused most clearly by Job's friends and expressed throughout the Psalms. Calvin's dogged defense of the theory of retributive suffering places him in the familiar but uncomfortable position of supporting those who are reproved in the end. Like previous commentators, Calvin feels compelled to rescue what he considers the incontrovertible moral truths taught by Job's companions. He too is convinced that one cannot deny the teachings in such statements as Job 4:7–8 ("Think now, I pray you, who that was ever innocent perished? Or were the upright ever cut off?"), 4:17 ("Can man be more just than God? Can man be more pure than his Creator?"), and 8:3 ("Does God pervert justice? Or does the Almighty abolish what is right?").

Calvin adopts the traditional principle formulated by Gregory to defend the truth of these verses: Although the friends wrongly applied their teachings to Job's case, they taught doctrine that was true in itself.[48] Explaining the rule that governs his exegesis of chapters 4, 5, 8, 11, 15, 18, 22, 25, and 29, Calvin says that "those who maintain the poor case . . . speak beautiful and holy sentences; there is nothing in their propositions that we ought not to receive as if the Holy Spirit had not pronounced it, for it is pure truth. These are the foundations of religion;

they discuss the providence of God, they discuss his justice, they discuss the sins of men. Here, then, is a doctrine which we have to receive without contradiction and yet the result that these people try to throw Job into despair and to destroy him completely is wrong."[49]

On the basis of Job's friends, Calvin can argue that as a "general rule" a direct cause exists between suffering and sin.[50] He finds it particularly important to be able to preach the truths expounded by Job's companions both because he can thereby defend divine justice and because he is determined that his hearers not apply Job's claims of innocence to themselves and assume that they were afflicted for something other than past sins. Like Gregory, Calvin is concerned to make clear that for most people the response to suffering should begin with confession. When we suffer, Calvin insists, we must attribute our adversities to our "infinite sins."[51] At every opportunity he warns his listeners that, unlike Job's case, their afflictions are corrective penalties.

In the speeches of Job's friends Calvin finds the opportunity to preach about the beneficial purpose of suffering. For the elect, adversity is intended not as mere vengeance but rather as medicine for the soul. Calvin's particular interest in the beneficial character of affliction gravitates toward his emphasis on the noetic effect of sin. In his view, sin wreaked epistemological or perceptual havoc on the human mind so that people lost their knowledge of God and could not recognize their own sinfulness. As he states in the *Institutes,* "we always seem to ourselves righteous and upright and wise and holy—this pride is innate in all of us—unless by clear proofs we stand convinced of our own unrighteousness."[52] Human beings now function in a reality dominated by self-deception, delusion, and blindness. Interpreting Job 19:1–12, Calvin cites Rom. 1:28 to show that the worst of all evils is to be so blinded and hardened by Satan that we cannot sense our sins when God strikes us.[53] As scriptural justification for the view that penitential suffering restores self-knowledge and leads to confession, Calvin, like Gregory, believes the words of Eliphaz in 5:17: "Behold the man whom God corrects is happy; refuse not the chastening of the Almighty."[54]

However, when Calvin looks for an example of how one properly endures corrective suffering, he often turns not to Job but to David. Calvin so frequently appeals to David throughout the sermons on Job because the figure of Job presents him with a twofold problem: Job did not exemplify corrective suffering, and he did not endure inexplicable suffering particularly well. Arguing that David was a model for both types of affliction, Calvin repeatedly appeals to David at Job's expense. Calvin is delighted, for example, that David expressed Eliphaz's same insight in passages such as Ps. 119:67 ("Lord it has been for my profit that thou has humbled me").[55] This verse, cited in the Job sermons, explains Calvin's preference for David over Job.[56] Ironically, for Calvin David is the bigger hero because he was the greater sinner; David's frequent confessions of sin endear him to the Reformer. Throughout the *Sermons on Job* and the commentary on the Psalms, Calvin commends David for attributing his adversities to his own guilt. Unlike the wicked, Calvin's David endured his tribulations by first confessing his own sin before God.[57]

Calvin draws on the penitential passages from the Davidic Psalms throughout the sermons on Job in order to use David's confessions as a corrective to Job's self-justification. Calvin knows that the Prologue excludes the possibility that Job was scourged for past sins. Nonetheless, Calvin insists that God *could* have afflicted Job for sin. That God did not choose to punish Job was not a reflection on Job's innocence but rather a result of God's hidden purpose. By using David to correct Job, Calvin wants to insist that the proper attitude in all suffering, regardless of the cause, is confession and humility. We can see why Job makes only rare appearances in the Psalms commentary, while David accompanies Job on almost every page of the Job sermons.[58] Calvin draws on David to teach Job how to endure suffering well.

If we turn to Sermon 53, we can see that the difference between Job and David is expressed most forcefully by Calvin's comparison between Job 14:4 and Psalm 51. In 14:4 Job cried, "Who can bring a clean thing out of impurity?" Like earlier exegetes, Calvin interpreted this verse as referring to original sin. But in Calvin's eyes, Job did not confess his own guilt readily enough in this statement; instead he sought "some subterfuge in order to lessen the condemnation that is upon all men." In contrast to Job, Calvin continues, David willingly confessed the guilt of original sin in Psalm 51 "not in order to have some pretext with which to justify himself before God, but to condemn what he was."[59] The importance of this comparison becomes clearer when we see that the same argument recurs in the sermon on 23:8–12 where David, unlike Job, is said to have confessed that he would not have "come out like gold" if judged according to the Law.[60] Repeatedly in the *Sermons on Job* Calvin opposes Job's impatient and passionate outbursts with David's humility, sobriety, and recognition that his afflictions were merited and necessary.[61] While Job often complained, became angry, and "spoke excessively," David was humble, "bridled" himself, and submitted to God. Unlike Ambrose, who placed Job and David on equal footing as model sufferers, Calvin sees a disjunction between these two anguished biblical figures. Although Calvin repeats the traditional view, defended by Gregory, that Job was intended as a "mirror of patience"[62] for future generations, the reader quickly realizes that this title more rightly belongs to David.

We see, then, that throughout the Psalms commentary as well as in the *Sermons on Job*, Calvin uses David to support his retributive theology of suffering, which construes adversity as an educational chastisement, the proper response to which is repentance. He finds this theory appealing primarily because it confirms his own view of human sinfulness and supports his belief that affliction is medicinal. Equally important, a retributive explanation for suffering affirms the moral intelligibility and rationality of history. Calvin knows that in the moral world of Job's friends, divine justice is knowable and visible. According to their retributive theology of suffering, God's actions are rational, history is predictable, and God always rewards and punishes according to the Law. By affirming the teachings of the friends as true in themselves, Calvin retains an intelligible moral system that guarantees the rationality of history. In his exegesis of both Job and the Psalms, the Reformer reminds his audience that there are times in history when God does act as Job's friends argued, by restoring order and punishing the wicked; in such ages one can see divine justice at work in the earthly realm.[63] Because God's justice is at times knowable, Calvin can recommend the reading of history through which one can discern God's providential rule in the past.[64]

Nonetheless, Calvin is well aware that there are periods in history when divine providence is not discernible. In his distinction between the truth of the doctrine of the friends and the erroneous application of their doctrine lies the division between hiddenness and visibility that cuts through all of Calvin's sermons on Job. Gregory formulated this distinction, and it was, to a certain extent, assumed by Aquinas. But because Gregory attributed such perceptual and virtuous superiority to Job, this distinction did not create in the *Moralia* the perceptual dilemma or sense of noetic urgency that we find in Calvin's interpretation. The text of Job forces Calvin to go beyond the defense of retributive suffering and pose the question of suffering and justice in terms of Job's particular situation. The opening dialogue between God and Satan compels him to ask the question from Job's very limited perspective: Would a just God permit someone to be scourged for something other than past sins? Would God afflict someone for a *hidden* reason? What would be the purpose of such suffering? Remaining faithful to the perspectival structure of the Book of Job, Calvin recognizes that neither Job nor his friends knew the reason for the divine scourges. From the human perspective Job was truly afflicted "without cause," a phrase Calvin interprets to mean that God struck him for a purpose unknown to human reason.[65] By maintaining the perceptual tension that characterizes the Joban story, Calvin confronts the problem of inexplicable suffering.

Again he turns to David. Although Calvin eagerly draws on David throughout the Job sermons to support his penitential view of suffering, he knows that the tragedies of Job and David cannot be explained only in terms of chastisement and repentance. In the stories of these two figures, Calvin also explores the reality of unexplainable affliction. A careful reading of the *Sermons on Job* allows us to detect an ongoing second comparison between Job and David, which parallels Calvin's praise of David's penitential attitude toward affliction. In the second comparison, Job and David are more nearly equal and represent not retributive but inexplicable suffering. According to Calvin, both Job and David were accused falsely by their detractors of being punished for past sins; the accusations leveled by Job's friends were equaled by Shimei who blamed David's troubles with Absalom on God's avenging the house of Saul against David because he was a man of blood.[66] For Calvin, both the story of Shimei (2 Sam. 16:7–9) and Psalm 41 serve as warnings against a hasty and false judgment about the cause of another person's suffering. Commenting on Ps. 41:1 Calvin makes a comparison, rare in the Psalms commentary, between Job and David, both of whom were wrongly accused by those who witnessed their suffering. Cautioning against the error of misjudging the cause of someone's adversities, Calvin describes the many reasons why God may afflict someone:

The error of which we speak, namely, that of judging wrongly and wickedly, is one that has prevailed in all ages of the world. The scriptures, in many places plainly and clearly state that God, for various reasons, tests the faithful by adversities. At one time [he tries them] in order to train them to patience; at another to subdue the sinful affections of the flesh; at another to cleanse; and, as it were, to purify them from the remaining desires of the flesh; sometimes to humble them; sometimes to make them an example to others; and at other times to stir them up to the contemplation of the celestial life.[67]

Preaching on Job 19:26–29 ("And you have said, 'Why is he persecuted? And the root of the cause you have found in me.'") Calvin briefly paraphrases this explanation of Ps. 41:1.[68] In so doing he uses David as an example that one must judge carefully regarding the cause of another's suffering, since God does not strike in response to sin only. Comparing Psalm 41 to the story of Job, Calvin argues that "we must be sober and modest when we see our neighbors afflicted and let us recognize the hand of God, in order that what happened to Job's friends does not happen to us."[69] Here Calvin shifts his position and aligns David with Job in opposition to the retributive theology of suffering preached by the friends. In both Job and David he recognizes the type of suffering endured by the faithful not because of sins but because they are caught in a world where God seems to be "asleep," appears to have "forgotten" the universe, seems to have "turned away," and "hides his face."[70]

We are now able to understand the particular view of temptation articulated by Calvin in the *Sermons on Job*. For Gregory, the discussions about temptation focused on moral vices or spiritual pride and were located primarily in the moral level of the text. For Calvin, however, the "temptation" felt by Job and David was not that of moral transgression or spiritual arrogance but rather a temptation caused by the hiddenness of God in history. Moving within the realm of inexplicable suffering and the glad triumph of the wicked, Calvin bases his comparisons of Job and David on the fact that both men underwent the same "spiritual combat" or "temptation" caused by the disordered appearance of human events. Throughout the commentary on the Psalms and the *Sermons on Job*, Calvin portrays both men as gazing upon the "confusion" of human history and watching as the wicked prosper and the good suffer. Repeatedly in the *Sermons on Job*, Calvin intersperses Job's complaints with verses from the Psalms in order to define the "temptation" of Job and David as the fear that God had abandoned them or forsaken the realm of human events.[71] The happiness of the wicked, described in Psalm 73, caused Calvin's David to succumb to the same temptation about providence as that experienced by Job when his wife told him to "curse God and die." At these moments, Calvin says, both men despaired or feared that God had "become their enemy" and had "abandoned his office" so that he no longer governed the world justly or cared about human affairs.[72] Job's cry that "God has become cruel to me and ravishes me with the force of his hand" reminds Calvin of similar statements by David in Ps. 22:15–16, 31:10–11, and 69:2–4.[73] Calvin makes such comparisons in order to define the specific form of spiritual agony felt by the faithful when God "hides" and "turns away."

For Calvin this spiritual torment was far more painful than the loss of family, honor, and material goods. The ultimate sorrow felt by Job and David was not poverty, rebellion, or illness but the feeling that God "no longer heard their prayers." As Calvin remarks in his sermon on Job 14:13–15, "There is nothing man ought to fear more than to be forgotten by God."[74] Describing this anguish, Calvin says, "So then we see Job, beyond the illnesses which he endured, was tormented by his wife and above all by those who came to tempt him spiritually." He explains, "Now I call it spiritual temptation when we are not only beaten and afflicted in our bodies, but when the devil so works in our imaginations that God is a mortal enemy to us and we can no longer have recourse to him. . . . But these spiritual struggles are much more difficult to bear than all the evils and adversities that we can suffer when persecuted."[75] He adds that Satan bombarded Job with "evil fantasies" by asking, "Do you believe that God thinks about you? Do you not know that he has abandoned you? Do you believe that God deigns even to have regard for human creatures?"[76]

In Calvin's interpretation both Job and David become paradigmatic figures for the type of spiritual anguish he saw as lying at the heart of

Job's story, namely, the suffering caused by the hiddenness of God. According to Calvin this divine hiddenness is a temptation unique to the faithful when they contemplate the chaos of their personal lives or the injustice and confusion evident in historical events. When God does not intervene and "restore order" in human affairs or put an end to inexplicable suffering, believers feel that he is "far off," has "forsaken the work of his hands," has "hidden his face," and has "concealed his purposes" from human beings. In the Psalms commentary Calvin explains that God delays in this way as a test of faith.[77] The inner "spiritual combat" endured by Job and David typified the conflict all believers must undergo, the conflict between trust and doubt, faith and despair, the judgment of the flesh and the perception of faith. The faithful, Calvin insists, must close their eyes to the present appearance of things, rise above the judgment of "carnal sense," the "clouds," "mist," or "darkness," and "celebrate the providence of God."[78]

When we recognize that the composition of the Psalms allows Calvin to believe that David "rose above the clouds" more quickly than did Job, we can see why he is consistently more at ease with the former than with the latter. In describing the search for a way to trust in God's justice during times of God's hiddenness, the Joban text is simply more obfuscating than the Psalter. In comparison to Calvin's David, Job took longer to arrive at this trust; he traveled more detours, complained more bitterly, fell into blasphemy, argued his own self-justification, accused God of wielding a tyrannical power, and challenged God's justice more deeply than did David. Frequently Calvin notes that David began a psalm by expressing his sorrow and doubts about divine providence but concluded by conquering temptation and celebrating the order, reason, and justice of God. Even David's prayers that God "awake" or "rouse himself" are interpreted by Calvin as proofs of David's unfaltering hope in God's care and justice.[79] While in the *Sermons on Job* Calvin emphasizes that God silenced Job, he observes repeatedly in the Psalms commentary that David often concluded his own laments with the praise of God.[80]

Double Justice: Calvin's Search for an Answer to Job

More so than the Psalms, the *Sermons on Job* drive Calvin to explore the deeper dimensions of God's hiddenness. It is the often convoluted character of the text of Job and the fact that Job was said to have "spoken rightly" before God that make Calvin probe more thoroughly the nature of divine justice and the relationship between divine justice and divine power. Briefly, the concept of double justice posits a higher, hidden justice in God that transcends the Law and could condemn even the angels. This idea, which appears in Calvin's works before the *Sermons on Job*, grew out of his fascination with Job 4:18, Eliphaz's statement that even the angels could not withstand the judgment of God. In the 1539 *Institutes* Calvin translates this verse, "Shall man be justified in comparison with God? Or shall he be purer than his maker? Behold, they that serve him are not faithful and even in his angels he finds wickedness."[81] In the 1559 *Institutes* he adds to this citation the concept of double justice in order to emphasize that no creaturely justice can satisfy the righteousness of God.[82] In his commentary on Col. 1:20, he uses Job 4:18 to show that even the unfallen angels needed a mediator before they could be joined fully to God.[83]

Calvin thus approaches the story of Job with a theological insight culled from the Joban text. In the course of these sermons he elaborates upon this insight and argues that there is in God both a created or clear justice (*iustice ordinaire, notoire, manifeste*), which is revealed in the Law, and a secret justice (*iustice cachee, secrette*), which surpasses the Law and is incomprehensible to human reason.[84] He proceeds to interpret Job by asking how these two justices are related: Does God's created justice have any claim on his secret justice? Is God free to override his ordinary justice "without cause" (Job 2:3) and to act tyrannically? Does Job come face to face with a God whose sovereignty is out of control? To answer these disquieting questions, Calvin develops a theory of justice that draws rather loosely on the Scotist-nominalist vocabulary of his day: the radical freedom of God, the contingency of the created order of justice, the idea of divine acceptation, the references to God's absolute power, and the identification of God with justice.[85]

We turn now to the specific texts to which Calvin applied his interpretive device of double justice in his search for an answer to Job's question about unjust and inexplicable suffering. Decisive for both Calvin and the medieval tradition, these verses determined how the exegete would find divine justice in the midst of Job's tragedy. By analyzing these texts in a comparative manner, we will be able to determine Calvin's similarity to, extension of, and divergence from the medieval exegetical tradition.

Both Calvin and medieval exegetes considered the question of divine justice inseparable from the issue of Job's innocence. If Job were truly sinless, his suffering seemed unjust and unwarranted. How could suffering benefit a sinless person? Claiming no more about himself than what was stated in 1:1 and 1:8, Job repeatedly asserted his righteousness: 9:15, 12:4, 13:16–18, 16:17, 23:7, 23:10–12, 27:5–6, 29:14–25. And always, there was verse 42:7, which declared that it was Job who had "spoken rightly" before God.

As we have seen, medieval exegetes also struggled with these texts. Can anyone really be "simple and straightforward," as 1:8 stated? Did Job retain his integrity throughout his scourges, especially in passages such as 3:1–23, 9:22–25, 19:6–7, and 21:7–33, where he appeared to attribute injustice to God? If Job did remain blameless, why did he repent in 39:33 (40:5) and in 42:1–6? But if he did fall into sin, Satan must have won the wager with God recounted in the Prologue. The medieval exegetes saw that the biblical text itself complicates the issue because in several verses Job confessed his sinfulness: 7:20–21, 9:20–21, 14:4, 14:16–17, 31:33–34. Job's claims to righteousness were further complicated by the doctrine of original sin. After all, it was Job himself who uttered one of the traditional proofs for original sin when he cried in 14:4, "Who can make clean one conceived of unclean seed?" (Vulgate).

Gregory concluded that although Job did not blaspheme during his scourges, he was still conscious of his sins.[86] Gregory thought that when Job argued that he would be "found just," he attributed wickedness to himself but righteousness to God.[87] When he claimed that he would "be like gold that passes through fire," he was saying that suffering would purify him.[88] When Job insisted that he would "hold fast" to his righteousness and not depart from his innocence, he was saying that he had not consented to the unlawful thoughts that tempted all mortals.[89] Gregory then proceeded to interpret the confession of Job as his recognition of the danger of spiritual pride.[90]

Aquinas agreed with Gregory that Job suffered from original sin, confessed his sins, and attributed his virtues to grace.[91] He also made clear that Job confessed only to venial sins but never to grave or mortal sins.[92] Moreover, Aquinas explained Job's apparent protests about divine justice in chapters 3, 10, and 21 by distinguishing three types of discourses: those words spoken by Job's sensual nature, those where he disputed rationally, and those uttered by divine inspiration.[93] Aquinas also argued that in 39:33–35 (40:3–5) and 42:1–6 Job confessed to using inordinate or careless speech.[94] By having "spoken lightly," Job scandalized his friends with words that seemed to taste of arrogance and appeared to derogate from divine justice. Nonetheless, both interpreters believed that Job confessed only to "sinning out of levity"; he did not have to repent for grave or mortal sins.[95]

Calvin also perceives the same textual problems. But the reader soon discovers that he is much more troubled by Job's behavior than were his predecessors. The reason for his uneasiness with Job's statements becomes evident if we consider a passage in the *Institutes*, which reflects his earlier reading of passages such as Job 1:3–22, 2:7–8, and 3:1–26. Calvin explains that various diseases, the ravages of war, ice and hail, poverty, death, and other chance happenings make "men curse their life, loath the day of their birth, abominate heaven and the light of day, rail against God and . . . accuse him of injustice and cruelty."[96]

In Calvin's thinking, the godly person does not "rail against God" nor "break forth into impatience and expostulate with God." Rather, by considering the righteousness and gentleness of God's chastening he will "recall himself to forbearance." Such a person is so "composed in mind" that whatever happens he "will not consider himself miserable nor complain of his lot with ill will toward God." Such a person "permits every part of his life to be governed by God's will." Calvin concludes by saying that "whatever happens, because he will know it to be ordained of God, he will undergo it with a peaceful and grateful mind."[97]

Calvin's problem, of course, is that Job, who was "as an angel of God,"[98] hardly endured his miseries with a "peaceful and grateful mind." To Calvin's mind, the literal meaning of the text simply does not allow for such an interpretation; Calvin's Job was not a model of detachment. We can see, then, how Calvin struggles with the Joban text as he tries to reconcile the proper endurance of suffering with the accusations and laments found throughout the text. At times he tries to maintain the traditional sympathetic interpretation of Job by saying that Job was a virtuous man, an example of holiness, obedience, patience, and faith. Nonetheless, he explicitly rejects Gregory's solutions by dismissing those who wish to excuse Job completely "as if he had been transported in his misfortune, without blaspheming against God." His discomfort is evident in the opening sermon, where he quickly qualifies the references to Job as "perfect [entier]" and upright; in Job, Calvin insists, there was an integrity that served God without hypocrisy and an uprightness in dealing honestly with his neighbors, but there was no absolute perfection that would render grace unnecessary.[99] Calvin's uneasiness is further evident in his qualification of the divine affirmation in 42:7. Arguing like Aquinas, Calvin claims that Job often gave expression to his passions or sorrows, without fully consenting to them.[100] For example, when Job cried, "Why did I not die at birth?" Calvin argues that words escaped his mouth to which he never really consented.[101] When Job asked in 3:20, "Why is light given to those who are in misery?" he was tempted but not "conquered."[102]

Nonetheless, Calvin is much more critical of Job's statements than the medieval exegetes were. Unlike Gregory, Calvin does not allow the divine approval in 42:7 to govern his interpretation of all Job's words. And unlike Aquinas, Calvin believes that Job's sin was greater than mere "levity of speech."[103] According to Calvin, Job did blaspheme during his scourges and did speak in an impassioned manner; he uttered words that were confused, excessive, unbridled, rebellious, and condemnable.[104] In some instances, Calvin even concedes that Job did want to "contend" with God and did distrust divine providence.[105] Calvin portrays Job both as fighting despair about providence and as falling into the suspicion that God was indeed cruel and unjust.

In such instances the reader can detect that Calvin's Job ceases to be an "example" or "model" for future generations and becomes instead a warning. When Calvin's Job gave vent to words such as those in 6:2–3 ("Oh that my troubles were weighed and my sorrows weighed in the balances! For it would be heavier than the sands of the sea and my words would be engulfed!), 9:16 ("If I invoke him and he responds to me, still I would not believe that he heard me"), and 19:4 ("If I have failed [or erred], my fault will remain with me"), he became a warning of how even a holy, patient, and faithful person could fall.[106] Continually Calvin transposes Job from a model to be imitated into a symbol of caution by asking, "If such words could escape from Job, what will happen to us?"[107] Calvin's Job, then, actually taught future generations to "beware," to be "on their guard," and not to fall prey to blasphemy, impatience, and temptation.

We can best appreciate Calvin's dilemma when we discern how uncomfortable the Reformer becomes when dealing with those verses in which Job seemed to claim a real justice before God and to imply that God was acting unjustly. Rather than reading these texts only as further examples of Job's impatience or blasphemy, Calvin is led by them to delve more thoroughly into the nature of God's justice and providence. Here we discover the path that leads him to argue that there are levels of justice within God. He deals with these passages by arguing that Job's words would be "difficult to understand" unless they referred to a twofold or double justice. According to Calvin, Job knew that God's "revealed justice" set the standard for creaturely perfection. God freely entered into a "pact [paction]" and agreed to "accept [accepte]" the perfection of this lower justice and not impute sins so that he who obeys the Law shall live.[108] Calvin then explains that in his assertions of righteousness Job was referring to this lower justice. Arguing that he would plead his case and be declared just, that he would "hold fast" to his righteousness, and that he would not "let go of his justice," Job was hoping that God would return to the "half justice" of the law and "content himself" with his "revealed" or "common" justice.[109]

Calvin's difficulty both with the text and with his own hermeneutical device of double justice begins to emerge in his argument that Job was both right and wrong when he appealed to God's lower justice. On the basis of 1:1 and 1:8 Calvin thinks that Job argued fairly that God was not treating him according to this lower justice. He explains that God had a "secret intention" for striking Job, that is, as a test of his patience in contest with Satan.[110] Although this "secret intention" was unknown to Job, it bore no reference to his sins. But Calvin also believes that Job was wrong to claim he would "come out as gold" according to the "common rule of the Law" or the "average" or "median" justice of the Law.[111] Here

Job spoke "excessively."[112] Even Job's integrity could not satisfy the purity of God's Law. Calvin frequently notes the metaphor of the "trial [procez]" in the Book of Job. He warns that if God wanted to "enter into a trial [entrer en procez]" with anyone, including Job, they would be annihilated.[113] In Calvin's reading, Job failed to recognize that God *could* have imputed his sins and chastised him justly for his offenses even against this lower justice. That God did not do so was due to the nonimputation of sins but not to any sinlessness on the part of Job.

We should note that this criticism of what Calvin sees as Job's excessive claims to righteousness protected Calvin's theological anthropology. It also helped him to interpret those passages where Job supposedly confessed his sins against God's revealed justice. Therefore, for Calvin, Job's integrity refers only to a human justice that relies on God's gratuitous acceptance and the nonimputation of sins. Job 10:2, Calvin argues, must be interpreted by Jer. 10:24 ("Chastise me Lord but only according to measure"). He believes that both Job and Jeremiah exemplified how one ought to pray that God would judge only according to the lower justice of the Law; for all its pain, this lower judgment will be far less frightening than to be hauled before the secret justice of God.[114] Nonetheless, the Joban text does not allow Calvin to stop with his interpretation of Job's claims to righteousness. The story of Job leads him to a deeper and more transcendent level of God's inscrutable and terrifying justice.

Double Justice and the Fear of a Tyrannical God

If Calvin had had to deal only with Job's assertions that God was not punishing him according to the Law, he might not have used the doctrine of God's secret justice. Although Job was not punished for past sins, he was not blameless even according to God's lower or revealed justice. But we can see that the text pushes Calvin further by stating that even if one *were* just, God could still condemn him. Here Calvin must confront the verses that state that God could condemn both the just and the angels. Was it simply blasphemy when Job said, "If I were just I could not respond to him . . . if it is a matter of justice, who could enter into it with him. . . . It was all one, he destroys the just and the wicked equally. . . . If I wash myself with pure waters . . . yet you will plunge me into the dirt. . . . If I am just, still I will not lift up my head." Like his medieval predecessors, Calvin wrestles with these verses throughout the Book of Job: 9:15, 9:19–22, 9:30–35, 10:7, 10:15–17.

Medieval interpreters saw these verses as expressing the vast difference between divine and human justice, wisdom, and purity. Gregory believed that these texts proved that God's justice so transcends human justice that "all human righteousness would be proved unrighteous if it be judged by strict rules."[115] Job's cry, "If I be righteous, I cannot lift up my head," demonstrated that the faithful must be buffeted by the assaults of the flesh "lest our mind, presuming on its own security, dare to lift itself up in pride."[116] When Job lamented, "If I wash myself with snow waters . . . yet thou shall stain me with filth," he was confessing that the more we attempt to rise up to God by good works, "the more exactly we know the filthiness of our life, by which we are rendered at variance with his pureness."[117] When Gregory's Job cried, "[God] destroys both the innocent and the wicked," he was saying that the purity of the perfect man is swallowed up by the "pureness of divine immensity."[118] Gregory explained that "although we are careful to preserve pureness, yet by the consideration of interior perfection, it is made clear that what we practice is not purity."[119]

To describe the gulf that separates divine and human justice, Gregory argued that if judged by the "secret judgments," "strict inquiry," or "standard of interior perfection," all the saints would be condemned.[120] Gregory's discussion reaches fullest expression in his exegesis of the whirlwind speech and in his understanding of Job's confessions. Interpreting 38:18–20 and 39:1, Gregory depicts the distance between human beings and God in graphic detail. Speaking from the whirlwind, Gregory's God declared: "For you know now what progress you yourself have made, but you do not know what I still secretly think of you. For you think about your acts of justice but you do not know how strictly they are weighed by me. Woe even to the praiseworthy life of men, if it is judged without pity. When strictly examined, the conduct which one imagines is pleasing to God, is overwhelmed by the presence of the judge."[121]

Aquinas also thinks the human justice found in a person such as Job could not withstand the scrutiny of divine judgment. According to Aquinas, when Job cried that "God would stain him with filthiness even if he were clean," he was confessing that human beings cannot claim purity before God because "man's purity, however great it may be, is found deficient when referred to divine examination."[122] So too, Aquinas argued, "divine justice exceeds human justice since the latter is finite and the former is infinite."[123]

In comparison to Calvin's sermons on Job, however, these earlier discussions about the transcendence of divine justice always remained a subordinate theme. Calvin does express this view but applies the emphasis on divine transcendence to his theory of double justice. In his search for the cause of his suffering, Calvin's Job "passed beyond" God's Law and glimpsed the reality of God's hidden and secret justice. When Job cried, "If I were just, still I would not lift up my head," he was aware that even if he fulfilled the Law perfectly, he could be condemned before the secret justice of God.[124] Even if he had "washed himself clean," God could "throw him into the mud" because the secret justice of God could condemn all human justice.[125] Calvin agrees, then, that these texts expose the deficiency of all human justice before God, including the justice of the Law. Although God revealed a perfect rule for living in the Law, the Law is still only a "median" or "half justice" compared to the secret justice of God.

The critical importance Calvin places on the vast transcendence of God's higher justice becomes evident when we see that, in his view, the text of Job threatens not only human but also angelic justice. What can Eliphaz's words in 4:18 mean when he declares that "those who serve him are not stable and in his angels he has found wickedness?" On the basis of the Vulgate translation, Gregory and Aquinas argued that the references to "instability" in these verses show that because the angelic nature is mutable, some angels fell and became wicked while others adhered to God through grace.[126]

Calvin disagrees with this traditional interpretation and reads Job 4:18 as, "Voici il ne trouve point fermeté en ses serviteurs, et a mis vanité en ses Anges." Eliphaz's words in both 4:18 and 15:15 ("Behold he finds no stability in his holy ones and the heavens are not clean before Him") push Calvin to the limits of transcendence. He refuses to interpret these statements by Eliphaz as references to the devils or fallen angels; Job 4:18 charges the angels with "vanity," not apostasy or rebellion.[127] Therefore, Calvin contends, even the good angels are full of "folly" or "vanity" and are incapable of withstanding the severity of God's higher justice.[128] If God willed, God could judge even the unfallen angels "with rigor" and find them guilty, for "what comparison is there between the infinite and the finite?"[129] Arguing that there is "no proportion" between the infinite and the finite, Calvin says that the unfallen angels and the just share in a common creaturely justice that is embodied in the Law but is "as smoke when one comes before the infinite majesty of God."[130] Calvin's insistence on the immense distance between the righteousness of God and the righteousness of creatures is never muted by the implication that all human deeds are imperfect. It is crucial to remember that Calvin does not place the insufficiency of creaturely justice in the context of the Fall, in terms of venial sins, or in the "instability" of all creatures; even the unfallen angels could be condemned if God exercised the extreme rigor of his secret justice. For Calvin, the Book of Job teaches that all creaturely perfection, even that of the angels, is "accepted" by God only insofar as God "contents" himself with the lower, median, or created justice revealed in the Law.[131]

We must recognize that in Calvin's interpretation, Job's cries that the just could be condemned meant that God's secret justice could condemn the purity of the Law. Before this higher justice, even the angels of paradise would be confused. In Calvin's view, Job's search for justice led him to acknowledge that God is not so bound to the Law that he is "subjected to it."[132] If he willed to do so, Calvin's God could judge both Job and the angels according to the "extreme rigor" of his hidden justice—before which everyone would perish. Calvin describes Job's deepening insight:

> But there is another kind of justice which is most strange to us; namely, if God were to treat us not according to the Law but according as he can justly act. The reason? When the Lord gives us his lesson in the Law and commands us to do what it contains (although that surmounts our powers and no mortal man would be able to accomplish what God commands), nevertheless, we will owe more and be obliged to him. The Law is not so perfect or exquisite as is that infinite justice [iustice infinie] of God . . . according to which he could find iniquity in his angels and the sun would be unclean before him. See, then, how there is a justice more perfect than the Law. If one accomplished everything in the Law, he could still be condemned if God wanted to use this justice. True, the Lord does not wish to use it since he accommodates himself to us and receives and accepts that justice which he has commanded.[133]

Thus the Book of Job drives Calvin to a more radical and increasingly uncomfortable view of divine justice. In Calvin's reading, Job's sufferings compelled him to recognize the depths of divine justice; although the Law contained the rule of creaturely perfection, it was an accommodated justice that lay far below the justice of God. We can see how crucial verse 4:18 is to Calvin's view of Job's knowledge by observing a striking exegetical move: Although 4:18 was originally uttered by Eliphaz, by the later sermons Calvin attributes this insight and these words to *Job!*[134]

Calvin gradually becomes uneasy with his own theory of twofold justice. Although this hermeneutical device allows him to explain various passages, it also leaves him with a terrifying question: Can God override the lower justice and judge according to the rigor of his secret justice? Having made use of the now developed theory of a twofold justice, Calvin is caught. Although Calvin's Job gained a deeper understanding of God's justice, he was forced to the brink where he glimpsed a God who, acting "without cause," might be "playing with men like balls." Calvin's increasing discomfort is most evident in his awareness that the distinction between revealed and secret justice looks suspiciously like that dreaded "nominalist" distinction between God's absolute and ordained power.

We can understand why Calvin dreads this distinction only when we realize that he misinterprets the term *absolute power* to mean that God acts tyrannically. Throughout the *Sermons* he worries that Job's God seems to have acted precisely according to such an "absolute" or, in

Calvin's view, "cruel power." More threatening to Calvin than Job's claims to justice or even God's ability to condemn the angels is the suggestion that God is a tyrant.

Chapters 9 and 23 worry him the most. In these chapters Job protested that God "afflicted him in a whirlwind" and wounded him "without cause." "Behold," Job shouted, "if he snatches away and carries one away by force, who will snatch me back from his hands? Who will say, 'what are you doing?' If one proceeds by force, behold he is strong! If it is a matter of justice, who can enter into it with him? . . . He destroys both the just and the wicked equally." And in 23:13–16, Job cried that God does "whatever he wishes" and confessed that he was "terrified" of this deity: "When I think of him, I dread him. God has made my heart grow faint; the Almighty has troubled me."

These verses were not particularly troublesome for Gregory, and Aquinas, who saw chapters 9 and 23 as further confessions by Job of his nothingness before the infinite purity and righteousness of God. As Gregory argued, Job realized that even the righteous person fails before divine scrutiny. When Job asked, "What are you doing?" he recognized that "all God's judgments must be revered since they cannot be unjust."[135] Aquinas stressed that although Job was speaking "passionately," he was not "contending" with God.[136] In his interpretation, Job was showing the profundity of divine wisdom and praying for mercy.[137] In chapter 23, Aquinas argued that Job saw the inability of the human being to know God perfectly; since God cannot be comprehended, he can be neither resisted nor judged.[138]

But for Calvin, Job is a more difficult hero. Uncomfortable with his outbursts, Calvin worries that Job accused God of exercising a tyrannical or absolute power. Calvin's discomfort with these texts accounts for his vacillation on this point. In some sermons he insists that Job did not blaspheme by attributing to God an "unregulated," "capricious," or "absolute power."[139] But elsewhere Calvin admits that Job has finally fallen prey to "temptation" and has accused God of wielding such a power.[140] In Calvin's sermons, Job's fear about God's "absolute power" exemplified human dread before the incomprehensibility and hiddenness of God. Commenting on 23:1–7, Calvin criticizes such fear:

But let us examine if indeed Job speaks rightly. Certainly he does not, for he speaks excessively. . . . Job, then, supposes that God uses toward him an absolute power [puissance absolue] as it is called; that is, "I am God and I will do whatever will seem good to me although it has no form of justice. I will act with an excessive domination." But here Job blasphemes God. Although the power of God is infinite, to make it "absolute" is to imagine a tyranny in God which is completely contrary to his majesty. Our Lord cannot be more powerful than he is just; his justice and power are inseparable.[141]

If we once again compare the commentary on the Psalms and the sermons on Job, we can see how Calvin struggles theologically and exegetically to find a reliable and providential God. We discover that the principle that protects Job's God from tyranny is the same that protects David's God from cruelty: the inseparability of the divine attributes. Throughout the Psalms commentary Calvin portrays David as rising above temptation by clinging to the truth that God cannot be idle or unjust because of his "nature." It is, Calvin explains, God's "office" to govern the world, an office God cannot abdicate.[142] So, too, throughout the *Sermons on Job* Calvin argues that when governing human events, God acts with a power inseparable from the divine attributes of justice, goodness, and mercy.[143] In his reading of Job, Calvin argues that the friends correctly warned Job not to separate God's power from God's justice, wisdom, goodness, and reason. To separate these attributes is to imagine a lone, tyrannical power in God; such an idea, Calvin insists, is the error of the "theologians of the Papacy," or the "Sorbonne doctors."[144]

But Calvin is still haunted by 2:3, which states that God acted "without cause." Repeatedly he assures his hearers that this was not true; the phrase "without cause" cannot mean that God acts tyrannically or irrationally. Calvin's concern with this phrase stems from his insistence that despite all appearances, the hiddenness or inscrutability of God's judgments do not allow us to posit a naked or absolute power in the divine being.[145] Calvin fondly recalls Elihu's statement in 34:12: "God does not condemn in vain. The Almighty will not pervert the right." On the basis of such verses Calvin reminds Job of the "Scotist" emphasis that "God's will is the rule of justice." After all, Calvin insists, God's hiddenness is a secret *justice*, not a secret power.[146]

Calvin, however, grows uncomfortable when he asks whether God actually judged Job according to the strict purity of his secret justice. Here the reader sees Calvin at his most difficult juncture. Although he argues that Job would be guilty before this secret justice, Calvin will not say that Job was punished because of his sins before this higher standard. Consequently, he is forced to admit that while God can "act" according to this secret justice, God cannot "judge" according to it. The reader must remember that Calvin sees Job's lot not as a punishment but as a test. By interpreting the celestial conversation between God and Satan as a test, Calvin avoids the possibility that Job was judged "with rigor." Every time he verges on saying that Job was judged for sins against God's secret justice, he switches vocabulary and says that God "tested" Job according to "another reason," a "higher cause," a "secret counsel," or a "secret intention,"—that is, as proof of his patience and as a model for future generations.[147] Calvin's listeners are told that the fairness of this test was guaranteed by God's higher justice because God's will is the rule of justice.

Although the notion of a higher justice guaranteed that God always acted justly, Calvin pulls back from using this idea to justify Job's suffering as punishment before the purity of God's secret justice. As Calvin says, "It is certain that he is not afflicted as an evil man."[148]

Why doesn't Calvin, in his usual unblinking way, come right out and say that God applied the standard of his secret justice to Job? Such a statement would have made his argument less convoluted and more coherent and consistent. The reason is twofold. First of all, the Prologue precludes punishment as the cause of Job's afflictions. Second, and more important, Calvin does not want his hearers to fear an unreliable God who would suddenly apply to them a secret justice, before which even the angels would perish. Therefore, he does not want to admit that God ever did this in any historical instance, including the case of Job. Repeatedly he insists that God will not arbitrarily break that promise to accept the lower, revealed justice. Calvin's God will not suddenly begin to judge "with rigor." Calvin warns his readers not to speculate about what God *can* do but only to remember what God has *promised* to do: "It is not a question of what God will do but a question of what he could do. But he does not will to act [according to his secret justice]. It is sufficient that if we have regulated our lives according to the Law of God, we will be reputed as just before him. Certainly . . . God could be displeased with us if he wanted. He could find such perfection in himself so that everything we do would be as nothing. Not that he does this, as I have said."[149]

Consequently, for Calvin, God's secret justice serves only to assure Job that God's incomprehensible judgments and purposes are, by definition, just. But Calvin backs off from saying that God applied this standard of double justice to Job. By this refusal he seeks to prevent the idea of a secret justice from being interpreted as a tyrannical "absolute power," and he promises his congregation that God will not cancel that immutable promise to act according to the ordinary or common justice and suddenly haul them before the court of a higher secret justice.

FROM CALVIN'S EXEGETICAL struggle with Job's question of suffering and justice, we can draw several preliminary conclusions.

First, the sermons show that Calvin interpreted the Book of Job with the help of the earlier exegetical tradition. Although he rejects Gregory's allegorical explanations, he adopts some of Gregory's exegetical solutions, especially those regarding the interpretation of the friends. He clearly appreciates the literal tradition of interpretation established by Aquinas and repeated by many late medieval and sixteenth-century commentators.

Second, Calvin stood in a long line of exegetes who tried to affirm, in various ways, all the competing views of justice articulated in Job's story.

The penitential or retributive nature of suffering, expounded by Job's friends and expressed in the Psalms, created no problems; all interpreters, including Calvin, saw the purpose of such affliction as educational, bringing purification, repentance, restoration, and self-knowledge.

Third, an important difference exists between Calvin and the medieval tradition of tropological and allegorical exegesis (as represented by Ambrose and Gregory) on the subject of inexplicable suffering. Like earlier Joban exegetes, Calvin believes that suffering changes perception; the sufferer can perceive truths or dimensions of reality that the nonsufferer cannot understand. In this sense, Calvin stands in continuity with the tradition by remaining faithful to the perspectival and perceptual implications of the biblical text of Job, a theme we will explore more thoroughly in the following chapter. However, compared with this medieval tradition, Calvin sees a distinct difference in the object of the perception that is changed by inexplicable suffering.

In the medieval tradition of Joban commentary, inexplicable suffering (personified by Job) teaches something about the nature of the self. For Calvin, such suffering gives insight into the nature of God. According to Ambrose and Gregory, suffering, particularly inexplicable suffering, was linked intrinsically to wisdom and freedom. Through affliction, including spiritual anguish and temptation, the soul is purified and freed from earthly entanglements and materiality. Loss produces freedom. Suffering effects detachment as the soul, extricated from the temporal realm, turns inward and ascends to the eternal realm. The purpose of such suffering is to teach the soul to recognize its true home above the realm of time and change. In this Neoplatonic view of suffering, affliction aims at an anthropological wisdom, a knowledge of the true nature and place of the soul in the hierarchy of reality.

For Calvin, the inexplicable suffering endured by Job and David is not defined as loss leading to detachment. It is not described in terms of interiority and freedom. The distinctive character of Calvin's interpretation emerges clearly when we see that he does not explain Job's laments as statements about the vanity or weariness of temporal existence. In Job's speeches Calvin confronts the darker, inscrutable, and more frightening side of the divine nature. In Calvin's interpretation, we see a suffering that aims not at anthropology but at theology. To be sure, Calvin's Job and David suffered real pain, a pain described as spiritual wrestling against a despair caused by God's hiddenness. That suffering, however, brought them not so much to the brink of self-realization as to the edge of the abyss. What they feared most was a world abandoned by God. Their greatness was their eventual triumph over despair. In the midst of their spiritual agony, Calvin's Job and David tried to pierce through the swirl of political and personal chaos to perceive the providential power of God and to cling with the eye of faith to the divine promises. In the midst of darkness they sought a God they could trust despite all experiential and empirical evidence.

Finally, the nature of inexplicable suffering, depicted in the Psalms and located at the heart of the Book of Job, led Calvin to explore the relationship between such suffering and divine justice. Job's suffering made Calvin examine a theme that was not central in his exposition of the Psalms or Samuel: that there are levels of justice within God, and that there is an infinite distance between divine and human righteousness.

When describing this vast gulf separating God and the human being, Calvin restated a common theme in precritical Joban exegesis: that before God's strict inquiry, creaturely purity, justice, and wisdom are nothing. Making this theme central to his exposition, Calvin explained that God's lower justice, to which Job clung, could not challenge the higher, secret justice of God. Although in many passages Calvin does sound like Gregory and Aquinas, by making Job 4:18 apply to the unfallen angels he widens the gulf between God and creation and portrays Job as confronting a darker and more hidden God. By distinguishing between God's lower and higher justice, Calvin also creates a problem: Did Job confront a God who could cancel the revealed justice and judge according to the rigor of the secret justice? To avoid this possibility, Calvin is careful to interpret God's revealed and secret justice according to a dialectic rather than an opposition. He thus attempts to distance himself from late medieval "nominalist" positions, which he feared made God tyrannical and the created order unreliable.

Revisionist historians of the last several decades have shown that such fears misinterpreted the intention of "nominalist" theology.[150] According to this revised assessment, the nominalist use of the distinction between God's absolute and ordained power did not render God capricious, arbitrary, or tyrannical. The idea of God's "absolute power" meant only that God was *exlex*, free from all claims external to the divine will. The only exceptions to this freedom were that God could not will God's own nonexistence or suspend the law of noncontradiction. As Steinmetz says, "Omnipotence does not extend to the production of nonsense."[151] Moreover, God placed self-limitations on his powerful will. Because of the *pactum* of his ordained will, God is committed unalterably to uphold the created order.[152] The present orders of creation and redemption are radically contingent but absolutely reliable.

But in the Job sermons when Calvin thought of "absolute power," he imagined an inordinate power that made the hiddenness of God a frightening abyss.[153] As we have seen, Calvin's thought is permeated by his awareness of God's hiddenness. The hiddenness of God is not unique to Calvin's thought; we have seen expressions of this theme in medieval Joban commentators as they described the transcendence of God's judgments and providence. Calvin's reflections on the hidden justice of God may stem from medieval discussions or from other sources, including Luther's distinction between the hidden and revealed God. Parallels between Luther and Calvin are striking. Like Luther, Calvin knew of a God hidden beyond nature, history, and Christ.[154] Calvin agrees with Luther that the hiddenness of God lies at the heart of the "horrible decree" of predestination. Nonetheless, the specific concept of double justice in the sermons on Job refers to a hiddenness that lies not so much beyond Christ as beyond the Law.[155]

This "extra" dimension of divine justice led Calvin to identify God's will with the rule of justice and to stress that God's freedom is not subject to external causality, including that imposed by the Law. But this omnipotence of God drives Calvin to search for a way to express God's reliability, to find a guarantee that God will not act contrary to his lower justice. To do so, Calvin appeals not only to the *pactum* but to the inseparability of the divine attributes. In these arguments Calvin is attempting to avoid what he considers to be the dangers in the nominalist use of the term *absolute power*.

According to nominalist theologians, however, the self-limitation of God's power (except those instances listed above) applies to God's ordained power. According to God's absolute power, the deity could have created a very different world with radically different laws of creation and salvation. The distinction between God's absolute and ordained power, did indeed invite speculation about what God could do and allowed for a hypothetical separation of God's power from God's justice.[156] In his search for a dependable God, however, Calvin seeks to find this limitation in the heart of the divine essence. He tries to place God's self-limitation not only in the ordained realm or *pactum* but also within God's justice *etiam extra legem*. God's rule over history may be inscrutable, but it is reliable because in the heart of the divine essence, God's power cannot act contrary to God's justice, goodness, and wisdom. To assert an "absolute power" in God would, in Calvin's words, "tear the divine essence apart" and attribute to God an action not in harmony with God's essence. For Calvin, then, the nature of the divine essence keeps the divine omnipotence in check.

Though inaccurate, Calvin's fear of the term *absolute power* reveals his central concern throughout his sermons on Job: the search for a God who is both completely sovereign and totally reliable. While Job's God certainly satisfied the former, Calvin's argument about the nature and self-limitation of God's essence satisfied the latter. Frankly, the sovereignty of Job's God scared even Calvin; the ruler of history cannot be a

God who afflicts "without cause" or by a will unformed by goodness or justice. This fear of an unreliable or tyrannical God haunts Calvin's use of the idea of double justice as a hermeneutical device throughout the sermons. The further he read into the text, the more Calvin saw Job facing the inscrutability of providence and the darker side of God's nature. Just when that darkness became unbearable, Calvin quickly rooted God's freedom in God's unchangeable promises and in the inseparable nature of the divine essence.

Because of the radical transcendence of God, this constant appeal to the inseparability of the divine attributes did not leave the realm of hiddenness. Job (and David) were simply told to trust in the divine essence, even when they could not understand it. But Calvin knew that people like Job and David could not endure forever the suffering caused by the hiddenness and silence of God. Therefore, despite his constant gravitation toward discussions of God's hiddenness, Calvin does not leave Job with a totally inscrutable God. We shall see that Calvin continually directs Job not merely to God's incomprehensibility but to God's knowable revelation, which stands, he promises, in continuity with God's hiddenness.

It is not the concept of double justice but the works of God in nature and history that finally provide Calvin with a way of holding together the tension between hiddenness and visibility that runs throughout the sermons on Job. However, nature and history are not a text easily read. Although God's providence can be discerned in the orderliness and beauty of nature, history is, in the words of St. Paul, a more clouded mirror. According to Calvin, the friends rightly appealed to the providence of God evident in creation. But Job "spoke rightly" before God because he alone discerned that in the historical present there is a disjunction between the visibility of God's revelation in nature and the hiddenness of God in history. As we will see in chapter 4, Calvin's understanding of Job's dilemma centers not on the anthropological and transformative power of suffering but rather on the limitations of fallen human knowledge. He articulates more fully than his predecessors the darker implications of the Thomistic or literal tradition of Joban interpretation. Calvin's interpretation of the debate between Job and his friends is, then, a discourse on the inscrutability of divine providence in history. The revelatory character of nature and the ambiguity of history provide the counterforces that produce the tempest Job must confront. To reap the whirlwind, Calvin's Job had to struggle to cling to the hope that the promise offered by creation will finally redeem history.

IV

BEHOLD BEHEMOTH!

Nature and History in Calvin's *Sermons on Job*

A man said to the universe:
"Sir, I exist!"
"However," replied the universe,
"The fact has not created in me
A sense of obligation."

Stephen Crane

THE FURTHER WE read into Calvin's *Sermons on Job*, the more we find ourselves enveloped in discussions of providence that emphasize the hiddenness and inscrutabiity of God. This concern with divine hiddenness occupied Calvin throughout his life. In the *Institutes* he describes the often obscure nature of divine governance, an obscurity that leads many to believe that human events are whirled about by chance or the "blind urge of fortune."[1] Even the salvific destinies of individuals are connected with God's hiddenness since the "horrible decree" of predestination points to the hidden will of God.[2] His commentaries on the Old Testament often describe the confusion that appeared when God seemed to abandon Israel. Calvin is acutely aware that the faithful always suffer; in David's laments he finds the temptation endured by the elect when God seemed "idle" or "asleep" in heaven.[3] No biblical text, however, drives Calvin further into the realm of hiddenness than the Book of Job. Several reasons account for this. The laments found elsewhere in the Bible—in the Psalms, Isaiah, Jeremiah, and the other prophets—are often concerned with judgment upon Israel and thus link divine silence and human suffering with past sin; the truly inexplicable or nonretributive character of affliction is not so central a theme as it is in Job's story. Most important, however, is the inherently perspectival structure of the biblical text of Job, which drives Calvin to examine honestly the meaning of Job's bitter complaints. Because Job was said to speak rightly before God, Calvin finds that the correct perspective was one that took full account of the incomprehensibility of God and the obscurity of divine providence.

The *Sermons* show that once again in the history of exegesis, the problem of perception surfaces as the dominant structuring element for interpreting the Book of Job. But this perceptual issue assumes both a more dramatic and a more unsettling character for Calvin than for earlier commentators. Calvin's understanding of providence as a dialectic between revelation and concealment is invested with a unique existential urgency. In his reading, Job did not view history from the transcendent viewpoint found in Gregory's *Moralia* nor from the more rationalistic perspective evident in Aquinas's *Expositio*. Since Calvin rejects allegory, he cannot portray Job as a prophet. Thus Calvin's Job was not engaged in the elevated and tranquil survey of sacred history that the typological or allegorical level provided for Gregory's Job. Furthermore, Calvin does not portray Job as one who suffered well by virtue of his inner detachment. Like Aquinas, Calvin casts the story of Job in terms of what the mind can actually *see* within history. But that which Aquinas calls the "evidence of experience" becomes for Calvin an agonized cry about the incomprehensibility of providence. In Job's words, Calvin finds more than a debate about the nature of history; Job was not simply refuting false premises and erroneous conclusions, he was fighting spiritually for his life. This fight is depicted in stark perceptual terms. Calvin's exploration of the problematic and limited nature of human perception places him, in some ways, closer to Maimonides than to his Christian predecessors.

Yet Calvin finds that he must rely to some extent on human perception. In addition to discussions about the inscrutability of providence, the *Sermons* are filled with passages depicting God's revelation. We discover metaphors for both darkness and light. We encounter descriptions of human blindness as well as exhortations to "open our eyes." Dispersed among the anguished descriptions of God's hiddenness are references to "mirrors," "lamps," and the manifestation of divine glory in the "theater" of creation.[4] By focusing on the perceptual implications of Calvin's doctrine of providence, we are led to the heart of the tension between visibility and concealment that runs throughout Calvin's *Sermons on Job*. This tension finds expression in two ways: in his use of the doctrine of immortality to set up, as did Aquinas, a perceptual opposition between Job and his friends, and in his continual juxtaposition of nature and history.

Job and His Friends: The Inscrutability of Providence

We first become aware of the tension between the perceptible and the hidden in Calvin's treatment of the dispute between Job and his friends. Like Aquinas, Calvin identifies the hope in the future life as the doctrine that divided Job from Eliphaz, Bildad, and Zophar. He defines the error of Job's opponents as their insistence that God executes judgment in this life—a view that, as Calvin says, "reserved nothing for the last day."⁵ Commenting on 22:15 ("Have you not observed the ancient way by which the wicked have walked?"), Calvin remarks that Eliphaz made it a general rule that the wicked are punished in this world. But if we follow this principle, Calvin asks, "what will become of the immortality of the soul? What will happen to the hope we have in the resurrection?" All such hope, he concludes, would be "annihilated."⁶ Explaining the divine rebuke of "Eliphaz and his two companions," Calvin again focuses on the issue of immortality:

> Job maintained a good cause although he proceeded poorly. . . . On the contrary, Job's friends had beautiful reasons from which we have received holy doctrine. But the fact remains that their foundation [fondement] was wrong. They take a general argument and apply it wrongly; that is, that Job was being punished because of his crimes and they considered him as an evil and abominable man. . . . Moreover, they therefore have a false and perverse doctrine, saying that God treats people in this world as they have deserved. But that doctrine would take away hope of the eternal life and would enclose all of God's grace within this fallen and fragile life. This, then, is to pervert everything.⁷

As we saw in chapter 3, Calvin believes the friends had a "good cause" because they defended the justice of God by associating suffering with sin. On the basis of this argument he proceeds to make the same interpretive move as Aquinas: Since Job's friends denied the afterlife, they were forced to restrict providence to earthly existence. To defend the justice of this providence, Eliphaz, Bildad, and Zophar claimed to see within history a just and equitable order whereby the wicked are always punished and the good always rewarded.⁸ We can argue, then, that by exploring the perceptual implications of the doctrine of immortality, Calvin focuses the Book of Job on the nature of history. Like Aquinas, Calvin understands the source of the controversy between Job and his opponents to be the alleged perception of order within human events, an order that is unchanging and consistent throughout history. More clearly than Aquinas, however, Calvin identifies the theology of the friends with the doctrine of the Law. By making this identification, he wrestles openly with the danger that the Book of Job contradicts the Book of Deuteronomy. The following passage reveals both Calvin's ambivalence toward Job's position and his attempt to reconcile the Law with what he sees as the Joban view of history. In chapter 11, Zophar promised Job that if he were pure, his life would be "brighter than the noonday." The wicked, however, "will fail and all way of escape will be lost to them." Calvin interprets Job's refutation of these seemingly orthodox statements by saying, "Job responds contrary to that which has been said in order to show that although this doctrine is taken from the Law, nevertheless, it is poorly applied." He then defends the doctrine of retribution and explains how Zophar has misinterpreted the Law:

> When, therefore, it is said in the Law that we will be in peace and rest when we have followed the Law of God, why are we tormented and troubled by men, except that we have made war on God? . . . If we are persecuted by men, let us see if we have been at peace with God. Let us see if we have provoked his wrath. . . . Let us note, then, that it is not without cause that this benediction is given in the Law; i.e., that we will be in peace if we adhere to God without contradiction. . . . This promise is not frustrated but sometimes God will permit men to hurt and molest us in order to test our constancy. . . . We see, therefore, how he chastises people in this world, some more and some less, and at the same time he reserves many punishments for the last day. We must not, then, pronounce such a sentence in general as Zophar has done. . . . By this Job shows that it is a great folly to pronounce in general and without exception that God punishes in this life all those who have offended him and that as soon as a man does evil, God rebukes him. . . . We see the opposite.[9]

In this passage we can detect Calvin's continual uneasiness with the possible tension between Job's laments and the Law. His sympathies often gravitate toward the friends. He reminds his congregation that Job's companions were frequently correct: God does sometimes punish sinners in this life.[10] Eliphaz was right when he said that God punishes the wicked. "But it is true that God . . . has always given some signs of his judgments in order that men would be held in fear, following that which is said in Isaiah 26:9, 'The Lord will execute his judgments and the inhabitants of the earth will learn what justice is.'" Calvin goes on to say that "at all times God has given some signs which make it necessary for men to come to account before him so that their iniquity will not remain unpunished."[11] Commenting on 9:24 ("The earth is given into the hand of the wicked, he covers the faces of its judges"), Calvin argues that "confusion" in history is the result of our disobedience against God.[12] Repeatedly, he insists that there are times when divine providence is discernible and when the promises of the Law are visibly executed within the earthly realm. The recurrence of such statements throughout the *Sermons* allows the reader to perceive Calvin's discomfort with the intensity of Job's complaints and his preference for the knowability and predictability of that justice taught by the Law.

Despite Calvin's obvious fondness for the Deuteronomic view of providence, he must come to terms with the Joban philosophy of history. His appreciation for the friends is coupled with a recognition of their perceptual inadequacy. Unlike Aquinas, who leads the reader very gradually toward a recognition of the perceptual dilemma posed by the Dialogues, Calvin seizes an imaginative construal that makes the issue of perception the hermeneutical linchpin of Job's cause. The controversy becomes an open battle over perception: who actually *sees* correctly? We must recognize that Calvin interprets both the error of the friends and the refutation by Job in perceptual terms. From this flows the imagery of sight and blindness. Eliphaz's words in 4:7–9 ("Think, I pray you, who that was innocent ever perished or when have the righteous been cut off?") make Calvin uneasy. He approves of the sentiment but warns that Eliphaz applied his principle badly by concluding that Job was not righteous. We must not, Calvin insists, make a general rule about how God exercises judgment in this world. We must not limit God's judgments "to that which we see in the present."[13] Eliphaz was wrong to think that we can always visibly perceive God's providential rule.[14] Calvin responds to Bildad's words in 8:20 ("Thus God will not reject a blameless man and will not take the hand of the wicked") by insisting that we cannot expect God always to hold to such a rule in this life: "If the judgments of God were all clear there would be no hope of salvation."[15] Against Bildad, Calvin argues that we "see" that things are confused in this world so that our life is "hidden" until Christ appears.[16] Commenting on Zophar's statement in 20:10–11 that the children of the wicked "will give back his wealth," Calvin reminds his listeners that they must contemplate by faith that which they cannot yet "see with the eye."[17]

In such passages we uncover a presupposition that emerged in the previous chapter: the equation of the Law with visibility. Although Calvin's discussions of how the friends expounded the Law do not always lead to the subject of God's double justice, he consistently describes the "lower" justice of the Law as "revealed," "clear," and thus knowable to the human mind. This is a justice that is comprehensible rather than "secret and hidden." The Law comes to represent for Calvin the visibility of providence. Still, on the basis of this revealed justice the friends wrongly concluded that all sufferers, including Job, must be sinners. Their error stemmed from a false application of the Law, which led to a misperception about human history. The friends, Calvin says, insisted that God immediately rewards and punishes people in an observable and "equal measure [d'une façon visible]."[18] Above all else, the friends argued that one could see God's rule "visibly [à veuë d'oeil]."[19]

But Calvin's Job argued that his opponents were "blind [aveugles]."[20] We might say that, in Calvin's view, the friends were not born blind. Rather, they lost their sight by denying the resurrection and thereby misinterpreting the Law. These errors caused their perception to become skewed. Job, on the other hand, saw things as they really were, a perspective that was correct but caused him great pain. In contrast to the "blindness" of the friends, Job knew that the rule of God's Law was true but not always apparent in the earthly life. Job insisted that God does *not* execute his judgments in an "equal fashion." He knew that we cannot limit our view to what "we see," to "present things," or to "that which appears."[21] The "justice of God is not always perceived by men, it is not known in such a way that we can point to it [qu'on y touche au doigt]."[22] Job's intention, Calvin explains, was to argue that "we cannot always see with the eye the judgments of God in this world, in order to draw a certain conclusion that one is punished according to whether he lived well or evilly. . . . Rather [we see] that things are confused in this transitory life."[23] Commenting on the opening verses of chapter 24 ("Are the times hidden from the Almighty"), Calvin again warns his congregation about the obscurity of providence. While Aquinas saw in this chapter Job's defense against charges that God did not know singulars, Calvin sees Job as warning that God does not always exercise his judgments "à veuë d'oeil."[24] After all, Job insisted, "the judgments of God are not always visible and one cannot perceive [apperçoit] them immediately."[25] According to Calvin, "Job wants to show that his adversaries are, as it were, blind and that they judge foolishly when they stop at that which one now sees visibly . . . our judgment, then, is neither right nor equitable, to the extent that we stop ourselves at visible things. We must look further."[26] Because his own suffering personified the ambiguity of human history, Calvin's Job knew that there are times when "God hides."[27]

In the Job sermons, Calvin's appeals to God's double justice are intricately connected with his understanding of providence. In the discussions of both double justice and providence, Job argued against his opponents that God's purposes transcend human reason and, therefore, remain hidden and obscure. An *honest* view of history must acknowledge this inscrutability of providence in human affairs. Thus Calvin's Job argued repeatedly that "we see the opposite" of the order claimed by the friends. What we actually "see" in the present life is "confusion."[28] Commenting on 12:6 ("The house of robbers prosper"), Calvin says that we often see the opposite of those punishments and rewards promised in the Law; thieves are favored while the good are despised and afflicted. This apparent inequity does not make God a mockery but shows "that the judgments of God are not of an equal measure in this world."[29]

Like Aquinas, Calvin interprets Job's laments as appeals to "experience." Calvin proceeds to contrast the "paradise" claimed by the friends to the world of real experience depicted by Job. While Zophar had insisted that God was "visibly [visiblement]" near to his own in this life, Job argued that "experience shows us that God will not execute his judgments so soon but, rather, that he holds them hidden and suspended until the hour which seems good to him."[30] Job recognized that one who looks at "present and visible things" sees the course of human events is "confused [confuses]," disordered, and "mixed up [meslees]." Repeatedly Calvin says that "things are confused in this world" and that "we will certainly be confused, if we stop with what is visible."[31] Interpreting Job's words in 17:8 ("The just will be astonished over this"), Calvin explains that "we know by experience how difficult it is for people to judge rightly about the works of God . . . for God does not execute his judgments in this world in such a way that everything is regulated and so that there is nothing to criticize. But, on the contrary, things are confused and if we see an evil man punished, the just man will be punished still more."[32] When Job cried in 9:24 that "the earth is given into the hand of the wicked," Calvin thinks he was simply being honest: "Job, in sum, shows here that during the present life things are so mixed up that we will not know black from white."[33] Throughout his laments, Calvin's Job looked at the inequities or confusion in human events and insisted that God did not seem to act rationally, "for God does not exercise his judgments in such a way that we can observe them. No, no. But often he will be as hidden . . . that is to say, he allows things to be in disorder [en desordre] for a time."[34]

In Job's confrontation with the disorder of history, Calvin finds a horrible spiritual temptation caused by the inscrutability of providence. We recall that for Gregory, Job's descriptions of the injustices in human events were intended both as moral lessons about justice and as expressions of detachment from the temporal realm. For Aquinas, Job was engaged in a debate in which he often merely assumed the position of his opponents. Calvin's interpretation is somewhat more complex. Like Aquinas, Calvin sometimes thinks that Job was arguing by taking on the viewpoint of his opponents. In so doing Job's purpose was always to demonstrate that God is the judge of the world even when we cannot discern the divine judgments "à l'oeil."[35] But Calvin is not content with this more rationalistic argument; he is drawn to the existential dimension of Job's words. In contrast to Aquinas, Calvin does not portray Job as always in control of his "sensual nature"; Job's "reason" did not always rise above his pain and sadness. Calvin's Job spiritually faced a world that appeared to be forsaken by God and "given into the hand of the wicked." Commenting on 24:1 ("Are not the times hidden from the Almighty and why do those who know him not see his days?"), Calvin moves beyond the Aristotelian or Averroistic view of providence discussed by Aquinas, namely, that God rules the world in general but exercises no providence over individual events.[36] He gives the passage an experiential meaning by referring to the spiritual temptation Job endured because of the inscrutability of divine providence:

It seems that God is hidden and that he withdraws from this world, that he separates himself in order to abandon it completely. Briefly, except when God makes us experience his providence and we are convinced that he governs high and low, we are as in the night, in an obscure time. . . . We do not see [God's judgments] according to our apprehension. There are some times that are hidden from men, but known to God; that is, when God delays his judgments and does not execute them at once . . . it is, indeed, an evil temptation for the faithful when things are confused in the world and it seems that God does not get involved but, rather, that fortune rules and dominates.[37]

Giving expression to the "disordered passions" of his sorrow, Calvin's Job experienced the same temptation as Maimonides's Job: the haunting fear that God had abandoned the realm of earthly events. These discussions of Job's temptation to doubt even the *existence* of providence run parallel to Calvin's descriptions of Job's temptation to think that God was his enemy and exercised an "absolute power" against him. Calvin's Job, then, fell into what Maimonides referred to as the error of "Aristotelianism." Calvin explains that during times of "darkness" it seems that God "turns away," "hides his face," and does not care about terrestrial things. This God "turns his face away" and abandons human affairs.[38] Unlike Aquinas, therefore, Calvin believes that Job wrestled seriously against doubt, temptation, and the fear of God's abandonment.

Nevertheless, Calvin thinks that Job did rise above such temptation and did defend the providence of God. Like Aquinas, Calvin portrays Job as insisting that because of the future life, it is not incompatible with divine providence that the wicked prosper in this world. The real empirical "disorder" and "confusion" are, however, what we actually see in history. Faith in providence therefore cannot be faith in what is visible. In the person of Job, Calvin depicts an example of the "spiritual combat" that must take place for the believer to have faith in the existence and justice of providence.[39] He describes this struggle on the basis of Job's laments by opposing the "natural sense" to "faith." Preaching on Job's words in 29:2 ("I only wish that I was as in times past, as in the days when God watched over me"), Calvin explains that Job spoke according to his "natural sense," that is, the feeling that he had been forsaken by God.[40] Still, Calvin maintains that there is in the believer a twofold sentiment or apprehension: the "natural sense" and "faith." The object of the natural sense or reason is what we sense, see, and touch. Faith, however, "ought to restrain the natural sense [doit reprimer le sens naturel]" and must "rise above" what we see here below.[41] Faced with the confusion of history, people like Job were "elevated by faith [esleves par foy]" to know that, despite appearances, God does bridle the wicked and exercise his justice.[42]

In these sections Calvin combines the imagery of sight and obscurity. Occasionally he speaks of "pure eyes [yeux purs]" or the "eye of faith [l'oeil de la foi]," which belong to believers who somehow seem to discern divine justice.[43] Yet this "eye of faith" is contemplating that which is concealed.[44] While Calvin speaks of the way in which the faithful "know" the counsels of God and perceive the justice of God's rule, he indicates that "the judgments of God are hidden to us."[45] God works, he says, in a "fashion that is incomprehensible to us."[46] By faith we contemplate "invisible things."[47] Calvin's Job knew that faith must not be restricted to what he could see.[48] But faith attains to the trust that God is just and provident more than to a clear understanding of God's reasons and future plans. Just as Job had to trust in the higher or secret justice of God, he had to have faith in the existence of divine providence. In the laments of Job, Calvin finds proof that even the believer cannot invariably see God's providence at work; sometimes the rule and justice of divine governance can only be known through faith in what one cannot see.

The knowledge of faith is reserved, therefore, until the last day. As Calvin says, "Thus when we see things confused here below, what must we do? Let us know that, nonetheless, God disposes everything as becomes him and that he knows the reasons which are hidden from us and that on the last day that which is now hidden will be completely clear."[49] Calvin's Job was right to argue that we must "not stop contemplating by faith that which we cannot yet see with the eye."[50] Job's words in 21:7 ("Why do the wicked live, grow old, and increase in riches?") illustrate Calvin's concern with the perceptual battle of faith. We recall that for Gregory, this verse demonstrated Job's detachment. For Maimonides, it was proof of Job's early despair. For Aquinas, it was a rebuttal of Zophar's view of history. In his explanation of this verse, Calvin uses the imagery of the sun and clouds to describe the visual difficulties involved in the struggle of faith to trust what is now concealed:

It is as when the weather is troubled and we cannot see the sun. But we are not so deprived of our sense that we do not know that the sun shines always above the clouds. . . . The sun shines but the weather is not clear and we cannot perceive that which is hidden. Thus when our Lord sends troubles into this world and we see iniquity which is transported as though without restraint, which is as a deluge that spreads out over everything, we do not perceive that God wants to resist it. But, it seems that all things happen here as if he has abandoned [human events]: the good are oppressed . . . when, I say, we see all that, it is necessary to have a reason higher than our natural sense.[51]

Given this imagery of light and darkness, it is not surprising that Calvin uses 1 Cor. 13:12 ("Now we see through a mirror dimly, but then face to face. Now I know in part") as the hermeneutical key to interpret the Dialogues. He refers to this verse in commenting on several speeches by Job's friends; references by Eliphaz, Bildad, and Zophar to divine transcendence give Calvin the opportunity to tell his congregation that we now know God's goodness and providence only "in part."[52] He makes no consistent attempt, however, to conform these statements to his view that the friends were in error because they blindly argued that God's justice is visible. Still, the theology expressed by 1 Cor. 13:12 belongs to the Joban view of history.[53] Calvin uses this verse frequently to interpret Job's laments about the inequities and calamities that characterize human events. At present, he argues, one can see only some "signs" and "glimpses" of God's governance; what often appears to the human eye is confusion.[54] Because of his faith in the resurrection, Calvin's Job was able to understand that in this life one can see only "in part."[55] The knowledge or trust provided by the "eye of faith" is not a present or prophetic vision so much as a confidence that on the last day God will restore order.[56]

In contrast to the present period of "disorder," the future restoration of order will be a time when we see God "face to face."[57] The following passage from Sermon 82 comments on Job 21:22–34, where Job has complained that "one dies in full strength, at his ease and in rest. His entrails are full of milk and his bones are full of marrow. Another dies in agony and lacks any good. They both are buried in the dust and worms cover them." Recall that Maimonides used these same verses to demonstrate Job's early "Aristotelianism" or denial of providence. Calvin sees this passage as Job's victorious fight against the devil's attempt to make him fall into this same type of despair:

We will certainly be confused if we stop at what is visible. . . . We must climb still higher and know that God reserves a judgment which does not appear today, for faith regards things invisible, things hidden. . . . It is true that in death everything is confused but God will indeed know how to put all things back into order and into a state of perfection. As it is said, at the coming of our Lord Jesus Christ, when he will appear in order to judge the world, there will be a restoration of all things. . . . At first it looks as if you [God] are asleep, but, nonetheless, it is completely the opposite when we see that there is another judgment upon the wicked. . . . God, then, already gives a declaration of his justice; i.e., that there is a judgment reserved at which time all things will be put back into order and their [proper] condition. . . . Faith must rule in us and the word of God lead us. [The word] must be a lamp to show us the way in the midst of the darkness of this world, until we come to that celestial clarity where there will be no more knowledge in part [cognoissance en partie] but where there will be total perfection when we contemplate our God face to face [face à face].[58]

We now see that for Calvin, the Dialogues depict a conflict between a false and honest perception of reality. Both sides were engaged in a perceptual battle in which each one thought he was right and everyone argued from what was allegedly visible. Assuming that all afflictions were punishments for sins, the friends deduced from Job's visible adversities that Job was a sinner. Hence they claimed to perceive in Job's situation an order that was clear and visible. They reasoned from what they saw—or rather from what they thought they saw. Calvin's Job, however, also argued from the visible, from the realm of "experience." Because he knew that he was not punished for sins, Job confronted the empirical disorder of history. He insisted that the visible realm exhibited not order but confusion. In Calvin's reading, the Dialogues become an intense and impassioned debate over the reliability of human perception. Both parties claimed to be on God's side. The friends defended the righteousness of God, a defense that always sounded just about right to Calvin's ear. Job tried to find justice in the midst of experiential evidence to the contrary.

In Job's spiritual temptation, Calvin recognized the struggle of faith to surmount the empirical evidence of history. To describe that battle of faith, Calvin forged a hermeneutical alliance between the text of Job and Paul's words in 1 Cor. 13:12. As we have seen, Calvin's Job conquered the temptation to despair by believing that in the present he could see only through a mirror dimly or "in part" but that the future restoration of order would allow him to see "face to face." Calvin believed that until that last day, Job personified the way in which the faithful must endure times when God keeps silent and "hides his face."

Calvin and Elihu

There are few people in the Bible Calvin admires more than Elihu. We can exegetically demonstrate his partiality for Job's fourth companion by comparing his interpretation to those of Gregory and Aquinas. Because God rebuked only "Eliphaz and his two friends," both commentators distinguished Elihu from Bildad, Zophar, and Eliphaz. From Elihu's statement in 36:4 ("For truly my speeches are without falsehood and my perfect knowledge will be proved to you"), Gregory argued that Elihu was orthodox in his teaching but guilty of pride.[59] Aquinas believed that Elihu's knowledge was superior to the opinion of the other friends but that he was moved by "vainglory" so that he misinterpreted Job's words and did not express the whole truth.[60] Both Gregory and Aquinas thought that although Elihu was not rebuked by God in 42:7, he was reproved in 38:2 when God said, "Who is that man wrapping his opinion in ignorant speeches?"[61]

Calvin will tolerate none of this criticism. In 36:4 Elihu was not speaking proudly but rather as a true doctor of the church. According to Calvin, Elihu was saying that he would preach "the true doctrine perfectly, as he received it from God."[62] Moreover, in Calvin's view, the divine reproof in 38:2 was addressed to *Job,* not Elihu.[63] In the figure of

Elihu, Calvin sees proof that from ancient times some good "seed of religion" survived in the midst of darkness and produced "some good and holy doctrine."[64] Elihu spoke out of a "zeal for God" and as "an organ of the Spirit of God."[65] Commenting on 32:18 ("For I am full of words and the spirit within me constrains me"), Calvin explains Elihu's zeal and the importance of his teaching. Although Elihu was not "as one of the Prophets" or "one of the children of Israel," nonetheless "we see that God has imprinted such a mark on the doctrine of Elihu and that the celestial spirit has appeared in his mouth so that we ought to be moved to receive that which he says."[66] Elihu, Calvin remarks, did not speak as a mortal man; his heart was like a wineskin ready to burst because God had "incited him with such vehemence."[67] For Calvin, Elihu was an example of one who defended and upheld the truth of God's word in much the same way as the reformed church must defend true doctrine against the "Papists."[68] Calvin's elevation of Elihu is as decisive as that of Maimonides; like Maimonides, he sees Elihu as teaching essentially the same truth declared in the whirlwind speech. And like Maimonides, Calvin portrays Elihu as superior to both the friends and the "early" Job. Calvin eagerly makes it clear that "God has not condemned [Elihu]. He condemns Job. He condemns Job's friends and shows that they all have erred in one way or another. Nevertheless, Elihu alone is justified."[69]

What did Elihu know? Why did Calvin defend his words in such an unqualified way? Up to this point in his sermons Calvin has been forced to maneuver very carefully through the text of Job. Arriving at chapter 32, he no longer has to qualify his approval of the speaker by saying that Elihu only "spoke poorly" or was "overcome by passions" or that he had a "good cause but applied it wrongly." In his interpretation of Elihu's speeches Calvin does not have to rely on any of the caveats that recur throughout his sermons on the Dialogues. Elihu is really Calvin's mouthpiece. Calvin's interpretation of chapters 32–37 offers a straightforward presentation of his real attitude toward Job and his friends. According to Calvin, Elihu's anger at Job (32:2) was a "good and praiseworthy indignation."[70] Unlike Eliphaz, Bildad, and Zophar, Elihu did not think that Job was an evil man who was being punished for sins. Nonetheless, he rightly charged Job with being "impatient" and excessive in his passions.[71] Most important, Elihu correctly attacked Job because he thought himself "just before God."[72] In Calvin's view, Elihu was justified in saying that Job "walked with the wicked," not because Job was a murderer or a thief but because he had not glorified God as he ought to have done.[73] For Gregory and Aquinas, these passages indicated that although Elihu said many true things, he was also moved by pride. As we have seen, Gregory thought that Elihu contradicted God's words in 1:8 ("Have you considered my servant Job, that there is none like him on the earth").[74] Aquinas believed that Elihu "abused" or misinterpreted Job's words, saying, "It is clear that the whole debate which follows is not against Job."[75] Calvin disagrees; in his view, Elihu was right.

The sermons on chapters 32–37 provide a summary of Calvinist theology. Elihu understood the sinfulness of human nature, the impossibility of merit, the justice of all suffering, and the inability of any human being to plead against God.[76] Calvin even finds in Elihu's words the doctrine of imputation.[77] He embraces Elihu's defense of divine justice.[78] Like Calvin, Elihu knew that God's will is the rule of justice. The verses about divine transcendence, so frequent in these chapters, prove that Elihu understood the infinite distance between God and humans and between divine and human justice.[79] Elihu also understood the inseparability of the divine attributes, a principle that allowed him to recognize that God's justice and power are inseparable from God's goodness.[80] Because he understood the inseparability of the divine attributes, Calvin's Elihu rightly charged Job with wrongly accusing God of acting according to an absolute or tyrannical power.[81]

For Calvin, the most crucial element of Elihu's teaching was his correct doctrine of providence. The reader of his sermons gradually becomes aware that in all its essentials, this doctrine was the same as that of Calvin's Job. In Elihu's words Calvin finds affirmation of both divine justice and divine hiddenness, of the occasional inexplicableness of suffering as well as the promised judgment of the wicked. Moreover, the design of chapters 32–37 allows us to detect an argument that goes beyond a mere summary of Calvin's doctrine of providence as expounded by Elihu and Job. In these chapters Calvin also finds an extensive use of nature imagery. In his interpretation of Elihu's speeches, he makes use of these images to exploit what he sees to be an interplay between nature and history that is, in reality, a dialectic between revelation and hiddenness. His treatment of this dialectic in chapters 32–37 epitomizes the structure of the *Sermons on Job* as a whole.

First let us examine the doctrine of providence expounded by Calvin's Elihu. In passages such as 36:6–14 ("He does not keep the wicked alive but gives judgment to the afflicted"), Calvin reaffirms his earlier teaching that the purpose of affliction is usually to make us sense our sins and to lead us to repentance. Earlier in the *Sermons* Calvin explains that it is "a special privilege" if God afflicts us for something other than sin, "for he would always have just reason to punish us even if we were the most just people in the world."[82] According to Elihu, afflictions are medicinal and testimonies of divine love.[83] In such statements we find a reassertion of the traditional view of suffering as beneficial or pedagogical. We see, further, Calvin's insistence on the complete inability of even the most righteous person to plead against the purity and justice of God. Finally, we recognize that by arguing that suffering is often due to sin, Calvin's Elihu can support the Deuteronomic view of history: there are indeed times within history when providence is predictable, just, comprehensible, and visible.

In the sermons on Elihu's speeches we also find some of Calvin's strongest statements about God's hiddenness and the inscrutability of divine providence. According to Calvin, Elihu understood that Job's friends had argued an "evil and false" principle and had "disguised the truth" by insisting that Job was being punished for past sins.[84] Although Calvin's Elihu criticized Job for his conduct during his adversities, he did not identify those adversities with punishments. In Calvin's interpretation, Elihu perceived that the reasons for divine judgments, especially suffering, are not always clear. The following passage demonstrates the extent to which Calvin is determined to find in Elihu's words the recognition that providence is often inscrutable and that justice is not always exercised clearly in the present historical realm. Calvin is preaching here on 34:10–12 ("Can there be injustice in God or iniquity in the Almighty? For God will render to man according to his work, according to the ways of each one, he will judge him"). In the mouth of Bildad, Eliphaz, or Zophar these words most certainly would have been interpreted by Calvin as the erroneous belief in the visibility of God's governance and the knowability of God's earthly justice. In short, if these words had been spoken by Job's other friends, they would have illustrated a naive misperception of history. For Calvin, however, these words bear the opposite meaning when uttered by Elihu:

This is not to be understood as if God immediately punishes the transgressors of his Law and as if he supports the good. . . . He [God] can, indeed, act (as happens all the time) so that he will support the wicked for awhile. We see that he hides [dissimule] when men have burst forth into evil and it does not seem as though he thinks about it or sees them. . . . Thus, God does not punish the wicked immediately and Elihu does not intend to say that he does. . . . God does not execute his judgments on the first day such that we can visibly perceive [appercevoir à l'oeil] that he renders to each according to his works. . . . St. Paul speaks of the justice of God saying not that he renders every day each according as he has deserved. . . . When? On the last day. Elihu does not contradict this sentence. But when he says "God renders," he presupposes what is true; i.e., that we must hold our spirits in suspense until God shows us that which is hidden for a time.[85]

Calvin finds in Elihu an explicit teaching that providence is often inscrutable and undetectable in the historical realm. Repeatedly he bases his argument on words that seem to justify instead the knowability and visibility of providence. Commenting on 36:6–7 ("He does not keep the wicked alive but gives judgment to the afflicted. He will not turn his eyes away from the just"), Calvin says that Elihu is speaking only "generally" because God does at times give us perceptible signs of his justice.[86] On the basis of these same verses, however, Calvin goes on to describe the "confusion" that marks the historical sphere during times of divine hiddenness. As always, he appeals to a future judgment:

We must remember that which has been declared before; i.e., that when we see things are not yet put back into such order and wholeness as we desire, that this is a warning to us that God will judge the world in the person of his Son . . . if everything were disposed as we desire, where would we be? We would have no faith in the last resurrection. Do we not see, then, that God does not execute all his judgments, but that he reserves them? . . . in order that he might appear in his majesty to regulate things which are now confused and to reestablish them . . . and when today [our works] are hidden and are not perceived [or judged] immediately, nevertheless, we must not stop being guilty when we must come before him . . . for leaving many unpunished, he hides [dissimule].[87]

Calvin portrays Elihu as facing history with the same realism as Job. To the honest observer it is clear that the wicked have their way and that God seems to have abandoned human events. If we follow our "fantasy," we can conclude only that human affairs are unjust and "confused."[88] Commenting on 34:29 ("When he will have hidden his face, who will be able to see him?"), Calvin sees Elihu expressing the horrible "temptation" caused by the inscrutability of divine providence. It is, he says, a "hard temptation," or a "great temptation," to think that God acts "without reason"; for when it "seems that God has no regard for us, we see only darkness and the clarity which ought to guide us does not shine."[89] When we see the "confusion" in the world, it truly is "as if God had hidden his face [avoit caché son visage]."[90] In this realm of apparent confusion and disorder, Calvin's Elihu told Job that we can only "wait in patience" until God fully reveals that which is today hidden; during this life we can only "know in part."[91]

Nature and History

Juxtaposed to Calvin's descriptions of the hiddenness of God in history is his emphasis on the revelation of God in nature. In Elihu's words, particularly in chapter 37, Calvin finds references to the wonders of creation. The heavens, thunder, lightning, snow, rain, the skies, and animals are all "mirrors" in which one should "contemplate the majesty of God."[92] Nature, Calvin says, allows us to see God "in a mirror."[93] Divine providence, therefore, is indeed visible in the order constituted in nature. Preaching on Elihu's statement in 37:5 ("God does marvelous things which we cannot comprehend"), Calvin argues: "We see, then, that if we have our eyes open to contemplate the providence of God and the natural order which is proposed to us, that order ought to serve as instruction so that we put our full trust in him."[94] Both the "order" of nature and the sudden changes in the cosmos are evidence of God's powerful rule and control over creation.[95] Although God's essence is invisible, we are intended to contemplate God in his "visible majesty in the heaven and the earth."[96] Although God often "hides his face" in history, Calvin's Elihu knew that nature is "as the face of God," which reveals God's wisdom, glory, goodness, and power.[97]

Perhaps Calvin's contrast between nature and history is clearest in Elihu's speeches because the passages about providence in chapters 32–36 are juxtaposed directly to the verse about nature in chapter 37. But throughout the *Sermons,* nature becomes for Calvin a counterpoint to the darkness of history. Consider his comments on Job's words in 9:7–10 ("Who commands the sun and it does not shine? Who seals up the stars as in a bag? Who stretches out the heavens and walks upon the sea? Who has made Arcturus and Orion, the Pleiades and chambers of the South?"):

And is it not a great shame that we live here in the world as in a beautiful and spacious theater where God gives us a view of all his creatures . . . but, we forget who is their author. We forget him who willed that the heaven and the earth and all that is contained therein are as mirrors of his glory. As it is said, through visible things we are able to see invisible things (Rom. 1:20). Thus, when he has put us in the world and we do not take account of all these things, is it not necessary to say that we have a very evil spirit?[98]

The threatening phenomena of water always draw forth from Calvin praise of divine power and providence. Whenever he finds water imagery in the text, he calls his congregation's attention to the revelation of divine governance evident in the seas, rains, or rivers. These passages presuppose the traditional cosmology, which allotted relative weights to the elements: Since water is lighter than earth, heavier than air, and circular in nature, why does it not engulf the earth?[99] Why does water stay in the clouds? Why does it stay within the confines of the sea and not overflow the dry land? Considering the position of human beings placed between the sea and the rain clouds in the heavens, Calvin says that God has placed human creatures as in a "grave."[100] Commenting on Job's words in 26:8 ("He binds up the waters in the clouds and the cloud is not rent under them"), Calvin says:

Is it not a miracle that the waters thus hang in the air and that they are held firmly there? We see the waters overflow and likewise that the air is so fine that it will always give place to them. By their nature the waters are heavier than the air. It is necessary, then, that they fall. Nonetheless we see that they are retained as in barrels, as is said in Ps. 33:7, for the prophet uses this likeness to express the miracle that is so poorly recognized by men.[101]

Preaching on 9:8 ("He walks upon the water"), Calvin explains that the existence of dry land proves that God continually restrains the waters:

Would it be possible that the sea would remain in the state which it is if it were not restrained by a miraculous power? We know that the nature of water is to overflow. But behold the sea which is raised up like a mountain. There are limits which are imposed. . . . If the sea were not restrained, the earth would necessarily be completely covered immediately. Let us not think that we would have some dry place in order to live except to the extent that God wants us to lodge here. And thus he holds the sea locked up [serree]. He has set its limits, not by rocks or trees, but by his power alone. The sea has so great a vehemence that it seems nothing could restrain it; nonetheless, God, by his word alone [i.e., that there be some dry land where men would live], restrains the sea even today.[102]

The stars also provide Calvin with the opportunity to reflect on the providence evident in the order of nature. He repeatedly tells his listeners to contemplate the heavens: "Behold God has given us eyes in order to perceive this beautiful order [ce bel ordre]."[103] Reflecting on Acturus, Orion, and the Pleiades as described in 9:9, Calvin preaches:

Thus God has positioned these two stars which are as the spokes in a wheel of a chariot. And we see the sun has its circuit. When we have learned these things we see how the inestimable wisdom of God will be better known so that the least of men will have some taste and will be incited to magnify [that divine wisdom], saying, "Lord, what is the excellence of your work?"[104]

Such descriptions of creation are found throughout the *Sermons* wherever Calvin finds nature imagery. In such passages he portrays the cosmos as a "theater" or "mirror" of divine glory. By extolling the works of God in nature, Calvin discovers that the Book of Job teaches both the clarity and the obscurity of divine providence. In the "beautiful order" of nature as well as in the sudden changes in the cosmos, God reveals his infinite power, goodness, and rule over creation. But does Calvin harmonize the themes of obscurity and visibility that run throughout his *Sermons*? That he understands and wrestles with the distinction between nature and history is clear from his sermon on Bildad's words in 18:4 ("Will the earth be forsaken because of you? Will the rocks be moved from their place?"):

For Bildad proposes that God has created the heaven and the earth and has constituted this natural order which we see. Therefore, he says that God's judgment must take its course. That is indeed true, but he applies it poorly to the extent that he wants the judgment of God to be completely clear [notoire] and that one can know it and see it visibly [qu'on le voye à l'oeil]. . . . In this Bildad is deceived. Nonetheless, it is good to know his intention . . . he asks, then, "Will the world change because of you?" . . . For you dispute with God saying that he does not execute his judgments here below in such a way that one knows them. Did not God constitute this order in the heaven, in the air, in the earth, in such a way that he wills his judgments to be known? When we contemplate the works of God high and low, is it not in order that his goodness, wisdom, justice, and all his virtues are known to us? This is indeed certain. . . . That is true in part. . . . But Bildad extends it too generally. . . . But it is also necessary that we know how to discern properly between the works of God. . . . God wills that the sun rises and sets and by that we are shown that until the end of the world he will give us the things which are necessary to preserve us here. . . . But with reference to his judgments there is another reason, for he wills only that we have some taste therein during this life and that we wait in patience, so that [God's judgments] will appear on the last day. For at that time the things which are now confused will be put back into their proper condition. Until then, God will carry out his judgments only in part. And, therefore, this conclusion which Bildad draws here is neither good nor fitting, for he mixes two things together between which there is great diversity.[105]

In chapter 18, then, Calvin finds a fundamental principle with which to interpret the Book of Job. On the basis of Bildad's "misinterpretation," Calvin makes the same distinction formulated by Aquinas in chapter 5 on the basis of Eliphaz's words: The revelation visible in nature must be distinguished from the ambiguity characteristic of history.[106] Although God governs both realms, providence is not equally discernible in both spheres. This distinction between nature and history serves Calvin as both an exegetical tool and a perceptual one. To argue, as Bildad did, from the wonders and order in nature to an allegedly perceptible order in history was to fail to discern correctly between the "works of God." Only Job and Elihu appear to have distinguished properly between nature and history. In their speeches, Calvin finds descriptions of the inscrutability of providence in history as well as the revelation of divine governance in creation. Thus the juxtaposition between nature and history inherent in the text of Job becomes a hermeneutical strategy by which Calvin can emphasize the dialectic between the visible and the hidden, the knowable and the inscrutable.

The Whirlwind Speech

Having articulated the distinction between nature and history in chapter 18, Calvin confronts a serious problem with the whirlwind speech. Here it is God, not Job's friends, who describes the wonders of nature. Did God, too, fail to discern between the realms of creation and history?

Does Calvin see the irony in dealing with a divine response that appears to contradict his own principle regarding the proper distinction between the works of God? Does he see the apparent irrelevance of the whirlwind speech—that the deity answers questions about history by describing the cosmos? Does he perceive that by answering questions about justice through an appeal to power, the whirlwind speech appears to justify Job's suspicion that God acts by an "absolute power"?

To understand how Calvin resolves the problems inherent in the whirlwind speech, we must first determine why he thinks God responded to Job and, in particular, why God rebuked Job. Calvin is more critical of Job than earlier exegetes. Unlike Gregory and Aquinas, he does not allow verse 42:7 to govern completely his exegesis of the Dialogues; Calvin's Job simply did not always "speak rightly" before God. As we have seen, Job pleaded his case poorly, spoke too passionately, and acted in too unrestrained a manner. It would be a mistake, however, to think that Calvin believes God reproved Job only because he spoke too passionately or gave full vent to his temptation and sorrow. These aspects of Job's character make Calvin uneasy but, in his opinion, did not warrant the whirlwind speech. By comparing Calvin's reading of 42:2–6 to those of Gregory and Aquinas, we can determine what most bothered the Reformer about Job.

According to Calvin, the fault to which Job confessed was not merely "levity of speech" but a sin so "enormous" that it was a "mortal crime."[107] For Calvin, that crime is defined in 40:3 ("Will you overthrow my judgment? Will you condemn me in order to justify yourself?"). For Gregory and Aquinas, this verse was an unsettling intrusion into the text; since Job had "spoken rightly" throughout the Dialogues, they concluded that this verse indicated only that there had been a secret (and small) impulse of pride in what he said.[108] For Aquinas, although Job did not intend to charge God with iniquity, Job's words "seemed reprehensible."[109] For Calvin, however, this verse was central and demonstrated that the whirlwind speech finally addressed the overriding problem of Job's self-justification. In the divine response Calvin sees a vindication of Elihu's charge against Job, that Job tried to justify himself before God. Calvin, then, presents the whirlwind speech as a rebuke to those statements in which Job justified himself and thereby accused God of injustice. He quickly qualifies this interpretation by saying that it was not Job's intention to blaspheme the deity. Still, Calvin's real feeling about Job is revealed in his insistence that whenever someone maintains his own justice, he necessarily condemns God. We must conclude that Calvin distinguishes sharply between Job's nonretributive suffering and his self-justification—a point made earlier on the basis of Elihu.

Although he was not punished for past sins, Calvin's Job did fall into the sin of self-justification during his adversities. Commenting on 40:3–5, Calvin says:

> Here God takes up his cause and pleads against Job because Job wants to be more just [than God]. Not that it was Job's intention to blaspheme against God so wickedly. . . . But . . . when [he] wants to maintain his own cause, he necessarily reverses the judgment of God. . . . Let us note, then, that as soon as a man undertakes to maintain his own cause as if he were just, he wants to condemn God, although obliquely. Although he has not deliberately conceived that purpose, that is what he does. Why? Because God cannot be just and cannot be a judge unless we are completely damnable. Nevertheless, if men were to have some justice in themselves, how will God be their judge? But he condemns us completely. If there is some justice in us, he does us wrong. All of our justice, then, must be destroyed; that is to say, we must know that there is only iniquity in us, that we do not have a grain of virtue which is praiseworthy, and that we are nothing but smell, stink, and stench.[110]

Calvin's interpretation differs strongly from those of his predecessors, who tended to mitigate the meaning of the divine rebuke to Job. Unlike Gregory, Calvin does not think that God humbled Job because his virtue might cause him to fall prey to the sin of pride; Calvin's Job was not that virtuous. Unlike Aquinas, Calvin does not believe that Job only "seemed" scandalous to his friends or had merely been "driven inwardly by some proud thought."[111] When Calvin is most forthright, he admits that Job was indeed prideful not only before his friends but also before God. In Calvin's view, Job committed the serious sin of claiming justice before the Lord. The whirlwind speech addressed this "unbridled" and arrogant Job by demolishing all human justice. Like Gregory and Aquinas, Calvin discusses the transcendence of divine justice. But in comparison to his predecessors, Calvin strains this transcendence to the limit. His emphasis falls not only on the unsurpassability of God's justice and purity but also on the condemnation of Job's own alleged righteousness. The divine response destroyed all vestiges of pride, crushed all claims of human justice, and humbled Job by showing him "the master with whom he had to deal."[112]

Calvin admits that one could "find it strange that wanting to maintain his justice and shut the mouth of men so that they do not slander him, God talks about the stars, the labor of the earth, speaks in the fashion of a navigator, and refers to the nature of the beasts. To what purpose? It would seem, therefore, that God seeks here some extravagant arguments."[113] But he does not really find the descriptions of the universe to be strange; on the contrary, he revels in them. His explanation for the use of creation in God's answer to Job reflects his presupposed anthropology: Human beings are so radically fallen and yet so presumptuous that they are best humbled by the creatures and phenomena of this lower world. Thus, in the whirlwind speech Calvin sees the perfect scriptural proof for his principle that human pride is crushed by the wonders of nature.[114] The earth, stars, waters, and animals are all proofs for divine providence and testify against human stupidity, arrogance, ignorance, and ingratitude.

In Calvin's view, nature serves both a positive and negative function. He is always eager to praise the beauty of creation and to encourage the contemplation of the cosmos. He also knows that nature humbles human beings and renders them inexcusable.[115] The references to nature in the whirlwind speech serve both purposes. Because he is contemplating nature through the "spectacles of Scripture," Calvin can use chapters 38–41 to expound on the wonders of creation. Nonetheless, because of their exegetical purpose in the Book of Job, he understands that the references to nature in the whirlwind speech primarily serve the negative purpose. Creation demonstrated Job's nothingness and the inability to criticize God. Calvin believes creation could successfully humble Job because the functioning of the cosmos transcended both human power and human understanding, a point made earlier by Aquinas.

A significant question remains: How does Calvin use this demonstration of human inability to comprehend and control nature as an answer to the problems about history raised in the Dialogues? After all, Calvin refuses to allegorize Behemoth and Leviathan and so to introduce the theme of redemptive history or historical salvation. He resolves the problem by placing the tension between revelation and hiddenness within the heart of nature itself. He then proceeds to make the realms of nature and history a continuum rather than a division.

Following a strictly literal exegesis of chapters 38–41, Calvin emphasizes the revelatory power of nature, a power that finally silences Job. Because the functioning of nature is contingent, the power of God is evident in its continual existence and operation.[116] Moreover, the beauty of creation bears a fragile and dangerous aspect, so that if the forces of nature are not controlled and restrained, they will collapse into chaos and engulf the human race. When commenting on 38:4 ("Where were you when I laid the foundations of the earth?"), Calvin, like Aquinas, marvels at the heaviness of the earth, which is surrounded by water and hangs in the air with no underlying element sufficient to support it. The earth is, after all, heavier than the air. As Calvin says, "Behold a terrible mass . . . it seems impossible to find a foundation sufficient to sustain it." He goes on to describe the wonder of the earth:

And on what does [the earth] rest? Upon water. It is hanging in the air . . . it has water surrounding it. It is true that the philosophers have no regard for the fact that it is God who created it. They have, indeed, found good reason to explain how the waters surround the earth and how the whole thing hangs in the air. They have disputed very subtly about this . . . but, nonetheless, despite themselves they are constrained to confess that it is beyond nature that the waters are pulled back in order that people would have a place to live. This cannot happen by itself; it is necessary that there be some divine providence which works here . . . we are always guilty when we have not glorified God in his works which are so clear and manifest.[117]

Preaching on 38:8 ("Who shut the sea with doors when it burst forth from the womb?"), Calvin again finds occasion to describe God's providence as evident in the restraint of the waters. He tells his congregation that in order to make room for human life, God holds back the waters so that they do not overflow the earth.[118] In Calvin's view, the position and constitution of the earth are "mirrors" in which Job should have contemplated God's powerful and restraining providence at work in creation. The divine speeches also give Calvin the opportunity to praise the beauty of the heavens, whose order and regularity ought to amaze us. Calvin assumes that the beautiful order of the stars is fragile; such an order could not have formed by chance and could not stay in existence without the constant power, restraint, and guidance of God.[119] Even the beasts elicit this same admiration. According to Calvin, God recalls us to the "school of the beasts" because he has there as many "advocates and attorneys against us as birds in the air or fish in the sea and beasts on the earth."[120] The feathers of a peacock should suffice to make us glorify God.[121] If the power of the horse terrifies us, what will happen before the infinite power of God?[122] Over and over Calvin tells his listeners that the deity must govern the path of the stars, determine the seasons, send the rains, and restrain the waters and the beasts. To Calvin's mind, all Job had to do was "open his eyes" and look at these visible works of God; he would have seen there the testimonies of the infinite power and wisdom of God who created and still controls the cosmos. The creation, Calvin says, pleads the Lord's case.[123] God imprints his glory on the mute creation and rejects those who refuse to contemplate him in his works.[124] Even the angels are astonished when they behold the glorious works of God in nature.[125]

Calvin's literal exegesis of chapters 38–39 is fundamentally the same as that of Aquinas. Although Calvin more often exhorts his congregation to contemplate the divine glory in creation, both exegetes focus on the physical characteristics of the phenomena described in the text. But this similarity ends at chapters 40–41 with the appearance of Behemoth and Leviathan. Adhering to what he sees as a strictly literal interpretation, Calvin denies that these chapters contain allegorical reference to the devil. Although he briefly admits that one could say the great beasts might symbolize the power of the devil, he quickly draws back and argues that to find Satan in the figures of Leviathan and Behemoth is to turn the Scripture into a "nose of wax" and to lose the simple sense of the passage.[126] Scoffing at the elaborate allegories about the devil found in earlier commentaries, Calvin sneers that "we do not need these trashy details."

According to a literal exegesis, Behemoth is an elephant and Leviathan a whale.[127] To justify this literal interpretation, Calvin knows that he must deal directly with the traditional texts that were used to prove the allegorical or metaphorical significance of these beasts. Thus he argues that 40:10 ("Behold Behemoth whom I made along with you") refers only to the "admirable order" God instituted in the world, an order in which a creature as small as the human being is the "lord and master" over such a huge creature as the elephant.[128] Assuming the traditional view that beasts became wild only after the fall, Calvin also asks why animals such as the elephant do not devour everyone. Why are they content to eat grass in the mountains?[129] The fact that such beasts do not overtake human places of habitation proves that God holds back their fury with a "secret bridle [bride secrette]"—the bridle of providence that also restrains the waters and keeps them from engulfing the earth.[130] Leviathan is called the "king over all the sons of pride" (41:25) because when the prideful learn that they cannot subdue the whale by their own physical strength, they recognize their weakness and are thereby humbled before God.[131]

Calvin's refusal to "allegorize" or to find a "mystical sense" in chapters 40–41 makes his reading of the whirlwind speech differ significantly from those of Gregory and Aquinas. Like Maimonides, Calvin insists that the whirlwind speech is about creation. Calvin and Maimonides both follow a literal or naturalistic interpretation of chapters 38–41 by insisting that the divine revelation did not go beyond "natural matters." Because Calvin will not allegorize Behemoth and Leviathan, Satan makes no reappearance at the end of the story, and his importance is thereby diminished. This lessening of Satan's significance is evident as early as Calvin's comments on 1:6. His insistence on the sovereignty of God leads him to argue that Satan's original presence in the heavenly council demonstrates that God did not merely permit but rather commanded all the devil's actions against Job.[132] Calvin believes, of course, that Job was threatened constantly by the devil who "prowls around like a roaring lion seeking prey."[133] As we have seen, it was Satan who tempted Job to think that God exercised an "absolute power" and to fear that God had abandoned him to the apparently chaotic world of human events. Still, Calvin chooses not to reintroduce Satan at the end of Job's ordeal.

Calvin's refusal to find the devil in the figure of the great beasts cannot be attributed solely to his dislike of allegory, because in his comments on Isa. 27:1 he interprets Leviathan allegorically as Satan.[134] We can only conclude that his refusal to allegorize the great beasts is motivated by his concern to stress the sovereignty of God, by making the end of the story a confrontation of Job with the Creator. Without the reintroduction of Satan, the power struggle depicted in chapters 40–41 was not between God and Satan but between God and Job. The balance of the book shifts; in Calvin's reading there was no "third party" so that God and Job were aligned against a common enemy. Calvin's Job did not have to withstand the power and slyness of the devil so much as to find a way to stand before God. Moreover, the enemy with whom Calvin's God had to deal was not the devil per se but *human* pride and presumption. We might say that, in comparison with Gregory and Aquinas, Calvin believes that despite his good intentions Job was already one of Leviathan's sons.

Calvin's denial of any allegorical meaning in Behemoth and Leviathan has another important consequence. Without reintroducing Satan, Calvin cannot tie the whirlwind speech to the celestial contest recounted in the Prologue. He thus loses an opportunity to connect the divine speeches directly to the issue of history and to the great historical drama that links the Book of Job to the first chapters of Genesis. Like his predecessors, Calvin does emphasize the issue of God's power, but he does not explain that power in terms of the great battle fought by Christ against "Leviathan"; Calvin does not even comment on 41:8 ("Remember the battle and speak no more"). He is much more interested in 41:1 ("Who is he that can stand in my presence?").

If we read closely, we can discern that Calvin makes the connection between the whirlwind speech and the Dialogues by arguing that the world of creation surpasses not only human power but also human comprehension. We recall that Gregory stressed the reality of redemptive history throughout chapters 38–41 by interpreting the text typologically. In chapters 40–41 he focused that redemptive history on the battle between God and the "Ancient Enemy"—the great historical battle that had raged from the beginning of creation and in which Job was now involved. Aquinas moved from an emphasis on human ignorance to an emphasis on human weakness in chapters 40–41 and thus referred the divine response back to history through a demonstration of divine power in God's historical victory over the devil. Calvin's reasoning moves in the opposite direction. He too depicts the power of God evident in the cosmos, but he links the whirlwind speech to the problem of history by stressing human ignorance with respect to all the works of God.

Before the vast panorama of the earth, waters, stars, and animals, Calvin's Job learned that creation was truly, as Elihu said, the "face of God." But while stressing the revelatory power of creation, Calvin also insists that human beings can never fully comprehend the wonders of the cosmos. Even when we do "open our eyes," we fail to understand the reasons behind the composition and functioning of nature. After examining the works of creation, "we must always conclude that the wisdom of God is hidden from us (in all these clear things) and that there is some cause above us to which we cannot attain."[135] Calvin applies 1 Cor. 13:12 to both history and creation; in the contemplation of nature, he says, we can know only "in part."[136] The very majesty of creation infuses it with a kind of hiddenness. By arguing that the wisdom of nature surpasses the human mind, Calvin is placing within nature itself a dialectic between revelation and hiddenness. The mirror of creation reveals the majesty and power of God. Nevertheless, the miraculous aspects of the cosmos still transcend our comprehension and leave us with only a "glimpse" or "taste" of divine providence.[137]

This dialectic that places hiddenness at the heart of creation is expressed throughout the *Sermons*. In the whirlwind speech, however, the awareness of such inscrutability serves a special purpose: to demonstrate that all the works of God, both nature and history, have at their core the transcendent incomprehensibility of God. Calvin's aim in the articulation of this dialectic in chapters 38–41 is to argue that we cannot fathom or judge the secrets of the divine judgments in history. If Job could not comprehend the wonders of nature, how could he presume to question the secret workings of providence, which far surpass the natural realm? Over and over Calvin drives home the point that if Job could not understand the visible works "at his feet," he could not arrogate to himself the governing of history. As Calvin asks, "If we cannot tame the wild ass or some other wild beast, how will we govern the whole world?"[138] Concluding his sermon on 38:4–11, Calvin asks, if we are constrained to adore God, confessing that we are far too weak to comprehend his loftiness in the things that lie before our eyes, "what will happen before his incomprehensible secrets, his narrow and hidden counsels when he works . . . in a fashion that seems strange to us and completely surmounts our capacity?"[139] If "visible things" are beyond our reasons, Calvin argues, then God must bridle human beings and show us "that we are too rude" and "too weak to climb so high" that we could fathom God's hidden counsel.[140]

It is the appeal to the incomprehensibility of *nature* that finally ties the whirlwind speech to *history*. In Calvin's view, Job had "exceeded his measure" by questioning the rigor of God's power and the justice of God's judgments. The whirlwind speech proved to Job that the governing of history required a wisdom and power even beyond what was revealed in creation. In short, Calvin argues that since nature itself astounds us, history is beyond our judgment. By placing the dialectic of hiddenness and revelation within the heart of nature, Calvin blurs his own distinction between the two realms. But he does so for a reason. By merging the two spheres, he forms a continuity between nature and history, a continuity that finally leads to trust. The argument works insofar as we remember that, for Calvin, God is the sovereign ruler over both spheres. Further, Calvin continues to presuppose that God is unchangeable and that the divine attributes are inseparable. Thus, the wonders of nature must lead the believer to trust that God governs human history with the same power and wisdom evident in creation. The demonstration of God's might and control over the cosmos cannot lead to a fear about God's "absolute power"; the God of the whirlwind speech is not a tyrannical deity but a God whose goodness is inseparable from his power. Job may not have understood the justice and wisdom of this providence but he could have faith in these aspects of the divine nature until the last day when he would see God "face to face."

Calvin's Job learned that the proper answer to the revelation in nature was not further questions about the justice of history but rather silence and awe. Consequently, instead of the passages about Behemoth and Leviathan, Calvin's hermeneutical key for unlocking the meaning of the whirlwind speech is the same as that of Maimonides: Job's confession and final silence. In his first confession Job properly "laid his hand upon his mouth" and "renounced" his earlier replies to God.[141] In the second confession Calvin eagerly notes Job's acknowledgment that "I have uttered what I did not understand, things too marvelous for me which I did not know." Commenting on Job's final act of repentance and silence, Calvin concludes that when speaking about God's "works," we must confess the weakness of our minds and admit that "we cannot climb so high" as to know God's secrets.[142]

Job's Restoration

Calvin's decision to preach on the Book of Job meant that he had to confront the view (or views) of providence found in the Joban text. The reader of his sermons gradually discovers that to come to terms with the Joban understanding of providence, Calvin makes the issue of human perception the central question of the book. In so doing, he makes the dialectic between revelation and hiddenness the principal theme by which he interprets Job's story. In chapter 3 we examined how the issues of suffering and justice led Calvin toward the problem of perception and the reality of divine hiddenness. In Calvin's interpretation, Job's nonretributive suffering led to the realization that there are in God levels of justice, a lower justice revealed in the Law and a higher, secret justice before which even the angels could be condemned. Job's confrontation with this higher justice was an encounter with the frightening hiddenness and inscrutability of God. Although Eliphaz's words best articulated the principle of double justice (4:18), it was Job who confronted the terrifying reality of this unknowable aspect of the deity. We have seen that this theory of double justice caused Calvin serious theological problems regarding the power and justice of God. Nonetheless, the theory of God's twofold justice demonstrates how the Book of Job continually steered Calvin toward an exploration of the limits of human comprehension and toward an increasing awareness of God's inscrutability.

The Reformer's assumptions about the visibility of the Law reappear in the passages where he must identify the error of the friends. To align himself with Job, Calvin portrays the Dialogues as a battle over human perception. Here he employs the basic Thomistic framework—the use of the belief in immortality as a way to explain Job's perceptual advantage regarding the nature of history. According to Calvin, the misinterpretation of the Law was the cause of a serious perceptual mistake by the friends. Insisting that the rewards and punishments of the Law are found in this life, they argued that Job's suffering belonged to the visible order of providential history. Calvin construes their argument perceptually: The friends interpreted history according to what they thought they saw. Calvin interprets the position of Job's friends so that their theology was in many ways correct although their perception was wrong.

Calvin counters the pious but misperceived view of history advocated by the friends with Job's true insight about the nature of human events. The perceptual superiority afforded him by his belief in the resurrection allowed Calvin's Job to see that disorder and confusion appeared to characterize the world. However, the emphasis on Job's correct perception of disorder makes the Epilogue particularly troublesome for Calvin. For all our commentators, one of the main problems posed by the text was the Epilogue, because these final chapters require the commentator to explain Job's final restoration. The difficulty the Epilogue posed to a commentator is directly related to whatever issue governed the exegesis of his commentary. For Gregory, the problem was how to defend Job's detachment in the face of his material reward. Aquinas and Calvin faced the problem of visibility—that is, how to explain why Job was right to say that God's judgments were not clear in this life when Job was visibly restored with earthly fortune.

The meandering and unconvincing nature of Calvin's comments on chapter 42 demonstrates his uneasiness with this passage. He offers one explanation by saying that Job's restoration was typical of Old Testament times; God bestowed earthly prosperity because there was not at that time "such a revelation of the celestial life as there is today in the Gospel."[143] We saw the same argument in the *Expositio*—that the Epilogue represented God's loving condescension to the people of the Old Covenant.[144] Calvin's discomfort is revealed most clearly in his statements that the twofold restoration was not for Job's instruction but for our own. "It is true," Calvin explains, "that here the Holy Spirit wanted to leave a memorial of the grace of God upon the person of Job, but this is not for his instruction but for ours."[145]

In this odd argument Calvin struggles to return to the pedagogical theory of suffering. In Job's story, he says, we see that afflictions are medicinal and aim ultimately at salvation—an argument that is rather hard to defend on the basis of Job's situation. Calvin also explains that the "history" of Job's suffering and restoration was written for "our" benefit in order to show that adversities are temporal and that God will not tempt us more than we can bear (James 5:11). He goes so far as to claim that Job's restoration demonstrates that the "issue" or "result" of suffering will be a happy one. But immediately he catches himself and hastens to add that it is not common for God to redouble his graces toward those who have been afflicted "so that it would appear that they are much richer than they were before and that they have children and progeny, and that everything is desirable according to the world. We see that this does not always happen for God does not treat us in an equal measure."[146] Calvin's retraction of his earlier statement as well as his inability to give a straightforward and consistent explanation of Job's reward does not show him at his exegetical best. Still, the problematic nature of his comments does allow us to discern how the issues of revelation and hiddenness determine his exegesis of the text.

Calvin proceeds in chapter 42 as he did earlier on the basis of Elihu's speeches. Confronting a verse that clearly supports the visibility of God's judgments, Calvin invests the passage with an affirmation of the inscrutability of providence. In this way he tries to keep the message of the book consistent: Human history appears disordered during those times when God "hides his face." Thus Calvin does not use the Epilogue to qualify Job's (or his own) earlier statements about the ambiguity and confusion of history.[147] Faced with the incomprehensibility of providence, Calvin's Job did not argue his view of human history in a serene or rational manner. His laments were those of a man who feared that he had been abandoned by God to the seemingly chaotic realm of human events. In the figure of Job, Calvin portrays the perceptual struggle of faith: to rise spiritually above what one actually sees. It is no accident that 1 Cor. 13:12 becomes the heuristic principle for interpreting the story. Calvin is determined both to explain the text literally and to defend Job's perspective. In the exegesis of both Calvin and Aquinas, we can detect a recurring rationale: that Job's world view can only be justified if it is a statement about incompleteness (we now see only dimly or "in part").

The assumption of or implicit appeal to incompleteness is also the hermeneutical principle behind Calvin's interpretation of the whirlwind speech. This appeal radically separates his exegesis from those of Gregory and Aquinas. To appreciate the use made of the whirlwind speech by all these precritical commentators, we must ask what question they thought God was answering. Gregory, Aquinas, and Calvin all seek in the Book of Job a confirmation that the world is in the control of a just and powerful God. For them, the whirlwind speech addressed the need for this control by portraying a God who governed both nature and history. All three are concerned to provide Job with the God he needed. Both the *Moralia* and the *Expositio* are filled with references to the "assaults," "attacks," "war," and "battle" waged by Satan. What Gregory's and Aquinas's Job needed was protection. By allegorizing Behemoth and Leviathan, they allowed Job to find in the whirlwind speech a God powerful enough to defeat this "Ancient Enemy" and to prevent him from becoming a member of Satan's kingdom of pride.

Calvin's Job learned less from God's answer than did the Job of Gregory or Aquinas. First of all, he lived in a more constricted universe. For Calvin, there is only one level of interpretation: the literal. There are only two protagonists: God and Job. There is only one argument: the uncompromised appeal to nature. There is, for Calvin, no transcendent viewpoint provided by an allegorical or metaphorical level of the text. For both Gregory and Aquinas, chapters 40–41 contained a message that went beyond the literal interpretation of the passage. Their reader travels from the surface inward toward a deeper significance. For Gregory, the result was a vast, comprehensive understanding of redemptive history as each verse took on typological meaning. In the *Expositio*, Aquinas's Job also gained a transcendent standpoint by viewing God's redemptive battle with Satan, a battle that had raged throughout history.

Refusing to move on the level of allegory, Calvin does not interpret the whirlwind speech as describing the exercise of God's power in the creation of the church, the governing of sacred history, or the victory over Satan. With Calvin, the reader's mind pierces neither through the text nor through the confusion of history. The inner meanings of the text are gone. Calvin does not permit Job to penetrate the phenomena of creation and history and thereby attain an eternal viewpoint. In the

Sermons the human mind cannot escape or fully understand the meaning of history. Moreover, because of his overriding concern with perceptual arguments and imagery, Calvin's reader (or listener) is like Job: Both are trapped within the disorder of history and caught in a swirl of perceptions and misunderstandings. The friends argued from what they thought was a revealed and visible order in the world. Calvin thinks they are partially right, since there are times when a perceptible order appears in human affairs. Over against the claims for visibility expounded by the friends, however, was the truer perception of Job. But that perception was an appeal to darkness, obscurity, incomprehensibility, and hiddenness. As if to complicate matters further, Calvin turns Elihu's statements about the visibility of providence into arguments for the hiddenness of God. These perspectives and this perceptual imagery have a dizzying effect, one that is much more disconcerting than what we encountered in the *Moralia*. For Calvin, the only ones who saw the situation clearly were Job and Elihu—who knew that they could *not* see.

Calvin finally attempts to stop the swirl of perceptions through the appeal to faith. In Job, Calvin portrays the insistence of faith that ultimately things are not what they seem. The darkness in history required a faith or trust that now only "glimpses" divine providence. Thus in the *Sermons on Job* we see a dialectical relationship among history, nature, and faith. Calvin argues that apart from nature, history is often a catalyst for despair. But, when coupled with the quasi-revelatory character of nature, history lays the basis for faith. In other words, history poses the options of despair or faith. Nature tips the balance toward faith, without thereby robbing faith of its quality of trust. We might say, then, that nature becomes like Maimonides's "filigree traceries" through which faith can glimpse the justice of divine providence.

By rejecting allegory, Calvin restricts those "glimpses" to the contemplation of nature. In his reading, the divine answer was only twofold: the transcendence of God and the limitations of human reason. This concern with the limitations of human knowledge causes Calvin to resemble Maimonides. Like the great Jewish thinker, Calvin also limits the whirlwind speech to the level of creation and insists that the human mind cannot transcend the realm of "nature." Repeatedly, Calvin argues that there is no continuity, between God and Job, the infinite and the finite, God's reason and human reason, divine justice and human justice, and divine power and human power.

When Calvin has to comment on 42:5 ("I have heard you with my ear, but now my eye has seen you"), he struggles to explain what Job really "saw." For both Gregory and Aquinas, this verse described the progress made by Job. Both argue that as "sight is superior to hearing," so Job made progress through "suffering," through "revelation," or through the "beholding of the light of truth." Hence Gregory's Job beheld the "light of truth" with the "inward eye" and thereby recognized the "darkness of his humanity."[148] Aquinas's Job admitted his "own guilt" as he confronted the higher justice of God.[149] Maimonides's Job saw that those things he had imagined to be happiness were not the ultimate goal, and therefore he repented of all he used to desire.[150] Consequently, Job's insight resulted in a deeper knowledge of his former ignorance, an ignorance that was reemphasized in Maimonides's argument that the whirlwind speech taught the limitations of human knowledge. Calvin also tried to explain Job's progress in understanding. We find that Calvin's Job learned to bear toward God a greater reverence and "to put all things into [God's] hands in order that he would have all authority and rule over us."[151] Fundamentally, however, Calvin sees in this verse the knowledge of faith, a sensing of the divine majesty that results in trust. Job's new "sight" really consisted of a deeper sense of his own ignorance and hubris, a faithful submission to God, but not a full understanding of divine rule. Therefore, although they presuppose very different, even opposing, conceptions of God, history, and providence, both Calvin and Maimonides understand that the whirlwind speech gave Job a wisdom characterized by the realization of his noetic limitations and of God's unknowability.

Calvin's God is not as transcendent as that of Maimonides. Nor is Calvin's view of history the same as that of the Jewish thinker. We see in the *Sermons,* as in the *Expositio,* that the appeal to the judgment in the afterlife creates a continuity between divine and human concepts of justice. Although Calvin may not have admitted this continuity, the argument from immortality means that justice is delayed, not unknowable. After his death, Calvin's Job would not simply become united in contemplation with the Active Intellect but rather would witness the final judgment of the wicked as well as his own vindication. The deity does indeed have his own purposes, but the attributes of Calvin's God are not completely incomprehensible. These attributes are revealed in Scripture, they are guaranteed by the unchangeability and inseparability of the divine essence, and they are manifest to some degree in nature. Furthermore, Calvin's view of history and providence is not that of Maimonides. For Calvin, there is a higher, although indiscernible, order in human events, a providential plan that guides all events of history from creation to the last judgment. Therefore, the promise that Job will one day see "face to face" means that human notions of justice and the desire for providential order are postponed, not irrelevant.

Rather than a full understanding of God's actions or a God powerful enough to defeat Leviathan, what Calvin's Job needed was a promise. He needed a promise that history was in some way an extension of nature. Both to make the whirlwind speech meaningful and to retain a purely literal exegesis, Calvin had to reconnect the spheres of nature and history. In so doing, he merges the imagery of light and darkness. In Calvin's interpretation, the imagery of "nature," "visibility," "reflection," "light," "brightness," and "mirrors" finally shades off into darkness. The providential rule of human history is inexplicable, incomprehensible, and beyond human reason. And yet nature points beyond itself and promises that the same God who brought the beauty and order of creation into being is wise and powerful enough to bring order out of what appears to be present confusion. Although Calvin insists that there is no continuity between God and Job, he holds out the promise of a continuity between God's revelation in nature and God's governance of history. For Calvin, then, Job had to rely on the promise offered by the mirror of nature and trust that the wisdom and power reflected in the cosmos are inherent and inseparable aspects of God's rule. In the "disorder" of the historical present, Calvin's Job was left not with "knowledge" but with faith and hope. Job "spoke rightly" before God because he alone perceived the necessity for trust and faith in the midst of the dark and seemingly abandoned realm of human events. This faith led him to believe that in the afterlife there would be a restoration of order when the believer would see God "face to face."

Conclusion

The commentaries we have studied span the sixth to the sixteenth centuries. We turned to the earlier commentaries by Gregory, Maimonides, and Aquinas to gain a perspective on Calvin's exegesis in the *Sermons*. In doing so, we were met with a welter of interpretive programs in which the metaphysical presuppositions, theological assumptions, and exegetical methods all differed. I have made a case that one issue emerges as a touchstone for determining the coherence of this varied tradition: the concern with human noetic perception. For all these commentators, the Book of Job begged for reflection on what the human mind could discern and how one could endure the difficult path to wisdom. Discussions about human noetic abilities or inabilities govern these works because questions about suffering, evil, providence, and history ineluctably led these thinkers toward the ambiguous nature of experience, understanding, knowledge, perspective, prophetic insight, revelation, and faith. To determine why Job "spoke rightly" before God, precritical exegetes were thrown directly into the problematic and disturbing world of perception.

Recalling the conclusions reached in earlier chapters, we can identify several factors that drew these exegetes toward the often problematic nature of human understanding. These include the subject matter of the story and the inherently perspectival structure of the biblical text. The Book of Job is composed as an argument about suffering, providence, evil, and history. Throughout the biblical Joban story there are competing perspectives: the views of the early and late Job, the outlooks of the sufferer and the nonsufferer, the human and divine perspectives. Viewing the Book of Job as a unity, these commentators were immersed in a text that demanded attention to clashing viewpoints and changing perspectives.

Other factors were equally important in explaining this concern with perception. Underlying assumptions about suffering, metaphysics, immortality, history, and providence also determined how these exegetes would develop to their own advantage the perspectival structure of the Book of Job. Gregory's presuppositions about the importance of affliction allowed him to find in the Joban text an affirmation of the enlightening power of suffering. His metaphysic of hierarchy and interiority led him to explore the perceptual dimensions of Job's detachment and transcendence. Maimonides's metaphysic was also instrumental in his discovery of perceptual themes in Job. His belief in the remoteness of God, his portrayal of the ten spheres and the Active Intellect, and his interpretation of the "evil spirit" caused him to see Job as stressing the limitations of human understanding. Interpreting the Book of Job without Gregory's theology of suffering, Aquinas explained Job's perceptual advantage by his belief in personal immortality. Both Aquinas and Calvin used the doctrine of the afterlife to focus the meaning of the Joban story on the perception of providence within history. They appealed to Job's experiential knowledge of apparent disorder in human events to construe the Book of Job as a perceptual battle over the nature of history.

Even more than Aquinas, Calvin depicted Job as traveling farther and farther into the realm of divine hiddenness, darkness, and incomprehensibility. Calvin's whole discussion of double justice is an exploration of the hiddenness of God. In Job, Calvin saw a man whose afflictions drove him toward the darker side of God. That darkness threatened to overwhelm history. Calvin's belief in the revelatory power of nature, the noetic fall of the human being, the hidden and revealed justice of God, the empirical disorder of history, and the providential rule of the deity make his *Sermons on Job* a constant dialectic between hiddenness and revelation. For all these exegetes Job became a symbol of what they saw as the fundamental message of the book. For Gregory, Job was the symbol of detachment and wisdom. For Maimonides, Job symbolized both transcendence and noetic limitation. For Aquinas and Calvin, Job was the symbol of the incompleteness of life. And furthermore, for Calvin,

Job became the personification of the triumph of faith over the noetic nightmare of history.

The noetic and perspectival issues are central to this interpretive tradition in another way as well, in the parallel relationship that emerges between exegesis and perception. As the hermeneutical method evolved from a highly allegorical to a more literal approach, *Job's perceptual abilities became increasingly restricted.* The exegetical method thus holds certain noetic or perceptual implications for the interpretation of Job. Similarly, as the literal commentaries turned toward the discernment of providence, Job's noetic abilities became more and more limited. The nature of reality presumed by the allegorical method—that truth about reality lies hidden under the surface of what can be seen—allowed the Job of the *Moralia* to probe levels of existence in ways that Calvin's Job could not.

The corollary between exegesis and perception is best illustrated by comparing the different views of history reached by the Jobs of our various commentators. By finding different levels of meaning in the Joban story and by placing the reader and speaker on shifting levels of discernment, Gregory makes questions of perspective and insight central to his reading of the book. When applied to the question of history, this hermeneutical practice causes different aspects of history to appear. On the literal and moral levels of the Book of Job, Gregory finds descriptions of the vanity and perishability of temporal existence. This view changes on the allegorical level of the Joban text. On this higher perspective, redemptive history is revealed through typological exegesis. Job's elevated standpoint makes possible discussions about the simultaneity of sight gained through prophecy. We encounter descriptions of the comprehensive view of sacred history that encompasses God's acts from creation to the end of time. This allegorical method ties the whirlwind speech back to the Prologue and even to Gen. 1–3. Gregory's Job gained deeper insight into the nature of his soul, the purpose of his suffering, and the redemptive plan of history.

This perceptual vista becomes increasingly leveled in later commentaries. Maimonides's Job progressed from a naive understanding of religion to the feeling of divine abandonment and, finally, to a true perception about the nature of providence. In so doing, Job did gain a transcendent view of history through union with the Active Intellect. Nonetheless, his deepening insight was, in reality, a greater appreciation for the limits of human knowledge. Maimonides's reading of Job's laments, the words of the friends, and the whirlwind speech leads him to interpret the story in terms of providence. His decision to read chapters 38–41 as a description of "natural things" means that he interprets the whirlwind speech as a restriction of the human mind to the natural realm. The final prophetic revelation did not lead Job to a comprehension of redemption within history or to an insight regarding the purpose of his adversities. Rather, Job came to understand that God was too distant to take an interest in human affairs. He also learned that human understanding could not surpass the lowest level of the Active Intellect—the realm of nature and history.

Aquinas and Calvin believe that the doctrine of personal immortality granted Job a superior perspective by which to judge historical reality. Nevertheless, both portray Job's immediate perception of history in the same way as Maimonides: History is a sphere of apparent disorder and injustice. Neither Aquinas nor Calvin sees Job as a prophet, offering a view of redemptive or typological history. Aquinas follows Gregory's interpretation of Behemoth and Leviathan as Satan and thereby allows Job to understand the reason for his afflictions and the role of suffering within the larger plan of God's providential history. In contrast, Calvin's thoroughly literal exegesis of the whirlwind speech limits Job to the present realm of nature and history. Throughout his ordeal Calvin's Job experienced the existential despair caused by the inscrutability of providence and the apparent abandonment of God. Even the direct revelation spoken through the whirlwind did not lift Job beyond the often confused world of human events. In Calvin's interpretation Job never gained a clear understanding of God's actions in the Prologue or of the justice of divine providence in history. Calvin's Job did, however, attain to faith in the invisible and the incomprehensible. Thus, while Job's noetic perception was hemmed in by the darkness of history, his faith was enlarged.

V

MODERN READINGS OF JOB

If he didn't have bad luck, he wouldn't have had none.

The Thin Blue Line, film directed by Errol Morris, 1988

CALVIN'S READING OF Job anticipates a perceptual *Götterdammerung.* In twentieth-century interpretations of Job, this twilight becomes all-enveloping. Here is an encroaching darkness that is not held back by light of revelation, immortality, or illumination. The precritical commentaries examined in the preceding chapters can inform our understandings of the dark modern interpretations of Job and make us more self-aware. The analysis we have undertaken affords us a fresh perspective on contemporary treatments of Job, indicative of our age. Like William and Adso in Umberto Eco's *The Name of the Rose,* we stand in an exegetical Aedificium where books murmur to books across the centuries. We are able to enjoy our own interpretive maneuvers better when we have understood those of others.

As Besserman noted, the Book of Job was read throughout the Middle Ages in a variety of artistic, literary, and ecclesiastical contexts.[1] His observation holds for the twentieth century as well. The Joban legend has been a wellspring for contemporary exegetes, novelists, playwrights, and poets. In this chapter, we turn to several forms of recent Joban interpretation: critical/exegetical, psychoanalytic, and literary. Our study proceeds by self-consciously analyzing such works in the light of our premodern commentaries on Job. Like earlier commentaries, modern interpretations of Job or the Joban theme are characterized by an interest in human perception. In contrast to earlier treatises, however, these later readings illustrate, in varying degrees, how the phenomenon of human perception is measured by the increasing remoteness, absence, or inaccessibility of the transcendent. As a result of this remoteness of God, human perception turns in on itself and finally collapses.

Modern Biblical Commentaries on Job

Commentaries and studies on Job have poured forth throughout the latter half of the twentieth century. We can divide these commentaries into two categories. One includes works that concentrate on the findings of the historical-critical method. The unparalleled studies by Fohrer and

156

Pope best represent this approach.[2] With these exegetes we receive a careful, encyclopedic *Forschungsbericht*-type commentary on the Book of Job. These and similar works address a complex of problems: the historical context; linguistic issues regarding syntax, vocabulary, and grammar; the literary precursors, parallels, and prehistory of the text; and the date, authorship, and redaction of the book.

From such studies we learn that the Book of Job in its present form dates from the fifth to the third centuries B.C.E. The text took its shape gradually. The Joban legend passed through perhaps four stages, evolving from (1) a pre-Israelite tale; (2) a pre-exilic version dating from the ninth–eighth centuries B.C.E.; (3) an exilic version in which Deuteronomic phraseology was added; and (4) the postexilic version in which the figure of Satan and elements of Wisdom teaching were incorporated.[3] Placing the book against its Near Eastern background, historical-critical exegetes study the nature of the Hebrew language as well as its literary parallels in ancient Mesopotamia. These scholars are primarily interested in the gradual formation of the present text and also in the original intention of the authors/redactor. They do not ignore the theology of the book, although it is not the primary emphasis in these studies. Rather, they examine the theological message historically and comparatively by analyzing various religious issues against the background of those same themes as they appear in manuscripts from the ancient Near Eastern world.

These studies have undoubtedly advanced our knowledge of the meaning of the Book of Job. Our present purposes, however, are better served by looking to a second group of commentaries, which reflect a more literary approach to the biblical narratives in addition to a grounding in the historical-critical method. Our analysis will focus in part on the influential works of Robert Gordis (*The Book of God and Man*) and Samuel Terrien (*Job: Poet of Existence*).[4] Our main focus will be two commentaries that best represent the literary approach to the text: Normal Habel's *Book of Job* and Edwin Good's *In Turns of Tempest*.[5] Although Habel and Good draw on insights from preceding historical studies of Job, they are concerned less with questions of textual emendation and historical background than with the literary integrity and meaning of the book as a whole. They read Job as an "integrated literary and theological work." Good employs a striking combination of historical criticism and the literary theory of desconstruction, a theory that emphasizes the "play" and indeterminacy of the text. But unlike pure deconstructionists, Good readily admits that "some interpretations are better than others."[6] In their attempt to find what Gordis calls the "architectonic structure" and "inner unity" of the Book of Job,[7] these four authors stand closest to the outlook of our precritical commentators.

We should not be surprised to find that modern biblical commentaries bear the least resemblance to Gregory's *Moralia*. This dissimilarity is not due simply to the rejection of allegory. More essential differences lie in diverging assumptions about the nature of reality and the purpose of suffering.[8] Modern exegetes do not work with a metaphysic of hierarchy; for the twentieth-century scholar, reality has been made thoroughly historical. Moreover, no contemporary interpreter finds in Job any message of detached transcendence or any belief in the beneficial and curative power of suffering. The modern Job did not embrace his adversities or turn inward to ascend toward God. Contemporary interpreters do not believe that providence is most indiscernible when the wicked suffer and the good prosper. This denial of the pedagogical value of Job's afflictions cannot be explained only by the modern focus on the literal-historical meaning of the book, since Gregory based his theology of suffering precisely on the moral and literal levels of the text. Most probably, the negative modern interpretation of Job's suffering is due to a combination of historical and cultural factors. Scholarly sensitivity to the historical context of the book leads exegetes to attribute to Job anything but an affirmation of suffering. In a limited way, however, contemporary exegetes do recognize that Job's suffering drove him to a deeper knowledge of God and of reality. This progress toward deeper insight is understood more in terms of the insights expressed by Maimonides, Aquinas, and Calvin; Gregory's view of Job's suffering as medicinal, purgative, and pedagogical has vanished.

If we omit Gregory's *Moralia* to focus on the exegetical tradition from Maimonides to Calvin, we can see that many themes reappear in the modern commentaries. Like the precritical commentators, recent exegetes recognize that the Book of Job challenges the teaching of moral retribution. Habel explains that Job and his friends initially espoused an orthodoxy that assumed "a moral order in the world where retributive justice is the norm."[9] According to Terrien, the Joban poet made the teaching of the friends attractive precisely to show the fallacy of their beliefs. In the speeches of the friends, Terrien says, we see "the failure of ethical monotheism to cope with existence."[10] Thus, while these scholars are not interested in defending the value of retributive suffering, they do understand that retributive justice cannot explain the experiential reality of history. This opposition between the doctrine of retribution and experience is a theme modern exegetes share with the earlier tradition.

Modern authors do not use the belief in resurrection or immortality as a framework within which to justify God's providence or to explain Job's perceptual superiority. Scholars recognize that the text leaves Job's belief in the afterlife ambiguous. Gordis notes that the idea of a life after death was emerging in Job's day but was ultimately rejected by Job.[11] Habel and Good note the ambivalence of Job's various statements about "seeing God" and returning from Sheol to face the deity. Explaining verses 14:13–17, 16:16–17:1, 11:15–16, and 19:26–27, Habel argues that Job believed there was a figure in heaven who could testify on his behalf, even if this testimony took place after his death. Habel states that in chapter 19 Job expressed the wish to be present to see his divine adversary face to face, even if that "seeing" was a post-mortem event.[12] Similarly, Terrien argues that in chapter 19 Job thought he would see God after death.[13] Good, on the contrary, insists that while Job may have entertained the possibility of life after death, he rejected such an idea in 14:16–17. Moreover, according to Good, although Job's avenger or $gō'ēl$ might live, Job himself expected a quick death.[14] None of these commentators read Job's elusive remarks about life after death as an extension of history in which the wicked are punished and the good rewarded. The possibility of "seeing God" is interpreted as only a moment for the vindication of Job's innocence, not as a way of defending the justice of God's providence in the moral order of history. As Terrien writes, "Job, of all men, did not think up this so-called 'proof' of immortality."[15] Any perceptual superiority granted to Job, therefore, is not attributed to his belief in a personal or impersonal immortality. Thus Job does not become a symbol of incompleteness.

Left in a world that did not extend to the afterlife and did not make sense according to human ideas of retributive justice, the Job of modern commentaries experienced many of the same spiritual torments and perceptual dilemmas as did the Job of Maimonides, Aquinas, and Calvin. Both Habel and Good clearly understand that the Book of Job is about contradictory experiences and perceptions of reality. Both exegetes chronicle Job's appeals to his own "experience" of undeserved suffering, an experience that contradicted the claims for moral order espoused by the friends. According to Habel, the Joban poet employed traditional forms and structures to create distinctive designs that emphasize a paradoxical interpretation of reality. From Habel we learn that "ambiguous images of the world are interwoven with conflicting perspectives about the world. . . . Subtle ironies, blatant sarcasm, ambiguities of language, and complexities of plot all unite to portend a theology of paradox."[16] Hence Job and his companions "explore numerous realities of their world, including the ground of knowledge, the nature of the wicked, the rule of God and the moral order."[17] Good also examines the story as a conflict of perspectives. According to Good, the friends consistently argued for their idea of the "world's moral structure," a structure

they insisted on applying to Job's situation. Job, however, saw the traditional world view shattered as he wondered if God punishes people
"without cause":

What Job has received is deeply, devastatingly frightening. The entire system of
laws, assumptions, assurances, truths behind his comfortable life has been
snatched rudely away. . . . Nothing solid is there anymore. That appalled shud-
dering terror points toward what Job is about to say. It is fearful enough to see
your whole worldview evaporate, leaving nothing in its place. It is at least as fearful to find in its place a new interpretation of the world exactly opposite to the
one that has gone. In the rest of this speech [chapter 21], Job propounds an
understanding of life that reverses what he and his friends held before.[18]

   For the Job of Habel and Good, "things fall apart: the center cannot
hold." The "paradoxical" experience of reality stood opposed to the
moral order preached by the friends. Both exegetes, then, interpret
Job's story as a perceptual battle about conflicting perspectives on the
world. In so doing they stand (perhaps unknowingly) in a long line of
Joban interpretation that stretches back at least to Maimonides. Furthermore, Habel and Good portray the same spiritual torments afflicting Job that Maimonides and Calvin described. Like Maimonides,
Good comments that Job experienced "god's absence" and felt that the
deity had abandoned those who ought to be under his care.[19] Like
Calvin, both commentators recognize that Job perceived God as an enemy and adversary. As Habel explains, Job saw himself as mortal and
God as an "oppressive celestial spy."[20] In language also reminiscent of
Calvin, Habel argues that "Job exposes the dark side of God."[21] In these
passages, Habel and Good repeat a theme developed also by Terrien
who writes, "In the end [Job's] torture is made of a vast complex, not
only physical and social humiliation but also and especially divine es-
trangement."[22]

   Most important, Terrien and Good glimpse an issue that was more
fully explored by Calvin: that this absent, hidden, and adversarial God
was problematic because his power might be seen as outstripping his justice. Like Calvin, they see that Job feared the arbitrariness of a potentially tyrannical deity. For Calvin, this fear resulted from the failure to
recognize the unity of the divine attributes. However, the unity of the divine essence is not a doctrine that informs these modern commentaries.
Terrien's Job wondered if God's omnipotence had gotten out of hand
and acted without "the control of inner standards or the check of out-
siders."[23] Good reflects on the same issue:

Here [Job] wants to be dead because the structure of things has fallen apart. He
had thought that divine power and divine justice were positively related, and

that divine power supported those weak ones who deserved divine justice. Sure that he deserves justice, he is also sure now that, like those wicked people who ought not to be supported, he is being attacked by the divine power. Distinction has dissolved into darkness, and Job would rather be dead.[24]

Good's Job and Calvin's Job stared into the same abyss. Both experienced what Good calls the "terrorism" of God or the "absent and arbitrary force" of the deity.[25] In the midst of darkness, the Job of all these interpreters searched for the face of God. The modern Job, however, did not find God's face in the world of nature. Here we notice a crucial contrast between the interpretation of Habel and Good and that of Calvin. The difference signals the gradual narrowing of Job's perceptual horizon, a narrowing that is even more pronounced in other twentieth-century treatments of Job. Like Calvin, Habel sees that the Book of Job challenges the attempt to derive moral order in history from the order evident in nature. According to Habel, the author of Job developed his imagery and analogy within the "broad parameters of a wisdom cosmology" in which "analogies were drawn from nature to confirm principles and axioms in the social and moral order of things, since a consistent ordering principle was assumed in all domains of the cosmos."[26] Habel explains that according to Job's friends and Elihu, God "acts righteously in all things and upholds the principle of distributive justice within the social and natural orders."[27] We recall that on the basis of Bildad's words in chapter 18 Calvin also identified this principle as the error of Job's friends.

Like Calvin, Habel and Good see that Job challenged this view of a continuity between the natural and historical orders. But they argue very differently from the Reformer. For Calvin, nature was indeed ordered, although that order was not visible in the moral disorder of history. Only in the whirlwind speech did Calvin reconnect nature and history by holding out the promise that human events are governed by the same unchangeable God who rules the cosmos. Although often indiscernible, the justice of providence is anchored in the wisdom of that deity who reveals himself in creation. Habel and Good read Job's attitude to nature in a way diametrically opposed to Calvin's view. For Good, even Job's "cosmological outburst" in chapter 26 was not a positive doctrinal statement but an expression of the fact that "the cosmos is under the thumb of a cruel, harshly present tyrant." Job's vision was one of "cosmic disorder." For Good's Job, then, "the disorder is both cosmic and social."[28] So too Habel argues that "living creatures will verify that there is no consistent operation of a moral principle of just retribution in the natural realm."[29] For Habel, the nature imagery in the Book of Job is a part of the "collage of paradoxes" that constitutes the book. "The same phenome-

non of nature, be it plant, cloud, light, thunder, or lion is subject to diverse interpretations and used as analogy for differing views of reality."[30]
As Habel says, "the natural order is amoral."[31] In these commentaries,
then, nature does not serve as the counterpoint to the darkness of history. Unlike Calvin, these modern exegetes see nature as a source of
paradox, tyranny, and disorder. Because nature too is disordered, the
realm of creation cannot act as a revelatory counterpoint to the disorder
of history. The "confusion" of history is unrelieved.

Not surprisingly, the Job of Habel and Good learned something significantly different than Calvin's Job. In these modern interpretations
we find no promise of an eventual transformation of the present moral
disorder of history. An ordered nature does not point beyond itself to a
future restored order in the afterlife or on judgment day. Rather, the
whirlwind speech now makes final the rejection of a retributive moral
order. Perhaps it is the complete denial of personal immortality and distributive justice that makes the interpretations of Habel and Good most
resemble that of Maimonides. According to Habel, the Joban poet
knows that "to deduce eternal moral principles on the basis of the natural order . . . is foolhardy."[32] For Habel, Job's God was never "bound by
any laws which operate within it [the cosmos], least of all any presumed
law of reward and punishment."[33] He concludes that

Job may be ignorant of the higher wisdom principle which governs God's design,
but he has gained sufficient understanding to know that pursuing litigation is fu-
tile. He knows, at least, that the design of God is not governed by a necessary law
of reward and retribution. God's wisdom is of a higher order—and remains a mystery. Thus the conflict is resolved on a formal level within the narrative plot and
the hero gains a new level of knowledge about reality, yet the enigma of the cosmic design remains. The hero comes to terms with the reality of God and his cosmos without understanding the full dimensions of that reality.[34]

Again, since there is no afterlife in which order and justice would be revealed, the lack of understanding for Habel's Job is the final reality.

Good concludes in a similar way. For Good, the whirlwind speech
teaches that "events in the world cannot be explicated simply as reactions to Job's and Job's friends' moral actions . . . morality has no cosmic
reverberations at all."[35] Following what was originally Maimonides's insight into the translation of 42:6 ("Therefore I despise and repent of
dust and ashes"), Good ends with an interpretation the Jewish thinker
would have applauded:

to "repent of dust and ashes" is to give up the religious structure that construes
the world in terms of guilt and innocence. It is to repent of repentance. The
world's events are not responses to human moral activity and inward disposition. Job has indeed heard the crucial question of 40.8, and has come to realize

not merely that he need not proceed with his trial but positively that the issue of repentance and the admission of sin, with its concomitant restoration of the former sinner to favor with the deity, is the wrong issue. That structure of guilt and innocence was the focus of the friends' argument. But the world spins on its own kind of order, of which Job had very little sense.[36]

Not all modern commentaries on the Book of Job exhibit an interest in the noetic or perceptual issues that concerned our precritical exegetes. The commentaries that do evince an interest in the perceptual dimensions of the story tend to be the "literary-critical" approaches exemplified here by Habel and Good. However, as we have seen, crucial differences divide these modern readings from the earlier tradition. The assumptions about suffering, revelation, nature, and moral justice have changed in the intervening centuries. The modern Job was left in a much more unsettling world where suffering, nature, history, or God did not resolve his spiritual agony. Unlike their precritical predecessors, modern commentators seem content to leave Job in his perceptual conundrum. There is little effort to "rescue the appearances."

Jung's *Answer to Job*

In addition to literary treatments, twentieth-century interpretations of Job encompass a wide variety of other genres. One is the psychoanalytic study. Such an analysis of Job was made by one of the preeminent psychoanalysts of our time, Carl Jung, in his *Answer to Job*.[37] In Jung's interpretation we see the major themes that recur in modern literary formulations: the loss or reinterpretation of transcendence, the absence of a transcendent revelation, and the consequent emphasis on the human subject. These themes have serious implications for the noetic abilities of Job; indeed, the perceptual or noetic abilities of "Job" collapse altogether. In these works we can trace the trajectory that ends in the crisis of human perception.

For Jung, the Book of Job is not about the confrontation with a transcendent deity, at least as the concept of transcendence has been traditionally understood in Western metaphysics. Jung reads the Joban story as an expression of ancient experience with the "archetype of the deity"—that is, the God-image in the collective unconscious. We cannot interpret the *Answer to Job*, then, by placing it within the context of strictly metaphysical and theological assumptions. Rather, we must read it in terms of what Homans has called Jung's "core process."[38] According to Jung, the ego or center of consciousness is formed primarily by the persona or the "collective consciousness." This is a process of rational adaptation to social reality. Below the ego, the collective consciousness, and the personal unconscious lies a larger impersonal or "transpersonal" collective unconscious. This psychic level is the *Urgrund* of our collective being.[39] The collective unconscious is a mythopoeic substratum or "ocean" of primordial images and archetypes that bear a universal character throughout time.[40] Central to Jung's theory is the process of individuation. In this process the persona is weakened, and the archetypes emerge from the collective unconscious into the conscious level of being. During individuation the archetypes are gradually assimilated into the ego. The goal of individuation (and the purpose of therapy) is to achieve a balance between the contents of the ego and the collective unconscious; at this point the whole and authentic self comes into being.

The individual confronts several archetypes during individuation, most notably the shadow, the animus or anima, and God. The last of these is connected with the self. In the Book of Job, Jung sees the human encounter with a certain aspect of the archetype of the deity, which came to consciousness around the years 600–300 B.C.E., the period to which Jung dates the Book of Job.[41]

For Jung, the Book of Job portrays the period of psychic evolution when humanity confronted the darkness of God. In Job's story, Jung finds a God who readily submits to Satan's deceit, who tortures a guiltless man, and who finally turns on Job with a display of ruthless and brutal force. In the person of Job, he sees a man who could not stop seeking justice from God but who encountered only a God of power. Job believed in God's justice but "in this [Job] is mistaken, as Yahweh's subsequent words make clear. God does not want to be just; he merely flaunts might over right. . . . [Job] looked upon God as a moral being. He had never doubted God's might, but he had hoped for justice [Gerechtigkeit] as well."[42] According to Jung, Job came face to face with God's "contradictory nature," with a God whose character is a "totality of inner opposites."[43] Job's superior insight allows him to see that God is a totality: "He [Yahweh] is everything in its totality; therefore, among other things, he is total justice and also its total opposite."[44] Jung's Job discovered an "antinomy" or dual nature in God:

Job, in spite of his doubt as to whether man can be just before God, still finds it difficult to relinquish the idea of meeting God on the basis of justice and therefore of morality. Because, in spite of everything, he cannot give up his faith in divine justice, it is not easy for him to accept the knowledge that divine arbitrariness [göttliche Willkür] breaks the law. On the other hand, he has to admit that no one except Yahweh himself is doing him injustice and violence. He cannot deny that he is up against a God who does not care a rap for any moral opinion and does not recognize any form of ethics as binding. This is perhaps the greatest thing about Job, that, faced with this difficulty, he does not doubt the unity of God. He clearly sees that God is at odds with himself [dass Gott sich in Widerspruch mit sich selber befindet]—so totally at odds that he, Job, is quite certain of finding in God a helper and "advocate" against God. As certain as he is of the evil in Yahweh, he is equally certain of the good in Yahweh. . . . [Yahweh] is both a persecutor and a helper in one, and the one aspect is as real as the other. Yahweh is not split but is an antinomy—a totality of inner opposites [Antinomie, eine totale innere Gegensätzlichkeit]—and this is the indispensable condition for his tremendous dynamism, his omniscience, and omnipotence.[45]

Seeing the "inner antinomy" in the deity, Jung's Job realized that God's goodness and justice could contradict his injustice and power. Like the forces of creation, God had an amoral nature.[46] Jung explains that "Yahweh is a *phenomenon* 'not a man.'"[47] This latter insight was articulated in varying ways by our premodern commentators, all of whom knew that the Book of Job revealed the otherness of God. For Maimonides, the Joban parable affirms the utter transcendence of God; neither the highest deity nor the Active Intellect can be comprehended by human standards of justice or providence. But Maimonides never posits within God a dark or arbitrary nature. Gregory and Aquinas both recognize that the story of Job demonstrates the incomprehensibility of God's wisdom and justice. But neither exegete portrays this incomprehensibility as an inner contradiction within the deity, a contradiction that would place real evil and injustice in God's nature. For Gregory and Aquinas, God's incomprehensibility is explained in terms of transcendence; divine justice surpasses human justice but does not contradict it. The *Moralia* and the *Expositio* appeal to mystery, not to the shadow or evil side of God.

Jung's description of Yahweh as including both justice and brutal power immediately recalls us to Calvin's explorations of double justice. Jung's insight most closely resembles Calvin's view that Job glimpsed the terrifying possibility of God's tyrannical nature. Calvin foreshadows Jung when he speaks of Job's fear that God could disregard his "lower justice" and act by a power unformed or unregulated by his goodness and justice. For both Calvin and Jung, therefore, Job confronted the prospect of God's "absolute power." Both thinkers recognize that the Book of Job comes "to terms with the divine darkness."[48] Most important, they understand that the dark side of God took the form of a division of the divine attributes, a separation between power and justice. Both authors see that Job's story leads one to ponder the idea of a self-contradictory and dual deity. Jung's references to God's antinomy, inner opposites, dual or contradictory nature are rooted in the same insight expressed by Calvin when he speaks of the fear that God sometimes seems to act independently of his justice.

There are, of course, decisive differences between Calvin and Jung in their understanding of God. What was a temptation for Calvin's Job becomes moral and noetic superiority for Jung's Job. Calvin identifies Job's fear of God's tyrannical or absolute power as despair, temptation, or lack of faith. To see God as unregulated by justice is to blaspheme the deity. Thus Calvin continually recalls Job to the inseparability of the divine attributes: God's power is inseparable from his justice. In Calvin's theology, therefore, divine power can never act independently of divine justice. The appearance of brutal or tyrannical power is explained by the noetic effect of sin in the human subject, not as anything real in God. He roots the problem not in God but in human perception. Calvin, then, restrains the apparently dark side of God's nature by appealing to the inherent unity of the divine essence. By defining that unity as an inseparability of the divine attributes, Calvin explains the darkness of God in terms of a transcendent incomprehensibility.

For Jung, however, Job did not at all find God incomprehensible. Jung reverses the roles of God and Job by arguing that Job understood God better than God understood himself. In comparison with Yahweh, Jung's Job had a "keener consciousness based on self-reflection."[49] According to Jung, "without Yahweh's knowledge and contrary to his intentions, the tormented though guiltless Job had secretly been lifted up to a superior knowledge of God which God himself did not possess. Had Yahweh consulted his omniscience, Job would not have had the advantage of him. . . . Job realizes God's inner antinomy and in light of his realization his knowledge attains a divine numinosity."[50] Jung's Job gained greater perception than God, or at least than the traditional archetype of God present in the human consciousness before the Joban era. Job's greater insight was his new awareness that God was indeed dual, that the deity was composed of a totality of opposites.

In the Book of Job, Jung finds further confirmation for his belief that the archetype of the deity is most fully perceived or experienced as a *complexio oppositorum*.[51] This means that God is ideally conceived as an image of wholeness. Jung's point, however, is that wholeness requires the inclusion of all aspects of reality within the divine nature, including evil. The most authentic experience of the archetype of the deity is that of a quaternity, the symbol of which is the mandala. Therefore, the evil, unjust, brutal, or dark side of God must be recognized as being as real as the goodness, love, and justice of God.

This experience of the deity as a quaternity is the result of a long psychic evolution that had not yet reached final fruition at the time of Job. According to Jung, the Book of Job recorded only one decisive stage in that process, which signaled that a "momentous change" was imminent.[52] That change was the "answer" to Job: the incarnation. Jung sees the incarnation as a "world-shaking transformation of God," for at this point the loving side of God came into consciousness.[53] In Christ, Yah-

weh identified "with his light aspect and becomes the good God and loving Father."[54] According to Jung, in the incarnation Yahweh caught up
with Job who had previously been his moral superior.[55]

Nevertheless, Jung argues that the incarnation cannot be considered
the ultimate experience of God because Christianity has not yet incorporated the dark side of the deity. Jung's vehement polemics against the
symbol of the Trinity, the concept of God as the *Summum Bonum,* and the
notion of evil as the *privatio boni* are all warnings against a dangerously
truncated experience of the God-archetype.[56] These traditional Christian doctrines all deny God's evil side and thereby prevent our psyche
from experiencing the wholeness that requires the presence of evil in
God. Jung would have insisted that our precritical commentators had
committed the error of conceiving God as the summum bonum, a view
that places evil outside the deity. We can imagine Jung's critique of
Calvin's argument for the inseparability of the divine attributes; by this
argument Calvin attributes the experience of injustice to the human
subject, either to the noetic fall or to sinfulness. For Jung, this attribu-
tion of evil to the human being is a failure to perceive the wholeness of
God as a conjunction of opposites.

Not surprisingly, the symbol of Satan becomes critical for Jung's argument. Satan proves, on the one hand, that evil cannot be imputed simply
to the human being because the biblical myth shows that humans did
not create the devil. On the other hand, the figure of Satan demonstrates that the evil side of God remained unincarnated and therefore
separate from the deity.[57] For Jung, the Book of Revelation illustrates
that the repressed image of the destructive God has yet to be assimilated
into Christianity. According to Jung, John also predicted the enantiodromian development of the Christian æon and the next stage of the incarnation, the age in which modernity now lives.[58] That era will be, in
effect, a second answer to Job; the dark side of God will be integrated
into a structure of wholeness.[59] The image of the Trinity will finally give
way to the image of quaternity or the mandala, and humanity will finally
experience the fullness of the deity.

In Jung's interpretation of Job we see, among other things, the rejection of traditional notions of transcendence and a turn to the world of
the psyche. The Book of Job is about the encounter with that vast and
psychic "hinterland," the collective unconscious. Throughout his career
Jung was criticized for rejecting the concept of transcendence. One of
his most important critics was Buber, who argued that Jung was not simply an interpreter of religion but the proclaimer of a new religion, "the
religion of pure psychic immanence."[60] Commenting on Jung's views,
Buber maintains that "if religion is a relation to psychic events, which
cannot mean anything other than to events of one's own soul, then it is

implied by this that it is not a relation to a Being or Reality which, no matter how fully it may from time to time descend to the human soul, always remains transcendent to it. More precisely, it is not the relation of an I to a Thou."[61] However, it is not quite fair to say that Jung sees religion as the relation to events of one's own soul; rather, religion is a relationship to those events that stem from the psychic level of being, which gives rise to the individual soul.[62] Understandably, Jung was asked repeatedly whether he believed in God. He replied that he regarded the "psyche as real."[63] When requested to expand on this statement, Jung explained:

An *archetype*—so far as we can establish it empirically—is an *image*. An image, as the very term denotes, is a picture of something. An archetypal image is like the portrait of an unknown man in a gallery. His name, his biography, his existence in general are unknown, but we assume nevertheless that the picture portrays a once living subject, a man who was real. We find numberless images of God, but we cannot produce the original. There is no doubt in my mind that there is an original behind our images, but it is inaccessible. We could not even be aware of the original since its translation into psychic terms is necessary in order to make it perceptible at all.[64]

Jung does reject the traditional notion of transcendence; God is not the One who stands over and against the individual. His search is for the archetype of the deity in the depths of the psyche, a depth that encompasses far more than the conscious self. Still, he does unite the archetype of the fourfold God with the experience of wholeness in the self. According to Jung, the mandala image always symbolizes to people something in themselves, something that belongs "intimately to themselves as a sort of creative background, a life-producing sun in the depths of the unconscious mind." It is a "systematic blindness," he argues, to conceive that "the deity is outside of man"; he speaks, therefore, of the "God within." He defines the self as the "totality of man, the sum total of conscious and unconscious existence."[65] As a "midpoint" between these psychic levels, the self might also be called the "god within."[66] Jung explains that the modern mandala contains no deity in the center, for "the place of the Deity seems to be taken by the wholeness of man."[67] Living in an era in which we have "withdrawn our projections" from the outside world, "everything of a divine or demonic character must return to the soul, to the inside of the unknown man." The experience of the mandala is "typical of people who cannot project the divine image any longer." The dweller in the mandala is now not a god but "rather an apparently most important part of the human personality."[68]

And yet the experience of wholeness or the reconciliation of light and dark, evil and good, male and female, has not yet been achieved by modernity—and it may never be achieved at all. This noetic and psychic failure on the part of human beings is catastrophic. As Jung writes in *The Answer to Job*, "Everything now depends on man."[69] Jung believes that the "uniting of [God's] antinomy must take place in man . . . for the dark God has slipped the atom bomb and chemical weapons into his hands. . . . Since he has been granted an almost godlike power, he can no longer remain blind and unconscious. He must know something of God's nature and metaphysical processes if he is to understand himself and thereby know God."[70]

Jung's treatises are filled with dire warnings about the spiritual crisis of the modern age. This involves the failure to achieve individuation and the alienation from the deepest psychic level of our being, the collective unconscious. We manifest a spiritual and perceptual crisis that signals our death. According to Jung's diagnosis, the psychic life of humanity can no longer be invested in what have become "obsolete forms of religion." As he argues in *Aion*, "the bridge from dogma to the inner experience of the individual has broken down. . . . Dogma no longer formulates anything, no longer expresses anything; it has become a tenet to be accepted in and for itself, with no basis in any experience that would demonstrate its truth."[71] For Jung, our rationality and modern secular consciousness are alienated from dogma as well as from the archetypal symbols in the "ocean" of our collective unconscious. Modernity has been cut off from the deepest level of being, and Jung warns that "when a living organism is cut off from its roots, it loses the connections with the foundations of its existence and must necessarily perish. When that happens, anamnesis of the origins is a matter of life and death."[72] From Jung we learn that the modern person is cast adrift. There is no transcendent revelation from which to gain insight into reality; projections have been withdrawn. Nor is modernity connected to its vast psychic unconscious, which nourishes its religious life and allows entrance into the depth dimension of reality. From Jung's analysis of the Joban story we learn that as a result of this spiritual crisis, the spiritually perceptual powers of the modern human being are threatened with atrophy.

Images of Job in Modern Literature

"Everything now depends on man." Without pursuing a Jungian analysis, we can detect that this turn toward the human subject is characteristic of modern literary interpretations of Job. This is not to deny that earlier interpretations of Job focused on the human subject. No one devoted more analysis to Job's spiritual and perceptual abilities than Gregory. Maimonides, Aquinas, and Calvin all discussed, in varying ways, Job's inner nature and the extent of his understanding. But for these precritical commentators, the turn to the self prompted by suffering was, in some way, to tap into the cosmos, or at least into the deeper levels of reality. The contemporary turn toward the subject is without revelation or transcendence: there is no "God" with regard to the self. Increasingly the responsibility for reaching a deeper understanding of reality is placed only on the person of Job. As the promise of an external revelation recedes, that reality becomes more and more unbearable.

Four works representative of contemporary treatments of the Joban story illustrate this subjective turn: H. G. Wells's *Undying Fire* (1919); Archibald MacLeish's *J. B.* (1958); Elie Wiesel's *Trial of God* (1979); and Franz Kafka's *Trial* (1914).[73] In all these stories, the concentration on the human subject has perceptual implications: The burden of understanding falls not on an external revelation but on Job himself. In fact, God is either conceived subjectively, is absent, or is totally inaccessible. Transcendence is clearly problematic. Moreover, several of the solutions to the story of Job found in our precritical commentaries reappear in these modern works only to be criticized or rejected. Traditional theological answers are clearly also troublesome. Consequently, the wisdom or insight achieved by Job becomes fleeting, fragile, or nonexistent. In these works we observe the ultimate collapse of human perception.

WE BEGIN WITH the works of Wells and MacLeish in order to demonstrate a certain parallel development: the narrowing of perception and the reliance on inner human resources. According to both authors, Job came to reject a morally ordered view of history in which virtue is always rewarded and sin always punished. In both stories Job saw the cosmos as cold and without purpose. Both Wells and MacLeish depict Job's heroism not as a confrontation with God but as a confrontation with meaninglessness. Both writers discover the answer to this chaotic and aimless world in an element within Job himself.

In *The Undying Fire*, the figure of Job is called Job Huss, a schoolmaster of an institution called Woldingston. Throughout his ordeal, he clings to his belief in reason and the power of education. After a series of disasters, his "friends" come to visit him. In the course of the ensuing conversation they discuss faith, God, and providence. Is there a purpose and justice evident in nature and history? According to Wells, Job never fully believed in the doctrine of moral retribution, although he did believe that the "God of Light" pervaded the cosmos. His undeserved suffering, however, opens his eyes to the true nature of the cosmos. Once again we encounter the appeal to an experientially based perception of reality:

I [Job] have been forced to revise my faith and to look more closely than I have ever done before into the meaning of my beliefs. . . . I have been wrenched away from that habitual confidence in the order of things which seemed the more natural state for a mind to be in. . . . I am thrown now into the darkest doubt and dismay; the universe seems harsh and black to me; whereas formerly I believed that at the core of it and universally pervading it was the will of a God of Light. . . . I have always denied, even when my faith was undimmed, that the God of Righteousness ruled this world in detail and entirely, giving us day to day our daily rewards and punishments. These gentlemen, on the contrary, do believe that. They say that God does rule the world traceably and directly, and that success is the measure of his approval and pain and suffering the fulfillment of unrighteousness.[74]

In this passage Wells sets up the same perceptual opposition between Job and his friends that was established by our precritical commentators. According to Job Huss, the friends believe that God rules the world "traceably and directly." Job's suffering, however, gives him a perceptual superiority that allows him to see clearly the real nature of history. Job Huss appeals to an experiential knowledge that cannot conform to the belief in a moral order. For Wells, Job's vision of the world was born of World War I. "Loneliness and littleness," says Huss, "harshness in the skies above and in the texture of all things. If so it is that things are, so we must see them. . . . Many men and women have lived and died happy in that illusion of security. But this war has torn away the veil of illusion from millions of men. . . . Mankind is coming of age. We can see life at last for what it is."[75]

"Mankind is coming of age" in an amoral universe. Job Huss looks "squarely at this world" and asks, "What is the true lot of life?" His realistic perception tells him that "life is a weak and inconsequent stirring amidst the dust of space and time, incapable of overcoming even its internal dissensions, doomed to phases of delusion . . . and at last to extinction." According to Huss, this is the "reality of life; this was no exceptional mood of things, but a revelation of things established. I had been blind and now I saw." Job's new perception of reality makes him ask if there is "the slightest justification for assuming that our conceptions of right and happiness are reflected anywhere in the outward universe?"[76]

In the midst of this "darkling sky of a frozen world,"[77] Wells deprives Huss of the traditional solutions that Gregory, Aquinas, and Calvin granted to Job. Once again, we find no affirmation of suffering; although affliction opens the eyes of Job Huss, there is no sense that the endurance of adversity serves a beneficial purpose. Suffering remains an unjust evil. The doctrine of personal immortality is explicitly rejected. *The Undying Fire* actually reverses the argument of Aquinas and Calvin. According to them, Job defended his belief in the afterlife against Eliphaz, Bildad, and Zophar. But according to Wells, Job's friends are the ones who argue for the personal immortality of the soul. Eliphaz, for example, takes on the argument that Aquinas and Calvin attributed to Job. Hence Eliphaz replies to Job Huss that history does not display a perfectly ordered justice; the afterlife, however, functions as a extension of history where order and justice are restored: "I admit that in this world nothing is rationalized, nothing is clearly just . . . the reason? Because this life is only the first page of the great book we have to read. . . . All this life is like waiting outside, in a place of some disorder, before being admitted to the wider reality, the larger sphere, where all cruelties, all these confusions, everything—will be explained, justified—and set right."[78] Wells's Job refuses to adopt such an answer. He will not hear of a God who is "just a means for getting away." Such a doctrine of immortality is merely a comfort "thrust now upon a suffering world."[79] Ultimately, however, that comfort fails. And because the traditional appeal to a life after death is no consolation, the perceptual horizon of this modern Job is limited to the temporal realm of existence. The depth dimension of reality assumed by our precritical commentators has been narrowed.

Nor is the revelation of nature any help to Job Huss. According to Wells, Job forcefully denies that creation gives evidence of any order or goodness in the world. Job Huss lives in a cold cosmos where humankind spins upon "a ball of rock and nickel steel"; where the sun and stars are "mere grains of matter scattered through a vastness that is otherwise utterly void." This is the world of evolution where life began as a "mere stir amidst the mud." But there is no "crescendo of evolution" here. Huss sees only "change and change, without plan and without heart."[80] Nature reveals no benevolence, wisdom, or justice. Contemplating the natural order, Wells's Job sees a world very different from that envisioned by Aquinas and Calvin. Huss's vision of creation is that of the commentaries by Habel and Good. Observing the world of nature, Huss says, "Suddenly it seemed to me that scales had fallen from my eyes and that I saw the whole world plain. It was as if the universe had put aside a mask it had hitherto worn, and shown me its face, and it was the face of boundless evil. . . . It was as if a power of darkness sat over me and watched me with a mocking gaze, . . . I could think of nothing but the feeble miseries of living things."[81]

Compared to the assumptions that informed our earlier commentaries, *The Undying Fire* presents us with an inverted world view. We find no defense of suffering. There is no personal immortality. Nature is brutish, cruel, and "without heart." Perhaps Wells's vision comes closest to that of Maimonides's "sea of chance," but the latter did not describe the universe in terms of "boundless evil." In the midst of cosmic meaninglessness, Wells's Job does not ascend but rebels. For Wells, the triumph of Job is not his wisdom and virtue gained through suffering, ascent, repentance, or faith. For Wells, Job is a rebel who stands defiant in the face of an aimless and dark universe.

Finally, however, in Job Huss's cries of rebellion we do catch a glimpse of something vaguely divine. In Wells's interpretation, Job does not receive an external revelation; he does not find faith in a justice he cannot see. Instead Job Huss looks inward and rebels in the name of the "undying fire" or "spirit of God in man."[82] By means of this element within the human soul Wells grants to Job a belief in impersonal and earthly immortality: "The immortal thing in us is the least personal thing. It is not you or I who go on living; it is Man that lives on, Man the Universal, and he goes on living, a tragic rebel in this same world and no other."[83] Within the human being there burns an "undying fire" that urges one to combat the cruelty and meaninglessness of the world. Wells conceives "God" subjectively; the divine is something that dwells in but is not identical with the human soul. Reflecting on that day when "the earth will be as dead frozen as the moon," Huss exclaims, "A spirit in our hearts, the God of mankind cries 'No!' but is there any voice outside us in all the cold and empty universe that echoes that 'No'?"[84]

Since the answer to this agonized question appears to be negative, Job Huss must turn to himself and oppose the chaos in the world around him. He fights in the name of reason or education, which he hopes will cast a "light" into this darkness. Only this undying fire can impose order and reason on a world of change, brutality, and confusion. Thus, in the name of education, Job cries, "I am the servant of a rebellious and adventurous God who may yet bring order into this cruel and frightful chaos in which we seem to be driven hither and thither like leaves before the wind."[85]

Job's hope is a subjective and fragile one. By means of the "undying fire," Huss fights against the cosmos. His cry for justice is not aimed against a transcendent God but rather against a meaningless universe. The answer to cosmic and human cruelty is not faith in the ultimate providence of God. It is found within the human heart, for "everything now depends on man." Nonetheless, this battle against chaos and absence of meaning is not guaranteed victory. Wells portrays Job as crying out against a vast darkness. He leaves the reader with the haunting fear that the darkness may win: "There is no reason anywhere, there is no creation anywhere, except the undying fire, the spirit of God in the hearts of men . . . which may fail . . . which may fail . . . which seems to me to fail."[86]

When we turn to MacLeish's *J. B.* we discover a world very similar to that of Job Huss, a world characterized by coldness, silence, cruelty, and emptiness. MacLeish also interprets the story of Job as a battle not against God but against meaninglessness. To portray the emptiness and

amorality of the modern world, MacLeish reverses the original arguments of Job and his friends. He portrays J. B. as clinging to his belief in
divine justice until scene 9, when Bildad, Zophar, and Eliphaz appear.
Until this point, however, it is J. B. who argues against his wife, Sarah,
that "God will not punish without cause" because "God is just."[87] Unlike
the biblical Job or the Job of our precritical commentaries, J. B. defends
the notion of retributive justice as long as he can, even to the extent of
confessing sins he did not commit. J. B. insists that "[God] knows the
guilt is mine. He must know: / Has He not punished it? He knows its
/ Name, its time, its face, its circumstance."[88]

Why does MacLeish invert Job's argument in this way? If we read
scene 8 carefully, we see that he places the notion of retributive suffering
in J. B.'s mouth as a last defense against total meaninglessness. J. B. begins to confront this horrifying alternative at the close of scene 8 when
he says, "We have no choice but to be guilty. God is unthinkable if we are
innocent."[89] Even more significant are his words to Sarah: "What I *can't*
bear is the blindness / Meaninglessness—the numb blow / Fallen in
the stumbling night."[90] In the exchange between J. B. and Sarah, it is the
latter who takes on the traditional defiance of the biblical Job. Sarah will
have none of J. B.'s guilt. Referring to her children she cries, "They
are / Dead and they were innocent: I will not / Let you sacrifice their
deaths / To make injustice justice and God good!"[91]

Most surprising of all, however, is MacLeish's portrayal of Job's comforters. Unlike all of our other interpreters, he does not present their
argument as a defense of divine justice. Instead he uses the friends to
mock the search for meaning and justice. In this way he deepens the
sense that the world is drifting before a silent God. Through Job's
friends, MacLeish expresses a disquieting argument: God does not care
about J. B. Human beings feel the need for sin and guilt in order to separate themselves from the universe and to see themselves as different
from the animals. J. B. says, "Guilt matters. Guilt must always matter. / Unless guilt matters the whole world is / Meaningless. God too is
nothing."[92] Zophar answers:

> If it were otherwise we could not bear it. . . .
> Without the fault, without the Fall,
> We're madmen: all of us are madmen . . .
> Without the Fall
> We're madmen all.
> We watch the stars
> that creep and crawl. . . .
> Bildad: Like dying flies
> Across the Wall
> Of night . . .

Eliphaz: and shriek . . .
           And that is all.
Zophar: Without the Fall.[93]

In MacLeish's interpretation, guilt is a human need; God has no interest in guilt or innocence. As Job's friends say: "Why should God reply
to *you* / From the blue depths of His Eternity? / Blind depths of His Un-
consciousness? / Blank depths of His Necessity? / God is far above in
Mystery. / God is far below in Mindlessness. / God is far within in History— / Why should God have time for you?"[94]

This feeling of God's utter remoteness and indifference was initially a
sign of despair for Maimonides's Job and a deadly temptation for
Calvin's Job. For J. B., however, this feeling becomes the final reality. In
the end J. B. has to give up his belief in divine justice: "Shall I repent of
sins I have not / Sinned to understand it? Till I / Die I will not violate my
integrity. . . . I cry out of wrong but I am not heard . . . / I cry aloud but
there is no judgment."[95] J. B. cries out to a world that is cold and meaningless, far from God, and uncaring for the human being. MacLeish depicts this vast and empty cosmos through visual descriptions of "eyes"
and "staring stars." At the beginning of the play Mr. Zuss (God) and Nickles (Satan) are reminiscing about the ancient Job. "Satan" remarks: "Job
was honest. He saw God— / Saw Him by that icy moonlight. / By that
cold disclosing eye / That stares the color out and strews / Our lives . . .
with light . . . for nothing."[96] Referring to the dangling light bulbs on the
stage, Nickles says: "Those stars that stare their stares at me— / Are those
the staring stars I see / Or only lights . . . not meant for me?"[97]

Images of "seeing" and "not seeing" as well as "staring stars" recur
throughout the play. Mr. Zuss says of God, "There is nothing those
closed eyes / have not known and seen." Nickles replies, however, that
Satan truly does *see:* "Those eyes *see* . . . / They see the *world*. They do.
They see it. / From going to and fro in the earth, / From walking up
and down, they see it. / I know what Hell is now—to *see*."[98]

In the world of J. B. the skies are made of "stone," God's eyes are
closed, the stars "stare," and only Satan really seems to see. But J. B. also
finally comes to see. His new perception, however, is not gained through
the revelation of the whirlwind speech. MacLeish finds the divine
speeches and Job's response distinctly unsatisfying. After God's "throwing the whole creation at him," Job repented. But why? Was his humility
sincere? Mr. Zuss thinks not: "You call that arrogant / Smiling, supercili-
ous humility / Giving in to God?"[99] And in a phrase Jung would surely
love, Mr Zuss says, "He'd heard of God and now he saw Him! / Who's
the judge in judgment there? / Who plays the hero, God or him? / Is
God to be *forgiven?*"[100]

When we examine J. B.'s "God" we can see why a meaningful external revelation is impossible. MacLeish makes both God and Satan laughable. Two "broken-down actors" play God and the devil. Throughout the play they speak from the "edge of the side-show stage" and provide a sardonic commentary on J. B.'s words and actions. But there is here no revelation or truth. In *J. B.* the element of divine transcendence is more thoroughly demoted and undermined than in *The Undying Fire.*

Whatever wisdom is to be gained from suffering, therefore, is left to J. B. We do find expression of the ancient insight that suffering leads to truth. But we quickly discover that this traditional belief is rejected. The words are uttered by Nickles (Satan), who says that Job must suffer

> To learn!
> Every human creature born
> is born into the bright delusion
> Beauty and loving-kindness care for him.
> Suffering teaches! Suffering's good for us!
> Imagine men and women dying
> Still believing that the cuddling arms
> Enclosed them! They would find the worms
> Peculiar nurses, wouldn't they? Wouldn't they?

This is the same reality encountered by Job Huss, who tears off this same "veil of illusion" and sees life for "what it is." For both MacLeish and Wells, suffering opens one's eyes only to the coldness of a universe without providence and without a transcendent God. In the end, this harsh reality is exactly what J. B. and Sarah learn:

> J. B.:   Curse God and die, you said to me.
> Sarah: Yes
>   You wanted justice didn't you
>   There isn't any. There's the world . . .
>   Cry for justice and the stars
>   Will stare until your eyes sting. Weep.
>   Enormous winds will thrash the water.
>   Cry in sleep for your lost children.
>   Snow will fall . . . Snow will fall . . .
> J. B.:   Why did you leave me alone?
> Sarah: I loved you
>   I couldn't help you any more.
>   You wanted justice and there was none—
>   Only love.
> J. B.:   He [God] does not love. He
>   IS.
> Sarah: But we do. That's the wonder. . . .
> J. B.:   Its too dark to see

Sarah: Then blow on the coal of my heart, my darling.
J. B.:   The coal of the heart.
Sarah: It's all the light now.
        Blow on the coal of the heart.
        The candles in churches are out
        The lights have gone out in the sky.
        Blow on the coal of the heart
        And we'll see by and by.[101]

Job Huss turns inward to the "undying fire" and rebels through reason against the cosmic chaos of the universe. So, too, J. B. and Sarah depend on themselves to find a response to the staring stars. In neither of
these works does "Job" call out to a transcendent deity. God is too subjective, nonexistent, absent, or trivial to be the object of Job's anger and
sorrow. In *The Undying Fire* and in *J. B.,* Job confronts not God but the
universe. Specifically, he opposes the meaninglessness of the world.[102]
The enemy, then, is not God's injustice but God's absence. These Joban
interpretations give literary expression to what Buber termed the
"Eclipse of God" or Sartre the "silence of the transcendent." This absence of transcendence places an enormous weight on the perceptual
powers of the human being. In these works one must either conceive
God subjectively or call on human resources to survive in a silent world.
For Wells and MacLeish, the answer is reason, education, or human
love. The interpretations of Wiesel and Kafka throw into full relief the
extreme fragility of the hopes of Job Huss and J. B.

IN THE WORKS of Wiesel and Kafka we find an even deeper immersion
in the perceptual implications of a meaningless world. Wiesel's *Trial of
God* and Kafka's *Trial* are not exact re-creations of the Book of Job; we
do not hear God and Satan talking in heaven, there is no whirlwind
speech, and the Epilogue is missing. Instead of the structure, both texts
dramatize the main theme of the Joban story. Wiesel's play depicts the
innocent sufferer who wants to call God to account for the persecutions
endured by the Jews. In this play Wiesel gives dramatic form to his earlier
essay "Job: Our Contemporary."[103] Both Wiesel and Kafka make God
the defendant, while "Job" refuses to submit.

Kafka never mentions Job by name, yet modern scholars have recognized that his books are an extended interpretation of the Book of Job.
Buber considered Kafka's work to be the most important Joban commentary of our time.[104] Frye sees the writings of Kafka as a "series of
commentaries on the Book of Job." He characterizes *The Trial* "as a kind
of 'Midrash' on the Book of Job."[105] In *The Trial* Kafka portrays the
search for justice and for the understanding of guilt by one who has
been accused of a mysterious and unknown crime. There is an impor-

tant reason behind Wiesel's and Kafka's choice not to restate explicitly the Joban scenario: Their main theme is the *absence* of God. These works achieve their effectiveness by implicitly exploring the Joban motif without the element of divine intervention. The Lord cannot talk to Satan in the Prologue or to Job in the whirlwind because the central reality is confrontation not with a transcendent (or a subjective) deity but rather with the silence and inaccessibility of God.

Wiesel sets his play in a "lost village" named Shamgorod in 1649, after a pogrom. Three Jewish minstrels (Mendel, Avremel, and Yankel) arrive at a tavern to perform a *Purimschpiel*. *The Trial of God*, then, is a play within a play as the *Purimschpiel* puts God on trial for the unjust suffering of the recent pogrom. The Joban figure is the innkeeper named Berish who, along with his daughter Hanna, survived the pogrom. Berish never adopts the attitude of the pious Job of the Prologue. Berish is a rebel who rejects God. At first he refuses to have anything to do with the minstrels or the holiday of Purim. He declares that he has "resigned from membership in God." Asked why he rejects God, Berish exclaims, "God sought me out and struck me down. So let Him stay away from me. His company is annoying me. He is unwelcome in my house. And in my life."[106]

But Berish cannot silence his anger at God. An old priest comes to the tavern to warn that yet another pogrom is imminent. The minstrels wonder why they should not beg God for mercy. Berish replies,

Because God is merciless, don't you know that? How long will you remain His blind slaves? I no longer rely on Him. I'd rather rely on the drunkenness of the priest. What is it? You don't like the way I speak? How do you expect me to speak, unless you want me to lie? God is God, and I am only an innkeeper. But He will not prevent me from letting my anger explode. He will not succeed in stifling my truth. . . . Yes I am boiling with anger. . . . To mention God's mercy in Shamgorod is an insult. Speak of His cruelty instead. . . . I would refuse to understand so as not to forgive Him.[107]

Finally Berish allows the *Purimschpiel* to take place. He demands, however, that the play be a *Din Toire*, a trial. Here we can see another example of how contemporary literature inverts the Joban motif. Berish does not ask for a trial to defend his innocence before God; he wants to put God on trial. He makes God the defendant, and he presses his case "against the master of the Universe!" Berish is determined to accuse "the *real* accused."[108] The minstrels agree to act as judges. The servant woman, Maria, will play "the people." Berish, of course, plays the prosecutor.

But a crucial problem remains. No one will consent to defend God. Accusing his companions of cowardice, Berish insists that, "I'll play without you. I'll yell for the truth all by myself! I'll howl words that have been howling inside me and through me! I'll tear off all the masks of Him whose face is hidden! With or without an attorney present, Your Honor, the trial will take place." Still, no one will "plead on behalf of the Almighty."[109] In this search for a defense attorney, Wiesel emphasizes the stark silence and absence of this God "whose face is hidden." In the world of Shamgorod, neither God nor his defenders will speak. Finally a stranger named Sam arrives who offers to defend God.

In Act III we can observe how traditional theological solutions are rejected, including some of those found in our precritical commentaries. The trial opens with Sam voicing a vindication of divine justice which reminds us of Calvin:

Mendel: Under the authority vested in us, I open this grave and solemn trial. We shall listen to the accusation and hear the defense. And we swear that justice shall be done.

Sam: Justice? Whose justice? Yours?

Berish: What kind of question is that? Justice is justice. Mine, yours, his: it's the same everywhere. Is there another?

Sam: There is that of God.

Berish: And it isn't mine? If that is so, then, with your permission—or without it—I reject it, and for good! I don't want a minor secondary justice, a poor man's justice. I want no part of a justice that escapes me, diminishes me and makes a mockery out of mine! Justice is here for men and women—I therefore want it to be human, or let Him keep it!

Sam: You want to reduce God's justice to yours? Why not elevate yours to His?[110]

Berish persists in his refusal to accept a "secondary justice." Sam then puts forth the argument that God is not the cause of evil. Human beings commit massacres: "Why involve, why implicate their Father in heaven?"[111] After all, Sam insists, God identifies with those who suffer and is to be found among the victims. Berish responds by appealing to divine power: "He could use His might to save the victims but He doesn't. So—on whose side is He? Could the killer kill without His blessing—without His complicity?"[112] Berish refuses to elevate suffering or to excuse God. In a speech that reverses Job's cry, "Yea though He slay me, I will hope in Him," Berish says, "Let Him crush me, I won't say Kaddish. Let Him kill me, let Him kill us all, I'll use my last energy to make my protest known. Whether I live or die, I submit to Him no longer."[113]

But Sam argues that one must humbly submit to the will of the Creator. In words that remind us once again of Calvin, Sam claims that "God is God, and His will is independent from ours—as is His reasoning." Maintaining that "God is just and His ways are just," Sam concludes: "I am His servant. He created the world and me without asking for my opinion; He may do with both whatever He wishes. Our task is to glorify Him, to praise Him, to love Him—in spite of ourselves."[114]

Sam's piety seems unshakable. The three judges are impressed with his reverence, faith, and love of God. They wonder who he is. Fearing the impending pogrom, Mendel asks, "Who are you, Stranger? A saint? A Penitent? A prophet in disguise? . . . You are a *tzaddik,* a Just, a Rabbi, a Master—you are endowed with mystical powers; you are a holy man. Do something to revoke the decree! If you cannot, who could? You are God's only defender. . . . Oh holy man, we beg you to save God's children from further shame and suffering."[115]

At the end they put on their Purim masks—and the perceptual theme takes a terrifying and evil twist. Sam's mask reveals his true identity so that the others finally *see* who it is that has so piously defended God: it is Satan. Sam [Satan] cries, "So—you took me for a saint, a Just? Me? How could you be that blind? How could you be that stupid?" Wiesel closes the play with the following, horrifying stage directions depicting the onset of the pogram:

Satan is laughing. He lifts his arm as if to give a signal. At that precise moment the last candle goes out, and the door opens, accompanied by deafening and murderous roars.[116]

Berish meets his death in a world abandoned by God. His is a universe where "the stars are soaked in blood," where "night is screaming and its screams become stars."[117] He experiences the same dread as Calvin's Job: the feeling that "God Himself is on the side of the enemy."[118] We are struck by how Sam or Satan expresses the arguments that were once defended by Calvin so many centuries earlier. Actually they are in large part the arguments of Elihu. In fact, the audience expects Sam to be Job's fourth companion. Wiesel may be using here a Talmudic tradition that relates Elihu and Satan.[119] In so doing he shows that traditional appeals to the will of God or to divine justice collapse before the reality of the Holocaust. In Wiesel's play God makes no answer, and Berish finds no solution. He gains no deeper insight into the justice or reason of God's action or lack of action in history. His suffering remains inexplicable and indefensible. There is no defense of suffering, no appeal to the afterlife, no hope in providence. Nor does the ability of human perception make up for the lack of a transcendent answer. We do not find any reliance on reason, education, or human love. In Wiesel's interpretation, human perception is deluded by the encounter with Satan. The silence of God is deafening as "Job's" story ends not with restoration but with death.

At least Berish has his faith. To the end he clings to his Jewish identity and cries to a God who does not answer. Refusing to escape the pogrom by feigning Christian conversion, he says, "I lived as a Jew and it is as a Jew that I shall die—And it is as a Jew that, with my last breath, I shall shout my protest to God! . . . I'll tell Him that He's more guilty than ever!"[120] When we turn to Kafka we find that in *The Trial* Kafka offers no such religious identity or tradition to which his hero can cling. We learn no more about the Joban figure than that he is Joseph K., an anonymous bank official. Like Wiesel, however, Kafka depicts a universe closed to revelation, insight, resolution, or divine intervention. In *The Trial* Kafka pushes the perceptual dilemma of Job's story to its unrelenting and catastrophic limit.

Kafka opens his novel with the following sentence: "Someone must have been spreading lies about Joseph K. for without having done anything wrong, he was arrested one morning." The Joban figure is arrested for an unidentified crime. Unlike the biblical Job, he does not immediately realize the seriousness of his situation; he tries not to take his arrest seriously and assumes that a mistake has been made.[121] Moreover, he feels total contempt for the Court with its bureaucracy, corruption, and "pettifogging lawyers." Nonetheless, as his trial wears on, his dealings with the Court become an all-consuming task. By chapter 7 Kafka tells us that "the thought of his case never left him now."[122] For the rest of his life K. tries to find out the nature of the crime of which he is accused. He continually defends his innocence. He seeks to confront the Judge, he fights for acquittal, and he endlessly works on his written defense. He finds, however, that at the higher stages of the judiciary process all written documents and pleas are not admitted as relevant: they have become "mere waste paper."[123] He passes through endless bureaucratic levels trying to gain access to the Court. He uses acquaintances, relatives, clerks, assistants, lower officials, and various women but never manages to penetrate beyond the lowest layers of this massive hierarchical judiciary. Finally, at the very end, he is executed without ever confessing to guilt or knowing the reason for his arrest.

In *The Trial* the two trends we have been examining are fully expressed: the incomprehensibility of the transcendent and the consequent narrowing of human perception. Kafka articulates the problem of transcendence in his portrayal of the Court. K.'s "God" is the unseen and inaccessible Judge who presumably stands at the head of a massive, incomprehensible, and impenetrable Court. Mann has characterized Kafka as a religious humorist who depicts the transcendent world "as an Austrian 'department'; as a magnification of a petty, obstinate, inaccessible, unaccountable bureaucracy; a mammoth establishment of documents and procedures, headed by some darkly responsible official hierarchy."[124]

The Court and its unseen Judge are portrayed from two conflicting perspectives. On the one hand, the Court is all-powerful, secret, and in a sense majestic. The Court makes a claim on K. and declares him guilty. It makes the arrest, carries on its secret proceedings, and executes the death sentence.[125] The climactic chapter of the book, "In the Cathedral," portrays the Law as a "light" or "radiance" that shines into the darkness of the everyday human world. On the other hand, the Court as seen from K.'s perspective is both ridiculous and tyrannical. With unfailing satirical humor Kafka points out the laughable elements of this colossal judiciary that takes control of one's life. The Court is located in dirty, cramped, unlit attics in buildings on the poorer side of town. During K.'s first interview with the minor officials of the Court, the proceedings are interrupted by the orgasmic shrieks of a couple in the back row.[126] Kafka relates the story of another accused man named Block who left his family and business to devote himself entirely to his trial. He moved into the lawyer's house and slept in the corner of a closet. The lawyer's method finally caused Block "to forget the whole world and have no hope but to drag himself along this illusory path until the very end of the case. The client ended up, therefore, not as a client but as the lawyer's dog. If the lawyer had ordered this man to crawl under the bed and beg as if in a kennel and bark there, he would have enjoyed doing it." All to no avail: in the end Block found out that his case had not actually *begun* yet.[127]

But Kafka's wit is gallows humor. His descriptions are indeed funny, but they are also infused with a sense of dread and unreality. Critics have noted that the whole "trial" may be a projection of K.'s mind, a paranoid fantasy, a delusory dream or nightmare. In the episode where he repeatedly sees two men being flogged in a lumber room, all sense of time seems to stop and the reader senses that the character "is looking into a concealed corner of his own mind."[128] As Robertson notes, however, "the argument that the Court is an emanation from K.'s mind should not be pressed too far . . . the terror of the Court seems rather to reside in its ambiguity, in its being both inside and outside K.'s mind."[129] *The Trial* is, above all, a *perceptual* novel, and in K.'s perception the Court stands outside, over, and against him. This judiciary is experienced both as ridiculous and increasingly as oppressive, menacing, and powerful. Above all else, the Court is *inaccessible* and is ominous precisely for this reason. From K.'s perspective his crime is unidentified because the legal records and charge sheets were not available to the accused or his lawyers. "The hierarchical structure of the Court was unending, parts of it were invisible even to the initiated. Proceedings in the Court were generally kept secret from the lower officials so that they could hardly ever follow up completely the subsequent course of the cases they were working on." At some point the case would take a turn where the lawyer could no longer follow it. "The case had simply reached a stage where no more help could be given, where it was being dealt with by courts that could not be reached and where even the defendant was no longer accessible to his lawyer."[130]

Kafka uses the idea of bureaucratic inaccessibility to portray the hiddenness and absence of God. He is not declaring the nonexistence of the Law or of God; he is describing a world where an unbridgeable chasm exists between the Absolute and the human being.[131] Twice he represents the remoteness of God through K.'s encounter with several paintings. In chapter 6, K. sees a portrait of a man whom he assumes to be a Judge. When he asks the man's rank, however, K. is told that he was an Examining Magistrate. "'Only an Examining Magistrate again,' said K., disappointed. 'The highest officials certainly hide away.'"[132] In chapter 7, K. sees another picture of a Judge. He is told that the portrait is of a man the painter has never seen. Now the Judge takes on the aspect of terror. The picture is actually "Justice and the goddess of Victory in one"; the Judge is not only remote and hidden but also frightening. Observing the picture of Justice, K. notes how "little by little this play of shadow surrounded the head like a piece of finery or a sign of high distinction. But the figure of Justice was left bright apart from an imperceptible tinge, and this brightness brought the figure into prominence so that it no longer recalled the goddess of Justice, nor the goddess of Victory, but now looked far more like the goddess of the Hunt."[133]

This is precisely the deity described in chapter 23 of the Book of Job—a God who cannot be found but who inspires terror and dread. This "goddess of the Hunt" recalls the fear experienced by Calvin's Job when he thought that God acted by an absolute and tyrannical power. Kafka's K. certainly feels the tyrannical nature of the Court's actions. He is convinced that behind his arrest and interrogation a great organization is at work, an organization that has an "indispensable and vast retinue of servants, clerks, police, and other assistants, perhaps even hangmen . . . and the significance of this great organization, gentlemen? It consists in securing the arrest of innocent persons."[134] In K.'s experience, this Court exercises a power that is cold, impersonal, distant, and inexorable. There is a sinister inevitability to the guilty verdict that will eventually be passed on K. An usher of the Court tells him, "But generally we don't institute proceedings unless they look promising."[135] K.'s uncle remarks that "having a case of that kind means having lost it already."[136] A painter, Titorelli, tells K. that he knows of no cases where the accused was found innocent, although there are distant legends about acquittals: "Certainly these legends do include instances of real acquittal, such legends are indeed even in the majority, they can be believed but they can't be proved." Finally, Titorelli informs K. that "it is never possible to budge the Court [from a conviction of guilt]."[137]

The question of K.'s guilt is the most frustrating aspect of the novel. Nowhere does Kafka explicitly define the charge and, to K.'s mind, the reason for his arrest remains maddeningly ambiguous. Certainly K. defends his innocence. He refuses to act like other accused men. Unlike the defendant Block, K. does not bark like a dog; he even fires his lawyer and takes his defense into his own hands.[138] He states at the beginning of his ordeal that he "cannot discover the slightest grounds for any accusation."[139] He insists that "it is the organization that is to blame. It is the high officials who are guilty."[140] K. hopes for "an absolute and final acquittal."[141] When asked by Titorelli whether he is innocent, K. answers, "I am completely innocent."[142]

Yet there are some indications that K. experiences a nagging feeling of guilt that he continually denies. He seeks reassurance from Frau Grubach that he is innocent and that his arrest is not very serious.[143] He is only too eager to apologize to Fräulein Bürstner for the imposition on her living quarters made by the Court officials who arrested him. And again he seeks reassurance that he is innocent or that at least he could not have committed a very serious crime.[144] When Titorelli begins to advise his defense on the basis of his complete innocence, he grows increasingly agitated.[145] At one point he sternly tells himself that "it was necessary that he should exclude from the very beginning any idea of possible guilt. There was no guilt."[146]

The most extensive discussion of guilt and innocence is found in the chapter "In the Cathedral," which corresponds to the whirlwind speech in the Book of Job. On a wet, murky, and dark day K. goes to the Cathedral intending to meet a bank client. He enters a sanctuary the size of which strikes him as bordering "on the very limits of what a human being could bear."[147] Instead of meeting his client, K. is confronted by a priest who tells him that his case is going badly: "I'm afraid it will end badly. You are considered to be guilty. Your case may not get beyond a lower Court at all. For the moment at least, your guilt is taken as proven."[148] To this K. answers, "But I am not guilty . . . it's a mistake. How can any man be [called] guilty? Surely we are all human beings here, one like the other." The priest replies, "That is true . . . but that's how the guilty talk."[149] When K. asserts that he is going to get more help, the priest warns him, "You search too much for outside help."[150] The implication, of course, is that he should turn to himself and recognize his own guilt.

At this point the priest tells K. the parable of the doorkeeper who stands as one of many doorkeepers before the countless doors leading to the interior of the Law. A man from the country comes seeking entrance to the Law. The doorkeeper says that he cannot admit the man at the present time. The man spends the rest of his life waiting to gain access to the Law. Just before he dies, as his eyes grow dim, he perceives "a radiance glowing from the door of the Law." The man asks the doorkeeper why no one else has come to this door seeking admittance to the Law. The doorkeeper answers: "No one could gain admittance through this door because this door was intended only for you. Now I am going to shut it."[151]

How could the man have gained entrance? Is K. a victim in need of external help, or is he guilty and in need of confession? The issue of K.'s guilt is a debated point in Kafka scholarship. For some critics, K. is a victim of a cruel and tyrannical power that hunts him down and kills him. The fact that Titorelli's painting makes the deity look like the "goddess of the Hunt" seems to lead inevitably to K.'s brutal execution. Moreover, K.'s alleged guilt seems totally incomprehensible from within the structure of the novel itself. Hence Politzer argues that "K.'s guilt may remain undecipherable as long as it is sought within the confines of the novel. . . . For within the parabolic framework of the novel K.'s guilt acquires a mysterious air of impenetrability."[152] According to Heller, "it is impossible to derive from the novel itself any exact notion of the 'lesson' or of K.'s guilt, and the meaning of *The Trial*."[153]

Other critics see evidence for K.'s guilt within the novel. Lasine argues that the first sentence of the novel reflects only K.'s own assumption that he has done nothing wrong. This is an important point since it shows that there is no external voice that objectively acquits K. in the way the Prologue does for the biblical Job. Furthermore, Lasine continues, K. contradicts the "oath of clearance" uttered by Job in chapter 31. K. was attracted to a married woman, raised his hand against poor children, and rejoiced at the idea of the enemy's ruin. Moreover, Titorelli's picture looked like the goddess of the Hunt *only* to K.; the novel itself does not identify Justice with "the Hunt." According to Lasine, K. adopts the "pose of victim" to evade his personal responsibility. For this, K. is held accountable by the Court and tried in very much the way that God tries the guilty in the Hebrew Bible.[154]

Robertson also finds that the novel itself confirms K.'s guilt. In this he explicitly defends the thesis originally put forth by Henel who argued that "Kafka sees the only path to the 'law' or the 'highest judge' in the acknowledgment of guilt."[155] For critics such as Henel, Lasine, and Robertson, K.'s guilt concerns the moral law and the failure of moral responsibility. At the outset of his ordeal, K. insists that he doesn't "know this Law." To this declaration the Court official replies, "He admits that he doesn't know the Law and at the same time he claims he is innocent."[156] K. is guilty not according to the civil law but under the moral law, a point symbolized by his first act after his arrest: eating an apple. According to Robertson, "K.'s ignorance of the moral law constitutes his guilt under this law." Therefore, K. is guilty because "his guilt consists in the belief that he is innocent." In Robertson's view, K. is too weak to confront his guilt; every time he has the opportunity to ask about the nature of the Court and the source of his guilt, he becomes faint and unable to breathe as if "he comes uncomfortably close to the truth."[157]

Perhaps the strongest condemnation of K. is that of Buber. Buber understands Kafka's "metaphysics of the door" in terms of guilt.[158] The doorkeeper of the Law opens the door only to one who makes a confession. Buber denounces K.'s categorical denial of guilt as "presumptuous words that are not proper to any human mouth." Hence he insists that "the thread that leads out of the labyrinth is not to be found in the book; rather this thread exists only when just that happens which did not happen, the 'confession of guilt.'" To support his analysis, Buber cites an entry from Kafka's notebooks, which he believes interprets the parable of the doorkeeper: "Confession of guilt, unconditional confession of guilt, door springing open, it appears in the interior of the house of the world whose turbid reflection lay behind walls." For Buber, "the confession is the door springing open."[159]

This brief review illustrates the very problematic nature of *The Trial*. No wonder that the "darkness" of Kafka's work "compels endless interpretation."[160] The crucial point is that the question of K.'s guilt turns the focus of the novel to the problem of perception. This problematic nature of K.'s guilt remains deliberately enigmatic because it is presented from two opposing perspectives.[161] If we read the novel as an interpretation of the Book of Job and recall the perspectival structure of the story, we can see how Kafka plays on the perceptual dilemma inherent in the biblical text. There are two perspectives in *The Trial:* that of the Court and that of K. From the perspective of the Court, K. is clearly guilty. As the arresting official tells K., the Law "is attracted by guilt."[162] Moreover, several characters in the story repeatedly express the viewpoint of the Court. Throughout, K. is told that only one thing can help him: a confession of guilt. At the beginning of his trial, the Inspector tells K: "And don't make such an outcry about your feeling innocent; it spoils the quite good impression you make in other respects."[163] K.'s mistress, Leni, implores him, "Don't be so inflexible from now on. There is no way you can defend yourself against this Court, you must admit your guilt. Make a full confession the first chance you get. Only then will you be able to escape from them and not until then."[164]

Nonetheless, K. insists on his innocence, maintaining that he is "completely innocent." And yet the text does, I think, support the conclusions of critics such as Henel, Robertson, and Lasine: Kafka presents a deeply flawed character whose central moral failure is his refusal or inability to take responsibility for his actions and to confront the essential truth of his guilt. Joseph K. is not the virtuous hero of the biblical Joban text. In fact, Kafka inverts the Joban story by making K. guilty but deluded. K.'s claim of innocence is based on the dangerous illusions of his own mind. Kafka deepens the perceptual dilemma of the Book of Job by emphasizing K.'s self-deception; K. engages in endless explanations and assertions of self-defense and self-justification. But he is not the voice of the innocent sufferer found in the laments of Job. Rather, K. is surrounding himself with illusory "motivations" that blind him to human sinfulness.[165] K. is not so much "presumptuous" as myopic. He cannot see himself; he cannot accept or fulfill "the invitation to discover himself in search of his guilt." His is an "aborted voyage" of self-discovery, a voyage that should lead to the confession of guilt.[166] If we assume that K. is guilty, the central theme of the book is self-delusion, the inability to see, and deception. K. is blind. K. speaks as all guilty men speak; by defending his illusory innocence he confirms his guilt. He never reaches the courage to know himself and accept responsibility. K. never repents "in dust and ashes." Therefore, K. never finds the insight, understanding, or perspective that would allow him an escape from his nightmare; not accidentally does *The Trial* bear the quality of a dream from which one cannot wake up.[167]

In total contrast to our precritical commentators, Kafka gives us a "Job" with no perceptual superiority. Where our earlier exegetes presented Job as gaining access to a larger reality, Kafka's K. finds neither self-knowledge nor insight into God, providence, immortality, or history. The novel is about self-blindness, not about sight. Kafka presents K. as refusing to turn inward, projecting all his guilt and all sources of evil as outside himself so that the external world becomes hostile and malevolent.[168] So too he turns outward for help, instead of facing the arduous and painful task of internal self-discovery. Hence the priest says to him, "You are looking too hard for outside help . . . especially from women. Don't you see that it isn't the kind of help you need?"[169]

The only true source of illumination is the light that streams out from under the door of the Law—but that illumination or self-knowledge is inaccessible to K. because of the iron grip of self-deception. Hence the priest shouts at K., "Can't you see two steps ahead of you?"[170] After K. fails to grasp the meaning of the parable of the doorkeeper the imagery of darkness invades the scene: The lamp has gone out, and K. cannot see his way out of the Cathedral. In fact, the imagery used throughout the novel illustrates K.'s inability to see—the failure to see himself, the Judge, the interior of the Law, or the reason for his situation. With the exception of the Cathedral, Kafka describes rooms that are overcrowded, dark, small, airless, and dim. Repeatedly K. goes up narrow winding stairways and through long passages. He squints because there is never enough light. He is always trying to get fresh air. K.'s world is truly closing in on him; this portrayal of the Joban story is set in a universe that is Escher-like, labyrinthine, and claustrophobic.

Kafka commentators have noted the gnostic character of *The Trial*.[171] The various doorkeepers and officials resemble the gnostic archons and planetary spheres the soul must overcome to reach God. K., however, cannot break the iron grip of these rulers; he has no secret knowledge or pass to continue on his journey. The realm of light is cut off from him forever. As Politzer says, we see in *The Trial* "the nihilistic turn the Gnostic vision has taken in Kafka's imagination."[172] Kafka turns Job into a gnostic myth, one in which there is no revelation, illumination, or liberation of the soul. Kafka presents the Court as a vast hierarchy, but this hierarchy is the opposite of the one in the *Moralia*. While for Gregory the idea of hierarchy was a means of ascent and illumination, for Kafka it is a sign of inaccessibility and blindness. The total inaccessibility of the transcendent results in the complete collapse or disintegration of human perception. K. is always wandering around infinite numbers of hallways and lobbies because he cannot ascend; there seems to be no exit from this nightmare. Because K. never attains to true self-knowledge or recognition of guilt, he cannot ascend; in *The Trial* there is no redemptive gnosis. With K. we find no salvific *Verwandlung*. K.'s failure demonstrates the character of the human situation in a gnostic world where the human being remains "ignorant" and God becomes inaccessible and, finally, silent. This silence is indicated by the priest's final words to K.: "The Court wants nothing from you. It receives you when you come and it dismisses you when you go."[173] K. refuses to find redemptive gnosis, and therefore he "dies like a dog." The Judge for whom K. allegedly searches never becomes visible, and consequently K. never finds understanding; his situation remains inscrutable to the end. Kafka describes the scene in which K. is executed by two men in a quarry. K.'s end signifies the complete absence of redemptive insight and the total opposite of Job's vindication:

Just like a light flashing on, the casements of a window suddenly flew open; a human figure, indistinct and tenuous at that distance and height, leaned abruptly forward and stretched both arms still farther. Who was it? A friend? A good man? Someone who cared? Someone who wanted to help? Was it one person only? Or was it all of mankind? Was help still possible? Were there arguments in his favor that had been overlooked? Of course there must be. Logic may indeed be unshakable, but it cannot withstand a man who is determined to live. Where was the Judge whom he had never seen? Where was the High Court, to which he had never penetrated?[174]

In this Joban interpretation the universe has become incomprehensible and meaningless. Kafka gives us a Book of Job where revelation is stifled. The revelation of the whirlwind speech never occurs because the "door" to the Law remains closed to K. Therefore, the transcendent element remains to the end inscrutable, inaccessible, and hidden. Kafka presents the Joban world as a perceptual nightmare. Unlike Wells and MacLeish, Kafka does not leave K. with the power of reason or the warmth of human love. Unlike Jung, he does not allow K. to "know more than Yahweh" or to delve into the vast human psyche to find the answers to the evil of human existence. And, of course, the solutions of the premodern Job are denied him. Gregory, Maimonides, Aquinas, and Calvin had all recognized the darker side of reality. Nonetheless, these thinkers found a way out for the sufferer—through the enlightening power of suffering, union with the Active Intellect, or belief in immortality or the external revelation of God. For these precritical exegetes the injustice and suffering of history were real but not ultimate. There was a depth dimension to reality, and human perception finally attained insight into that reality.

With Kafka insight is gone; perception has utterly failed. The Court dismisses K. and withdraws into its inscrutable and impenetrable silence.[175] The voice or view of the Judge recedes into silence. There is no depth dimension to reality, which becomes accessible to the human mind, and no transcendent deity to deliver one from a hopeless and inverted world. The confidence in perception that in various ways permeates our precritical commentaries has vanished. The fragility of the perceptual abilities offered by Wells, Jung, and MacLeish come to a crashing end in both Wiesel and Kafka.

In the contemporary treatments of Job we observe the gradual overturning of the "nobility of sight" that once dominated the Western metaphysical tradition. Hans Jonas, founder of gnostic studies, wrote a groundbreaking essay discussing the role of perception and the imagery of vision in Western thought. Jonas describes the priority attributed to a form of knowing patterned after the visual that presupposes an abstracted gaze, a distance between viewer and object. It was a world view that placed supreme confidence in the ability of the viewer to apprehend the object. Analyzing the priority given to the sense of sight, Jonas summarizes his findings:

We turn back to the beginning, the partiality of classical philosophy for one of the bodily senses. Our investigation has shown some grounds for this partiality in the virtues inherent in sight. We even found, in each of the three aspects under which we treated vision, the ground for some basic concept of philosophy. *Simultaneity of presentation* furnishes the idea of enduring present, the contrast between change and the unchanging, between time and eternity. *Dynamic neutralization* furnishes form as distinct from matter, essence as distinct from existence, and the difference of theory and practice. *Distance* furnishes the idea of infinity.[176]

Thus the mind has gone where vision pointed.

IN THE WORKS of modern Joban interpretation studied in this chapter, this partiality for metaphors of sight to express confidence in the power of perception has come to an end. Vision points nowhere. Confidence in sight has disappeared. In these modern literary readings, visual imagery is used rather to depict a claustrophobic, inscrutable, and impenetrable world, a world of darkness and confusion. Recalling the words of Clifford Geertz quoted at the beginning of this study, we are left in a universe where "reality threatens to go away unless we believe very hard in it." These modern Joban interpretations are further reflections of the twentieth-century preoccupation with the instability of human knowledge or the deeply felt ambiguity about human perception. These contemporary interpretations of Job are a part of the "infinite whirl" or "drift" that characterizes our age. Jung argued that insight and spiritual growth now "depended on man." If these literary works are any indication, the contemporary world has failed him. We are left with a view of Job's universe as cruel and meaningless—a view our earlier Joban commentators would have been unable to accept. Gone are appeals to the ascent through suffering, the union with the Active Intellect, the hope of personal immortality, and the faith that history is ruled by the same God who governs the beautiful order of creation. Job's world is now a world without justice, without revelation, without hope, and without understanding. It is a world, however, in which the twentieth-century Job still struggles to survive.

ABBREVIATIONS

CCSL	*Corpus Christianorum: Series Latina* (Turnhout: Brepols, 1954–)
CO	*Ioannis Calvini opera quae supersunt omnia,* ed. Wilhelm Baum, Edward Cunitz, and Edward Reuss, 59 vols., *Corpus Reformatorum* 29–87 (Brunswick: C. A. Schwetschke and Son, 1863–1900). The sermons on Job are in *CO* 33–35.
CSEL	*Corpus scriptorum ecclesiasticorum latinorum* (Vienna: Hoelder-Pichler-Tempsky, 1866–)
De interpellatione	Ambrose, *De interpellatione Iob et David,* in *Sancti Ambrosii Opera,* ed. Carolus Schenkl, *CSEL,* vol. 32.2 (1897), pp. 209–96
Expositio	Thomas Aquinas, *Expositio super Iob ad litteram,* in *Opera Omnia,* iussu Leonis XIII P.M. edita, cura et studio Fratrum Praedicatorum, vol. 26 (Rome, 1965)
Guide	Moses Maimonides, *The Guide of the Perplexed,* trans. Shlomo Pines (Chicago: University of Chicago Press, 1963)
HEz.	Gregory the Great, *Homiliae in Hiezechihelem Prophetam,* cura et studio Marcus Adriaen, *Corpus Christianorum: Series Latina* 142 (Turnhout: Brepols, 1971)
Inst.	John Calvin, *Institutio Christianae religionis,* in *Ioannis Calvini opera selecta,* vols. 3–5, ed. Peter Barth and Wilhelm Niesel (Munich: Chr. Kaiser, 1926–36)
Mor.	Gregory the Great, *Moralia in Iob,* cura et studio Marci Adriaen, *Corpus Christianorum: Series Latina* 143, 143A, 143B (Turnhout: Brepols, 1979–85)
PL	J.-P. Migne (ed.), *Patrologiae cursus completus: Series latina,* 221 vols. (Paris, 1841–64)
SC	*Sources chrétiennes* (Paris: Editions du Cerf, 1940–)
SCG	Thomas Aquinas, *Summa contra gentiles, Opera Omnia,* vols. 13–15 (Rome: Apud Sedem Commissionis Leoninae, 1918–30)
Sententia	Thomas Aquinas, *Sententia libri Ethicorum,* in *Opera Omnia,* iussu Leonis XIII P.M. edita, cura et studio Fratrum Praedicatorum, vol. 47, pts. 1–2 (2 vols.) (Rome, 1969)
ST	Thomas Aquinas, *Summa theologiae,* 60 vols. (New York: Blackfriars and McGraw-Hill, 1964–)

NOTES

Introduction

1. David Tracy, *The Analogical Imagination: Christian Theology and the Culture of Pluralism* (New York: Crossroad, 1989), pp. 159, 163.
2. Ibid., pp. 113, 154. Selections from and analysis of various interpretations of Job can also be found in Nahum Glatzer, *The Dimensions of Job: A Study and Selected Readings* (New York: Schocken Books, 1969).
3. Lawrence Besserman, *The Legend of Job in the Middle Ages* (Cambridge, Mass.: Harvard University Press, 1979).
4. Earlier writers who preached or commented on Job include figures such as St. Ambrose, St. Augustine, Julian of Eclanum, Origen, and St. John Chrysostom. As Robert Gillet points out, Gregory did not know Greek, and if he did know any of these works, he judged them to be of little value for his own exposition. See Robert Gillet, "Les sources des 'Morales,'" in *SC*, vol. 32 (1975), pp. 82–85. Jerome's interpretation of the names of the characters in the Job story in his *Liber de nominibus hebraicis* (*PL*, vol. 23 [1883], p. 838), was adopted by Gregory in *Mor.*, Praef., 16. Discussion of Chrysostom's commentary on Job can be found in the following: Ursula and Dieter Hagedorn, *Johannes Chrysostomos Kommentar zu Hiob* (Berlin: Walter de Gruyter, 1990), pp. xi–xiv; L. Dieu, "Le commentaire de S. Jean Chrysostome sur Job," *Revue d'histoire ecclésiastique* 13 (1912): 650–68; and John Chrysostom, *Commentaire sur Job*, introduction, critical texts, translation, and notes by Henri Sorlin with Louis Neyrand, S.J., *SC*, vols. 346 (1988) and 348 (1990). Although the literary tradition and exegetical chains indicated the existence of Chrysostom's Greek commentary on Job, Angiol Maria Bandini first explicitly called attention to it in 1762 in *Novelle letterarie di Firenze* 23:299–320. See also R. Devreesse, "Chaînes exégétiques grecques, Job," *Supplément au Dictionnaire de la Bible*, vol. 1 (1928): cols. 1140–45; and *SC*, vol. 346 (1988), pp. 9–74.

For a fuller list of Jewish and Christian commentaries on Job from the patristic era through the twentieth century, see David J.A. Clines, *Word Biblical Commentary, Job 1–20* (Dallas: Word Books, 1989), pp. lxi–cxv. This list should, however, be used with caution. For example, Martin Bucer did not write a commentary on Job. See also *Dictionnaire de spiritualité*, vol. 8, pp. 1218–25. A careful discussion of Gregory's predecessors who wrote on Job can be found in Gillet, "Les sources des 'Morales.'"

For the history of Jewish commentators on Job, see Nahum N. Glatzer, "The Book of Job and Its Interpreters," in *Biblical Motifs: Origins and Transformations*, ed. Alexander Altmann, Brandeis University Studies and Texts 3 (Cambridge, Mass.: Philip W. Lown Institute of Advanced Judaic Studies, 1966), pp. 197–220. A discussion of the role of Job's friends and wife in Haggadic and Arabic literature can be found in Hans-Peter Müller, *Hiob und seine Freunde: Traditionsgeschichtliches zum Verständnis des Hiobbuches*, Theologische Studien 103

(Zürich: EVZ-Verlag, 1970). Compare D. B. MacDonald, "Some External Evidence on the Original Form of the Legend of Job," *American Journal of Semitic Languages and Literature* 14 (1898): 137–64. For a discussion of the "patience of Job," see Bruce Zuckerman, *Job the Silent: A Study in Historical Counterpoint* (New York: Oxford University Press, 1991). For examples of the history of Joban interpretation with an emphasis on modern readings of Job, see Glatzer, *The Dimensions of Job*.

     5. Henri de Lubac, *Exégèse médiévale: Les quatre sens de l'Ecriture*, 4 vols. (Paris: Aubier, 1959–61), vol. 2, p. 38. For the views of Gregory and his influence in the patristic and medieval eras, see De Lubac, *Exégèse médiévale*, vol. 1, pp. 187–98; vol. 2, pp. 537–48, 586–99; vol. 3, pp. 53–98; H. Wasselynck, "La part des *Moralia in Iob* de saint Grégoire le Grand dans les Miscellanea victorins," *Mélanges de science religieuse* 10 (1953): 287–94; Wasselynck, "Les *Moralia in Iob* dans les ouvrages de morale du Haut Moyen Age latin," *Recherches de théologie ancienne et médiévale* 31 (1964): 5–13; Wasselynck, "L'influence de l'exégèse de saint Grégoire le Grand sur les commentaires bibliques médiévaux," *Recherches de théologie ancienne et médiévale* 32 (1965): 157–205; Wasselynck, "Présence de saint Grégoire le Grand dans les recueils canoniques (X–XIIe siècles)," *Mélanges de science religieuse* 22 (1965): 205–19; Wasselynck, "Les compilations des *Moralia in Iob* du VIIe au XIIe siècle," *Recherches de théologie ancienne et médiévale* 29 (1962): 5–32; Jean Leclercq, "The Exposition and Exegesis of Scripture: From Gregory to Saint Bernard," in *The Cambridge History of the Bible: The West from the Fathers to the Reformation*, ed. G.W.H. Lampe, 3 vols. (Cambridge: Cambridge University Press, 1976), vol. 1, pp. 183–97; Beryl Smalley, *The Study of the Bible in the Middle Ages* (Notre Dame, Ind.: University of Notre Dame Press, 1970), pp. 32–36. E. Ann Matter explains that Gregory's *Moralia* was often excerpted for florilegia and was circulated widely through three collections: the *Liber de expositione veteris et novi testamenti* of Gregory's chancellor Paterius (*PL*, vol. 79 [1862], pp. 685–916); the *Sententiarum* of Taio of Saragosa (*PL*, vol. 80 [1863], pp. 727–990); and the *Egloga de moralibus Iob* of the Irish monk Lathcen (ed. M. Adriaen, *CCSL*, vol. 145 [1969]). See E. Ann Matter, *The Voice of My Beloved: The Song of Songs in Western Medieval Christianity* (Philadelphia: University of Pennsylvania Press, 1990), pp. 8, 18 n.14.

     6. Carole Straw, *Gregory the Great: Perfection in Imperfection* (Berkeley: University of California Press, 1988), pp. 2–5; Jeffrey Richards, *Consul of God: The Life and Times of Gregory the Great* (Boston: Routledge and Kegan Paul, 1980); T. S. Brown, *Gentlemen and Officers* (London: British School at Rome, 1984); A.H.M. Jones, *The Later Roman Empire*, 2 vols. (Norman: University of Oklahoma Press, 1964). Compare Michel Rouche, "Grégoire le Grand face à la situation économique de son temps," in *Grégoire le Grand*, ed. Jacques Fontaine, Robert Gillet, and Stan Pellistrandi, Colloques internationaux du Centre National de la Recherche Scientifique, Chantilly, 15–19 September 1982 (Paris: CNRS, 1986), pp. 41–57.

     7. Brown, *Gentlemen and Officers*, pp. 8–20.

     8. *Mor.*, Ep. to Leander, 1. On Gregory's apocalypticism see also Claude Dagens, "La fin des temps et l'église selon saint Grégoire le Grand," *Recherches de science religieuse* 58 (1970): 273–88; Dagens, *Saint Grégoire le Grand: Culture et*

expérience chrétiennes (Paris: Etudes augustiniennes, 1977), pp. 345–430; René Wasselynck, "L'orientation eschatologique de la vie chrétienne d'après saint Grégoire le Grand," *Assemblées du Seigneur* 2 (1962): 66–80.

9. *Mor.*, Ep. to Leander, 5.

10. Mark Cohen, "Maimonides' Egypt," in *Moses Maimonides and His Time*, ed. Eric L. Ormsby (Washington, D.C.: Catholic University of America Press, 1989), p. 27. Norman Roth, however, argues that it is unlikely that the Almohads could have begun any serious practice of anti-Jewish measures in Spain much before 1163: Norman Roth, "The Jews in Spain," in *Moses Maimonides and His Time*, p. 20.

11. Cohen, "Maimonides' Egypt," pp. 21–34. For an account of the economic, political, and social history of the Jews in the Islamic Mediterranean from the eleventh through the thirteenth century, see S. D. Goitein, *A Mediterranean Society*, 5 vols. to date (Berkeley: University of California Press, 1967–88). See also E. Strauss, "Saladin and the Jews," *Hebrew Union College Annual* 27 (1956): 305–26.

12. Cohen, "Maimonides' Egypt," p. 32.

13. Ibid., p. 29.

14. Z. Diesendruck, "On the date of the Completion of the Moreh Nebukim," *Hebrew Union College Annual* 12–13 (1937–38): 496. Diesendruck argues that the *Guide* was completed by 1185.

15. James A. Weisheipl, O.P., *Friar Thomas d'Aquino: His Life, Thought, and Works* (Washington, D.C.: Catholic University of America Press, 1974), p. 368.

16. Ibid., p. 153.

17. Ibid.

18. On Calvin's preaching and the date of his sermons, see the following: W. de Greef, *Johannes Calvijn, zijn werk en geschriften* (Kampen: De Groot Goudriaan, 1989), pp. 101–8; Erwin Mülhaupt, *Die Predigt Calvins: Ihre Geschichte, ihre Form und ihre religiösen Grundgedanken*, Arbeiten zur Kirchengeschichte 18 (Berlin and Leipzig: Walter de Gruyter, 1931); Mülhaupt, "Calvins Auffassung von der Predigt," *Monatsschrift für Pastoraltheologie* (1930): 312–18; Karl Halaski, ed., *Der Prediger Johannes Calvin*, Beiträge und Nachrichten zur Ausgabe der Supplementa Calviniana, Nach Gottes Wort reformiert 17 (Neukirchen-Vluyn: Neukirchener Verlag des Erziehungsvereins, 1966), pp. 25–33; Paul Lobstein, *Etudes sur la pensée et l'oeuvre de Calvin* (Neuilly: Editions de "La Cause," 1927), pp. 15–49; Leroy Nixon, *John Calvin, Expository Preacher* (Grand Rapids, Mich.: Wm. B. Eerdmans, 1950); Rodolphe Peter, "Jean Calvin prédicateur," *Revue d'histoire et de philosophie religieuses* (1972): 111–17; Peter, "Rhétorique et prédication selon Calvin," *Revue d'histoire et de philosophie religieuses* (1975): 249–72; Richard Stauffer, *Dieu, la création et la providence dans la prédication de Calvin* (Bern: Peter Lang, 1978); Thomas Torrance, "Calvin's Sermons," *Scottish Journal of Theology* (1952): 424–27; T.H.L. Parker, *The Oracles of God: An Introduction to the Preaching of John Calvin* (London: Lutterworth Press, 1947). Parker has updated *The Oracles of God* in *Calvin's Preaching* (Louisville, Ky.: Westminster/John Knox Press, 1992). For his analysis of the date of the Job sermons, see pp. 163–71.

19. Alexandre Ganoczy, *The Young Calvin*, trans. David Foxgrover and Wade Provo (Philadelphia: Westminster Press, 1987). See also Heiko A. Oberman,

Initia Calvini: The Matrix of Calvin's Reformation (Amsterdam: Koninklijke Nederlandse Akademie van Wetenschappen, 1991), pp. 42–43.

20. For a history of sixteenth-century Geneva, see E. William Monter, *Calvin's Geneva* (New York: John Wiley and Sons, 1967).

21. *CO* 31:25–33.

22. *CO* 33:131; 34:271, 298, 319, 632, 635; 35:3, 204. On these issues see the brief discussion by Adelheid Hausen, *Hiob in der französischen Literatur: zur Rezeption eines alttestamentlichen Buches,* Europäische Hochschulschriften 13.17 (Bern: Peter Lang, 1972), pp. 68–69.

23. *CO* 33:256.

24. *CO* 33:672.

25. *CO* 35:719–20.

26. *CO* 33:611–12.

27. Ariste Viguié, "Les sermons de Calvin sur le livre de Job," *Bulletin de la Société de l'Histoire du Protestantisme Français* (1882): 471, 552. On Calvin's Job sermons see also Paul Lobstein, "Zu Calvins Predigten über das Buch Hiob," *Monatsschrift für Pastoraltheologie* (1909): 365–72; rpt. in *Etudes sur la pensée et l'oeuvre de Calvin,* pp. 51–67.

28. Viguié, "Les sermons de Calvin," pp. 471, 554.

29. Parker, *The Oracles of God,* p. 167; Parker, *Calvin's Preaching,* pp. 186, 190–91.

30. Robert N. Bellah et al., *Habits of the Heart* (New York: Harper and Row, 1985), p. 153.

31. Françoise Wendel, *Calvin: The Origins and Development of His Religious Thought,* trans. Philip Mairet (New York: Harper and Row, 1963), p. 19. Some of the literature is also reviewed in Heiko A. Oberman, *Initia Calvini,* pp. 10–19.

32. Wendel, *Calvin,* pp. 129, 228, 231.

33. Karl Reuter, *Das Grundverständnis der Theologie Calvins unter Einbeziehung ihrer geschichtlichen Abhängigkeiten,* Beiträge zur Geschichte und Lehre der Reformierten Kirche 15 (Neukirchen-Vluyn: Neukirchener Verlag des Erziehungsvereins, 1963).

34. T. F. Torrance, "Intuitive and Abstractive Knowledge from Duns Scotus to John Calvin," in *De doctrina Ioannis Duns Scoti,* Acta Congressus Scotistici Internationalis Oxonii et Edimburg, 11–17 Sept. 1966 celebrati cura Commissionis Scotisticae (Rome, 1968), pp. 291–305; Torrance, *The Hermeneutics of John Calvin* (Edinburgh: Scottish Academic Press, 1988), pp. 3–11, 72–95.

35. Hiltrud Stadtland-Neumann, *Evangelische Radikalismen in der Sicht Calvins: Sein Verständnis der Bergpredigt und der Aussendungsrede (Matt. 10),* Beiträge zur Geschichte und Lehre der Reformierten Kirche 24 (Neukirchen-Vluyn: Neukirchener Verlag des Erziehungsvereins, 1966).

36. Ganoczy, *The Young Calvin,* pp. 168–78.

37. Alister E. McGrath, *A Life of John Calvin* (Oxford: Oxford University Press, 1990), pp. 36–38.

38. *CO* 33:141, 559, 725; 34:261, 306, 464, 697, 707.

39. Nicholas of Lyra and Denis the Carthusian were two of the few medieval authors who were later collected by the library of the academy in Geneva: Alexandre Ganoczy, *La bibliothèque de l'Académie de Calvin,* Etudes de philologie et

d'histoire 13 (Geneva: Librairie Droz, 1969). Their inclusion in the library cannot, of course, be seen as evidence that Calvin used these authors, since the academy was not founded until 1559.

40. Heiko A. Oberman, *Initia Calvini*, p. 16. Oberman ends this passage by saying that "the traditional type of intellectual history is as treachorously reductionist as its twin brother 'Ahnenforschung' is racist. For this reason, intellectual history is badly in need of deconstruction, this time not to eliminate but to recover the authorial intention."

41. The phrase is from David Harlan. Although I find his conclusion unsatisfactory, his review and analysis of the problems posed to intellectual history are excellent: David Harlan, "Intellectual History and the Return of Literature," *American Historical Review* 94/3 (June 1989): 581–609. On this issue see also the essays by Dominick LaCapra, Martin Jay, and Hans Kellner in *Modern European Intellectual History: Reappraisals and New Perspectives*, ed. Dominick La Capra and Steven L. Kaplan (Ithaca: Cornell University Press, 1982), pp. 13–136. For a discussion of the new trends in historical research, see Peter Burke, ed., *New Perspectives on Historical Writing* (University Park: Pennsylvania State University Press, 1992).

42. Edwin M. Good, *In Turns of Tempest: A Reading of Job with a Translation* (Stanford: Stanford University Press, 1990), p. 177.

43. Peter Novick, *That Noble Dream: The "Objectivity Question" and the American Historical Profession* (Cambridge: Cambridge University Press, 1988), pp. 537–46.

44. Hans-Georg Gadamer, *Truth and Method*, 2nd rev. ed., trans. Joel Weinsheimer and Donald G. Marshall (New York: Crossroad, 1990), pp. 271–77. On current hermeneutical discussions see David Couzens Hoy, *The Critical Circle: Literature, History, and Philosophical Hermeneutics* (Berkeley: University of California Press, 1982).

45. Ibid., p. 300.

46. Ibid., pp. 300–307.

47. Ibid., p. 306.

48. Ibid. See also David Tracy's chapters in Robert M. Grant and David Tracy, *A Short History of the Interpretation of the Bible*, 2nd ed. (Philadelphia: Fortress, 1985), pp. 153–87.

49. Gadamer, *Truth and Method*, p. 296.

50. Paul Ricoeur, *Interpretation Theory: Discourse and the Surplus of Meaning* (Fort Worth: Texas Christian University Press, 1976), p. 92.

51. Paul Ricoeur, *Hermeneutics and the Human Sciences*, ed. and trans. with introd. by John B. Thompson (Cambridge: Cambridge University Press, 1981), pp. 146–47.

52. Jacques Derrida, "Structure, Sign, and Play in the Discourse of the Human Sciences," in *The Structuralist Controversy: The Languages of Criticism and the Sciences of Man*, ed. Richard Macksey and Eugenio Donato (Baltimore: Johns Hopkins University Press, 1972), pp. 247–65. In *Of Grammatology*, however, Derrida reminds his readers of the necessary function of the instruments of traditional criticism: Derrida, *Of Grammatology*, trans. Gayatri Chakravorty Spivak (Baltimore: Johns Hopkins University Press, 1976), p. 157; cited by Umberto Eco, *The Limits of Interpretation* (Bloomington: Indiana University Press, 1990),

pp. 37, 54. See also Roland Barthes, *S/Z* (New York: Noonday Press, 1970). For a critique of deconstructionism, see David Lehman, *Signs of the Times: Deconstruction and the Fall of Paul de Man* (New York: Poseidon Press, 1991).

53. Umberto Eco, *The Limits of Interpretation* (Bloomington: Indiana University Press, 1990), p. 34.

54. Ibid., p. 52.

55. On the attempt to defend authorial intention, see Harlan's analysis of Quentin Skinner and J.G.A. Pocock in "Intellectual History and the Return of Literature," pp. 583–87.

56. Clifford Geertz, "Anti-Anti-Relativism," *American Anthropologist* 86 (1984): 264; cited by Novick, *That Noble Dream*, p. 552.

57. Patricia O'Brien, "Michel Foucault's History of Culture," in *The New Cultural History*, ed. Lynn Hunt (Berkeley: University of California Press, 1989), p. 25.

58. Hayden White, *Tropics of Discourse: Essays in Cultural History* (Baltimore: Johns Hopkins University Press, 1978), p. 234.

59. On these issues see André Glücksmann, "Michel Foucault's nihilism," in *Michel Foucault, Philosopher* (New York: Routledge, 1992), pp. 336–49; Paul Veyne, "Foucault and going beyond (or the fulfilment of) nihilism," in *Michel Foucault, Philosopher*, pp. 343–45; Ian Hacking, "The Archeology of Foucault," in *Foucault: A Critical Reader*, ed. David Couzens Hoy (Oxford: Basil Blackwell, 1986), pp. 27–40; Richard Rorty, "Foucault and Epistemology," in *Foucault: A Critical Reader*, pp. 41–50; Hayden White, *The Content of the Form* (Baltimore: Johns Hopkins University Press, 1987), p. 105.

60. White, *The Content of the Form*, p. 134.

61. Ibid., p. 114.

62. Ibid., p. 104; Rorty, "Foucault and Epistemology," pp. 43–47.

63. White, *Tropics of Discourse*, p. 233.

64. Michel Foucault, *The Archeology of Knowledge*, trans. A.M. Sheridan Smith (New York: Pantheon Books, 1972), p. 55.

65. Rorty, "Foucault and Epistemology," p. 45. On the epistemological implications of the "linguistic turn" on history, see John E. Toews, "Intellectual History after the Linguistic Turn: The Autonomy of Meaning and the Irreducibility of Experience," *American Historical Review* 92 (October 1987): 879–906. Reviewing *The Return of Grand Theory in the Human Sciences*, ed. Quentin Skinner (Cambridge: Cambridge University Press, 1985), Toews summarizes the "overall cultural point" of theorists such as Derrida, Gadamer, Foucault, and Habermas: "If we take them seriously, we must recognize that we have no access, even potentially, to an unmediated world of objective things and processes that might serve as the ground and limit of our claims to knowledge of nature or to any transhistorical or transcendent subjectivity that might ground our interpretation of meaning. Knowledge and meaning are not discoveries but constructions" (pp. 901–2).

66. Toews, "Intellectual History after the Linguistic Turn."

67. Foucault, *The Archeology of Knowledge*, p. 203. See also David Couzens Hoy, "Taking History Seriously: Foucault, Gadamer, Habermas," *Union Seminary Quarterly Review* 34 (1978): 85–95.

68. White, *Tropics of Discourse,* p. 81.

69. Ibid., pp. 1–134; Hayden White, *Metahistory: The Historical Imagination in Nineteenth-Century Europe* (Baltimore: Johns Hopkins University Press, 1973).

70. White, *Tropics of Discourse,* p. 127.

71. Ibid., pp. 72–76; White, *Metahistory,* pp. 1–264, 281–425.

72. White, *Tropics of Discourse,* p. 83.

73. Ibid., pp. 88, 128.

74. Ibid., p. 129.

75. Ibid.

76. Ibid., p. 117. On the question of relativism and perspectivism, see Lloyd S. Kramer, "Literature, Criticism, and Historical Imagination: The Literary Challenge of Hayden White and Dominick LaCapra," in *The New Cultural History,* ed. Hunt, pp. 118–28.

77. White, *Tropics of Discourse,* p. 117.

78. Ibid., p. 23.

79. Dominick LaCapra, *Rethinking Intellectual History: Texts, Contexts, and Languages* (Ithaca: Cornell University Press, 1983), pp. 23–71. On the comparison between White and LaCapra, see Kramer, "Literature, Criticism, and Historical Imagination," pp. 97–128.

80. LaCapra, *Rethinking Intellectual History,* pp. 38, 45.

81. White, *Metahistory,* p. 37.

82. LaCapra, *Rethinking Intellectual History,* pp. 34–35.

83. Ibid., pp. 60–69.

84. Gadamer, *Truth and Method,* p. 296.

85. LaCapra, *Rethinking Intellectual History,* p. 46.

86. Eco, *The Limits of Interpretation,* pp. 57–63. Denying that deconstructionism really points to infinite meanings, Eco notes (p. 60) that "no responsible deconstructionist has ever challenged such a position." Quoting J. Hillis Miller, Eco writes, "It is not true that . . . all readings are equally valid. Some readings are certainly wrong. . . . To reveal one aspect of a work of an author often means ignoring or shading other aspects. . . . Some approaches reach more deeply into the structure of the text than others."

87. David C. Steinmetz, *Luther in Context* (Bloomington: Indiana University Press, 1986), pp. 43–44.

88. On the inherently perspectival character of the Joban text, see Stuart Lasine, "Bird's-Eye and Worm's-Eye Views of Justice in the Book of Job," *Journal for the Study of the Old Testament* 42 (October 1988): 29–53.

89. On the denigration of sight in contemporary thought, see Martin Jay, "In the Empire of the Gaze: Foucault and the Denigration of Vision in Twentieth-Century French Thought," in *Foucault: A Critical Reader,* pp. 175–204.

1. Where Is the Place of Understanding?

1. F. Holmes Dudden, *Gregory the Great: His Place in History and Thought,* 2 vols. (London: Longmans, Green, and Co., 1905), vol. 2, p. 288.

2. Cuthbert Butler, *Benedictine Monachism,* 2nd ed. (London: Longmans, Green, and Co., 1919), p. 113.

200 NOTES TO PAGES 22–24

3. Smalley, *The Study of the Bible in the Middle Ages*, p. 34.

4. *Mor.*, Ep. to Leander, 2. The authoritative critical edition of Gregory's work is: St. Gregory the Great, *Moralia in Iob*, ed. Marcus Adriaen, *CCSL*, vols. 143, 143A, 143B (1979–85). Other, less critical editions include: *PL*, vol. 75 (1862), pp. 509–1162; and *PL*, vol. 76 (1878), pp. 9–782. A French translation based on the latter text and notes can be found in *SC*, vol. 32 (1975; books 1–2, ed. and introd. Robert Gillet, O.S.B., and trans. Dom André de Gaudemaris, O.S.B); *SC*, vol. 212 (1974) (books 11–14, ed., introd., trans., and notes by Aristide Bocognano); *SC*, vol. 221 (1975) (books 15–16, ed., introd., trans., and notes by Aristide Bocognano). See also the edition published in *Library of the Church Fathers* (Oxford: John Henry Parker, 1844–60). I have cited the *Moralia* by book, section, and paragraph numbers. References to the preface and the Epistle to Leander are cited by paragraph number only.

We should, perhaps, also take note of the Latin text of Job used by Gregory. In *Mor.*, Ep. to Leander, 5, Gregory explains that he is expounding the "new translation" (by Jerome) but that, on occasion, he consults both the new and the old translations for further testimony or proof. Pierre Salmon concludes, "Malgré son caractère éclectique, le texte de Job contenu dans les *Moralia* est un bon témoin de la Vulgate, qui a besoin seulement d'être contrôlé par les autres pour la dégager de ce qui proviendrait d'une source étrangère" (Pierre Salmon, O.S.B., "Le texte de Job utilisé par S. Grégoire dans les 'Moralia'," in *Studia Anselmiana*, Miscellanea Biblica et Orientalia 27–28 (1951), pp. 187–94. See also *CCSL*, vol. 143 (1979), pp. vi–vii. A more recent study of the diverse versions of the Bible used by Gregory is that by Jean Gribomont, "Le texte biblique de Grégoire," in *Grégoire le Grand*, ed. Fontaine, Gillet, and Pellistrandi, pp. 467–75.

5. Pierre Courcelle, *Les Confessions de saint Augustin dans la tradition littéraire: Antécédents et postérité* (Paris: Études Augustiniennes, 1963), pp. 225–34; Dagens, *Saint Grégoire le Grand*, pp. 170–76, 212–21; Gillet, "Les sources des 'Morales'," *SC*, vol. 32 (1975), pp. 86–88; Carole Straw, *Gregory the Great* (Berkeley: University of California Press, 1988), pp. 9–10, 13–14.

6. *Mor.* 16.37.45. See also *Mor.* 4.28.55, 4.32.65, 5.34.63, 9.47.72, 16.43.54–55, 18.50.82; Dagens, *Saint Grégoire le Grand*, pp. 201–5; Michael Frickel, O.S.B., *Deus totus ubique simul: Untersuchungen zur allgemeinen Gottgegenwart im Rahmen der Gotteslehre Gregors des Grossen*, Freiburger theologische Studien 69 (Freiburg im Breisgau: Herder, 1956), pp. 28–44. On the background of the concept of the hierarchy of reality, see A. H. Armstrong, *The Architecture of the Intelligible Universe* (Cambridge: Cambridge University Press, 1940); Arthur O. Lovejoy, *The Great Chain of Being: A Study in the History of an Idea* (Cambridge, Mass.: Harvard University Press, 1936, 1961); Bernard McGinn, *The Golden Chain: A Study in the Theological Anthropology of Isaac of Stella* (Washington, D.C.: Consortium Press, 1972), pp. 53–54, 61–102. For further bibliography and for a thorough discussion of this concept in later thinkers, see Edward P. Mahoney, "Metaphysical Foundations of the Hierarchy of Being according to Some Late-Medieval and Renaissance Philosophers," in *Philosophies of Existence, Ancient and Medieval*, ed. Parvis Morewedge (New York: Fordham University Press, 1982), pp. 165–257; and Marion Leathers Kuntz and Paul Grimley Kuntz (eds.), *Jacob's Ladder and*

the Tree of Life: Concepts of Hierarchy and the Great Chain of Being, American University Studies 5, 14 (New York: Peter Lang Publishing, 1987).

7. Straw, *Gregory the Great,* p. 30.

8. Dagens, *Saint Grégoire le Grand,* pp. 173–201; Paul Aubin, S.J., "Intériorité et extériorité dans les *Moralia in Job* de saint Grégoire le Grand," *Recherches de science religieuse* 62/1 (1974): 117–66. See also Pierre Courcelle, "'Habitare secum,' selon Perse et selon Grégoire le Grand," *Revue des études anciennes* 69 (1967): 266–79.

9. *Mor.* 5.11.20; 7.35.53; 13.13.25, 29; 23.20.37–38; 25.7.18; 26.13.20; 31.12.18–19. Dagens, *Saint Grégoire le Grand,* pp. 165–204.

10. On Gregory's understanding of contemplation see: A. Ménager, "La contemplation d'après Saint Grégoire le Grand," *Vie spirituelle* 9 (1923): 242–82; Ménager, "Les divers sens du mot 'contemplatio' chez saint Grégoire le Grand," *Vie spirituelle,* suppl. 59 (1939): 145–69, and suppl. 60 (1939): 39–56; Franz Lieblang, *Grundfragen der mystischen Theologie nach Gregors des Grossen Moralia und Ezechielhomilien,* Freiburger theologische Studien 37 (Freiburg im Breisgau: Herder, 1934); Cuthbert Butler, *Western Mysticism,* 2nd ed. (London: Constable, 1922) (and for an evaluation of Butler, see Courcelle, *Les Confessions de saint Augustin,* pp. 226–27); Grover A. Zinn, Jr. "Silence, Sound, and Word in the Spirituality of Gregory the Great," in *Grégoire le Grand,* ed. Fontaine, Gillet, and Pellistrandi, pp. 367–75; Straw, *Gregory the Great,* pp. 225–34. See also Patrick Catry, "Désir et amour de Dieu chez saint Grégoire le Grand," *Recherches augustiniennes* 10 (1975): 269–303; Dagens, *Saint Grégoire le Grand,* pp. 211–15.

11. *Mor.,* Praef., 13; 1.25.34; 9.31.47; 23.1.2; 32.15.25. As did Augustine, Gregory uses water imagery extensively to depict the mutability of historical existence: *Mor.,* Ep. to Leander, 1; 6.36.57; 18.43.68; 28.18.39.

12. *Mor.* 25.3.4; compare 8.10.19. See also Lieblang, *Grundfragen der mystischen Theologie nach Gregors des Grossen Moralia und Ezechielhomilien,* pp. 29–43.

13. See also Patrick Catry, "Lire l'Ecriture selon saint Grégoire le Grand," *Collectanea cisterciensia* 34 (1972): 177–201.

14. *Mor.,* Ep. to Leander, 3. On ancient theories regarding inspiration and the "spiritual" exegesis of the biblical text, see Robert M. Grant, *The Letter and the Spirit* (London: SPCK, 1957). See also Dagens, *Saint Grégoire le Grand,* pp. 55–64, 233–44; Dudden, *Gregory the Great,* pp. 304–7. For an analysis of Gregory's contribution to the "fourfold" sense of Scripture, see de Lubac, *Exégèse médiévale,* vol. 1, pt. 1, pp. 187–90. The classic fourfold division included, of course, history, allegory, tropology, and anagogy. De Lubac argues that while Gregory usually expounds only the first three senses, he sometimes includes in the moral sense what came to be called the "anagogical" sense. In *Mor.* 16.19.24 he distinguishes a contemplative sense from the moral sense, and in *HEz.* 1.2.9 he explicitly refers to four senses. For Gregory this "fourth sense" is that which lifts the soul in contemplation to things on high. De Lubac concludes that Gregory was one of the principal initiators of the medieval doctrine of the fourfold sense (p. 189). Smalley, however, states that Gregory's "typical" (or allegorical) sense included both Cassien's allegorical and anagogical senses, "that is, the finding of types of the church past and present, and of the Last Things" (Smalley, *The Study of the Bible in the Middle Ages,* p. 34). One's definition of the anagogi-

cal sense determines where one finds it in Gregory. If it refers to a contempla-tive-mystical sense, then Gregory does occasionally place it after the moral sense, although often not explicitly. If it refers to future predictions about the church, then it is located in the allegorical or "typical" sense.

15. On Gregory's exegesis see: de Lubac, *Exégèse médiévale*, vol. 2, pp. 537–48; Dagens, *Saint Grégoire le Grand*, pp. 38–82, 233–44; G. R. Evans, *The Thought of Gregory the Great* (Cambridge: Cambridge University Press, 1986), pp. 87–96; Smalley, *The Study of the Bible in the Middle Ages*, pp. 32–35; Jean Leclercq, "From Gregory the Great to St. Bernard," in *The Cambridge History of the Bible* (Cambridge: Cambridge University Press, 1969), vol. 2, pp. 183–87; Judith McClure, "Gregory the Great: Exegesis and Audience" (diss., Oxford University, 1978); Catry, "Lire l'Ecriture selon saint Grégoire le Grand," pp. 177–201.

16. *Mor.*, Ep. to Leander, 2–4; 18.18.24; 20.1.1. See also Catry, "Lire l'Ecri-ture selon saint Grégoire le Grand," pp. 185–86; Catry, "Amour du monde et amour de Dieu chez saint Grégoire le Grand," *Studia monastica* 15 (1973): 256–59; Dagens, *Saint Grégoire le Grand*, pp. 40–45, 165–98, 233–44. As Maureen Quilligan has demonstrated, this "vertical conceptualization of allegory" is mis-leading if applied indiscriminately to every type of allegorical work. These meta-phors of hierarchy and depth derived from the imposition of allegorical exege-sis on texts that were originally nonallegorical, such as Homer and the Bible. "Actual" or "narrative" allegories, such as *Piers Plowman, The Faerie Queene,* and *The Pilgrim's Progress,* employ an allegorical process quite different from the glossing of biblical texts. Citing Northrop Frye in his *Anatomy of Criticism*, Quil-ligan explains the error of confusing the two types of allegory:

> The second and more important thing we must realize before we can become inured to the charm of this traditional definition [i.e., of think-ing of allegory in terms of a "vertically organized spatial hierarchy"] is that this whole conception of allegory—derived from the process of im-posing it on nonallegorical texts—was then applied whole to the actual allegorical narratives, that is, to those poems taking place in a special-ized, often dreamlike landscape peopled by personified abstractions. The theory of literary composition assumed in *allegoresis* was predicated of both kinds of allegories—for "imposed" and for "actual" allegories. Yet poets, we must be ready to remember, may do something quite dif-ferent from critics, and the poetic use of personification to mirror an extrasensuous world implies a process quite different from glossing bib-lical passages or moralizing Ovid, if only because *allegoresis* assumes that meaning is not manifest and must be dug for, while personification manifests the meaning as clearly as possible by naming the actor with the concept. Allegories do not need *allegoresis* because the commentary, as Frye has noted, is already indicated by the text. (Maureen Quilligan, *The Language of Allegory, Defining the Genre* [Ithaca: Cornell University Press, 1979], p. 31)

See also ibid., pp. 224–25. Other major works on "actual" or "narrative" al-legory include: Gay Clifford, *The Transformation of Allegory* (London: Routledge and Kegan Paul, 1974); Angus Fletcher, *Allegory: The Theory of a Symbolic Mode*

(Ithaca: Cornell University Press, 1964); Edwin Honig, *Dark Conceit: The Making of Allegory* (Oxford: Oxford University Press, 1966); C. S. Lewis, *The Allegory of Love* (London: Oxford University Press, 1936); Michael Murrin, *The Veil of Allegory* (Chicago: University of Chicago Press, 1969); Murrin, *The Allegorical Epic* (Chicago: University of Chicago Press, 1980).

17. *Mor.* 20.1.1.

18. Dagens, *Saint Grégoire le Grand,* p. 220, and pp. 203–44, especially 216–20, 233–40; Aubin, "Intériorité et extériorité dans les *Moralia in Job* de saint Grégoire le Grand," p. 134; Catry, "Lire l'Ecriture selon Saint Grégoire le Grand," pp. 185–87.

19. See Dagens, *Saint Grégoire le Grand,* pp. 165–98. Dagens distinguishes between Augustine's "metaphysic of interiority" and the moral emphasis found in Gregory (p. 182).

20. *Mor.* 5.5.8.

21. *Mor.* 35.4.5. Gregory is commenting on Job's confession (42:5), "I have heard Thee by the hearing of the ear, but now my eye sees Thee."

22. Straw, *Gregory the Great,* p. 237.

23. Ibid., pp. 236–60; Carole Straw, "Adversitas et Prosperitas: Une illustration du motif structurel de la complémentarité," in *Grégoire le Grand,* ed. Fontaine, Gillet, and Pellistrandi, pp. 277–88.

24. Gregory, of course, was not the first thinker to analyze the beneficial nature of suffering. Biblical, Greek, and early Christian thought reflects, in differing ways, the recognition that adversity is profitable to the human soul. Early Christians such as Cyprian usually explored the importance of suffering, endurance, and patience within the wider context of martyrdom (Cyprian, *De bono patientiae,* ed. C. Moreschini, *CCSL,* vol. 3A [1976], p. 120). The salutary character of suffering, however, also found expression in other contexts. Perhaps the most articulate spokesperson for the medicinal and pedagogical purposes of suffering in early Christianity is John Chrysostom. For a thorough analysis of his views, examined against the background of Stoic and Jewish thinking, consult Edward Nowak, *Le chrétien devant la souffrance: Etude sur la pensée de Jean Chrysostome,* Théologie historique 19 (Paris: Éditions Beauchesne, 1972). See also Jean Coste, "Notion grecque et notion biblique de la 'souffrance éducatrice'," *Recherches de science religieuse* 43 (1955): 481–523; M. Spanneut, "Le stoïcisme dans l'histoire de la patience chrétienne," *Mélanges de science religieuse* 39 (1982): 101–30; Étienne Borne, "Sens et non-sens de la souffrance," *La vie intellectuelle* 27 (April 1956): 5–16. Compare Borne, *Le problème du mal,* 4th ed., Initiation philosophique 33 (Paris: Presses Universitaires de France, 1967). For an overview of the problem of suffering and religion, see John Bowker, *Problems of Suffering in Religions of the World* (Cambridge: Cambridge University Press, 1980).

On Gregory's understanding of suffering, see also Patrick Catry, "Epreuves du juste et mystère de Dieu: Le commentaire littéral du Livre de Job par saint Grégoire le Grand," *Revue des études augustiniennes* 18/1–2 (1972): 124–44. In the following analysis I do not pretend to examine fully Gregory's various views of suffering. I limit myself to the assumptions that exegetically structure the *Moralia.* For a much more thorough discussion of Gregory's understanding of suffering and penitence, see Straw, *Gregory the Great.*

25. Straw, *Gregory the Great,* pp. 236–56.

26. *Mor.,* Praef., 6.

27. On Gregory's understanding of patience, see Straw, *Gregory the Great,* pp. 199, 221, and passim. Straw is quite right to point out (p. 199 n.28) that the distinction Spanneut makes between Stoics who seek autarchy through the conquest of suffering and the biblical traditions that attempt to "enlarge the soul" through suffering does not hold for Gregory; for Gregory, "suffering is both an opportunity for gaining self mastery and of improving the soul." Compare Spanneut, "Le stoïcisme dans l'histoire de la patience chrétienne," pp. 101–5.

28. *Mor.* 23.25.51.

29. *Mor.,* Praef., 6–7, 12.

30. *Mor.* 19.6.11, 23.19.34. The Vulgate translation of 2 Cor. 12:9 reads, "Sufficit tibi gratia mea: nam virtus in infirmitate perficitur." Gregory interprets this to mean that human, not divine, strength is made perfect in weakness.

31. *Mor.* 26.13.21, 24. Compare Nowak, *Le chrétien devant la souffrance,* pp. 167–72.

32. *Mor.* 8.22.38.

33. *Mor.* 26.45.82.

34. *Mor.* 3.9.15, 5.1.1, 6.23.40, 6.25.42, 7.5.39, 8.54.92, 23.24.47–48, 24.9.23, 26.13.21, 26.34.62, 26.45.82, 29.17.31, 33.19.35. It is important to note that in these passages Gregory speaks of both external and internal scourges, the latter identified as temptation. See, for example, *Mor.* 23.30.51.

35. *Mor.* 5.1.1, 8.54.92, 10.16.32, 23.24.47, 26.13.20–21, 27.13.25–26. See also Catry, "Amour du monde et amour de Dieu chez saint Grégoire le Grand," pp. 259–75.

36. *Mor.* 5.1.1, 5.40.72, 6.25.42, 7.5.39, 8.54.92, 10.16.32, 23.24.47, 23.30.51, 26.13.20–21, 27.13.25–26, 29.17.31.

37. *Mor.* 23.24.47.

38. *Mor.* 26.13.21.

39. *Mor.* 5.40.72, 10.16.32, 26.13.20–21.

40. *Mor.* 6.13.15, 6.25.42.

41. *Mor.* 7.16.19.

42. *Mor.* 6.25.42. For an analysis of this passage against the background of patristic spirituality, see Jean Doignon, "'Blessure d'affliction' et 'blessure d'amour' (*Moralia* 6.25.42): Une jonction de thèmes de la spiritualité patristique de Cyprien à Augustin," in *Grégoire le Grand,* ed. Fontaine, Gillet, and Pellistrandi, pp. 297–304. For various aspects of Gregory's "logic of antithesis," see Straw, *Gregory the Great,* pp. 143–46. As Straw explains (p. 144), God's dispensation "is an economy of antithesis and paradoxical contrast." Rist analyzes this idea in ancient Stoicism, namely, "that things go by contraries, that there cannot be pleasure without pain; that the existence of local pain, even to the good, is justified by the 'economy' or necessary arrangement of the world." See John Rist, *Stoic Philosophy* (London: Cambridge University Press, 1969), p. 50. I owe this citation to Straw, *Gregory the Great,* p. 144 n.96.

43. *Mor.* 5.1.1; compare 10.16.32.

44. *Mor.* 5.40.72.

45. *Mor.* 27.14.26.

46. *Mor.* 5.1.1.

47. I am dependent here on the "Epilogatio in Librum Job," by Denis the Carthusian. In this treatise Denis summarized and discussed the problems the Book of Job posed to earlier medieval exegetes. See Denis the Carthusian, *Doctoris ecstatici D. Dionysii Cartusiani opera omnia,* vol. 5 (Monstrolii, 1898), pp. 73–80.

48. *Mor.* 9.24.26, 11.38.51, 12.17.21, 13.30.43, 14.31.38, 18.5.9–11.

49. *Mor.* 11.52.70. Gregory reads this verse as a reference both to original sin and to Job's prophecy of the incarnation.

50. *Mor.* 9.45.68, 13.30.34, 18.5.9–11, 23.16.32; compare 21.6.11.

51. *Mor.* 18.5.9; compare 23.30.34.

52. *Mor.,* Praef., 8.

53. *Mor.* 5.11.26, 6.1.2, 7.1.1, 14.31.38, 35.7.9–10.

54. *Mor.,* Praef., 12.

55. Ibid.

56. Ibid. The "contest" between God and Satan is not a Manichaean dualism in Gregory's theology. God always remains in control of the affliction caused instrumentally by the devil. Carole Straw analyzes the "deeply complementary" relationship between God and Satan, a relationship that makes Gregory's God seem at times to be a very ambivalent figure:

> The devil and God have a deeply complementary relationship. The devil and his wickedness are not purely evil, but are salutary expressions of God's indignation and severe judgment. The devil serves God as his *exactor,* chastising and punishing man's errant ways, and the devil's sheer cruelty is useful pedagogy, teaching man how much more God should be loved as deliverer. But if the devil and his evil are partly transformed, God is also changed, at least from man's point of view. Where man once wholly feared the devil, he now learns to fear God all the more as God is acknowledged as the true source of man's affliction. (Straw, *Gregory the Great,* p. 64)

See also ibid., p. 257. It is important to note that the devil's work as God's "exactor" more easily fits with the theology of Job's friends than with Job's own situation: namely, that Satan was allowed to strike Job "frustra." Gregory strains to accommodate this view of pain and the work of the devil to the Joban prologue. Nonetheless, as we shall see in Gregory's interpretation of the epilogue, all human action, even of the just man, pales before majesty of God.

57. *Mor.* 3.7.11. For other examples of Gregory's discussion about the suffering of the just in the Bible, see *Mor.* 8.8.15, 9.56.85, 19.27.49, 20.27.56, 33.19.35. Gregory, of course, had a rich biblical tradition upon which to draw. For an excellent study of the biblical conception of the suffering of the just, see Karl Theodor Kleinknecht, *Der leidende Gerechtfertigte* (Tübingen: J.C.B. Mohr, 1984). For this notion in Greek philosophy, see Thomas C. Brickhouse and Nicholas D. Smith, *Socrates on Trial* (Princeton: Princeton University Press, 1989). See also Ernst Betz, "Christus und Sokrates in der alten Kirche," *Zeitschrift für die neutestamentliche Wissenschaft und die Kunde der Älteren Kirche* 43 (1952): 195–224; Jean Paulus, "Le thème du Juste Souffrant dans la pensée grecque et

hébraique," *Revue de l'histoire des religions* 121 (1940): 18–66. For an overview of this theme in ancient Near Eastern literature (Assyrian-Babylonian, Egyptian, Armenian, Arabian, Hindu, and Greek), see Jean Lévêque, *Job et son Dieu,* 2 vols. (Paris: J. Gabalda, 1970), pp. 13–116.

58. *Mor.,* Praef., 6.

59. *Mor.* 5.16.33.

60. Ibid., cited by Straw, *Gregory the Great,* p. 214. This is an important theme throughout her book.

61. *Mor.* 10.1.1.

62. *Mor.* 23.1.1.

63. *Mor.,* Praef., 9.

64. *Mor.* 8.13.28.

65. *Mor.* 4.1.1.

66. *Mor.,* Praef., 7.

67. *Mor.* 4.1.1.

68. As noted above, chapter 3 presents Gregory with more problems regarding the literal meaning than do Job's other laments. This is because Job's cursing of the day of his birth is, to Gregory's mind, irrational and because the "outer meaning" of the words is either impious or meaningless. Hence the reader is told to seek the inner meaning of the words. Gregory insists that Job's words must be understood in the "pious sense" in which they were intended and that the reader must seek the inner meaning of those verses which "on the surface" contradict reason (*Mor.,* Praef., 7; 4, Praef.). However, Gregory distinguishes this task from the allegorical meaning of Job's words, which he also expounds. On the literal and moral levels of the text, the reader is searching for the real intention or meaning of Job's words.

69. *Mor.* 4.1.1.

70. *Mor.* 4.1.4.

71. Ibid.

72. *Mor.* 8.11.26–13.28.

73. Ibid.

74. *Mor.* 8.7.12. As Gillet points out, Gregory differs from a thinker such as Ambrose who taught that the Christian is actually to love death. Gregory, Gillet explains, departs from Ambrose and the sages of antiquity by seeing corporeal death in terms of a "précis et redoutable passage." In his discussions about the "desire for death," Gregory speaks of a "death to the world" and not of a desire for corporeal death. See Robert Gillet, "Désir de la mort," *SC,* vol. 32 (1975), pp. 48–50. However, Rush places Gregory's view of death as a struggle with the devil in continuity with many figures in Christian antiquity. For the devout, Rush explains, Gregory is said to have "softened and beautified death and he encouraged the faithful to hope for a happy death." Nonetheless, "among the beliefs which Gregory echoed from patristic times and which he transmitted to the future ages, colored with the originality of his own moralizings, was the ancient Christian belief in death as a struggle with the devil" (Alfred C. Rush, "An Echo of Christian Antiquity in St. Gregory the Great: Death as a Struggle with the Devil," *Traditio* 3 [1945]: 369–80). On the theme

of detachment, separation, or freedom from the world as expressed in ancient and medieval monasticism, see Jean-Claude Guy, S.J.,"La place du *contemptus mundi* dans le monachisme ancien," *Revue d'ascétique et de mystique* 41 (1965): 237–49; and Réginald Grégoire, O.S.B., "'Saeculi actibus se facere alienum': Le 'mépris du monde' dans la littérature monastique latine médiévale," *Revue d'ascétique et de mystique* 41 (1965): 251–90. In the same volume see also the concluding comments by Jean Leclercq, O.S.B., pp. 287–90. These authors explain that this expression did not indicate any hatred of the world or of creation. Rather, separation from the world was a means to a higher end: the total love of God. Gregory's statements about death to the world or freedom from transient pursuits and earthly life support the argument found in these articles; he is not condemning the world as such but seeks to turn the soul away from the world to redirect it toward a total love of God. On this theme see also Leonhard Weber, *Hauptfragen der Moraltheologie Gregors des Grossen: Ein Bild altchristlicher Lebensführung* (Freiburg in der Schweiz: Paulusdruckerei, 1947), pp. 116–28.

75. Weber, *Hauptfragen der Moraltheologie Gregors des Grossen,* pp. 116–28. Weber argues that Gregory does not reject the world but speaks of leaving it for heaven (pp. 125–28).

76. *Mor.* 5.1.1.

77. Ibid.

78. Ibid.

79. *Mor.* 15.43.49.

80. *Mor.* 8.13.28.

81. *Mor.* 20.33.65, 31.38.55.

82. Ibid.

83. *Mor.* 31.28.55.

84. *Mor.* 22.2.4.

85. Ibid.

86. *Mor.* 22.16.35.

87. *Mor.* 22.16.37.

88. *Mor.,* Praef., 14.

89. *Mor.* 3.14.26–27; compare 1.12.16.

90. *Mor.* 3.16.29.

91. *Mor.* 14.41.49.

92. *Mor.* 9.27.41–42.

93. *Mor.* 9.28.44.

94. *Mor.,* Praef., 14–15; 3.22.42; 5.12.29; 12.23.28; 12.26.31; 13.2.2; 14.30.35; 16.16.21.

95. *Mor.* 13.7.9, 13.13.16.

96. *Mor.* 4.29.56, 4.31.62, 7.3.2, 7.6.6, 9.16.25, 11.20.31, 16.33.41.

97. *Mor.* 4.32.65.

98. St. Gregory the Great, *Homiliae in Hiezechihelem Prophetam,* ed. M. Adriaen, *CCSL,* vol. 142 (1971), p. 5: "'Occulta cordis eius manifesta fiunt,' profecto monstratur quia per hunc modum prophetiae spiritus non praedicit quod futurum est, sed ostendit quod est. Quo autem pacto prophetiae dicatur

spiritus, qui nihil futurum indicat, sed praesens narrat? Qua in re animadvertendum est quod recte prophetia dicitur, non quia praedicit ventura, sed quia prodit occulta."

99. *HEz.*, pp. 5–16.

100. *Mor.* 4.31.62. At the beginning of this passage Gregory explains, "Vir igitur sanctus spiritu aeternitatis plenus quaeque futura sunt colligat; et quos longe post ventura saecula gignerent, laxato mentis sinu comprehendat."

101. *Mor.* 11.20.31.

102. Ibid. See also *Mor.* 4.29.56, 9.48.74–75.

103. *Mor.* 4.32.63.

104. *Mor.* 2.35.57.

105. *Mor.* 2.36.59.

106. *Mor.* 15.58.69.

107. *Mor.* 8.8.15–16.

108. *Mor.* 8.10.19.

109. *Mor.* 9.10.11, 9.11.15.

110. *Mor.*, Praef., 11–12.

111. *Mor.*, Praef., 15.

112. *Mor.* 23.1.4; compare Praef., 9. Gregory does believe that Elihu was rebuked by God in Job 38:2 but not in 42:7.

113. *Mor.* 5.11.27, 12.31.35.

114. *Mor.* 20.14.37.

115. *Mor.* 7.19.22.

116. *Mor.* 15.33.39.

117. *Mor.* 6.12.13.

118. *Mor.* 27.17.33.

119. *Mor.* 6.24.41.

120. *Mor.* 6.23.40.

121. *Mor.* 35.8.14.

122. *Mor.* 12.28.33, 13.3.3.

123. *Mor.*, Praef., 12.

124. *Mor.* 23.17.30–31; compare 20.9.20.

125. *Mor.*, Praef., 15; 5.11.27–28; 5.27.49; 11.1.1; 12.31.36; 18.16.26.

126. *Mor.* 23.20.37.

127. For example, on the literal level of the text Gregory impugns the reality of Eliphaz's vision, but when interpreting Job 4:12, he validates this vision on the allegorical level: *Mor.* 5.23.45–37.67.

128. Matitiahu Tsevat, *The Meaning of the Book of Job and Other Biblical Studies* (New York: Ktav Publishing, 1980), p. 8.

129. René Girard, *Job the Victim of His People*, trans. Yvonne Freccero (Stanford, Calif.: Stanford University Press, 1987), p. 142.

130. *Mor.* 28.6.15–7.18. On Gregory's theology of creation and the use of animals and nature in exegesis, see René-Jean Hesbert, "Le bestiaire de Grégoire," in *Grégoire le Grand*, ed. Fontaine, Gillet, and Pellestrandi, pp. 455–66. See also Straw, *Gregory the Great*, 31–33, 50–56.

131. *Mor.* 28.9.20.

132. *Mor.* 28.16.36.

133. *Mor.* 28.19.43.

134. *Mor.* 32.12.16.

135. *Mor.* 34.7.12–13.

136. *Mor.* 34.23.47.

137. Ibid.

138. *Mor.* 34.9.19.

139. *Mor.* 33.6.12. Gregory's interpretation of this verse is a gloss on Rev. 12:15–16: "Et misit serpens ex ore suo post mulierem, aquam tanquam flumen, ut eum faceret trahi a flumine. Et adiuvit terra mulierem, et aperuit terra os suum, et absorbuit flumen, quod misit draco de ore suo" (Vulgate).

140. *Mor.* 34.20.39–31.40.

141. *Mor.* 33.7.14–9.17.

142. *Mor.* 33.19.36.

143. Ibid.

144. *Mor.* 12.

145. *Mor.* 32.1.1–3.3: "sed ad verba locutionis intimae reum se juste cognovit."

146. *Mor.* 28.11.29, 29.18.34, 29.30.59, 29.30.62, 31.2.2, 31.41.82, 32.5.6; compare 4.1.1, 9.46.40.

147. *Mor.* 28.1.1. See also Matthew Baasten, *Pride according to Gregory the Great: A Study of the Moralia* (Lewiston, N.Y.: Edwin Mellen Press, 1986); and Weber, *Hauptfragen der Moraltheologie Gregors des Grossen,* pp. 224–33.

148. *Mor.* 5.11.21, 5.37.67, 9.15.22, 9.26.40, 17.15.21, 29.18.34, 32.1.1, 32.4.5, 35.2.3.

149. *Mor.* 43.4.5.

150. *Mor.* 35.2.3.

151. *Mor.* 32.1.1.

152. *Mor.* 35.1.2. In this interpretation of Job's confession we see Gregory's view that all human actions can only be understood as a sacrifice to God, so that all of life is continuous penitence; see Straw, *Gregory the Great,* pp. 218–33. Thus, even Job's very real virtue could not meet God's standard of purity. Still, since Job's suffering was not chastisement, we again see Gregory struggling to make Job's particular situation representative of the sinful human condition.

153. *Mor.* 35.14.24, 35.15.35–16.36, 35.16.41, 35.20.47.

154. *Mor.* 35.16.36.

155. *Mor.* 35.8.11, 35.14.26, 35.14.28–29, 35.15.35.

156. Some of the most important studies of Augustine's theology of sacred history include R. A. Markus, *Saeculum: History and Society in the Age of Augustine* (Cambridge: Cambridge University Press, 1970); and Alois Wachtel, *Beiträge zur Geschichtstheologie des Aurelius Augustinus,* Bonner historische Forschungen 17 (Bonn: L. Röhrscheid, 1960). See also Peter Brown, *Augustine of Hippo* (Los Angeles: University of California Press, 1969), pp. 313–29; Henri-Irénée Marrou, *L'ambivalence du temps de l'histoire chez S. Augustin* (Montreal: Institut d'Etudes Médiévales and Paris: J. Vrin, 1964); A. Luneau, *Histoire du salut chez les pères de l'église: La doctrine des âges du monde,* Théologie historique 2 (Paris: Beauchesne,

1964); Jaroslav Pelikan, *The Mystery of Continuity: Time and History, Memory and Eternity in the Thought of Saint Augustine* (Charlottesville: University Press of Virginia, 1986), pp. 34–51.

2. The Exulting of the Wicked Is Short

1. Moses Maimonides, *The Guide of the Perplexed*, trans. Shlomo Pines (Chicago: University of Chicago Press, 1963). The Pines translation is based on the Arabic text established by Solomon Munk, *Le Guide des Egarés*, 3 vols. (Paris, 1856–66), and edited with variant readings by Issachar Joel, *Dalālat-al-ḥa'irīn* (Jerusalem: J. Junovitch, 5691 [1930–31]). On the history of Jewish interpretations of Job, see Nahum Glatzer, "The Book of Job and Its Interpreters," in *Biblical Motifs: Origins and Transformations*, ed. Alexander Altman, Brandeis University Studies and Texts 3 (Cambridge, Mass.: Philip W. Lown Institute of Advanced Judaic Studies, 1966), pp. 197–200.

Thomas Aquinas, *Expositio super Iob ad litteram*, in *Opera Omnia*, iussu Leonis XIII P.M. edita, cura et studio Fratrum Praedicatorum, vol. 26 (Rome, 1965). I have cited the Latin text by book, verse, and line numbers, followed by page numbers. An English translation can be found in Thomas Aquinas, *The Literal Exposition on Job: A Scriptural Commentary Concerning Providence*, trans. Anthony Damico with notes and interpretive essay by Martin D. Yaffe (Atlanta: Scholars Press, 1989).

2. For the background to Maimonides's thought, see Joseph A. Buijs, "Introduction," in *Maimonides: A Collection of Critical Essays*, ed. Buijs (Notre Dame, Ind.: University of Notre Dame Press, 1988), pp. 1–18.

3. Raymond L. Weiss, *Maimonides' Ethics: The Encounter of Philosophic and Religious Morality* (Chicago: University of Chicago Press, 1991), pp. 5–6.

4. Isadore Twersky, ed., *A Maimonides Reader* (West Oreange, N.J.: Behrman House, 1972), p. 39, cited by Cohen, "Maimonides' Egypt," p. 39.

5. Z. Diesendruck, "On the Date of the Completion of the Moreh Nebukim," *Hebrew Union College Annual* 12–13 (1937–38), p. 496.

6. There was no critical edition of the *Guide* known to Thomas Aquinas. He appears to have used a Latin translation from the Hebrew version by Judah al-Harîzî. The Paris edition of 1520 is a printing of the medieval version with some revisions: *Dux seu Director dubitantium aut perplexorum*, ed. Augustinus Justinianus (Paris, 1520; rpt., Frankfurt: Minerva, 1964). I owe this citation to David B. Burrell, "Aquinas' Debt to Maimonides," in *A Straight Path: Studies in Medieval Philosophy and Culture: Essays in Honor of Arthur Hyman*, ed. Ruth Link-Salinger (Washington, D.C.: Catholic University of America Press, 1988), p. 211 nn.16–17. For discussions of the translation of Maimonides's works into Latin and his influence on the scholastics, see: J. O. Reidl, "Maimonides and Scholasticism," *The New Scholasticism* 10 (1936): 18–28; Wolfgang Kluxen, "Literargeschichtliches zum lateinischen Moses Maimonides," *Recherches de théologie ancienne et médiévale* 21 (1954): 23–50; Kluxen, "Maimonides und die Hochscholastik," *Philosophisches Jahrbuch* 63 (1955): 151–65; Kluxen, "Die Geschichte des Maimonides im lateinischen Abendland als Beispiel einer christlich-jüdischen Begegnung," in *Judentum im Mittelalter*, ed. P. Wilpert, Miscellanea mediaevalia 4

(Berlin: Walter de Gruyter, 1966), pp. 146–66; Kluxen, "Maimonides and Latin Scholasticism," in *Maimonides and Philosophy*, ed. Shlomo Pines and Yirmiyahu Yovel (Dordrecht: Martinus Nijhoff, 1986), pp. 224–32.

7. *Expositio*, Prol., 98–102.

8. Weisheipl, *Friar Thomas d' Aquino*, pp. 152–53. According to Weisheipl, the current text is an elaborated edition of Thomas's lectures given in the Dominican priory of San Domenico in Orvieto and is contemporary with books 2–3 of the *Summa contra gentiles* "in the sense that the commentary on Job and the *Summa contra gentiles* III, 64–113, deal with the problem of divine providence, and in the sense that both Job and the *Summa* utilize Moerbeke's new translation of Aristotle's work on animals" (p. 368).

9. The following discussion draws heavily on John H. Wright, *The Order of the Universe in the Theology of St. Thomas Aquinas*, Analecta Gregoriana 39 (Rome: Gregorian University, 1957).

On the concept of order in Aquinas's thought in general, see: Brian Coffey, "The Notion of Order according to St. Thomas Aquinas," *The Modern Schoolman* 27 (1949): 1–18; Joseph Marling, *The Order of Nature* (Washington, D.C.: Catholic University of America Press, 1934); E. A. Pace, "The Concept of Order in the Philosophy of St. Thomas," *New Scholasticism* 2 (1928): 51–72; A. Silva-Tarouca, "L'idée d'ordre dans la philosophie de saint Thomas d'Aquin," *Revue néoscolastique de philosophie* 40: 341–84.

10. *SCG* 2.24.4.

11. *SCG* 3.12; Wright, *The Order of the Universe*, pp. 86–108, 144–48, 156–58, 184–86.

12. Wright, *The Order of the Universe*, pp. 5–8 and passim.

13. *Expositio* 7:17, 361–94, p. 50.

14. Wright, *The Order of the Universe*, pp. 2, 138, 201.

15. *SCG* 3.12.8.

16. *SCG* 3.18.5.

17. *SCG* 3.7.1–12, 3.10.1–18, 3.12.1–7, 3.15.1–9.

18. Wright, *The Order of the Universe*, pp. 23–25, 108–12, 158–66, 190, 193–94, 204–5.

19. *Guide* III.22, p. 486. Pines notes that Maimonides is citing B.T. Hagigah 13a, but refers there to Ezekiel's vision.

20. *Guide* I, Introd., pp. 9–14. Scholars have debated the role of an esoteric sense in Maimonides's work. Among modern scholars, Strauss has been most influential in his analysis of the relationship between these two senses in the *Guide:* Leo Strauss, "The Literary Character of the *Guide for the Perplexed,"* in *Persecution and the Art of Writing* (Glencoe, Ill.: Free Press, 1952), pp. 38–94. Scholars have also differed, however, on the way in which these sense are related to one another. For a critique of Strauss's argument, see Joseph A. Buijs, "The Philosophical Character of Maimonides' *Guide:* A Critique of Strauss' Interpretation," *Judaism* 27 (1978): 448–57; rpt. in *Maimonides: A Collection of Critical Essays*, pp. 59–70. Buijs criticizes Strauss's view that the *Guide* is not a philosophical book and concludes that the *Guide* is "an attempt to present a systematic philosophy of Judaism or of religion." Some authors, such as Reines and Kravitz (see note 31 below), assume an oppositional relationship between the inner

and outer meanings. But by appropriating Hartman's analysis of the connection between reason and revelation, or the legal and philosophical works, one can also conclude that these senses are related to each other in a hierarchical but not necessarily oppositional manner. See David Hartman, *Maimonides: Torah and Philosophic Quest* (Philadelphia: Jewish Publication Society of America, 1976). For Twersky the "Archimedean point" of Maimonides's thought was the inseparability and the ultimate complementarity and harmony of the only apparently discordant disciplines of law and philosophy. Twersky emphasizes the "constant intersection of philosophy and halakah." According to Twersky, Maimonides's overarching objective was "to bring law and philosophy, two apparently incongruous attitudes of mind, two jealous rivals, into fruitful harmony" (Isadore Twersky, *Introduction to the Code of Maimonides [Mishneh Torah]* [New Haven, Conn.: Yale University Press, 1980], pp. 356–69). For a discussion of how Maimonides attempts to negotiate the philosophical conflict between Athens and Jerusalem in the area of ethics, see Raymond L. Weiss, *Maimonides' Ethics* (Chicago: University of Chicago Press, 1991).

It should also be noted that Maimonides explains (*Guide*, Introd., pp. 12–14) that the prophetic parables are of two kinds. In some parables each word has a meaning, while in others the parable as a whole indicates the intended meaning. In the latter kind, not every word adds something to the intended meaning, and hence one should not inquire into all the details.

21. *Guide* I, Introd., pp. 11–12. On the use of Prov. 25:11 in the history of Jewish exegesis, see Frank Talmage, "Apples of Gold: The Inner Meaning of Sacred Texts in Medieval Judaism," in *Jewish Spirituality*, ed. Arthur Green (New York: Crossroad, 1986).

22. *Guide* I, Introd., p. 12.

23. *Guide* I.33, p. 71. Pines notes that Maimonides is citing *B.T.* Yebamoth 71a; *B.T.* Baba Mesi'a 31b.

24. *Guide* I.33, p. 71. The citation as a whole reads:

Similarly, these true opinions were not hidden, enclosed in riddles, and treated by all men of knowledge with all sorts of artifice through which they could teach them without expounding them explicitly, because of something bad being hidden in them, or because they undermine the foundations of the Law, as is thought by ignorant people who deem that they have attained a rank suitable for speculation. Rather have they been hidden because at the outset the intellect is incapable of receiving them; only flashes of them are made to appear so that the perfect man should know them. On this account they are called *secrets and mysteries of the Torah*, as we shall make clear. . . . This is so because it is presented in such a manner as to make it possible for the young, the women, and all the people to begin with it and to learn it. Now it is not within their power to understand these matters as they truly are. Hence they are confined to accepting tradition with regard to all sound opinions that are of such a sort that it is preferable that they should be pronounced true and with regard to all representations of this kind—and this in such a manner that the mind is led toward the existence of the objects of these opinions and representations but not toward grasping their essence as it truly is.

On Maimonides's comments regarding the study of metaphysics, see Armand A. Maurer, "Maimonides and Aquinas on the Study of Metaphysics," in *A Straight Path*, ed. Link-Salinger, pp. 206–15.

25. Hartman, *Maimonides: Torah and Philosophic Quest*, pp. 193–94. Compare *Guide* I, Introd., pp. 8–9, and III.52, pp. 629–30 (cited by Hartman).

26. On the "love of God" in Maimonides's thought, see the following: Hartman, *Maimonides: Torah and Philosophic Quest*, pp. 210–14; Simon Rawidowicz, "Knowledge of God: A Study in Maimonides' Philosophy of Religion," in *Jewish Studies, Issued in Honor of the Chief Rabbi J. L. Landau* (Tel-Aviv: Publication Committee, 1935), pp. 96–106; Charles Touati, "Les deux théories de Maïmonide sur la providence," in *Studies in Jewish Religious and Intellectual History, Presented to Alexander Altmann on the Occasion of His Seventieth Birthday*, ed. Siegfried Stein and Raphael Loewe (Tuscaloosa: University of Alabama Press in Association with the Institute of Jewish Studies, London, 1979), pp. 339–41; Georges Vajda, *L'Amour de Dieu dans la théologie juive du moyen âge* (Paris: J. Vrin, 1957), pp. 137–40.

27. *Guide*, Introd., pp. 6–7: "Hence you should not ask of me here anything beyond *the chapter headings*. And even those are not set down in order or arranged in coherent fashion in this Treatise, but rather are scattered and entangled with other subjects that are to be clarified. For my purpose is that the truths be glimpsed and then again be concealed, so as not to oppose that divine purpose which one cannot possibly oppose and which has concealed from the vulgar among the people those truths especially requisite for His apprehension." Given statements such as this, it is difficult to understand how Leaman can conclude that "there is no reason to believe that Maimonides was consciously doing what he ought not to be doing, and therefore had to conceal his message from the ordinary reader . . . He uses arguments and explains texts in his analysis; he does not proceed by assembling contradictions and repetitions which mislead the naïve reader and instruct the more intelligent concerning his real purpose" (Oliver Leaman, *Moses Maimonides* [London: Routledge, 1990], p. 17). For a recent discussion of Maimonides's secretive style, see Leonard S. Kravitz, *The Hidden Doctrine of Maimonides' Guide for the Perplexed: Philosophical and Religious God-Language in Tension*, Jewish Studies 4 (Lewiston, Mass.: Edwin Mellen Press, 1988), pp. 277–81; and Marvin Fox, *Interpreting Maimonides: Studies in Methodology, Metaphysics, and Moral Philosophy* (Chicago: University of Chicago Press, 1990), pp. 3–90.

28. *Guide* I, Introd., pp. 5–7.

29. Ibid. See also Strauss, *Persecution and the Art of Writing*, pp. 46–55.

30. *Guide* III.22, p. 486; I.35, p. 80: "as well as the discussion concerning His creation of that which He created, the character of His governance of the world, the 'how' of His providence with respect to what is other than He, the notion of His will, His apprehension, and His knowledge of all that He knows; and likewise as for the notion of prophecy and the 'how' of its various degrees, and the notion of His names, though they are many . . . it should be considered that all these are obscure matters. In fact, they are truly *the mysteries of the Torah* and the

secrets constantly mentioned in the books of the prophets and in the dicta of the *Sages, may their memory be blessed.* They are matters that ought not to be spoken of except *in chapter headings.*" Compare I.72, p. 193.

31. *Guide* III.22, p. 488. Compare III.16, pp. 363–64. On Maimonides's concept of providence, see Charles Raffel, "Maimonides' Theory of Providence" (diss., Brandeis University, 1983). Raffel's discussion of Maimonides's interpretation of Job is found on pp. 99–109. See also Raffel, "Providence as Consequent upon the Intellect: Maimonides' Theory of Providence," *Journal of the Association for Jewish Studies Review* 12 (1987): 25–72. Raffel's interpretation of Maimonides's work on Job in this article is found on pp. 52–57 and 63–68. Raffel's work criticizes that of Reines: Alvin Reines, "Maimonides' Concepts of Providence and Theodicy," *Hebrew Union College Annual* 43 (1972): 169–206. See also Alfred L. Ivry, "Providence, Divine Omniscience, and Possibility: The Case of Maimonides," in *Maimonides: A Collection of Critical Essays,* ed. Buijs, pp. 175–91; David Burrell, "Maimonides, Aquinas, and Gersonides on Providence and Evil," *Religious Studies* 20 (1984): 335–51; Leo Strauss, "Der Ort der Vorsehungslehre nach der Ansicht Maimunis," *Monatsschrift für Geschichte und Wissenschaft des Judentums* 81 (1937): 93–105; Kravitz, *The Hidden Doctrine of Maimonides' Guide for the Perplexed;* Haim (Howard) Kreisel, "Miracles in Medieval Jewish Philosophy," *Jewish Quarterly Review* 75 (1984): 99–133; Ralph Lerner, "Maimonides' Governance of the Solitary," in *Perspectives on Maimonides,* ed. Joel L. Kraemer (Oxford: Oxford University Press for the Littmann Library, 1991), pp. 33–46.

32. *Guide* III.16, pp. 461–64; III.19–21, pp. 477–85. See also Raffel, "Maimonides' Theory of Providence," p. 115.

33. Alvin J. Reines, "Maimonides' True Belief Concerning God," in *Maimonides and Philosophy,* ed. Shlomo Pines and Yirmiyahu Yovel (Dordrecht: Martinus Nijhoff, 1986), pp. 24–35; Raffel, "Maimonides' Theory of Providence," pp. 114–29; Tamar Rudavsky, "Maimonides and Averroes on God's Knowledge of Possibles," *Da'at* 13 (1984): xxvii–xliv; Alfred Ivry, "Providence, Divine Omniscience, and Possibility: The Case of Maimonides," pp. 175–94. On pp. 184–85 Ivry makes the following important point:

> It is we who appraise God's actions from the point of view of reward and punishment, we who personalize the actions of the divine overflow, which become individualized in the varied responses we—and all corporeal being—bring to it. . . . We could say therefore that the divine intellect is essentially impersonal and functions of necessity, but for the element of will which Maimonides . . . regards as essential to the divine being. . . . The divine will is perhaps most successful a term when taken as representing the outwardly oriented and purposive nature of the divine being, a purpose which, for Maimonides, should be said to extend to individuals, though not intended in the personal way we like to believe.

See also Ivry, "Neoplatonic Currents in Maimonides' Thought," in *Perspectives on Maimonides,* ed. Kraemer, p. 132: "The One, however, relates only indirectly to the realm of time and place, since his knowledge and actions are eternal. That which occurs here is thus removed from him and mediated through other eternal forces, specifically the intelligences of the spheres, and particularly the Active Intellect. The individual occurrences of particular forms within a physical frame thus stem from God originally, but they are known to him only in a general way, as members of a given species. His responsibility for what occurs here is, accordingly, indirect and remote." Compare Kreisel on God's "impersonal" governance of nature: "Miracles in Medieval Jewish Philosophy," pp. 113–14. Compare also Norman Roth, "Knowledge of God and God's Knowledge: Two Epistemological Problems in Maimonides," in *Maimonides, Essays and Texts: 850th Anniversary* (Madison: The Hispanic Seminary of Medieval Studies, 1985), pp. 69–87.

34. *Guide* I.56–60, pp. 117–18. Maimonides concludes that no positive attributes may be predicated of God. In I.53, pp. 118–19, he allows that attributes of action may be predicated of God after it is made clear that such actions are not carried out "by means of differing notions subsisting within the essence of the agent, but that all His different acts, may He be exalted, are all of them carried out by means of His essence and not, as we have made clear, by means of a superadded notion." The literature on Maimonides's theory of divine attributes is too extensive to be summarized here. Some of the most important discussions include: Joseph Buijs, "Comments on Maimonides' Negative Theology," *The New Scholasticism* 49 (1975): 87–93; David B. Burrell, C.S.C., *Knowing the Unknowable God: Ibn-Sina, Maimonides, Aquinas* (Notre Dame, Ind.: University of Notre Dame Press, 1986), pp. 51–70; Isaac Franck, "Maimonides and Aquinas on Man's Knowledge of God: A Twentieth-Century Perspective," in *Maimonides: A Collection of Critical Essays*, ed. Buijs, pp. 284–305; Arthur Hyman, "Maimonides on Religious Language," in *Studies in Jewish Philosophy*, ed. Norbert M. Samuelson (Lanham, Md.: University Press of America, 1987), pp. 351–65; Roth, "Knowledge of God and God's Knowledge: Two Epistemological Problems in Maimonides," pp. 69–87; Harry A. Wolfson, "Maimonides and Gersonides on Divine Attributes as Ambiguous Terms," in *Mordecai M. Kaplan Jubilee Volume on the Occasion of His Seventieth Birthday* (New York: Jewish Theological Seminary of America, 1953), pp. 515–30; Wolfson, "Maimonides on Negative Attributes," in *Louis Ginsberg Jubilee Volume on the Occasion of His Seventieth Birthday* (New York: American Academy for Jewish Research, 1945), pp. 411–46, rpt. in *Essays in Medieval Jewish and Islamic Philosophy: Studies from the Publication of the AAJR* (New York: KTAV, 1977), pp. 180–218.

35. In *Guide* II.16, p. 463, Maimonides states that "there are also some philosophers who believe, as we do, that He, may He be exalted, knows everything and that nothing secret is at all hidden from Him." In III.20, p. 480, Maimonides states, "After this has been demonstrated, we, the community of those who adhere to a Law, say that He knows with one single knowledge the many and numerous things." At the end of III.20, p. 483, however, Maimonides explains that, "All the contradictions that may appear in the union of these assertions are due to their being considered in relation to our knowledge, which has only its name in common with His knowledge. Similarly, the word 'purpose' is used equivocally when applied to what is purposed by us and to what is said to be His purpose, may He be exalted. Similarly, the word 'providence' is used equivocally when applied to what we are provident about and

to that of which it is said that He, may He be exalted, is provident with regard to it. It is accordingly true that the meaning of knowledge, the meaning of purpose, and the meaning of providence, when ascribed to us, are different from the meanings of these terms when ascribed to Him."

36. *Guide* III.20, p. 483.

37. *Guide* III.23, p. 490. Compare III.22, p. 487.

38. Maimonides identifies these opinions of Job's friends with those outlined in III.17, pp. 466–70. Eliphaz's opinion was the opinion of "our Law." Bildad's view was that held by the Mu'tazila. The view of Zophar was that of the Ash'ariyya.

39. *Guide* III.23, p. 491

40. *Guide* III.23, pp. 490–91.

41. *Guide* III.23, p. 494.

42. Maimonides describes what he believes to be Aristotle's view of providence in III.17, p. 465:

[Aristotle] holds that God, may He be exalted, takes care of the spheres and of what is in them and that for this reason their individuals remain permanently as they are. Alexander has formulated this, saying that in Aristotle's opinion God's providence ends at the sphere of the moon. This is a branch deriving from his root doctrine concerning the eternity of the world, for he believes that providence corresponds to the nature of what exists. Accordingly, with regard to the spheres, whose individuals are permanent, and what is in them, providence regarding them means that they remain permanent in a changeless state. But just as the existence of other things—whose individuals have not, but whose species have, an enduring existence—derives necessarily from theirs, there is likewise an overflow from the providence in question, which overflow necessitates the durability and permanence of the species, though the durability of the latter's individuals be impossible.

On the debate about Maimonides's Aristotelianism, see Fox, *Interpreting Maimonides,* pp. 10–13, and for a discussion about Maimonides's critique of Aristotelian cosmology and view of the eternity of the world, pp. 273–90. See also Raffel, "Providence as Consequent upon the Intellect: Maimonides' Theory of Providence," pp. 38–39, 43–51. For an analysis of Maimonides's view of Aristotelian method, see Joel L. Kraemer, "Maimonides on Aristotle and Scientific Method," in *Moses Maimonides and His Time,* ed. Ormsby, pp. 53–88.

43. *Guide* III.22, p. 487.

44. *Guide* III.23, p. 492.

45. *Guide* I.33, p. 71.

46. *Guide* III.23, p. 493.

47. *Guide,* p. 488.

48. *Guide* III.22, p. 489. On this point I am in agreement with Kravitz's identification of Satan rather than with that of Reines. Kravitz, "Maimonides and Job: An Inquiry as to the Method of the Moreh," *Hebrew Union College Annual* 38 (1967): 149–58. Compare Reines, "Maimonides' Concepts of Providence and

Theodicy," pp. 202–3. Reines identifies Satan with matter or, following Munk, with privation. The issue in III.22 is whether the term *evil inclination* refers to the discussion of evil in III.10 (matter and privation) or to the discussion of the "evil impulse" in II.12, p. 280. I have adopted the latter solution as proposed by Kravitz. This is not to deny, of course, that matter is the source of evil since it is that which causes change.

49. On the unreliability of the imagination, see *Guide* I.73, pp. 209–10, analyzed in Arthur Hyman, "Maimonides on Causality," in *Maimonides and Philosophy*, ed. Pines and Yovel, pp. 163–65. On the role of imagination in prophecy, see the following: Menachem Kellner, "Maimonides and Gersonides on Mosaic Prophecy," *Speculum* 52 (1977): 62–79; Jeffrey Macy, "Prophecy in al-Farabi and Maimonides," in *Maimonides and Philosophy*, ed. Pines and Yovel, pp. 192–97; Raffel, "Providence as Consequent upon the Intellect: Maimonides' Theory of Providence," pp. 57–59; S. Daniel Breslauer, "Philosophy and Imagination: The Politics of Prophecy in the View of Moses Maimonides," *Jewish Quarterly Review* (1980): 165–71; and Norbert Samuelson, "Comments on Maimonides' Concept of Prophecy," *Central Conference American Rabbis Journal* 18 (January 1971): 23–24. Samuelson is criticizing Alvin J. Reines, "Maimonides' Concept of Mosaic Prophecy," *Hebrew Union College Annual* 40–41 (1969–70): 325–61. See also Miriam Galston, "Philosopher-King v. Prophet," *Israel Oriental Studies* 8 (1978): 204–18. For Maimonides's discussion of the relation of the imagination to the intellect, see *Guide* I.73, pp. 209–11. On the relationship between philosophic and prophetic knowledge, see Breslauer, "Philosophy and Imagination: The Politics of Prophecy in the View of Moses Maimonides"; Galston, "Philosopher-King v. Prophet," pp. 210–18; Ithamar Grünwald, "Maimonides' Quest beyond Philosophy and Prophecy," in *Perspectives on Maimonides*, ed. Kraemer, pp. 141–57; Barry S. Kogan, "What Can We Know and When Can We Know It? Maimonides on the Active Intelligence and Human Cognition," in *Moses Maimonides and His Time*, ed. Ormsby, pp. 128–37. Kogan concludes that "all that ultimately distinguishes the prophets in kind from the most accomplished philosophers is their reliance upon the imaginative faculty in expressing what they know" (pp. 130–31). For a different view see Shlomo Pines, "The Limitations of Human Knowledge according to Al-Farabi, ibn Bajja, and Maimonides," in *Studies in Medieval Jewish Literature*, ed. Isadore Twersky (Cambridge, Mass.: Harvard University Press, 1979), pp. 82–109; rpt. in *Maimonides: A Collection of Critical Essays*, ed. Buijs, pp. 91–121.

50. *Guide* II.12, p. 280.

51. *Guide* III.23, p. 495.

52. *Guide* II.6, pp. 262–65: "Rather do all these texts state plainly that all this—including the various parts of that which exists and even the creation of the limbs of animals as they are—has been brought about through the intermediation of angels. For all forces are angels . . . that God has placed in the sperm a formative force shaping the limbs and giving them their configuration and that this force is the *angel*, or that all the forms derive from the act of the Active Intellect and that the latter is the *angel* and *prince of the world* constantly mentioned by the *Sages*" (pp. 263–64). For an analysis of this passage see Kravitz, "Maimonides and Job: An Inquiry into the Method of the Moreh," pp. 149–58.

See also Raffel, "Providence as Consequent upon the Intellect: Maimonides' Theory of Providence," p. 56.

53. For a brief description of Maimonides's cosmology, see Arthur Hyman, "Demonstrative, Dialectical and Sophistic Arguments in the Philosophy of Moses Maimonides," in *Moses Maimonides and His Time,* ed. Ormsby, p. 47; Reines, "Maimonides' Concepts of Providence and Theodicy," pp. 174–77. On Maimonides's theory of emanation see Ivry, "Providence, Divine Omniscience, and Possibility," pp. 179–85; Ivry, "Neoplatonic Currents in Maimonides' Thought," pp. 115–40. Compare Fox's analysis of Maimonides's view of Aristotle's theory of the supralunar world in *Interpreting Maimonides,* pp. 272–90. On the difficulties in Maimonides's understanding of the supralunar world, see also Tzvi Langermann, "The 'True Perplexity': The *Guide of the Perplexed,* Part II, Chapter 24," in *Perspectives on Maimonides,* ed. Kraemer, pp. 159–74.

54. *Guide* II.10–11, pp. 269–76. For the place of the human being in this hierarchy, see *Guide* III.12, p. 443.

55. Ivry, "Providence, Divine Omniscience, and Possibility," pp. 184–85.

56. *Guide* III.23, p. 495.

57. *Guide* III.17–18, pp. 474–75. Compare III.17, p. 471.

58. *Guide* II.42, pp. 388–90.

59. *Guide* II.36, p. 369.

60. On Maimonides's view of prophecy, see Galston, "Philosopher-King v. Prophet," pp. 204–18; Menachem Kellner, "Maimonides and Gersonides on Mosaic Prophecy," pp. 62–79; Kellner, *Maimonides on Human Perfection,* Brown Judaic Studies 202 (Atlanta: Scholars Press, 1990), pp. 29–32, 51, 86 n.20; Kellner, *Maimonides on Judaism and the Jewish People* (Albany: State University of New York Press, 1991), pp. 26–29; Macy, "Prophecy in al-Farabi and Maimonides," pp. 26–29; Raffel, "Providence as Consequent upon the Intellect: Maimonides' Theory of Providence," pp. 58–60; Raffel, "Maimonides' Theory of Providence," pp. 91–96; H. A. Wolfson, "Hallevi and Maimonides on Prophecy," *Jewish Quarterly Review* 32 (1942): 345–70, and 33 (1942): 49–82; Howard Kreisel, "Maimonides' View of Prophecy as the Overflowing Perfection of Man," *Da'at* 13 (1984): xxi–xxvi; Kreisel, "Miracles in Medieval Jewish Philosophy," pp. 99–133. For an interpretation of the political context of Maimonides's statements on prophecy, see Breslauer, "Philosophy and Imagination: The Politics of Prophecy in the View of Moses Maimonides."

61. In *Guide* II.32 Maimonides lists several views of prophecy: (1) that prophecy is miraculously or supernaturally revealed knowledge; (2) that prophecy is "a certain perfection in the nature of man," an opinion that Maimonides identifies with the philosophers; and (3) that prophecy is a natural event that may be stopped by the divine will, a view in accordance with "our Law" (p. 36). Scholars have debated whether Maimonides sees prophecy as the purely natural perfection of the individual who prepares himself through the perfection of rational and imaginative faculties, or whether the ability of God to withhold prophecy from a qualified individual means prophecy contains a miraculous element. The scholar who has most seriously opposed the naturalistic reading of Maimonides's understanding of prophecy is Zvi Diesendruck, "Maimonides' Lehre von der Prophetie," in *Jewish Studies in Memory of Israel*

Abrahams, ed. George Alexander Kohut (New York: Press of the Jewish Institute of Religion, 1927), pp. 74–134. For an analysis of the relationship between Maimonides's view on the miraculous element possible in prophecy and his belief in the creation or eternity of the world, see Lawrence Kaplan, "Maimonides on the Miraculous Element in Prophecy," *Harvard Theological Review* 70 (1977): 233–56. For the defense of the naturalistic view, see Alexander Altmann, "Maimonides and Thomas Aquinas: Natural or Divine Prophecy," in *Essays in Jewish Intellectual History* (Hanover, N.H.: University Press of New England, 1981), pp. 77–96; Kreisel, "Miracles in Medieval Jewish Philosophy," pp. 99–133; Kreisel, "Maimonides' View of Prophecy as the Overflowing Perfection of Man," pp. xxi–xxvi. In his dissertation, "Theories of Prophecy in Medieval Jewish Philosophy" (diss., Brandeis University, 1980), Kreisel further strengthens Reines's argument that in Maimonides's esoteric view, Mosaic prophecy, the Law, and miracles are to be considered natural phenomena. Compare Reines, "Maimonides' Concept of Mosaic Prophecy"; and Reines, "Maimonides' Concept of Miracles," *Hebrew Union College Annual* 45 (1974): 243–85. See also Reines, *Maimonides and Abrabanel on Prophecy* (Cincinnati: Hebrew Union College Press, 1970), pp. ccci–cccv.

    62. *Guide* III.23, p. 496.

    63. Ibid.

    64. For an analysis of Maimonides's interpretation of this verse see Touati, "Les deux théories de Maïmonide sur la providence," pp. 331–44. Touati links this passage to III.51 and argues that Maimonides depicts Job as one who surpasses the Aristotelianism of Elihu (who thought one could only have contact with the Active Intellect "two or three times") and attains true, uninterrupted knowledge of the Active Intellect. At this point the regenerated Job completely disregarded the contingencies and imaginary goods of the material world.

    65. *Guide* III.23, p. 497.

    66. *Guide* I.74, pp. 221, cited by Reines, "Maimonides' Concepts of Providence and Theodicy," p. 191 n.90. In this section Maimonides explains, "Now you know that regarding the things separate from matter—I mean those that are neither bodies nor forces in bodies, but intellects—there can be no thought of multiplicity of any mode whatever, except that some of them are the causes of the existence of others and that thus there is a difference among them since one is the cause and the other the effect. However, what remains of Zayd is neither the cause nor the effect of what remains of Umar. Consequently all are one in number." See also I.70, pp. 173–74: "For the *souls* that remain after death are not the *soul* that comes into being in man at the time he is generated. For that which comes into being at the time a man is generated is merely a faculty consisting in preparedness, whereas the thing that after death is separate from matter is the thing that has become actual and not the *soul* that also comes into being; the latter is identical with the spirit that comes into being. Because of this the Sages have numbered the *souls and spirits* among the things that come into being. What is separate is, on the contrary, one thing only." Compare *Guide* III.51, pp. 627–28. To counter the attacks against his teaching about the immortality of the soul and his alleged denial of resurrection, Maimonides wrote his *Treatise on Resurrection*. For an analysis of this work see Leaman, *Moses Mai-*

monides, pp. 115–21; R. Lerner, "Maimonides' *Treatise on the Resurrection,*" *History of Religions* 23 (1983): 140–55.

67. In Book III.24 of the *Guide* Maimonides dismisses the idea we saw Gregory expound: that "God sends down calamities upon an individual, without their having been preceded by a sin, in order that his reward be increased" (p. 497). See also Vajda, *L'amour de Dieu dans la théologie juive du moyen âge,* pp. 131–32.

68. *Guide* I, Introd., pp. 6–7.

69. Ibid.

70. *Guide* III.51, pp. 618–28. For a discussion of Maimonides's use of demonstrative and dialectical arguments, see Arthur Hyman, "Demonstrative, Dialectical, and Sophistical Arguments in the Philosophy of Moses Maimonides," in *Moses Maimonides and His Time,* ed. Ormsby, pp. 35–52.

71. *Guide* III.51, p. 621.

72. *Guide* III.23, p. 490. Recall that at the beginning of the story, Job and his friends agreed that "everything that had befallen Job was known to Him, may He be exalted, and that God had caused these misfortunes to befall him."

73. *Guide* III.23, pp. 492–93. Compare *Guide* III.10–12, pp. 438–48. In these sections Maimonides describes the nature of evil as privation and explains the evils that are an inherent part of human existence because the human being is associated with matter (pp. 443–44). On p. 447 he states that the attainment of material wealth and possessions is a "false imagining or a plaything." Compare Maimonides's list of evils in III.12 with Job's afflictions. For a discussion of the role of matter in the nature of evil, see *Guide* III.10, pp. 438–40, and III.12, pp. 441–48. See also Kravitz, *The Hidden Doctrine of Maimonides' Guide for the Perplexed,* pp. 200–236; and Raffel, "Providence as Consequent upon the Intellect: Maimonides' Theory of Providence," pp. 52–53.

74. *Guide* III.23, p. 497.

75. On Maimonides's translation of this verse, see Dale Patrick, "The Translation of Job XLII 6," *Vetus Testamentum* 26 (1976): 369–71.

76. *Guide* III.23, p. 493.

77. It is important to remember that for Maimonides the realm of nature includes the Active Intellect; see Reines, *Maimonides and Abrabanel on Prophecy,* p. xxix.

78. According to Maimonides, the ultimate human perfection is to become rational in actu:

> The Law as a whole aims at two things: the welfare of the soul and the welfare of the body. . . . Know that as between these two aims, one is indubitably greater in nobility; namely, the welfare of the soul—I mean the procuring of correct opinions—while the second aim—I mean the welfare of the body—is prior in nature and time. The latter aim consists in the governance of the city and the well-being of the states. . . . For the first aim can only be achieved after achieving this second one. . . . His [man's] ultimate perfection is to become rational in actu, I mean to have an intellect in actu; this would consist in his knowing everything concerning all the beings that it is within the capacity of man to know in accordance with his

ultimate perfection. It is clear that to this ultimate perfection there do not belong either actions or moral qualities and that it consists only of opinions toward which speculation has led and that investigation has rendered compulsory. (*Guide* III.27, pp. 510–11)

As Hartman has argued, however, Maimonides "distinguishes between morality before and after knowledge of God. On the one hand, the yearning for God is of more importance than moral actions. On the other hand, the theoretical knowledge of God does affect practice and changes one's actions and orientation to life" (Hartman, *Maimonides: Torah and Philosophic Quest*, pp. 200–206). See also Kogan, "What Can We Know and When Can We Know It? Maimonides on the Active Intelligence and Human Knowledge," pp. 132–37. Kogan argues that Maimonides's "fourth perfection," described in III.51, includes both intellectual apprehension and conduct. Lerner has argued, "Not some imposed duty, not even some proclaimed mission, but a profound human understanding leads the perfect one to re-enter the world of practice. Yet that re-entry is in no case a reimmersion in human concerns; the perfect one may be in the world of affairs but is not of it. In the highest instances, Maimonides has pointed out, domestic and practical governance were conducted by the Patriarchs and Moses 'with their limbs only,' or as we might say, with their minds elsewhere. . . . Because the end in view in all their actions was 'to bring into being a religious community that would know and worship God'" (Ralph Lerner, "Maimonides' Governance of the Solitary," in *Perspectives on Maimonides*, ed. Kraemer, p. 45). On the debate about Maimonides's understanding of ultimate perfection and political activity, see L. V. Berman, "The Political Interpretation of the Maxim: The Purpose of Philosophy Is the Imitation of God," *Studia Islamica* 15 (1961): 56–61; Shlomo Pines's foreword to Hartman, *Maimonides: Torah and Philosophic Quest*, pp. xi–xv; Galston, "Philosopher-King v. Prophet," pp. 216–17; Alexander Altmann, "Maimonides' 'Four Perfections,'" *Israel Oriental Studies* 2 (1972): 24. For an analysis of all these views, see Steven Harvey, "Maimonides in the Sultan's Palace," in *Perspectives on Maimonides*, ed. Kraemer, pp. 70–75. For a thorough discussion of Maimonides's views of perfection, see Kellner, *Maimonides on Human Perfection*.

79. See also Raffel, "Providence as Consequent upon the Intellect: Maimonides' Theory of Providence," pp. 63–71. Compare Reines, "Maimonides' Concepts of Providence and Theodicy," pp. 193–94.

80. *Guide* III.51, p. 625. See also Touati, "Les deux théories de Maïmonide sur la providence," pp. 335–41; and Rawidowicz, "Knowledge of God," pp. 89–93. For a discussion of how earlier thinkers interpreted this passage, see Zvi Diesendruck, "Samuel and Moses ibn Tibbon on Maimonides' Theory of Providence," *Hebrew Union College Annual* 11 (1936): 341–51. See also Fox, *Interpreting Maimonides*, p. 316 n.26.

81. *Guide* III.9, pp. 436–37: "Matter is a strong veil preventing the apprehension of that which is separate from matter as it truly is." See also *Guide* II.12, pp. 279–80; III.8, pp. 430–36; III.22, p. 488.

82. *Expositio*, Prol., 96–102, p. 3.

83. For a thorough discussion of the development of Aquinas's exegetical

method, see Maximinus Arias Reyero, *Thomas von Aquin als Exeget: Die Prinzipien seiner Schriftdeutung und seine Lehre von den Schriftsinnen* (Einseideln: Johannes Verlag, 1971). See also: de Lubac, *Exégèse médiévale*, vol. 2, pp. 272–302; Paul Synave, "La doctrine de saint Thomas d'Aquin sur le sens littéral des Écritures," *Revue biblique* 35 (1926): 40–65; Smalley, *The Study of the Bible in the Middle Ages*, pp. 300–302; J. R. Sheets, "The Scriptural Dimension of St. Thomas," *American Ecclesiastical Review* 144 (1961): 154–73. See also P. C. Spicq, *Esquisse d'une histoire de l'exégèse latine au moyen âge* (Paris: J. Vrin, 1944); Spicq, "Saint Thomas exégète," *Dictionnaire de théologie catholique*, vol. 15-A, pp. 694–738; A. Gardeil, "Les procédés exégétiques de saint Thomas," *Revue thomiste* 11 (1903): 428–57; Carl Siegfried, "Thomas von Aquino als Ausleger des A.T.," *Zeitschrift für wissenschaftliche Theologie* 37 (1895): 603–26; Hugh Pope, "St. Thomas as an Interpreter of Holy Scripture," in *St. Thomas Aquinas*, ed. Aelred Whitacre et al. (Oxford: Blackwell, 1925). For a discussion of the "literal" sense in medieval exegetes, see Anthony Nemetz, "Literalness and the *Sensus Litteralis*," *Speculum* 34 (1959): 76–89.

84. *ST* 1.1.10. See also James Samuel Preus, *From Shadow to Promise: Old Testament Interpretation from Augustine to the Young Luther* (Cambridge, Mass.: Harvard University Press, 1969), pp. 46–60.

85. Ibid.

86. *ST* 1.1.10 ad 3.

87. An exception is Job 1:6 ("Now on a certain day when the sons of God had come to stand in the presence of the Lord"). "Now this premise is proposed symbolically and enigmatically, in keeping with the usage of sacred Scripture, which describes spiritual things under the figures of corporeal things. . . . Now although spiritual things are proposed under the figures of corporeal things, nevertheless, the truths intended about spiritual things through sensible figures belong not to the mystical but to the literal sense because the literal sense is that which is primarily intended by the words, whether they are used properly or figuratively" (*Expositio* 1:6, 223–34, p. 7). On the other hand, Aquinas says that 40:10–14 "cannot refer literally to the devil," and at 40:19 he states that "by this passage is designated mystically the fact that Christ overcame the devil." Occasionally Aquinas allows for the possibility of alternate literal interpretations of a text; see *Expositio* 35:32–33, 41:16.

88. *Expositio*, Prol., 72–90, p. 3. Aquinas draws on the reference in Ezek. 14:14 to Noah, Daniel, and Job as proof that Job was a historical person. To deny his historical existence is to doubt also the reality of Noah and Daniel, thereby threatening the authority of Scripture. So, too, he draws on James 5:11. Gregory interpreted Ezek. 14:14 allegorically in *Mor.* 33.20.35.

89. On this aspect of the text see Yaffe, "Interpretive Essay," in Aquinas, *The Literal Exposition on Job*, pp. 13–16.

90. *Expositio*, Prol., 55–57, p. 3. See also 1:1, 1–4, p. 5: "Quia, sicut dictum est, intentio huius libri tota ordinatur ad ostendendum qualiter res humanae providentia divina regantur, praemittitur quasi totius disputationis fundamentum quaedam historia in qua cuiusdam viri iusti multiplex afflictio recitatur: hoc enim est quod maxime videtur divinam providentiam a rebus humanis excludere." For the notion of the debate or disputatio in Aquinas's interpreta-

tion of Job, see Yaffe, "Introduction," in Aquinas, *The Literal Exposition on Job*, pp. 25–60. Yaffe argues (p. 7 n.32) that Aquinas's reading of the Book of Job as a disputatio follows that of Albert the Great. Dondaine, however, dates Albert's commentary after that of Aquinas, c. 1272–74. See Antoine Dondaine, "Introduction," in Aquinas, *Expositio super Iob ad litteram*, p. 33. On the Job commentary of Albert the Great, see Antonin-M. Justras, O.P., "Le *Commentarium in Job* d'Albert le Grand et la disputatio," *Etudes et recherches* 9 (1955): 9–20. For an examination of Aquinas's doctrine of providence, see Wright, *The Order of the Universe;* Bernard McGinn, "Development of the Thought of Aquinas on the Reconciliation of Divine Providence and Contingent Action," *The Thomist* 39 (1975): 741–52.

91. Compare *Guide* III.17.
92. *Expositio*, Prol., 1–6, p. 3.
93. *Expositio* 7:1–95, pp. 46–52; 5:17–27, 281–417, pp. 38–40; 8:3–7, 45–119, pp. 53–54; 7:6, 124–34, p. 47. Yaffe notes such cross-references throughout the English translation by Damico: Aquinas, *The Literal Exposition on Job*.
94. *Expositio* 6:28, 307–9, pp. 44–45: "'Verum tamen quod coepistis, explete' ut ex mutua disputatione veritas elucescat."
95. *Expositio* 42:7, 50–65, p. 228. Compare 13:4, 32–40, 84–85: "quia hoc mendacium adinvenerant quod Iob iniquam vitam duxisset. In hoc autem mendacium devenerant propter hoc quod circa fidem qua Deus colitur errabant, credentes quod in hac vita tantum fieret meritorum ac poenarum retributio."
96. See, among others, *Expositio* 2:11, 195–219, p. 18; 4:7, 109–30, p. 28; 5:6, 92–100, p. 36; 5:17–18, 302–18, p. 38; 7:1, 1–53, p. 47; 8:1–2, 1–44, p. 53; 13:11, 160–65, p. 86.
97. *Expositio* 13:3–4, 22–46, p. 84.
98. Aquinas sees moments in the debate where Job becomes more assertive in such passages as *Expositio* 13:19, 280–84, p. 87; 14:6, 57–61, p. 91; 17:1, 5–7, p. 106; 19:23, 221–24, p. 116; 19:25, 245–94, pp. 116–17; 21:34, 340–50, p. 127; 27:8, 84–106, p. 148.
99. *Expositio* 19:25–26, 245–94, p. 116.
100. *Expositio* 20:18, 200–205, p. 120.
101. *Expositio* 22:30, 308–15, p. 132.
102. *Expositio* 37:24–25, 375–91, p. 197.
103. *Expositio*, Prol., 24–40, p. 3; compare *ST* 1.22.1–3.
104. *Expositio*, Prol., 24–40, p. 3: "Opinione igitur plurimorum firmata in hoc quod res naturales non casu sed providentia agerentur propter ordinem qui manifeste apparet in eis, emersit dubitatio apud plurimos de actibus hominum, utrum res humanae casu procederent an aliqua providentia vel ordinatione superiori gubernarentur. Cui quidem dubitationi maxime fomentum ministravit quod in eventibus humanis nullus certus ordo apparet: non enim semper bonis bona eveniunt aut malis mala, neque rursus semper bonis mala aut malis bona, sed indifferenter bonis et malis et bona et mala. Hoc igitur est quod maxime corda hominum commovit ad opinandum res humanas providentia divina non regi, sed quidam eas casualiter procedere dicunt nisi quatinus providentia et consilio humano reguntur, quidam vero caelesti fato eorum eventus attribuunt."

105. *Expositio* 3–6, 45–112, pp. 53–54.

106. *Expositio* 5:9–16, 148–280, pp. 37–38.

107. *Expositio* 9:17, 287–308, p. 38. Aquinas is commenting on Eliphaz's words in 5:17: "Beatus homo qui corripitur a Domino. Increpationem ergo Domini ne reprobes."

108. *Expositio,* Prol., 41–57, p. 3; 9:11–13, 286–380, pp. 61–62; 12:16, 241–56, p. 82; 7:17–18, 358–419, pp. 50–51. *Expositio* 14:6, 57–61, p. 91: "ubi primo Iob suam intentionem aperuit: non enim sic negat adversitates praesentes [esse punitiones] quasi Deus hominum actus non remuneret vel puniat, sed quia tempus retributionis proprie est in alia vita." See also *Expositio* 21:17–22, 164–206, p. 125; 24:18, 200–223, p. 139. On God's punishment of sinners see also *SCG* III.140–45.

109. *Expositio* 9:2, 17–23, p. 58; 12:1–4, 21–56, p. 79. Here Aquinas sees 12:3 as proof that on all essential points about God's goodness and majesty, Job agreed with his friends. See also *Expositio* 26:5–14, 51–210, pp. 144–46.

110. *Expositio* 2:11, 208–19, p. 18; 7:1, 11–53, p. 47; 14:6, 51–61, p. 91; 24:24, 301–16, pp. 140–41; 27:1–8, 1–106, pp. 148–49. It should be noted that Aquinas was not the first to make the argument about the afterlife. Gregory, too, believed that the friends wrongly accused Job of sin, that Job proved the doctrine of resurrection in chapter 19, and that God did not always punish sinners in this life. But Gregory did not make these arguments the interpretive key to the Book of Job or the explanation for Job's perceptual superiority; indeed, his criticism that the friends judged Job according to his present situation is based more in the belief that the friends loved the temporal life rather than in the conviction that they denied the afterlife. See *Mor.* 14.58.78–79, 15.56.67, 16.62.76, 24.18.44. What for Gregory were occasional and primarily doctrinal statements became for Aquinas the hermeneutical strategy for interpreting the book.

111. *Expositio* 42:7, 50–83, pp. 228–29. Unlike Job, who sinned "lightly," Job's friends sinned by asserting "unfaithful dogma."

112. *Expositio* 1:1, 17:43, p. 5.

113. *Expositio* 6:1–3, 1–41, p. 41; 13:23, 335–50, p. 88; 16:18, 234–35, p. 104; 16:19, 264–66, p. 104; 17:2, 29–45, p. 106; 27:6, 65–74, p. 148. Throughout these passages, Aquinas explains that Job was, of course, subject to original sin (14:4) and had committed venial sins or sins of omission. Nonetheless, since Job had committed no mortal sin, he was right to insist on his "innocence" and to argue that he was not being punished for past sins.

114. *Expositio* 1:8–9, 458–79, p. 10; 23:10, 160–70, p. 135.

115. *Expositio* 1:12, 553–74, p. 11.

116. *Expositio* 16:9, 90–99, p. 102; 16:12, 138–43, p. 102.

117. *Expositio* 16:12, 141–42, p. 102; 16:15, 190, p. 103.

118. *Expositio* 23:10, 160–70, p. 135.

119. *Expositio* 9:16, 426–45, p. 63:

hoc enim est conterere quod multiplicare vulnera, idest tribulationes, et hoc est *in turbine,* idest in horribili obscuritate, quod dicit *sine causa,* scilicet manifesta et ab homine afflicto perceptibili; si enim homo afflictus perciperet causam quare Deus eum affligit et quod afflictiones sunt ei utiles ad salutem, manifestum est quod crederet se exauditum, sed quia hoc non intelligit credit se non exauditum. Et ideo non solum exterius affligitur sed etiam interius, sicut infirmus qui nesciret se per medicinam amaram sanitatem consecuturum non solum affligeretur in gustu sed etiam in animo.

See also *Expositio* 10:1, 12–15, p. 68.

120. *Expositio*, conclusion, 368–79, p. 212.

121. *Expositio* 3:1, 1–15, p. 20; 3:3, 103–13, p. 21.

122. *Expositio* 3:1, 7, p. 20.

123. Ibid.: "Ratio enim condicionem naturae auferre non potest; est autem naturale sensibili naturae ut et convenientibus delectetur et gaudeat et de nocivis doleat et tristetur: hoc igitur ratio auferre non potest sed sic moderatur ut per tristitiam ratio a sua rectitudine non divertat."

124. *Expositio* 7 (conclusion), 527–37, p. 52: "Notandum est etiam quod Iob in verbis praemissis tres rationes tetigit quare aliquis in hac vita flagellatur a Deo: prima est ut cohibeatur eius malitia ne aliis nocere possit, et hanc rationem tetigit cum dixit 'Numquid mare sum ego aut cetus quia circumdedisti me carcere?'; secunda est ad hominis probationem ut virtus eius manifestetur, et hanc tetigit cum dixit, 'Visitas eum diluculo et subito probas illum'; tertia est in poenam peccatorum, et hoc tetigit cum dixit 'Peccavi, quid faciam tibi, o custos hominum' etc." See also *Expositio* 7:18, 399–406, pp. 50–51: "*et subito probas illum* per adversa in quibus apparet qualiter se habeat ad virtutem quia, sicut habetur Eccli. xxvii.6 'Vasa figuli probat fornax, et homines iustos tentatio tribulationis.'" See also *Expositio* 23:10, 160–70, p. 135.

125. *Expositio* 9:16–17, 419–21, p. 63: "ita Deus homini in tribulationibus constituto tribulationes non subtrahit, quamvis deprecanti, quia scit eas expedire ad finalem salutem." See, among others, *Expositio* 1:21, 847–61, p. 15: "Non enim esset placitum Deo quod aliquis adversitatem pateretur nisi propter aliquod inde proveniens bonum: unde adversitas, licet ipsa ex se amara sit et tristitiam generet, tamen ex consideratione utilitatis propter quam Deo placet debet esse iocunda, sicut et de apostolis dicitur, 'Ibant apostoli gaudentes' etc."

126. In contrast, of course, to Gregory's Job; compare *Mor.* 5.1.1.

127. *Expositio* 17:11, 159–65, p. 108: "Deinde proponit mala quae patitur cum subdit *cogitationes meae dissipatae sunt,* idest impeditae a quieta contemplatione sapientiae propter acerbitatem corporalis doloris, et hoc est quod subdit *torquentes cor meum,* quia videlicet eius cogitationes a suavi consideratione veritatis erant deductae in amaritudinem qua cor torquebatur."

128. *Expositio* 16:8, 67–72, p. 102.

129. Ibid.

130. *Expositio* 30:16–20, 182–217, p. 162.

131. *Expositio* 3:3, 110–13, p. 21; 3:8, 275–76, p. 23: "Sic igitur Iob quia secundum partem sensibilem vitam sub adversitate repudiabat . . . vult eam esse idiosam malis: nam adversitatem et boni et mali abhorrent." Throughout this passage Aquinas explains that Job is speaking in accordance with the "sensual side" of his nature—that is, the "lower part of the soul," which was affected by sadness.

132. *Expositio* 3:10, 312–18, p. 23: "non ipsam vitam propter se abhorreo sed propter mala quae patior; etsi enim vita secundum se desiderabilis sit, non tamen vita miseriis subiecta. Ubi considerandum est quod omnia quae supra figurative locutus est hac finali clausula exposuisse videtur, quod etiam in aliis eius dictis advertendum est."

133. *Expositio* 10:18, 382–84, p. 72.

134. *Expositio* 9:22–23, 508–40, p. 64; 21:6–8, 39–69, pp. 123–24; 21:23–26, 230–67, p. 126.

135. See, among others, *Expositio* 7:10–11, 237–41, 251, p. 49; 10:21, 423–25, 463, p. 73; 23:3, 50–51, p. 133.

136. *Expositio* 21:27, 268–72, p. 126: "Erat autem opinio amicorum Iob quod ratio praedictae diversitatis esset ex diversitate meritorum, quod est contra id quod experimento apparet de hoc quod impiorum quidam prosperantur, quidam adversa patiuntur."

137. Yaffe, "Interpretive Essay," in Aquinas, *The Literal Exposition on Job*, pp. 44–45.

138. *Expositio* 30:21, 220–21, 225–26, p. 163.

139. *Expositio* 13:1–13, 1–183, pp. 84–86.

140. *Expositio* 13:4–6, 42–60, p. 84. Compare 17:6, 103–5, p. 107.

141. *Expositio* 10 (conclusion), 495–506, p. 74.

142. *Expositio* 25:1, 6–8, p. 142; 24:24–25, 300–315, pp. 140–41; 37:7–8, 86–89, p. 148.

143. *Expositio* 38:3, 68–70, p. 199.

144. *Expositio* 33:12, 116–17, p. 175. Aquinas is commenting throughout the text primarily on 13:3 ("But yet I would speak with the Almighty and I desire to debate with God"). Explaining this verse, Aquinas says, "Non quidem ut eius iudicia improbare velim sed ut vestros errores destruam, quibus suppositis sequeretur quod esset iniustitia apud Deum" (*Expositio* 13:3, 30–32, p. 84). See also *Expositio* 9:1, 15–16, p. 58; 9:22, 509–10, p. 64.

145. *Expositio* 38:1, 5–17, p. 199.

146. Martin D. Yaffe, "Providence in Medieval Aristotelianism: Moses Maimonides and Thomas Aquinas on the Book of Job," *Hebrew Studies* 20–21 (1979–80): 73–74. A revised version of this essay can be found in *The Voice from the Whirlwind*, ed. Clark Gilpin and Leo Perdue (Nashville: Abingdon Press, 1991), pp. 111–28.

147. Idit Dobbs-Weinstein, "Medieval Biblical Commentary and Philosophical Inquiry as Exemplified in the Thought of Moses Maimonides and St. Thomas Aquinas," in *Moses Maimonides and His Time*, ed. Ormsby, p. 119.

148. *Expositio* 38:3, 76–84, p. 199.

149. *Expositio* 38:3, 75–83, p. 200.

150. *Expositio* 11:6, 51–74, pp. 75–76; 11:7–10, 103–65, pp. 76–77; 26:14, 197–210, p. 146; 23:8, 117–20, p. 134; 23:13, 206–15, p. 135; 36:23–31, 247–331, pp. 191–92.

151. *Expositio* 38:3, 77–81, p. 200.

152. *Expositio* 38:4, 102–8, p. 200; 38:37, 581–87, p. 206.

153. *Expositio* 38:8, 180–90, p. 201; 38:13, 257–79, p. 202.

154. *Expositio* 38:35, 608–11, p. 206.

155. *Expositio* 39:34–35, 343–67, p. 212.

156. *Expositio* (conclusion), 368–79, p. 212.

157. *Expositio* 40:7–9, 166–220, p. 215, especially lines 215–20.

158. *Expositio* 40:10, 269–81, p. 216.

159. *Expositio* 40:10, 282, 288–89, p. 216: "si referatur ad diabolum, de quo figuraliter sive metaphorice haec dicuntur."

160. *Expositio* 40:14, 395–97, p. 217.

161. *Expositio* 41:16, 293–95, p. 225.

162. *Expositio* 41:16, 299–301, p. 225.

163. *Expositio* 41:24, 451–57, p. 227.

164. *Expositio* 40:19–20, 475–544, pp. 218–19.

165. *Expositio* 40:19, 477, p. 218.

166. *Expositio* 40:27, 653–77, p. 221.

167. See *Expositio* 41:24, 451–57, p. 227, where Job is told to be careful of an attitude and words that "smacked [saperent]" of pride.

168. *Expositio* 42:3, 14–49, p. 228.

169. *ST* I.II.37.2 ad 2.

170. *ST* I.II.38.4.

171. Thomas Aquinas, *Sententia libri Ethicorum,* in *Opera omnia,* iussu Leonis XIII P.M. edita, cura et studio Fratrum Praedicatorum, vol. 47, pts. 1–2 (2 vols.) (Rome, 1969). I have cited this work by book, section, line, and page number: VII.13, 1153b, 20–27, p. 431; VII.14, 1154a.13, 65–72, p. 436. See also X.2, 1172b.18, 50–53, p. 555: "Manifeste enim apparet quod tristitia secundum se est omnibus fugienda."

172. *Sententia* VII.13, 1153b, 20–27, p. 431.

173. *Sententia* VII.12, 1153a.7, 141–43, p. 429.

174. *Sententia* VII.12, 1153b.31, 160–64, p. 433; VII.14, 1154a.26, 111–14, p. 436.

175. *Guide* III.51, p. 625.

176. *Expositio* 1:6, 235–65, pp. 7–8. In the *Expositio* Aquinas makes this point in order to show that Satan acted only by divine permission (1:12, 586–610, p. 12). See also *Expositio* 7:17, 362–94, p. 50; 11:6, 58–74, pp. 76–77.

177. *Expositio* 22:11, 103–54, pp. 129–30. Yaffe refers the reader to Averroes, *Aristotelis Metaphysicorum commentarium* XI.51, in Averroes, *Aristotelis omnia quae extant opera . . . Averrois Cordubensis in ea opera omnes, qui ad haec usque tempora pervenere, commentarii,* 9 vols. in 11 (Venice: Apud Junctus, 1562), vol. 8, p. 335, col. 1. An English translation from the Arabic is available in *Ibn Rushd's Metaphysics: A Translation with Introduction of Ibn Rushd's Commentary on Aristotle's Metaphysics, Book Lam,* trans. Charles Genequand (Leiden: E. J. Brill, 1984), p. 198. In this section Averroes is arguing that divine knowledge is not of the particular because the particulars are indefinite and no knowledge encompasses indefinite things. Aquinas cites Averroes's commentary in *Scriptum super libros Sententiarum,* I.d.35, a.3. Compare *ST* I.14.5–6, 11.

178. *Expositio* 24:1–3, 1–44, p. 137. Compare *Scriptum super libros Sententiarum,* I.d.38, q.1, a.5: "all knowledge is after the mode of the knower, as has been said. Since therefore God is eternal, it is proper that his knowledge have the mode of eternity . . . and so in his knowledge he sees all temporal things,

although successive in themselves, as present to him." Cited by McGinn, "The Development of the Thought of Aquinas on the Reconciliation of Divine Providence and Contingent Action," p. 744. See ibid., p. 750, for McGinn's discussion of how Aquinas's argument has advanced in *SCG* III.c.94.

179. *Expositio* 42:10, 109–13, p. 229.

180. *Expositio* 9:3, 46–50, p. 58: "quod non potest homo Deo respondere unum pro mille ac si diceret quod nulla determinata numeri mensura metiri potest quantum divina iustitia humanam excedat, cum haec sit finita, illa autem infinita." See also *Expositio* 9:30–32, 658–719, p. 66; 25:6, 85–94, p. 143.

181. *ST* I.13.6.

3. Does God Pervert Justice?

1. As noted in chapter 1, the literal exegesis of Job was continued by such early sixteenth-century commentators as Tommaso de Vio (Cajetan), *In librum Iob commentarii* (Rome, 1535); Johannes Oecolampadius, *In librum Iob exegema* (Basel, 1532); and, to a lesser extent, Johannes Brenz, *Iob. Cum piis et eruditis Ioannis Brentii commentariis . . .* (Halle, 1546). All were later collected by the Academy Library. I have followed manuscript spelling. Oecolampadius and Cajetan follow the tradition established by Maimonides and Aquinas by stating explicitly that the Book of Job is a debate about the nature of divine providence. Cajetan, for example, writes, "quòd materia libri est divina providentia, praecipuè circa actiones humanas, & qualitas eius; nam disputatio inter Job & amicos eius, circa qualitatem divinæ providentiæ versatur: an videlicet sit talis, quòd etiam iustis mala præsentis vitae dispenset. Principium autem libri de divina providentia erga humanas actiones tractat: finis verò etiam circa alia divinam manifestat providentiam" (*In librum Iob commentarii*, p. 401). Oecolampadius agrees that the nature of providence is the subject matter of the book and, like Aquinas, begins by listing the erroneous opinions about providence held by such groups as the Epicureans and Aristotelians. For Brenz, the Book of Job is about the suffering of the faithful, "whose life may be impure but whose doctrine is pure." "Porro inter eos sanctos, in quibus & misericordia & iudicium Domini manifestantur, vel inter præcipuos, Iob primus est. . . . Igitur quod Dominus fateatur, se Iobem sine caussa adflixisse, non in legem & peccati maledictionem, respicit, sed in Evangelion & in fidem, quam in Iob, se donante, invenit. Est autem hoc libri huius Thema, Dominū sine caussa, hoc est, non propter peccatum solere affligere pios" (*Iob. Cum . . . commentariis . . .*, pp. 2A, 8A; see also p. 20A). Brenz goes on to explain that by these afflictions, God was "testing" his holy man.

2. *CO* 33:272–73, 443, 448; *CO* 34:51–52, 261, 370, 575; *CO* 35:246, 464–67. On Calvin's exegetical method see the following: Alexandre Ganoczy and Stefan Scheld, *Die Hermeneutik Calvins: Geistesgeschichtliche Voraussetzungen und Grundzüge* (Wiesbaden: Franz Steiner Verlag, 1983), pp. 90–187; Hans-Joachim Kraus, "Calvins exegetische Prinzipien," *Zeitschrift für Kirchengeschichte* 79 (1968): 329–41; T.H.L. Parker, *Calvin's Old Testament Commentaries* (Edinburgh: T. and T. Clark, 1986); T. F. Torrance, *The Hermeneutics of John Calvin* (Edinburgh: Scottish Academic Press, 1988); Wilhelm de Greef, *Calvijn en het Oude*

Testament (Amsterdam: Ton Bolland, 1984), pp. 31–92; J. Marius J. Lange van Ravenswaay, *Augustinus totus noster: Das Augustinverständnis bei Johannes Calvin* (Göttingen: Vandenhoeck and Ruprecht, 1990), pp. 53–102. Compare Luchesius Smits, *Saint Augustin dans l'oeuvre de Jean Calvin*, 2 vols. (Assen: van Gorcum, 1957), vol. 1, pp. 268, 274; and Oberman, *Initia Calvini*, p. 119 n.31. Both Smits and Oberman point out that Calvin thought Augustine was sometimes wrong in his exegesis (*CO* 31:310b [Ps. 31:19]; *CO* 48:137b [Acts 7:14]; cited by Oberman). See A. de Pury, "Y a-t-il encore une spécificité de l'exégèse réformée?" in *Actualité de la Réforme* (Geneva: Éditions Labor et Fides, 1987), pp. 79–92. Compare Wilhelm Vischer, "Calvin, exégète de l'Ancien Testament," *Etudes théologiques et religieuses* 45 (1965): 213–31; George W. Stroup, "Narrative in Calvin's Hermeneutic," in *John Calvin and the Church*, ed. Timothy George (Louisville, Ky.: Westminster/John Knox Press, 1990), pp. 157–71; Roland M. Frye, "Calvin's Theological Use of Figurative Language," in *John Calvin and the Church*, ed. George, pp. 172–94.

Since Calvin does not give the Hebrew original when noting the meaning of a word, the Job sermons are not extremely useful for the question of Calvin's use of Hebrew. On this question see Antoine Jean Baumgartner, *Calvin hébraisant et interprète de l'Ancien Testament* (Paris: Librairie Fischbacher, 1889). A more recent discussion can be found in Parker, *Calvin's Preaching*, pp. 80–88. Parker notes that although he never cites the original, Calvin preached from a Hebrew Bible in his Old Testament sermons. He does not identify the particular edition and often cites the verse differently in the context of the sermon itself. The issue is even more problematic for both his Old and New Testament sermons and for his very ambiguous references to other interpreters who are referred to generally as *aucuns*. On the difficulty of Calvin's Old Testament text, see also T.H.L. Parker, *Calvin's Old Testament Commentaries* (Edinburgh: T. and T. Clark, 1986), p. 37 n.72. On page 5 Parker does suggest that Calvin made some use of Sebastian Münster's Hebrew Old Testament. Parker does not specify this, however, on the basis of the Job sermons. For a discussion of exegetical developments in the years leading to the Reformation, see G. R. Evans, *The Language and Logic of the Bible: The Road to Reformation* (Cambridge: Cambridge University Press, 1985). For further references, consult the bibliography in Ganoczy and Scheld, *Die Hermeneutik Calvins.*.

On the history of the concept of the literal sense, see Brevard S. Childs, "The Sensus Literalis of Scripture: An Ancient and Modern Problem," in *Beiträge zur Alttestamentlichen Theologie: Festschrift für Walther Zimmerli zum 70. Geburtstag* (Göttingen: Vandenhoeck and Ruprecht, 1977), pp. 80–93.

On Calvin's use of the French language, consult Francis M. Higman, *The Style of John Calvin in His French Polemical Treatises* (London: Oxford University Press, 1967); and Higman, ed., *Jean Calvin, Three French Treatises* (London: Athlone Press, 1970), pp. 26–36.

3. *CO* 33:406–10, 607–9; *CO* 34:61, 139, 301–2, 305, 322, 385, 445, 462, 464. Compare *CO* 34:221–22, 35:494.

4. *CO* 33:731; *CO* 34:89, 221–24, 263–64, 302, 307, 372, 385–86, 406–7, 444–45; *CO* 35:2–3, 28–29. See also *CO* 34:264: "Nous voyons que tout est esgal: mais Iob ici conclud contre ses ennemis, que combien que la fin soit pareille en

apparence, toutes fois il y a un iugement de Dieu par dessus cela, et qu'il ne faut point que les hommes s'abrutissent pour demeurer seulement au sepulchre et à ce qui apparoist là: mais qu'ils cognoissent, Dieu restaurera les choses, tellement que les boucs seront separez d'avec les agneaux, quand Dieu monstrera qu'il est Iuge du monde: mais le temps n'est pas venu encores."

5. On Calvin's view of providence and history, see the following: Josef Bohatec, "Calvins Vorsehungslehre," in *Calvinstudien: Festschrift zum 400. Geburtstage Johann Calvins* (Leipzig: Rudolph Haupt, 1909), pp. 340–441; Bohatec, "Gott und die Geschichte nach Calvin," *Philosophia reformata* (1936): 129–161; Heinrich Berger, *Calvins Geschichtsauffassung,* Studien zur Dogmengeschichte und systematischen Theologie 6 (Zürich: Zwingli-Verlag, 1955); Charles Partee, *Calvin and Classical Philosophy,* Studies in the History of Christian Thought 14 (Leiden: E. J. Brill, 1977); Richard Stauffer, *Dieu, la création et la providence dans la prédication de Calvin* (Berne: Peter Lang, 1978), pp. 261–302; Henri Strohl, "La pensée de Calvin sur la providence divine au temps où il était réfugié à Strasbourg," *Revue d'histoire et de philosophie religieuses* 22 (1942): 154–169; Susan Schreiner, *The Theater of His Glory: Nature and the Natural Order in the Thought of John Calvin* (Durham, N.C.: Labyrinth Press, 1991), pp. 7–37; Charles Trinkaus, "Renaissance Problems in Calvin's Theology," *Studies in the Renaissance* 1 (1954): 59–80.

6. *Inst.* 1.17.11.

7. Ibid.

8. *Inst.* 1.18.1.

9. *Inst.* 1.5.1.

10. Ibid.

11. Brian A. Gerrish, "'To the Unknown God': Luther and Calvin on the Hiddenness of God," *The Old Protestantism and the New* (Chicago: University of Chicago Press, 1982), p. 142.

12. *Inst.* 1.17.1.

13. *Inst.* 1.17.2.

14. *Inst.* 1.17.1.

15. *Inst.* 1.16.6.

16. *Inst.* 1.17.1.

17. After discussing the various purposes for which God sends afflictions, Calvin argues, "Now, to suffer persecution for the sake of righteousness is a singular comfort. For it ought to occur to us how much honor God bestows upon us in thus furnishing us with the special badge of his soldiery" (*Inst.* 3.8.7). See also Ronald S. Wallace, *Calvin's Doctrine of the Christian Life* (Grand Rapids, Mich.: Wm. B. Eerdmans, 1959), pp. 67–68.

18. *Inst.* 3.8.1. On this theme see also Wallace, *Calvin's Doctrine of the Christian Life,* pp. 41–74.

19. *Inst.* 2.10.10. In this section of the *Institutes,* Calvin is arguing against Servetus and the "Anabaptist" denigration of the Old Testament: "Now let us examine the chief point in this controversy: whether or not the believers were so taught by the Lord as to perceive that they had a better life elsewhere; and, disregarding the earthly life, to meditate on the heavenly. First, the manner of life divinely enjoined upon them was a continual exercise by which they were re-

minded that they were the most miserable of all men if they were happy in this life only."

20. *Inst.* 2.10.10–11.

21. *Inst.* 2.10.11.

22. *Inst.* 2.10.12.

23. *CO* 33:82–88, 286–87, 439; *CO* 34:61, 94, 97, 135.

24. For the dates of Calvin's Old Testament commentaries, see Parker, *Calvin's Old Testament Commentaries*, pp. 29–34; and Erwin Mülhaupt, *Die Predigt Calvins: Ihre Geschichte, ihre Form und ihre religiösen Grundgedanken* (Berlin: Walter de Gruyter, 1931), pp. 1–24; W. de Greef, *Johannes Calvijn: Zijn werk en geschriften* (Kampen: De Groot Goudriaan), pp. 93–101. See also the introductions by Hanns Ruckert and Erwin Mülhaupt to vols. 1 (1961) and 7 (1981) of the *Supplementa Calviniana*.

I treated the exegetical relationship between Job and David in my earlier essay, "'Why Do the Wicked Live?': Job and David in Calvin's Sermons on Job," in *The Voice from the Whirlwind*, ed. Gilpin and Perdue, pp. 129–43. However, limited space precluded extensive bibliographic references. The following paragraph includes many of the secondary sources pertinent to that essay and further amplifies that discussion.

For the history of the interpretation of David, see A. Gosselin, *The King's Progress to Jerusalem: Some Interpretations of David during the Reformation Period and Their Patristic and Medieval Background* (Malibu: Undena, 1976). On the interpretation of the Psalms in the sixteenth century, see R. Gerald Hobbs, "Hebraica Veritas and Traditio Apostolica: Saint Paul and the Interpretation of the Psalms in the Sixteenth Century," in *The Bible in the Sixteenth Century*, ed. David C. Steinmetz (Durham, N.C.: Duke University Press, 1990), pp. 83–99. On Calvin's view of and fondness for David, see R. A. Hasler, "The Influence of David and the Psalms upon John Calvin's Life and Thought," *Hartford Quarterly* 5 (1965): 7–18. Walchenbach's unpublished master's thesis also addresses the influence of David on Calvin: John Robert Walchenbach, "The Influence of David and the Psalms on the Life and Thought of John Calvin," (thesis, Pittsburgh Theological Seminary, 1969). On Calvin's Psalms commentary, see also: Hans-Joachim Kraus, "Vom Leben und Tod in den Psalmen: Eine Studie zu Calvins Psalmen-Kommentar," in *Leben angesichts des Todes. Beiträge zum theologischen Problem des Todes: Helmut Thielicke zum 60. Geburtstag* (Tübingen: J.C.B. Mohr, 1968), pp. 258–77; James Luther Mays, "Calvin's Commentary on the Psalms: The Preface as Introduction," in *John Calvin and the Church*, ed. George, pp. 195–205. Consult also the bibliography in De Greef, *Johannes Calvijn*, p. 96 n.33.

25. *CO* 34:586. Compare *Supplementa Calviniana*, vol. 1 (1961), p. 468; *CO* 34:602.

26. *CO* 34:350; compare *CO* 34:625.

27. *CO* 33:85, 286–87, 439, 625; *CO* 34:97, 135, 602, 607, 610. Compare *CO* 30:412, 416, 343–34; *CO* 31:373, 378, 382–83, 638–39; *SC* I.601, 645.

28. Ambrose, *De interpellatione Iob et David*, in *Sancti Ambrosii Opera*, ed. Carolus Schenkl, *CSEL*, vol. 32.2 (1897), pp. 209–96. Ambrose is often citing the Septuagint.

29. *De interpellatione* III.3.5; compare III.1.1.

30. *De interpellatione* I.1.1, I.9.30. Judith Baskin points out that Ambrose stressed Job's patience and steadfastness but, preferring to keep Job on the human plane, ignored typological parallels between Job and Christ. It was the "human suffering Job" that appealed to Ambrose as a tropological idea. See J. R. Baskin, "Job as Moral Exemplar in Ambrose," *Vigiliae Christianae* 35 (1981): 222–31. On Job as the Righteous Gentile, see Baskin, *Pharaoh's Counsellors: Job, Jethro, and Balaam in Rabbinic and Patristic Tradition*, Brown Judaic Studies 47 (Chico, Calif.: Scholars Press, 1983), pp. 7–44.

31. *De interpellatione* I.3.6, pp. 213–14. Ambrose cites Job 7:1–6 in conjunction with Sirach 23:18 and Luke 15:11–16.

32. *De interpellatione* I.1.3.

33. *De interpellatione* I.1.1.

34. *De interpellatione* II.2.3.

35. *De interpellatione* I.2.4.

36. *De interpellatione* II.1.2; compare II.3.7–3.8.

37. *De interpellatione* II.2.3., p. 235: "at vir sanctus Iob discernebat spiritu quomodo cuique eum oporteret loqui: fortior ergo quam illi qui sani et incolumes viderentur. et quid dico fortiorem inuentum ceteris? fortior [erat aeger quam cum sanus esset] se ipso inventus est; fortior enim erat aeger Iob quam sanus fuerat, secundum quod scriptum est quia virtus in infirmitatibus consummatur."

38. *De interpellatione* III.2.3.

39. *De interpellatione* III.3.9.

40. *De interpellatione* II.1.2–2.4, II.4.12 (citing 1 Cor. 2:14).

41. *De interpellatione* II.4.11.

42. *De interpellatione* III.2.3.

43. *De interpellatione* III.11.29; compare II.5.17.

44. *De interpellatione* I.9.28–29, I.4.13, I.4.16, IV.2.6.

45. *De interpellatione* II.4.15, II.5.17, III.3.8.

46. *De interpellatione* I.9.30, IV.5.19.

47. *De interpellatione* I.9.30, IV.2.6. Compare Ambrose's sermon *De fuga saeculi*, in *CSEL*, vol. 32.2 (1897), pp. 163–207.

48. *CO* 33:23–24; *CO* 34:268, 294, 317; *CO* 35:1, 28–29, 34, 131, and passim. When interpreting the words of the friends, Cajetan closely follows Aquinas. According to Cajetan, the friends were reproved because they denied that rewards and punishments extended to the afterlife. Cajetan also excludes Elihu from the final divine reproof in 42:7 (*In librum Iob commentarii*, p. 556A). Brenz argues that although the friends were reproved by God, not all their words were wrong. Their error consisted in concluding that Job was struck because of sin. Still, Brenz insists, they said many true things about the wisdom and power of God (*Iob. Cum . . . commentariis. . .* , p. 21A; compare pp. 96A, 245A). Oecolampadius is somewhat harder on Job's friends than is Brenz, identifying their arguments as the "internal cross" the just have to bear. Like Gregory, however, he notes that Paul cited the words of Eliphaz, and he admits that the friends said many true things about divine power and wisdom. Like Aquinas, Oecolampadius identifies the error of the friends with their denial of the afterlife and their restriction of

God's rewards and punishments to this life (*In librum Iob exegema*, pp. 18A, 19B, 252A).

49. *CO* 33:23–24. William James Bouwsma notes that Calvin can sometimes sound like Job's friends: *John Calvin: A Sixteenth-Century Portrait* (New York: Oxford University Press, 1988), p. 96. Like earlier commentators, Calvin excludes Elihu from the divine rebuke in 42:7. The exclusion allows him to use Elihu to correct the other friends. On the basis of Elihu's speeches, Calvin can appeal to the revelation in nature and to divine transcendence, themes pursued in the chapter 4.

50. *CO* 33:166, 262, 288, 375–76; *CO* 35:9–10. Compare *CO* 33:23; *CO* 34:268, 284, 294, 317; *CO* 35:1, 28–30, 34, 131, 175. Compare also Bouwsma, *John Calvin*, pp. 94–96.

51. *CO* 33:138, 166, 262, 268–69, 294, 301, 375, 478, 510, 585; *CO* 34:93–94, 291, 585, 590, 619; *CO* 35:118, 175, 198–200, 270–72, 285–86.

52. *Inst.* 1.1.2; compare *Inst.* 2.1.2–3.

53. *CO* 34:94. We can discern a parallel in Calvin's thought between the role of Scripture and that of suffering: Both restore the sinner to healed perception. Just as Scripture serves as a pair of spectacles to cure the noetic effect of sin so that we can once again come to see God in nature, suffering allows the sinner to perceive the character of the fallen self.

54. *CO* 33:257–70.

55. Calvin probably intended to cite Ps. 119:71. In his commentary on the Psalms Calvin admits that the authorship is uncertain, but he claims the right to attribute it to David since David surpassed all others in poetical and devotional skill.

56. *CO* 33:269; *CO* 35:508. Compare *CO* 34:277–78; *CO* 35:199–200. Bouwsma notes, however, that Calvin could also criticize David's excessive grief at the deaths of Saul and Jonathan (*John Calvin*, p. 94).

57. See, for example, Calvin's exegesis of Psalms 6, 32, 38, 51, 130, 143. (Calvin seems to read Psalm 130 as Davidic, as is evident in his interpretation of verse 4.)

58. Calvin refers to Job in his commentary on the following Psalms: *CO* 31:399 (Ps. 39:5); *CO* 31:418 (Ps:41:1); *CO* 31:807 (Ps. 88:6, non-Davidic); *CO* 31:676 (Ps. 73:4).

59. *CO* 33:666.

60. *CO* 34:350. Calvin cites Ps. 130:3 and 143:2 in David's defense.

61. *CO* 33:151–53, 269, 666; *CO* 34:277–78, 350; *CO* 35:114, 199–200, 508.

62. In his excellent study, Zuckerman analyzes in detail how Job came to be known as the model of patience, as evidenced by St. James's Epistle. Although this remained the traditional view for many later exegetes, it was not the only interpretation of Job's laments. We have already seen in Aquinas's *Expositio* that Job's words were often spoken from his lower nature. In Calvin we see a much clearer admission that Job was, indeed, often *impatient*. It is not quite fair to say, therefore, that "consequently, when he [James] celebrated the patience of Job, this concept remained fixed from then on as the precedent. Thereafter, especially once the New Testament had authority of its own as the canon that takes

precedence over the Old Testament canon, all Christian interpretation of Job had to begin with the assumption that first and foremost, he was the most patient of men" (Zuckerman, *Job the Silent: A Study in Historical Counterpoint*, p. 179).

63. *CO* 33:109, 383–88; *CO* 34:305–6, 483.

64. Calvin's recommendation that believers should study history should not, however, be taken to mean that the observer always sees providence within the historical present. It is by looking to the outcome of events recorded in the past that one can perceive the workings of divine providence. Compare Josef Bohatec, *Budé und Calvin, Studien zur Gedankenwelt des französischen Frühhumanismus* (Graz: Böhlau, 1950), pp. 280–300.

65. *CO* 33:103–16, 242, 372, 437–38, 649–50, 656. When interpreting this verse Cajetan is eager to explain that God was not "moved" by Satan but had decided to give power to the devil by a decision made "from eternity." He also argues that the word *frustra* means "sine causa meritoria ex parte ipsius Iob" (*In librum Iob commentarii*, p. 407A). Oecolampadius stresses that God permitted Satan to strike Job, but that Satan always remained subject to divine power (*In librum Iob exegema*, pp. 10–14). In his interpretation of 2:1–6, Oecolampadius does not emphasize the word *gratis* but rather stresses that the Prologue places the tragedies of Job in the wider context of God's contest with the devil. Brenz places the verse in the context of Law and Gospel. Under the Law, all are condemned for sin. Under the Law, penalties are imposed for sin. Thus, Brenz explains, the Lord acknowledges that he struck Job "sine caussa" because he regarded him not under the Law and the curse of sin but rather as "in the Gospel" and in faith (*Iob. Cum . . . commentariis. . . ,* pp. 7B–8A).

66. *SC* I:476; compare *CO* 31:350–51, 422, 641. Calvin also states the analogy between Job's friends and Shemei in *CO* 34:92, 586.

67. *CO* 31:418. Ps. 41:1 is cited repeatedly in the *Sermons on Job: CO* 33:135, 445, 494, 534. Compare *CO* 35:30.

68. *CO* 34:135.

69. Ibid.

70. *CO* 33:221, 240–42, 277–78, 442, 451, 463, 477, 653; *CO* 34:52, 241–52, 254, 374, 477, 487, 624; *CO* 35:93, 139, 175–76, 193–94, 264, 360, 370–76, 397, 455; *CO* 30:416–17, 434, 442, 458; *CO* 31:132, 673–74; *CO* 32:19, 23–26, 196; *Supplementa Calviniana*, vol. 1 (1961), pp. 130, 431–32, 444, 594. On the hiddenness of God in Calvin's theology, see Brian A. Gerrish, "To the Unknown God: Luther and Calvin on the Hiddenness of God," in *The Old Protestantism and the New* (Chicago: University of Chicago Press, 1982), pp. 131–49; Berger, *Calvins Geschichtsauffassung*, pp. 51–55, 224–26, 237–40.

71. *CO* 33:123, 135, 286, 649, 740; *CO* 34:100, 610; *CO* 35:140, 223. Compare *CO* 33:477; *CO* 34:53, 264, 624.

72. *CO* 33:120–24.

73. *CO* 34:610.

74. *CO* 33:683.

75. *CO* 33:23.

76. *CO* 33:685; compare *CO* 33:123, 341, 683. If we turn to Calvin's interpretation of David in the Psalms and later in 1 and 2 Samuel, we can see that he

explores further the nature of this spiritual suffering caused by God's hidden-ness. Commenting on Psalm 10, he describes David's temptation as the fear that God was idle and unconcerned about human events. David began to doubt the reality of divine providence when God's "hand and judgment are not seen" (*CO* 31:116). Repeatedly, Calvin depicts David as dismayed by the seeming disorder in human history, struggling to rise above its apparent confusions in order to behold God's justice with the "eye of faith." In his interpretation of Psalm 37, Calvin explains that according to carnal sense, God indeed seems to be idle and disinterested in human lives (*CO* 31:372-73). When in 1 Sam. 22:1-5 David left his cave and was exposed to the cruelty of Saul, Calvin argues that David must have experienced the gravest of temptations: the dread that God had aban-doned him (*CO* 30:410-11). In 2 Sam. 15:25-31 Calvin interprets David's weep-ing as his sorrow that God had "hidden his face" and forsaken him (*SC* I:444; compare *SC* I:432, 594). This temptation is best described for Calvin in Psalm 73 where David says, "They are not in the trouble that is common to man." Sym-pathizing with David, Calvin writes that "when we consider that the life of men is full of labor and miseries, and that this is the law and condition appointed for everyone, it is a terrible temptation to watch the despisers of God indulging themselves in their luxurious pleasures" (*CO* 31:677).

77. *CO* 31:372.

78. *CO* 31:673-75, 810 (non-Davidic), 828-29 (non-Davidic); compare *CO* 33:123, 440; *CO* 34:220; *CO* 35:459, 482.

79. *CO* 31:109, 133, 115-16, 220-21, 645; compare *CO* 31:695-96.

80. *CO* 31:56-57, 95-108, 117-20, 651-53, 684-90.

81. *Inst.* 3.12.1.: "et in angelis suis reperit pravitatem."

82. Ibid. Compare *Inst.* 1.17.2 on God's hidden will.

83. *Comm. on Col.* 1:20; *CO* 52:88-89 (published 1548).

84. On the concept of double justice in Calvin's thought, see Josef Bohatec, "Gott und die Geschichte nach Calvin," *Philosophia reformata* (1936): 146-47; Bo-hatec, *Budé und Calvin*, p. 280; Richard Stauffer, *Interprètes de la Bible, études sur les Réformateurs du XVIe siècle*, Théologie historique 57 (Paris: Editions Beauchesne, 1980), pp. 227-34; idem. *Dieu, la création et la providence dans la prédication de Calvin*, pp. 118-19; Bouwsma, *John Calvin*, p. 42. Stauffer locates only one allu-sion outside the Job sermons that resembles the idea of God's twofold justice: the fifty-fourth sermon on 2 Sam. (*Supplementa Calviniana*, vol. 1 [1961], p. 473), where Calvin says, "Or Dieu a deux façons de commander. Il y en a l'une qui est pour nostre reigle quant a nous et a nostre esgard, l'aultre pour executer ses iugemens secretz et pour accomplir ce quil a determiné en son conseil, et pour donner cours a sa providence. Quant est de la premiere facon de commander, elle est contenue en la Loy. . . . Or il y a une autre facon de commander, cest quand il execute ses iugemens." Portions of the following discussion of double justice are found in Susan Schreiner, "Exegesis and Double Justice in Calvin's Sermons on Job," *Church History* 58 (September 1988): 322-38.

Calvin's historical sensibilities cause him to question whether Job lived be-fore or after the Law. He vacillates on this issue. In *CO* 34:580 he states that we do not know if Job lived before or after the Law but that Job did live before the prophets. In *CO* 34:631 he makes essentially the same point and explains that

Job lived before the prophets who clarified much that was obscure in the Law. In *CO* 33:497 he states that the Law was not written at the time of Job. In *CO* 35:70 he states that Job and his friends lived without the Law and that knowledge was given to them in an extraordinary fashion, as in dreams. They did not have Scripture. In *CO* 35:182 he remarks that in 34:27 Elihu spoke of those pagans who lived without the Law. However, he reminds the reader that the pagans had the Law of God written on their hearts. Calvin appears to assume this last point in his references to Job and his friends. In *CO* 33:47 he states that Job was a sign that a seed of religion remains in all people, for Job invoked God in purity. (This judgment of Job differs, of course, from what Calvin attributes to the seed of religion in the *Institutes!*) Still, these statements are rare and scattered throughout the 159 sermons. On a regular basis Calvin simply assumes the Law in his exegesis of the Joban text. In *CO* 33:552 Calvin more explicitly presumes the Law, for on pp. 546–47 he sees Zophar as articulating the first and second tables of the Law. In *CO* 33:497 he states that the Law was engraved on the hearts of men. (See also *CO* 34:586; and *CO* 35:6 and passim.) Calvin's very occasional awareness that Job lived before the Mosaic revelation of the written Law makes no impact on his arguments about God's double justice and the lower justice of the Law. It appears that Calvin simply needs the concept of the Law and uses it throughout the *Sermons on Job* in order to defend divine justice.

85. Calvin's knowledge of nominalism has been a matter of debate. In his criticism of Reuter's *Das Grundverständnis der Theologie Calvins,* Ganoczy argued that Reuter attributed undue influence to John Major as a source of the young Calvin's thought. See Alexandre Ganoczy, *The Young Calvin,* pp. 174–78. Compare Reuter, *Das Grundverständnis der Theologie Calvins,* pp. 123–72. My analysis of Calvin's theory of double justice makes no claim for a sophisticated knowledge of nominalism by the Reformer. The Job sermons reflect only Calvin's use of general Scotistic-nominalist themes and vocabulary, which he may have derived from Luther or Scotus. However, these sermons are the product of the older Calvin who had read more late medieval sources than he had in his earlier years studied by Ganoczy. As Oberman points out, "there is a whole range of themes clustered around Calvin's presentation of the *ordo salutis* which a hundred years before would have earned him the school ranking 'Scotist.'" As Oberman notes, even the young Calvin used the medieval vocabulary of commitment encountered in Scotist and nominalist theologians ("the *pactum Dei* to which God is bound *de potentia ordinata*"). Oberman, *Initia Calvini,* pp. 117, 121.

86. *Mor.* 4.26.53, 8.6.8, 8.33.56, 18.5.10, 22.14.30.

87. *Mor.* 11.38.51.

88. *Mor.* 16.32.39.

89. *Mor.* 18.5.11.

90. *Mor.* 35.5.6.

91. *Expositio* 9:15–21, 9:30, 13:15–16, 14:4. Aquinas argues in 14:4 that "what [Job] had said of himself as an individual he applies generally to the whole human race." In 14:4 Aquinas's Job referred to the "infection of concupiscence" that now infects the human seed. Conceived from this unclean seed, the human being is made virtuous or clean only through the power of God.

92. *Expositio* 96:1–2, 39:33, 42:7.

93. *Expositio* 39:35; compare 3:2–3, 3:15, 6:4, 6:10.

94. *Expositio* 39:34–35, 42:1–3.

95. Ibid.

96. *Inst.* 3.7.10.

97. Ibid.

98. *CO* 34:625; compare *CO* 33:27–30, 57–70, 119, 155, 159.

99. *CO* 33:27–30, 141. Brenz stands closest to Calvin in the interpretation of 1:1. In the preface to his commentary, Brenz makes clear that the lives of the saints are impure. According to Brenz, Job's "simplicity" stems from his faith (*Iob. Cum . . . commentariis. . .* , p. 2). Oecolampadius explains the verse linguistically but concludes by the words of John that no one is free from sin (*In librum Iob exegema*, p. 4A–B).

100. *CO* 33:141–42, 171–72, 338–39, 506, 608–9, 625, 641, 645, 657, 669, 673; *CO* 34:115–16, 611; *CO* 35:7, 55.

101. *CO* 33:153–60. The interpretation of chapter 3 is crucial for determining how any of these exegetes will interpret Job's many laments. Cajetan insists that Job did not sin by cursing the day of his birth. Like Gregory, Cajetan allows 1:21–22, 2:10, and the contest with the devil recounted in the Prologue to govern his reading of Job's speeches. Thus he argues that if Job blasphemed, then the devil won his contest with God (*In librum Iob commentarii*, p. 400B). Cajetan also concludes that Job only cursed his "present life" in order to state the subject for the future disputation with his friends. Oecolampadius denies that Job blasphemed; Job spoke from great pain and in the custom of common people, but not from blasphemy (*In librum Iob exegema*, pp. 21A, 23B). However, in 42:7 Oecolampadius admits that Job said some things "in speciem blasphema" regarding the judgments of God. Like Gregory, Oecolampadius argues that if Job blasphemed, then Satan won his challenge to God (p. 20A). Of these three sixteenth-century exegetes, Brenz most clearly states that Job did fall into blasphemy (*Iob. Cum . . . commentariis. . .* , pp. 15A, 97B–98A, 245A–B; compare pp. 23–24). For Brenz, Job's lapses do not seem particularly troublesome because Job always retained a good cause and because Job was justified by faith, not by his conduct while under trial.

102. *CO* 33:166–67.

103. *CO* 35:490–91: "Notons bien donc que Job ne parle point ici d'une penitence commune: mais il cognoist que son offence est si grieve et si enorme. . . . Ainsi nous voyons en somme ce que Iob a voulu dire: c'est qu'en ayant repentence d'avoir parlé à la volee, il adiouste, que son peché n'est point leger ne petit: mais si enorme, qu'il est prest de se constituer un povre malfaicteur, qui a commis crime mortel, et qui a toute son attente et refuge à la pure misericorde de Dieu: et mesmes que devant les hommes il fera volontiers une telle protestation." Compare *CO* 35:495–96.

104. *CO* 33:171, 458, 464–65, 467–68, 478; *CO* 35:56.

105. *CO* 33:171, 302, 613, 625; *CO* 35:58, 131, 133, 217–20, 449–50.

106. *CO* 33:141, 154, 155, 157–58, 171–72, 287, 302, 435, 452; *CO* 34:92, 96.

107. *CO* 33:154–55, 435; *CO* 34:96.

108. *CO* 33:457, 461, 633, 726; *CO* 34:334, 337. See esp. *CO* 33:496:

c'est assavoir, que la Loi de Dieu nous est bien une regle parfaite de bien vivre et sainctement voire quant à nous. Notons donc que la iustice qui est contenue en la Loi sera bien nommee parfaite: oui, au regard des hommes, c'est à dire selon leur capacité et mesure. Mais ce n'est pas une iustice qui soit correspondante à celle de Dieu, ne qui y soit egale, il s'en faut beaucoup. Comme quoy? Cela sera mieux cognu aux Anges. Voila les Anges qui n'ont point de Loy escrite, mais tant y a qu'ils se conforment à l'obeissance de Dieu. . . . La iustice des Anges combien qu'elle soit parfaite au regard des creatures, si est-ce que ce n'est rien, ce n'est que fumee quand on voudra venir devant la maiesté infinie de Dieu. Notons bien donc que quand la Loy nous a esté donnee, ç'a bien esté une regle certaine de bien vivre: et quand nous pourrions faire et accomplir ce qui nous est là ordonné, alors nous serions tenus et reputez pour iustes devant Dieu en toute perfection, ouy bien, mais tant y a encores que nous ne serions point iustes, pour dire qu'il y eust quelque dignité en nous, pour dire, que nous eussions rien merité devant luy. Et pourquoy? C'est de pure grace quand il dit, Qui fera ces choses il vivra en icelles . . . Nous voyons donc maintenant, comme il y a double iustice en Dieu, l'une c'est celle qui nous est manifestee en la Loy, de laquelle Dieu se contente, pource qu'il luy plaist ainsi: il y a une autre iustice cachee qui surmonte tous sens et apprehensions des creatures.

Compare *CO* 33: 457–500, 497–500, 633–37, 726; *CO:* 237. Also *CO* 34:335:

Iob cognoissoit bien qu'il estoit un povre pecheur, il n'estoit pas si aveuglé d'orgueil, qu'il se fist à croire qu'il estoit du tout iuste, et que Dieu n'eust que mordre sur lui: mais il entend que si Dieu le vouloit traitter à la façon commune, c'est à dire, comme il a declaré en sa Loy, qu'il benira ceux qui l'auront servi, et les traittera si doucement, qu'ils pourront bien sentir qu'il est un bon Pere: en ceste façon et suivant ceste regle, il respondroit bien devant lui. Ainsi il veut dire que Dieu use à son endroit d'une iustice qui est secrette et cachee aux hommes qu'il ne le traitte plus selon la forme de sa Loy, mais qu'il a quelque consideration que les hommes ne peuvent pas apprehender, et qui surmonte toutes leurs pensees, et tous leurs sens.

109. *CO* 33:458, 464–65, 467–68, 471–73, 478, 495–96, 725; *CO* 34:335–38, 351. See also the passages in note 96 above.

110. *CO* 33:471–72, 634; *CO* 34:38, 89, 96, 618–23, 714.

111. *CO* 33:725; *CO* 34:343–51.

112. *CO* 33: 458, 464–65, 467–68, 478, 635; *CO* 34:351.

113. *CO* 34:715–19. Compare *CO* 33:457. Calvin does admit Job's right to be vindicated before God against the false accusation of his friends.

114. *CO* 33:473.

115. *Mor.* 9.18.28; compare 5.11.21, 17.15.21.

116. *Mor.* 9.56.85.

117. *Mor.* 9.36.57.

118. *Mor.* 9.26.40.
119. *Mor.* 9.11.23.
120. *Mor.* 32.1.1, 32.4.5, 35.5.6.
121. *Mor.* 29.18.34, 35.2.3.
122. *Expositio* 9:19, 29.
123. *Expositio* 9:29.
124. *CO* 33:494; *CO* 33:460, 630–34; *CO* 34:96, 344, 443.
125. *CO* 33:455–65.
126. The Vulgate translation reads: "Ecce qui serviunt ei, non sunt stabiles, et in angelis suis reperit pravitatem." *Mor.* 5.38.68; *Expositio* 4:18.
127. Calvin's translation reads: "Voici il ne trouve point fermeté en ses serviteurs, et a mis vanité en ses Anges." In his commentary on Col. 1:20, Calvin translates this verse, "Atque huc procul dubio spectat sententia ista ex libro Iob (4:18) 'In Angelis suis reperiet iniquitatem'" (*CO* 52:89). Commenting on this verse in the Job sermons, Calvin says:

Aucuns pource qu'il leur sembloit qu'il y eust de l'absurdité, que Dieu ne trouvast point ses Anges du tout iustes, ont conclu qu'ici il n'estoit point parlé des Anges qui ont persisté en l'obeissance de Dieu, mais de ceux qui sont cheus, et sont devenus apostats. . . . Voila donc comme plusieurs ont exposé ce passage. . . . Mais il ne faut point que nous cerchions des expositions contraintes pour magnifier les Anges: car il est ici parlé des serviteurs de Dieu, et ce titre est honorable. Eliphas n'eust point dit, Dieu ne trouve point de fermeté en ses serviteurs: mais il eust dit, Voila les diables qui estoyent auparavant deputez au service de Dieu: or ils sont trebuschez d'une façon si horrible que par leur cheute tout a esté esbranlé, que le genre humain mesme est venu en semblable perdition, qu'il a esté attiré à une mesme ruine. Eliphas eust parlé ainsi: mais il dit, Dieu ne trouve point de verité en ses Anges, il y trouve folie, ou vanité: il ne dit pas rebellion ou apostasie, mais il dit seulement vanité, il parle plus doucement. Ainsi donc quand tout sera bien consideré, il n'y a nulle doute qu'ici Eliphas ne parle des Anges qui servent à Dieu, et qui s'y adonnent du tout. . . . Quant à ce qui s'ensuit que Dieu y trouve, ou y met (car le mot emporte cela, que Dieu y met) folie ou vanité: ce n'est pas que la vanité qui est aux Anges soit de Dieu, mais il dit qu'il l'y met par iugement: c'est à dire que comme iuge il prononce qu'il y a folie et vanité aux Anges, c'est à dire qu'il y a de la faute, voire, et qu'ils ne pourroyent pas subsister devant luy, quand il les voudroit traitter à la rigueur. Il est vray que ceci semble nouveau à ceux qui ne sont point exercez en l'Escriture saincte: mais si nous cognoissons que c'est de la iustice de Dieu, il ne se faut point esbahir que les Anges mesmes soyent trouvez coulpables, quand il les voudroit accomparer à luy: car il nous faut tousiours revenir à ce point, que les biens qui sont aux creatures sont en mesure petite au pris de ce qui est en Dieu, qui est du tout infini. Il nous faut donc tousiours discerner entre l'un et l'autre: voila les Anges qui ont des vertus admirables, voire si nous regardons à nous (car cependant que les Anges demeureront au reng des creatures, nous les pourrons bien glorifier) mais quand nous viendrons à Dieu, il faut que la grandeur de Dieu engloutisse tout, ainsi que nous voyons le soleil qui obscurcit toutes les estoiles du ciel. Et qu'est-ce du soleil? c'est une planete aussi bien que les autres: neantmoins pource que Dieu a donné à ceste creature-la d'avoir plus de clarité que les autres estoiles, il faut que tout soit englouty qu'on n'apperçoive point les estoiles quand le soleil domine . . . c'est assavoir que quand on demeure aux degrez et au reng des creatures, il y aura aux Anges une perfection, voire comme aux creatures: mais quand ce vient à Dieu, ceste perfection-la est comme engloutie ainsi que les estoiles n'apparoissent plus quand le soleil donne sa clarté." (*CO* 33:206–8)

Calvin then goes on to repeat his earlier exegesis of Col. 1:20 where he said that if Job 4:18 referred to the devil, nothing of importance would have been said. Rather Paul is saying that even the angels have need of a mediator because there is "not on the part of the angels so much righteousness as would be sufficient for their being fully joined with God." Compare Calvin's discussion of these verses as they "recur" in 15:14–15 (*CO* 33:725–26).

Interpreting 4:18 through John 8, Brenz explains the verse as a reference to Satan and the fallen angels (*Iob. Cum . . . commentariis. . .* , p. 18B). Cajetan interprets 4:18 to mean that in the beginning God did not make the angels "firm" by nature but rather gave them an intellect and will that they could turn away from God. According to their "nature," then, the angels were not immutable (*In librum Iob commentarii*, p. 416A; compare p. 456A). Oecolampadius also argues that 4:18 means that, by nature, the angels are not stable; if left to their "nature" God could not "believe" in them. Oecolampadius also states that this verse can be interpreted to mean that God puts no trust in his prophets, in whom one can find iniquity or depravity (*In librum Iob exegema*, p. 25A; compare p. 888). Gregory had made a somewhat similar point regarding the human frailty of God's "holy doctors."

128. *CO* 33:206. Calvin does not use 25:4–5 to expound in detail the doctrine of God's twofold justice, except perhaps briefly in *CO* 34:415.

129. *CO* 33:726; *CO* 34:96–97.

130. *CO* 33:495–96.

131. *CO* 33:205–7, 457–59, 496, 633, 643, 726; *CO* 34:96, 337.

132. *CO* 33:633; compare *CO* 34:341, 496–97.

133. *CO* 34:334.

134. "Il [Job] a declaré ci dessus, qu'il savoit bien que les Anges n'estoyent pas purs devant Dieu: et qu'il y avoit une iustice si parfaite en Dieu, qu'il faut que tout ce que les creatures peuvent amener soit aneanti: que si la clarté du soleil obscurcit les estoilles, il faut bien encore par plus forte raison que la iustice de Dieu engloutisse tout ce que nous cuidons avoir" (*CO* 34:35). Calvin uses "Job's" insight in 4:18 to excuse his more passionate outbursts where he desired to plead his case before God.

135. *Mor.* 9.15.22; compare 9.24.21–15.22, 16.11.50.

136. *Expositio* 9:22, 9:35, 23:13.

137. *Expositio* 9:10–11, 17–18.

138. *Expositio* 23:13.

139. *CO* 33:437–42; *CO* 34:444–46, 611, 713; *CO* 35:55–56.

140. C0 34:336, 338–42, 345, 357–60; *CO* 35:54–56, 131.

141. *CO* 34:336; compare *CO* 34:338.

142. *CO* 31:83, 85, 253, 301, 591. Compare *CO* 34:174, 222, 256.

143. *CO* 33:339, 371–72; *CO* 34:36, 175, 222, 336, 339, 360, 362; *CO* 35:58–59, 131, 154, 315, 369, 454, 479–80.

144. *CO* 33:371, 540, 584; *CO* 34:36, 175, 335–40, 362; *CO* 35:59–60, 131, 144–46, 151, 154, 178, 222, 315, 369, 479.

145. *CO* 33:104–11, 242, 372, 437–38, 650–56; *CO* 34:254–55, 449; *CO* 35:169, 479.

146. *CO* 33:141; *CO* 34:98, 232, 258, 362, 483; *CO* 35:59–60, 141, 153–54, 174–78.

147. *CO* 34:335–40. Compare *CO* 33:494–501, 633–34; *CO* 34:96–98, 443, 714.

148. *CO* 33:501.

149. *CO* 33:461. Compare *CO* 33:495–96, 499; *CO* 34:333–35, 337; *CO* 35:479.

150. The term *nominalist* is debated. For a history of its changing assessment, see the following: William J. Courtenay, "Nominalism and Late Medieval Religion," in *The Pursuit of Holiness in Late Medieval Religion,* ed. Charles Trinkaus and Heiko Oberman (Leiden: E. J. Brill, 1974), pp. 26–59; Courtenay, "Nominalism and Late Medieval Thought: A Bibliographical Essay," *Theological Studies* 33 (1972): 716–34; Courtenay, *Covenant and Causality in Medieval Thought: Studies in Philosophy, Theology, and Economic Practice* (London: Variorum Reprints, 1984); Leif Grane, "Gabriel Biels Lehre von der Allmacht Gottes," *Zeitschrift für Theologie und Kirche* 53 (1956): 53–75; Grane, *Contra Gabrielem, Luthers Auseinandersetzung mit Gabriel Biel in der Disputatio contra Scholasticam Theologiam 1517* (Copenhagen: Gyldendal, 1962); Grane, *Modus loquendi theologicus: Luthers Kampf um die Erneuerung der Theologie (1515–1518)* (Leiden: E. J. Brill, 1975); Heiko Oberman, "Some Notes on the Theology of Nominalism," *Harvard Theological Review* 53 (1960): 46–76; Oberman, *The Harvest of Late Medieval Theology* (Cambridge, Mass.: Harvard University Press, 1963); Oberman, *Werden und Wertung der Reformation* (Tübingen: J.C.B. Mohr [Paul Siebeck], 1977); Oberman, *The Dawn of the Reformation* (Edinburgh: T. and T. Clark, 1986); David C. Steinmetz, "Scholasticism and Radical Reform: Nominalist Motifs in the Theology of Balthasar Hubmaier," *Mennonite Quarterly Review* (1971): 125–28; Paul Vignaux, *Justification et prédestination au XIVe siècle: Duns Scot, Pierre d'Auriole, Guillaume d'Occam, Grégoire de Rimini* (Paris: Leroux, 1934).

151. David C. Steinmetz, "Calvin and the Absolute Power of God," *Journal of Medieval and Renaissance Studies* 18 (1988): 65.

152. For the medieval background of this tradition of covenant and God's self-limitation, see Berndt Hamm, *Promissio, Pactum, Ordinatio: Freiheit und Selbstbindung Gottes in der scholastischen Gnadenlehre,* Beiträge zur historischen Theologie 54 (Tübingen: J.C.B. Mohr, 1977).

153. Oberman notes, however, that Calvin occasionally uses the term *abso-*

lute power. What he opposes is the *nuda potentia absoluta* (*CO* 31:402). Oberman, *Initia Calvini,* p. 121 n.44.

154. Compare *Inst.* 1.15.8, 1.16.9–17, 2.18.3; *CO* 32:12, 151–52. See also Gerrish, "To the Unknown God: Luther and Calvin on the Hiddenness of God," pp. 131–49. For studies on the hiddenness of God in Luther's thought, consult the extensive bibliography in Gerrish's article.

155. Heiko A. Oberman, "The 'Extra' Dimension in the Theology of Calvin," in *The Dawn of the Reformation* (Edinburgh: T. and T. Clark, 1986), p. 256.

156. Steinmetz, "Calvin and the Absolute Power of God," pp. 67–68.

4. Behold Behemoth!

1. *Inst.* 1.17.1. On Calvin's polemics against the notion of "fortune," see Bouwsma, *John Calvin,* pp. 167–69. For a historical perspective see C. N. Cochrane, *Christianity and Culture* (Oxford: Oxford University Press, 1940), pp. 99, 478–79; H. R. Patch, "The Tradition of the Goddess Fortuna," *Smith College Studies in Modern Languages* 3/3 (April 1922):131–77, and 3/4 (July 1922):179–235.

2. *Inst.* 1.16.9; 1.17.1; 3.23.4, 7.

3. See Calvin's comments on Isa. 45:15, 54:7–8, and Lam. 5:19–20.

4. *CO* 33:198, 237, 256, 388, 651; *CO* 34:63, 68, 91, 117, 266, 399, 405; *CO* 35:125, 185, 245, 261–62, 267, 304, 315, 353, 368–69, 406, 415, 461.

5. *CO* 33:609.

6. *CO* 34:302.

7. *CO* 35:494.

8. *CO* 33:23, 371, 406–14; *CO* 34:61, 204, 322, 533.

9. *CO* 33:556–59.

10. *CO* 33:451; *CO* 34:302, 305–6, 445, 483.

11. *CO* 34:302.

12. *CO* 33:447–51.Compare Bouwsma, *John Calvin,* pp. 169–70.

13. *CO* 33:196.

14. *CO* 33:385. Compare *CO* 33:195–96, 221–24; *CO* 34:305.

15. *CO* 33:403.

16. *CO* 33:402–6.

17. *CO* 34:163.

18. *CO* 33:82, 407, 414, 443; *CO* 34:100, 204, 216, 302, 385.

19. *CO* 33:224, 277–78; *CO* 34:77, 100, 241, 368, 462, 481, 534. Compare *CO* 34:385, 533.

20. "Nous avons dit, qu'icy il veut monstrer, que ses adversaires sont comme aveugles, et qu'ils iugent follement, d'autant qu'ils s'arrestent à ce qu'on voit maintenant à l'oeil" (*CO* 34:534). Compare *CO* 34:142.

21. *CO* 33:224, 277–78, 557; *CO* 34:53, 224, 241–42, 246, 250–51, 266, 307–8, 385–86, 469, 487, 533–34, 544.

22. *CO* 33:443. See also *CO* 33:221–24, 373–74; *CO* 34:100, 241, 245, 250, 252, 368–69, 462, 481.

23. *CO* 34:241. See also *CO* 33:277–78; *CO* 34:486–87.

24. *CO* 34:368.

25. *CO* 34:381. Compare *CO* 34:391; Bouwsma, *John Calvin,* pp. 167–72; Gerrish, "To the Unknown God," pp. 141–49.

26. *CO* 34:534, 544.

27. *CO* 33:451, 561, 653; *CO* 34:220–21, 369–73, 383, 487, 605–7, 624.

28. *CO* 33:224–25, 443–44, 559, 592; *CO* 34:220, 255, 368–69.

29. *CO* 33:559.

30. *CO* 33:561.

31. *CO* 33:123, 224–25, 259, 444, 447, 477; *CO* 34:52, 64, 241, 246–47, 252–53, 255, 258–59, 262–66, 369, 535.

32. *CO* 34:52.

33. *CO* 33:447.

34. *CO* 34:382–83.

35. *CO* 34:481.

36. *CO* 34:370. Actually, Calvin paraphrases the accusation of an Aristotelianism that Aquinas attributed to Eliphaz in 22:12–14. Aquinas believed that Job *refuted* Eliphaz's charge in chapter 24.

37. *CO* 34:370–71.

38. *CO* 33:120, 123, 190, 223, 302, 434–35, 439, 451–52; *CO* 34:52–53, 57, 65, 100–101, 224, 258–59, 263, 347, 370–74, 539, 624.

39. In *Inst.* 3.2.4, 17–21, Calvin explains the struggle of faith against the temptation to doubt that God is merciful. This understanding of faith recurs in the *Sermons on Job* when Calvin depicts Job as fearing that God had become his enemy. In the passages cited below, the struggle of faith refers directly to the idea that God does not exercise providence or justice. See the emergence of this theme in *Inst.* 1.16.9.

40. *CO* 34:538.

41. *CO* 33:224, 434, 441–42, 585; *CO* 34:38, 163, 242, 259, 266, 368–69, 480, 538–39, 604; *CO* 35:257, 487.

42. *CO* 34:242.

43. *CO* 34:405; *CO* 35:459. See also *CO* 33:224, 441; *CO* 34:163, 242, 259, 368–69, 385, 480, 487, 538–39. On the perception of faith in Calvin's theology, see the forthcoming dissertation by Barbara Pitkin, "What Pure Eyes Can See" (University of Chicago).

44. *CO* 34:369.

45. *CO* 34:406, 480.

46. *CO* 34:603.

47. *CO* 34:259.

48. *CO* 34:603.

49. *CO* 34:255. Compare *Inst.* 1.16.9, 1.17.1–2.

50. *CO* 34:163.

51. *CO* 34:220. Compare *Inst.* 1.16.9 and 1.17.1; and Trinkaus, "Renaissance Problems in Calvin's Theology."

52. *CO* 33:239, 273, 371–73, 535, 720.

53. *CO* 33:105, 160, 459, 585–86; *CO* 34:255–56, 266, 341, 348, 482–90, 514.

54. *CO* 33:224–26, 441–42, 447; *CO* 34:219–20, 255, 305–6, 383, 391; *CO* 35:263.

55. *CO* 34:266.

56. *CO* 34:189, 221–24, 259, 263–64, 395, 487. On Calvin's understanding of the restoration of order, see also Lucian Joseph Richard, *The Spirituality of John Calvin* (Atlanta: John Knox Press, 1974), pp. 111–22, 175–78; Ronald S. Wallace, *Calvin's Doctrine of the Christian Life* (Edinburgh and London: Oliver and Boyd, 1959).

57. *CO* 34:266: "Contemplons donc ce qui nous est monstré au miroir de la parole de Dieu: c'est assavoir, qu'il y a un jugement plus grand que Dieu reserve, lequel il executera lors qu'il se monstrera iuge du monde. Voila comme il nous faut avoir cognu les tentations, et les ayans cognues il nous y faut resister, et passer outre . . . Voila, di-ie, comme il nous faut considerer les choses presentes, et regarder que si nous en iugeons selon nostre sens humain, tout sera perverti, et c'est afin que la foi domine en nous, et que la parole de Dieu nous conduise, que ce soit comme une lampe pour nous monstrer le chemin au milieu des tenebres de ce monde, iusques à ce que nous en soyons parvenus à ceste clarté celeste, où il n'y aura point de cognoissance en partie: mais où il y aura toute perfection quand nous contemplerons nostre Dieu face à face."

58. *CO* 34:259, 263, 266. On the theme of "restoring order," see also Bouwsma, *John Calvin*, pp. 86–97.

59. *Mor.* 23.4.4, 26.24.42–43.

60. *Expositio* 32:17, 160–65; 35:15, 141–48.

61. *Mor.* 38.2.11; *Expositio* 38:2, p. 151.

62. *CO* 35:259. Cajetan also wrestled with the figure of Elihu. He admits that much of what Elihu said was true, especially regarding the hiddenness of God. Still, he was rebuked by God in chapter 38:

> Relege dicta ab Elihu, & perpendes veritatem hanc. Elihu siquidem multos veros sermones protulit: tum quòd Deus noviter loquitur non mutatus ipse, sed mutatione interveniente in nobis: tum quòd Deus nulli facit iniustitiam: tum quòd opera Dei sunt occulta hominibus, sic quòd partim cognoscuntur, & partim ignorantur, sed sermones isti quantuncunque veri, quia fuerunt absque notitia divini consilii circa præmia & poenas hominum, ideo tendunt ad obscurandum divinum consilium circa præmia & poenas hominum. Consilium siquidem divinum quod ab aeterno conclusit apud seipsum, & in tempore revelavit, est reservare præmia & poenas hominum in vitam alteram: & hoc loquendo de præmio & poenis simpliciter & absolutè, verissimum est. Elihu autem sermones reddunt hominibus obscurum hoc consilium, quoniam ad inferendum oppositum proferuntur, videlicet ad afferendum quòd adversitates & prosperitates praesentis vitæ, sunt simpliciter & absolutè poenæ pro peccato, & præmia pro iustitia hominum. meritò ergo reprobatur Elihu locutus in favorem Dei. (*In librum Iob commentarii*, p. 532)

> Brenz (*Iob. Cum . . . commentariis . . .*) attributes the rebuke to Job, not Elihu: "loquitur autē Dominus, non de Elihu, qui probe peroravit contra Iobem, sed de Iobe dicens: quem hic audio mihi resistentem, mea iuditia blasphemantem, me iniusticiæ arguentem: quis est iste Iob, qui adversus me, & occulto cordis cogitatu ac mumure, & sermone impio insurgit." In 42:7, however, Brenz says, "Tres amici male loquuti sunt, Iob bene, cum interim & Iob male, & amici bene

disputarint, amici enim impie sentiebant, ex adflictione iratum Deum, & impium Iobem statuentes, caetera probe de omnipotentia & sapientia Dei differŭt: & Iob bene loquitur, quod constanter asseverat adflictiones, nullo merito sibi accidisse, nec esse impietatis suæ, aut irati Dei signa: male vero, quòd iudicio Dei indignetur, & Deum blasphemet." See also Brenz's commentary on 42:3.

Oecolampadius argues regarding 38:2: "Quidā hac oratione Eliŭ obiurgatŭ putant, contra quem nihil dicitur, sed sermo eius cōfirmatur magna ex parte. Et pulchre servatur divinæ maiestatis decorŭ quod durius ad iudiciŭ vocatur Iob . . . Qualia omnia nostra sunt, quando loquimur de deo, etiāsi castigatissima proferamus" (*In librum Iob exegema*, p. 205).

63. *CO* 35:356. In his commentary, *In Turns of Tempest* (Stanford, Calif.: Stanford University Press, 1990), p. 341, Edwin Good observes that 38:2 could apply to either Job or Elihu.

64. *CO* 35:4.

65. *CO* 35:12, 123. Compare *CO* 35:7, 36.

66. *CO* 35:35–36. In *CO* 35:38, however, Calvin says that "mais quant à Eliu, Dieu l'a suscité comme son Prophete qui l'a servi de son bon gré."

67. *CO* 35:37.

68. *CO* 35:13, 37–38, 41–42.

69. *CO* 35:34.

70. *CO* 35:7.

71. *CO* 35:131, 135, 215, 217–20.

72. *CO* 35:7–8. Calvin makes clear that this was not Job's direct intention, but that nonetheless such words "escaped" from him: "Quand Iob s'abandonne ainsi à tant de murmures et despitemens, il n'y a nulle doute qu'il ne se face iuste par dessus Dieu." See also *CO* 35:131–32, 135–36.

73. *CO* 35:135.

74. *Mor.* 35.7.9.

75. *Expositio* 34:10, p. 180.

76. *CO* 35:9–10, 145, 174–75.

77. *CO* 35:88. Compare *CO* 35:93, 105, 195–96, 225–30.

78. *CO* 35:141. Compare *Inst.* 3.23.2, 4–5.

79. *CO* 35:60, 131, 174–75, 178.

80. *CO* 35:58–60, 131, 151, 154, 206, 222, 315.

81. *CO* 35:54–55, 58–60, 136, 150. See note 77 above for Calvin's qualifications regarding Job's intention.

82. *CO* 35:9–10.

83. *CO* 35:9–10, 30, 117–18, 270, 285–86.

84. *CO* 35:34, 134–35.

85. *CO* 35:145–46.

86. *CO* 35:263–66.

87. *CO* 35:263.

88. *CO* 35:142. See also *CO* 35:139–42, 223, 231–32, 263–64, 269.

89. *CO* 35:192–94. See also *CO* 35:140.

90. *CO* 35:193.

91. *CO* 35:28, 63, 141, 192.

92. *CO* 35:315–18.

93. *CO* 35:315.

94. *CO* 35:320. These passages about the contemplation of nature bear on the old debate in Calvin literature about the role of creation as a source of the knowledge of God. The Job sermons most closely support the position initially argued by Dowey but continued by his later students and followers. See Edward A. Dowey, *The Knowledge of God in Calvin's Theology* (New York: Columbia University Press, 1952), pp. 131–47. The debate, of course, was originated by Barth and Brunner: Emil Brunner and Karl Barth, *Natural Theology*, trans. Peter Fränkel (London: Geoffrey Bles, 1946). The original German work of Barth and Brunner dates from 1934; Barth noted that a divergence on this issue began to manifest itself about 1929. The debate prompted by Barth and Brunner was continued by others, including Dowey and T.H.L. Parker, *Calvin's Doctrine of the Knowledge of God* (Grand Rapids, Mich.: Wm. B. Eerdmans, 1952). See also Günter Gloede, *Theologia naturalis bei Calvin* (Stuttgart: Kohlhammer, 1935); T. F. Torrance, *Calvin's Doctrine of Man* (London: Lutterworth Press, 1949); Gerald J. Postema, "Calvin's Alleged Rejection of Natural Theology," *Scottish Journal of Theology* 24 (1971): 423–34. For a recent discussion of some of these issues, see David C. Steinmetz, "Calvin and the Natural Knowledge of God," in *Via Augustini*, ed. Heiko A. Oberman (Leiden: E. J. Brill, 1991), pp. 142–56. See also Bouwsma, *John Calvin*, pp. 103–4, 262 n.51.

On the place of nature in Calvin's thought, see Schreiner, *The Theater of His Glory*. That book was already in press when the following fine essay appeared: Christopher B. Kaiser, "Calvin's Understanding of Aristotelian Natural Philosophy: Its Extent and Possible Origins," in Robert V. Schnucker, ed., *Calviniana: Ideas and Influence of Jean Calvin*, Sixteenth-Century Essays and Studies 10 (Kirksville, Mo.: Sixteenth-Century Journal Publishers, 1988), pp. 77–92. Kaiser examines Calvin's appropriation and criticism of Aristotle's cosmology, including the place of the elements and the location of the earth.

95. *CO* 35:316–50. The *Sermons on Job* do not give rise to the kind of discussions about the decay or fall of nature that we find in Calvin's *Commentary on Genesis*, where he describes in detail the impairment and diminution of fertility and says that "in all the elements we perceive that we are cursed." Occasionally in the Job sermons Calvin does presuppose the fall of creation by saying that at times nature threatens human beings. His emphasis, however, is not on the disorder or fall of nature itself but on God's use of creation to punish human sin, a theme common in Calvin's theology. In floods, hail, famine, the wildness of animals, and so forth, nature remains a mirror of God's "just judgment"; thus, creation does not lose its revelatory quality. To my knowledge, in the *Sermons on Job* Calvin does not really explain why this aspect of nature clearly reveals God at work while the disorders of history often do not. See, for example, *CO* 34:275–76; *CO* 35:336–37, 394–95, 462. See also Berger, *Calvins Geschichtsauffassung*, pp. 232–36. Nature as a punishment for sin remains a very minor theme in these sermons; obviously the Job text more often leads Calvin to stress the restraint of nature and the subsequent remaining order and beauty in creation.

96. *CO* 35:304.

97. *CO* 35:341.

98. *CO* 33:419.

99. *CO* 34:431–32, 434–36; *CO* 35:332, 372–73, 376–77, 403–4. For the ancient discussion on the natural order of the elements, see Aristotle, *Physica* IV.8.213a, and *De caelo* IV.5.312a. Compare Aquinas, *Expositio* 5:10, p. 37, and 38:8, p. 201. On Calvin's knowledge of Aristotle's natural philosophy, see Kaiser, "Calvin's Understanding of Aristotelian Natural Philosophy," pp. 77–92.

100. *CO* 34:436; *CO* 35:332.

101. *CO* 34:431–32.

102. *CO* 33:420.

103. *CO* 33:425. See also Bouwsma, *John Calvin*, p. 104.

104. *CO* 33:421.

105. *CO* 34:68.

106. *Expositio* 5:9–11, p. 37.

107. *CO* 35:491. Cajetan explains the meaning of Job's confession in 38:3:

Perpende hîc prudens Lector peccatum Iobis, contra quod Deus tanquam indignatus loquitur: ut simul intelligas quò tendit tam prolixus Dei sermo, in istis siquidem primis verbis proponitur peccatum Iobis commissum, dicendo illa verba scripta in C. 13 peccavit siquidē Iob specie arrogantiæ: non dico quòd peccavit arrogantia, sed quòd peccavit specie arrogantiæ. Declaro singula non peccavit arrogantia, arrogando sibi scientiam non solùm parem, sed prævalentem scientiæ Dei: hoc enim tam stultum atque blasphemum est, ut nec cogitabile sit. peccavit autem specie arrogantiæ: quia verba eius prae se serunt arrogantiam, quia verba eius suapte natura sunt verba arrogantis, qui enim cupit disputare cum aliquo, & dat ei opinionem arguendi. (*In librum Iob commentarii*, p. 532b)

Compare ibid., p. 555, on verse 42:3. For Brenz's view of Job's sin see note 62 above.

108. *Mor.* 37.4.5.

109. *Expositio* 40:3, p. 211.

110. *CO* 35:449.

111. *Expositio* 42:2, p. 211.

112. *CO* 35:353.

113. *CO* 35:435.

114. Compare *Inst.* 1.5.1–14.

115. *CO* 35:367, 380, 409, 419, 431–32, 435, 437–38.

116. On Calvin's view of secondary causality, see Schreiner, *Theater of His Glory*, chap. 1.

117. *CO* 35:366–67. Compare Kaiser, "Calvin's Understanding of Aristotle's Natural Philosophy," pp. 77–92. Calvin is assuming, of course, a geocentric universe. Scholars have debated about whether Calvin could be said to be anti-Copernican. Rosen has argued that Calvin never mentions Copernicus and that "never having heard of him, Calvin had no attiude toward Copernicus." Ratner argues, however, that Calvin's silence about Copernicus cannot be used as evidence that he had never heard of him. Stauffer has pointed out a passage in Calvin's work that is obviously hostile to the Copernican theory, although he never names Copernicus or refutes him by the use of Scripture. For this debate

see Edward Rosen, "Calvin's Attitude toward Copernicus," *Journal of the History of Ideas* 21 (1960): 431–41; Joseph Ratner, "Some Comments on Rosen's 'Calvin's Attitude toward Copernicus,'" *Journal of the History of Ideas* 22 (1961): 382–85; Rosen, "A Reply to Dr. Ratner," *Journal of the History of Ideas* 22 (1961): 386–88; Richard Stauffer, "Calvin et Copernic," *Revue de l'histoire des religions* 179 (1971): 31–40; Rosen, "Calvin n'a pas lu Copernic," and Stauffer, "Réponse à Edward Rosen," *Revue de l'histoire des religions* 182 (1972): 183–85, 185–86. Another contribution to the debate comes from Pierre Marcel, "Calvin et la science: Comment on fait l'histoire," *La revue réformée* 17 (1966): 50–51; Marcel, "Calvin et Copernic: La légende ou les faits? La science et l'astronomie chez Calvin," *La revue réformée* 31 (1980), the entire issue devoted to this topic. See also B. A. Gerrish, "The Reformation and the Rise of Modern Science," in *The Old Protestantism and the New*, pp. 169–70; and Heiko A. Oberman, "Reformation and Revolution: Copernicus' Discovery in an Era of Change," in *The Dawn of the Reformation*, pp. 179–203. Oberman rightly reminds us that "pre-Copernican cosmology did not posit the earth at the static center as a place of glory but as a place of inertia, the farthest removed from divine movement so perfectly reflected in the circular movement of the stars. Man, not his earth, held the cosmic place of honor, reaching in the summit of his soul (*apex mentis*) the greatest proximity to God" (p. 181). Compare Calvin's sermon on Job 9:7–15, *CO* 33:417–30.

118. *CO* 35:372–73, 377, 391–92, 403–5.
119. *CO* 35:403.
120. *CO* 35:437.
121. *CO* 35:423.
122. *CO* 35:429.
123. *CO* 35:431–32.
124. *CO* 35:371–72.
125. *CO* 35:371.
126. *CO* 35:464–67:

Or devant que passer outre, nous avons à noter sur ce qu'il y a une si longue deduction de ceste espece de bestes terrestres que nous dismes hier estre elephans (combien qu'il le nomme ici du mot general *Behemoth*) et aussi une deduction plus longue de *Leviathan:* qu'on a cuidé qu'ici par allegorie il soit parlé du diable, plustost que d'elephans ou de baleines: et a on voulu approuver ceste phantasie par ce qui est dit en la fin, que *c'est le roi des enfans d'orgueil* que ceste baleine. Or en parlant de ceste espece de bestes que nous touchasmes hier, il estoit dit que *Dieu les fait manger le foin et l'herbe comme aux boeufs.* Nous voyons donc que c'est pour nous declarer la puissance de Dieu en choses visibles: et non point pour nous descrire le diable.

After grudgingly admitting that the beasts might well symbolize the *power* of the devil, Calvin says that he wants to retain the "simplicity of the texte [simplicité du texte]": "car de se iouër de l'Escriture saincte la transformant en allegorie, c'est une chose mauvaise: et les allegories ne doivent estre tirees sinon du sens naturel. . . . Revenons donc à ce propos qui a esté entamé. Dieu fait ici ses triomphes et par mer et par terre, afin que les hommes cognoissent, qu'ils seront tousiours confus en leur orgueil s'adressans à luy." The literal sense, he insists, is better than "subtle expositions": "Si nous avons retenu ceste simplicité-là, elle nous vaudra mieux que toutes les expositions subtiles qu'on pourra amener: comme quand ceux qui ont ici basti des allegories, ont espluché les os et les arestes des balaines, et ont aussi traitté de la peau, de cecy et de cela: bref, il n'y a rien où il n'y ait fallu trouver ie ne say quels menus fatras. Or c'est comme faire de l'Escriture saincte un nez de cire, la transfigurant hors de son sens naturel" (*CO* 35:467).

Cajetan argues (*In librum Iob commentarii*, p. 549): "ad hominem itaque docentem & tanquam ex aquis extrahentem ad hominum utilitatem Dæmones tanquam pisces, dicit Deus. extrahens quidem Leviathan (hoc est, Dæmonem) tanquam piscem ex aquis, hamo cultus trahentis ipsum." He further states (p. 546): "Et propterea literalem sensum prosequendo, appellatione Behemoth Dæmones sub nomine brutorum animalium demonstrantur, dicendo, *Ecce Behemoth* . . . quia Dæmones ad hiusmodi statum sunt deiecti, ideo demonstrantur sub nomine animalium brutorum, & in numero plurali, quia multi sunt, & ut multi descripti sunt superbi ac impii."

Brenz argues (*Iob. Cum . . . commentariis. . .*, chap. 40): "Sub Behemoth autem abscondite describitur hoc loco Satanæ potentia, sic enim Dominus Behemoth, quasi corporalem quandam bestiam proponit, cum interim in Satanam oculos dirigat, ut primum declaret se potentissimum esse qui solus Satanum vincere possit: dein, hominem esse maxime omnium imbecillem, qui vel sola nativitate, Satanæ captivus fiat." So, too, he argues that Leviathan signifies the power of the devil, as is indicated by Isa. 24. Oecolampadius relates the allegorical meaning of Behemoth and Leviathan as the power of the devil and the wicked on the earth but prefers the literal sense of the "elephant" and the "whale."

127. *CO* 35:464.
128. *CO* 35:460–61.
129. *CO* 35:462.
130. *CO* 35:462. See also *CO* 35:420–21.
131. *CO* 35:465.
132. *CO* 33:75, 91–92, 106–7. Compare *Inst.* 1.18.1.
133. *CO* 33:61, quoting 1 Pet. 5:8.
134. *Comm. on Is.* 27:1.
135. *CO* 35:396.
136. *CO* 35:388, 397–98.
137. *CO* 35:383–84, 403, 429.
138. *CO* 35:416.
139. *CO* 35:375.
140. *CO* 35:481.
141. *CO* 35:445.
142. *CO* 35:481–83.
143. *CO* 35:512.
144. *Expositio* 42:10, p. 229.
145. *CO* 35:508.

146. *CO* 35:510.

147. Calvin does not emphasize the upcoming Epilogue in passages such as *CO* 33:593; *CO* 34:361, 371, 398, 498; *CO* 35:244. Thus in the body of the *Sermons* Job's restoration does not serve as evidence of a counterpoint to the visibility of providence.

148. *Mor.* 35.4.5.

149. *Expositio* 42.5.35–43, p. 228.

150. *Guide* III.23, p. 493.

151. *CO* 35:488.

5. Modern Readings of Job

1. Lawrence Besserman, *The Legend of Job in the Middle Ages* (Cambridge, Mass.: Harvard University Press, 1979).

2. Georg Fohrer, *Das Buch Hiob,* Kommentar zum Alten Testament 16 (Gütersloh: Gerd Mohn, 1963); Marvin Pope, *Job: Introduction, Translation, and Notes,* 3rd ed., vol. 15 of the Anchor Bible (Garden City, N.Y.: Doubleday, 1973).

3. Georg Fohrer, "Überlieferung und Wandlung der Hioblegende," in *Studien zum Buche Hiob* (Gütersloh: Gerd Mohn, 1963), pp. 44–67; Fohrer, *Das Buch Hiob,* pp. 29–58. See also Walter E. Aufrecht, *Studies in the Book of Job,* Canadian Corporation for Studies in Religion/Corporation Canadienne des Sciences Religieuses Supplements 16 (Waterloo, Ontario: Wilfrid Laurier University Press, 1985), pp. 1–18.

4. Robert Gordis, *The Book of God and Man: A Study of Job* (Chicago: University of Chicago Press, 1965); Samuel Terrien, *Job: Poet of Existence* (Indianapolis: Bobbs-Merrill, 1957).

5. Normal C. Habel, *The Book of Job: A Commentary,* The Old Testament Library (Philadelphia: Westminster Press, 1985); Good, *In Turns of Tempest.*

6. Good, *In Turns of Tempest,* p. 188.

7. Gordis, *The Book of God and Man,* p. vii.

8. For a historical analysis of the problem of theodicy and suffering, see Kenneth Surin, *Theology and the Problem of Evil* (Oxford: Blackwell, 1986). Surin discusses the issue of "taking suffering seriously" (pp. 142–53). See also Dorothee Soelle, *Suffering* (Philadelphia: Fortress Press, 1975). For an excellent analyis of attitudes toward suffering in modern literature, see Walter J. Slatoff, *The Look of Distance: Reflections on Suffering and Sympathy in Modern Literature: Auden to Agee, Whitman to Woolf* (Columbus: Ohio State University Press, 1985).

9. Habel, *The Book of Job,* p. 61.

10. Terrien, *Job: Poet of Existence,* p. 68.

11. Gordis, *The Book of God and Man,* pp. 151–52.

12. Habel, *The Book of Job,* pp. 302–9.

13. Terrien, *Job: Poet of Existence,* p. 153.

14. Good, *In Turns of Tempest,* pp. 240–41, 258–60.

15. Terrien, *Job: Poet of Existence,* p. 130.

16. Habel, *The Book of Job,* p. 60.

17. Ibid., p. 61.

18. Good, *In Turns of Tempest,* p. 266.

19. Ibid., pp. 276–79.

20. Habel, *The Book of Job,* pp. 43, 49.

21. Ibid., pp. 53, 61.

22. Terrien, *Job: Poet of Existence,* p. 186.

23. Ibid., pp. 108–9.

24. Good, *In Turns of Tempest,* p. 229; compare pp. 235, 278, 285–87, 307.

25. Ibid., p. 278.

26. Habel, *The Book of Job,* p. 57.

27. Ibid., p. 61; see also pp. 450, 505, 511–13, 543, 563–66.

28. Good, *In Turns of Tempest,* pp. 235, 285.

29. Habel, *The Book of Job,* p. 58; see also pp. 219–20.

30. Ibid., p. 58.

31. Ibid., p. 65.

32. Ibid., p. 59.

33. Ibid., pp. 59, 534–36, 543.

34. Ibid., p. 579.

35. Good, *In Turns of Tempest,* p. 356.

36. Ibid., p. 377.

37. Carl Jung, *Antwort auf Hiob,* in *Zur Psychologie westlicher und östlicher Religion* (Freiburg im Breisgau: Walter-Verlag, 1971), pp. 387–506. An English translation can be found in Carl Jung, *Answer to Job,* trans. R.F.C. Hull, in *The Portable Jung,* ed. Joseph Campbell (New York: Viking Press, 1971), pp. 519–650; and also in Carl Jung, *Psychology and Religion: West and East,* trans. R.F.C. Hull, in *Collected Works,* vol. 11 (Princeton: Princeton University Press, 1969), pp. 355–470. Citations of the English translation in this chapter refer to *The Portable Jung.*

38. Peter Homans, *Jung in Context* (Chicago: University of Chicago Press, 1979), pp. 23–24. The *Answer to Job* is usually analyzed in terms of Jung's relationship with and split from Freud. See, for example, Homans, "Narcissism in the Jung-Freud Confrontations," *American Imago* 38 (April 1981): 81–95.

39. Jung, *Antwort auf Hiob,* pp. 390–92. See also June Singer, *Boundaries of the Soul* (New York: Doubleday, 1972), p. 72; Anthony Storr, *Jung* (London: Fontana, 1973), pp. 39–61.

40. "The psyche reaches so far beyond the boundary line of consciousness that the latter could be easily compared to an island in the ocean. While the island is small and narrow, the ocean is immensely wide and deep, so that if it is a question of space, it does not matter whether the gods are inside or outside" (Jung, *Psychology and Religion* [New Haven: Yale University Press, 1966], p. 102). See also Storr, *Jung,* pp. 42–43.

41. Jung, *Antwort auf Hiob,* p. 414 (*Answer,* p. 550). Jung opens the treatise with the statement: "Das Buch Hiob ist ein Markstein auf dem langen Entwicklungswege eines göttlichen Dramas" (p. 392).

42. Ibid., p. 405 (*Answer,* p. 541).

43. Ibid., pp. 396, 399, 404 (*Answer,* pp. 530–31, 534, 540–41).

44. "Er ist jede Eigenschaft in ihrer Totalität, also u.a. die Gerechtigkeit schlechthin, aber auch das Gegenteil, und dies ebenso vollständig" (ibid., p. 399 [*Answer,* p. 534]).

45. Ibid., p. 396 (*Answer,* pp. 530–31).

46. "Die Reden Jahwes haben den zwar unreflektierten, aber nichtsdestoweniger durchsichtigen Zweck, die brutale Übermacht des Demiurgen dem Menschen vorzuführen: 'Das bin Ich, der Schöpfer aller unbezwingbaren, ruchlosen Naturkräfte, die keinen ethischen Gesetzen unterworfen sind, und so bin auch ich selber eine amoralische Naturmacht, eine rein phänomenale Persönlichkeit, die ihren eigenen Rücken nicht sieht'" (ibid., p. 413 [*Answer,* p. 549]).

47. "Diese Symbolik erklärt das—von einem menschlichen Standpunkt aus betrachtet—unerträgliche Verhalten Jahwes. Es ist das Benehmen eines vorzugsweise unbewussten Wesens, das man nicht moralisch beurteilen kann: Jahwe ist ein *Phänomen* und 'nicht ein Mensch'" (ibid., p. 411 [*Answer,* p. 547]).

48. Ibid., p. 393 (*Answer,* p. 527).

49. Ibid., p. 403 (*Answer,* p. 538).

50. Ibid., p. 404 (*Answer,* p. 540):

> Wir müssen aber ein Auge auf dem Hintergrund dieses Geschehens behalten: es wäre nicht unmöglich, dass etwas in diesem Hintergrund allmählich deutlicher wurde, nämlich eine Kompensation für das unverschuldete Leiden, welche Jahwe, auch wenn er sie nur von Ferne ahnen sollte, nicht gleichgültig lassen konnte. Der unschuldig Gequälte war nämlich ohne sein Wissen und Wollen in aller Stille zu einer Überlegenheit der Gotteserkenntnis, die Gott selber nicht besass, emporgehoben worden. Hätte Jahwe seine Allwissenheit befragt, so hätte ihm Hiob nichts vorausgehabt. Dann wäre aber allerdings so viel anderes auch nicht passiert.
>
> Hiob erkennt die innere Antinomie Gottes, und damit erlangt das Licht seiner Erkenntnis selber göttliche Numinosität.

51. Jung explores this concept in sections 12–14 of the *Answer to Job* where he analyzes the Book of Revelation. A fuller analysis can be found in his "Psychological Approach to the Dogma of the Trinity," in *Collected Works,* vol. 11, pp. 107–200. For a study of this treatise see Murray Stein, *Jung's Treatment of Christianity* (Wilmette, Ill.: Chiron Publications, 1985), pp. 115–35.

52. "Eine grosse Wendung steht bevor: *Gott will sich im Mysterium der himmlischen Hochzeit erneuern . . . und will Mensch werden*" (Jung, *Antwort auf Hiob,* p. 426 [*Answer,* p. 563]).

53. "Man vergegenwärtige sich, was das heisst: *Gott wird Mensch.* Das bedeutet nichts weniger als weltumstürzende Wandlung Gottes" (ibid., p. 431 [*Answer,* p. 568]).

54. Ibid., p. 440 (*Answer,* p. 579).

55. Ibid., pp. 434–36 (*Answer,* p. 573):

> Der Sieg des Unterlegenen und Vergewaltigten ist einleuchtend: Hiob stand moralisch höher als Jahwe. Das Geschöpf hatte in dieser Beziehung den Schöpfer überholt. Wie immer, wenn ein äusseres Ereignis an ein unbewusstes Wissen rührt, kann letzteres bewusst werden. Man erkennt das Ereignis als ein "déjà vu" und erinnert sich an ein präexistentes Wissen darum. Etwas derartiges muss mit Jahwe geschehen sein.

Die Überlegenheit Hiobs kann nicht mehr aus der Welt geschafft werden. Damit ist eine Situation entstanden, die nun wirklich des Nachdenkens und der Reflexion bedarf. Aus diesem Grunde greift Sophia ein. Sie unterstützt die nötige Selbstbesinnung und ermöglicht dadurch den Entschluss Jahwes, nun selber Mensch zu werden. Damit fällt eine folgenschwere Entscheidung: er erhebt sich über seinen früheren primitiven Bewusstseinszustand, indem er indirekt anerkennt, dass der Mensch Hiob ihm moralisch überlegen ist und dass er deshalb das Menschsein noch nachzuholen hat. Hätte er diesen Entschluss nicht gefasst, so wäre er in flagranten Gegensatz zu seiner Allwissenheit geraten. Jahwe muss Mensch werden, denn diesem hat er Unrecht getan . . . *Weil sein Geschöpf ihn überholt hat, muss er sich erneuern.*"

56. Ibid., p. 449 (*Answer,* p. 589). See also Jung, *Aion: Researches into the Phenomenology of the Self,* in *Collected Works,* vol. 9, pt. 2 (Princeton: Princeton University Press, 1968, rpt. 1978), pp. 45–53; see also chap. 5, "Christ, a Symbol of the Self." See also Stein, *Jung's Treatment of Christianity,* pp. 151–53.

57. Jung, *Antwort auf Hiob,* pp. 430–31, 441, 463–64, 477 (*Answer,* pp. 568–69, 579, 604–5).

58. Ibid., p. 480 (*Answer,* p. 622). For an explanation of Jung's concept of the "enantiodromian process" as a return of the repressed and the motion of reversal, see Stein, *Jung's Treatment of Christianity,* pp. 151–54, 158, 167, 176.

59. Stein, *Jung's Treatment of Christianity,* p. 168.

60. Martin Buber, *Eclipse of God: Studies in the Relation between Religion and Philosophy,* trans. Norbert Guterman et al. (New York: Harper and Brothers, 1952), p. 111.

61. Ibid., pp. 105–6.

62. "It is, to my mind, a fatal mistake to consider the human psyche as a merely personal affair and to explain it exclusively from a personal point of view" (Jung, *Psychology and Religion,* p. 16). "Someone may object that the so-called unconscious mind is merely my own mind and that, therefore, such a differentiation is superfluous. . . . My psychological experience has shown time and again that certain contents issue from a psyche more complete than consciousness" (ibid., pp. 46–69). "But since modern research has acquainted us with the fact that an individual consciousness is based upon and surrounded by an idefinitely extended unconscious psyche, we needs must revise our somewhat old-fashioned prejudice that man is his consciousness" (ibid., p. 99).

63. "Man hat mich aber so oft gefragt, ob ich an die Existenz Gottes glaube oder nicht, dass ich einigermassen besorgt bin, man könne mich, viel allgemeiner als ich ahne, für einen 'Psychologisten' halten. Was die Leute meist übersehen oder nicht verstehen können, ist der Umstand, dass ich die Psyche für wirklich halte" (Jung, *Antwort auf Hiob,* p. 497 [*Answer,* p. 642]).

64. "Jung and Religious Belief," in *Psychology and Western Religion,* trans. R.F.C. Hull (Princeton: Princeton University Press, 1984), p. 259. This section consists of extracts from H. L. Philp, *Jung and the Problem of Evil* (London: Rockliff, 1958), and includes correspondence between Philp and Jung in the form of questions and answers (in English).

65. Jung, *Psychology and Religion*, pp. 71–73, 100.

66. Homans, *Jung in Context*, p. 108.

67. Jung, *Psychology and Religion*, p. 99. He also states, "Since modern mandalas have amazingly close parallels in ancient magic circles, in the center of which we usually find the deity, it is evident that in the modern mandala man—the complete man—has replaced the deity" (p. 106).

68. Ibid., pp. 103, 105.

69. Jung, *Antwort auf Hiob*, p. 493 (*Answer*, p. 636).

70. Ibid., pp. 494–95 (*Answer*, pp. 638–39).

71. Jung, *Aion*, p. 178. I owe this citation to Stein, *Jung's Treatment of Christianity*, p. 156.

72. Jung, *Aion*, p. 180.

73. H. G. Wells, *The Undying Fire* (New York: Macmillan, 1919); Archibald MacLeish, *J. B.* (Cambridge, Mass.: Riverside Press, 1958); Elie Wiesel, *The Trial of God*, trans. Marion Wiesel (New York: Schocken Books, 1979); Franz Kafka, *Der Process*, ed. Malcolm Pasley (Frankfurt am Main: S. Fischer, 1990); Kafka, *The Trial*, trans. Douglas Scott and Chris Waller (London: Pan Books, 1977). The "definitive" English translation is Kafka, *The Trial*, trans. Will Muir and Edwin Muir (New York: Alfred A. Knopf, 1937, and Schocken Books, 1935). I have referred readers to the translation by Scott and Waller, since this is a better translation. For an analysis of the difficulties with the translation by Muir and Muir, see Irmgard Hobson, "The Kafka Problem Compounded: *Trial* and *Judgment* in English," *Modern Fiction Studies* 23 (Winter 1977–78): 511–29. Kafka wrote *Der Prozess* between August 1914 and January 1915, and in 1920 he presented a manuscript to his friend Max Brod. Kafka died in 1924; the text was edited by Brod and published in 1925. For an analysis of the works by Wells and MacLeish, see Jon Douglas Levenson, *The Book of Job in Its Time and in the Twentieth Century* (Cambridge, Mass.: Harvard University Press, 1972).

74. Wells, *The Undying Fire*, p. 103.

75. Ibid., p. 106.

76. Ibid., pp. 81, 84–87.

77. Ibid., p. 118.

78. Ibid., p. 121.

79. Ibid., pp. 128–29.

80. Ibid., pp. 106–7, 116.

81. Ibid., pp. 84–85.

82. Ibid., pp. 60, 103, 132, 137, 153–54.

83. Ibid., p. 132.

84. Ibid., pp. 107–8.

85. Ibid., pp. 147–48.

86. Ibid., pp. 153–54.

87. MacLeish, *J. B.*, p. 109.

88. Ibid.

89. Ibid., p. 111.

90. Ibid., p. 108.

91. Ibid., p. 110.

92. Ibid., p. 121.

93. Ibid., pp. 126–27.

94. Ibid., p. 119.

95. Ibid., pp. 125, 127.

96. Ibid., p. 12.

97. Ibid., p. 5.

98. Ibid., pp. 16, 22.

99. Ibid., p. 135.

100. Ibid., p. 140.

101. Ibid., pp. 49, 151–53.

102. As Levenson says in commenting on the interpretations of MacLeish, Wells, and Frost: "for twentieth-century man has known disaster but no revelation" (*The Book of Job in Its Time and in the Twentieth Century*, p. 69).

103. Elie Wiesel, *Messengers of God: Biblical Portraits and Legends*, trans. Marion Wiesel (New York: Random House, 1976), pp. 211–35. In this essay, Wiesel portrays Job as defying God and making God the defendant. He concludes his interpretation in "Job: Our Contemporary" in much the same way as he ends *The Trial of God*. In the former essay he writes, "I prefer to think that the Book's true ending was lost. That Job dies without having repented, without having humiliated himself; that he succumbed to his grief an uncompromising and whole man. . . . Job personified man's eternal quest for justice and truth—he did not choose resignation" (pp. 233, 235). For a more extended exposition of Job, see Wiesel's conversation with Josy Eisenberg, *Job ou Dieu dans la tempête* (Paris: Librairie Arthème Fayard and Editions Verdier, 1986).

104. Martin Buber, *Darko shel Mikra* (Jerusalem: Mosad Bialik, 1964), p. 357; cited by Nahum Glatzer, *Dimensions of Job* (Schocken Books, 1969), p. 48.

105. Northrop Frye, *Anatomy of Criticism* (Princeton: Princeton University Press, 1971), p. 42; Frye, *The Great Code* (New York: Harcourt Brace Jovanovich, 1982), p. 195. So, too, Susman states that Kafka's work bears the traits of Job's primeval dispute with God more profoundly than any other achievement of Western Jews: Margarete Susman, "Das Hiob-Problem bei Franz Kafka," *Der Morgen* 5 (1929): 49. For these and other citations comparing Kafka's work with the Book of Job, see Stuart Lasine, "Job and His Friends in the Modern World: Kafka's *The Trial*," in *The Voice from the Whirlwind*, ed. Gilpin and Perdue, pp. 144–56.

106. Wiesel, *The Trial of God*, pp. 15, 26.

107. Ibid., pp. 42–43.

108. Ibid., pp. 55, 56.

109. Ibid., pp. 103, 109.

110. Ibid., p. 123.

111. Ibid., p. 127.

112. Ibid., p. 129.

113. Ibid., p. 133.

114. Ibid., pp. 132, 157.

115. Ibid., pp. 159, 160.

116. Ibid., p. 161.

117. Ibid., p. 49.

118. Berish states, "I don't believe you. When the whole world is our enemy,

when God himself is on the side of the enemy—when God *is* the enemy, how can one not be afraid? Admit it: You do fear Him. You neither love nor worship Him. All He evokes in you is fear" (ibid., p. 54).

119. Wiesel states, "Mais le Talmud dit le contraire: Élihou ne serait autre que le Satan qui, éliminé de l'histoire, y serait revenu déguisé en Élihou!" (Eisenberg and Wiesel, *Job ou Dieu dans la tempête*, p. 390).

120. Wiesel, *The Trial of God*, p. 156.

121. Rudolf Suter, *Kafkas "Prozess" im Lichte des "Buches Hiob"* (Frankfurt am Main: Peter Lang, 1976), pp. 39–48.

122. Kafka, *Der Process*, p. 149 (*The Trial*, p. 134).

123. Ibid., p. 163 (*The Trial*, p. 144).

124. Thomas Mann, "Homage," in Kafka, *The Castle* (New York: Alfred A. Knopf, 1956), p. xvi.

125. Politzer sees in this agressive action a paradox in the nature of the Court. See Heinz Politzer, *Franz Kafka, Parable and Paradox* (Ithaca, N.Y.: Cornell University Press, 1962), pp. 167–70. Politzer does not analyze *The Trial* in terms of the Book of Job.

126. Kafka, *Der Process*, p. 70 (*The Trial*, p. 63).

127. Ibid., pp. 265, 267 (*The Trial*, pp. 219–21). On the interpretation of the character Bloch in terms of the biblical figure Balaam, see Stuart Lasine, "Kafka's *The Trial*," *The Explicator* 43 (1985):34–36.

128. Ritchie Robertson, *Kafka: Judaism, Politics, and Literature* (Oxford: Clarendon Press, 1985), pp. 195–96.

129. Ibid. Robertson is responding to Ingeborg Henel, "Die Türhüterlegende und ihre Bedeutung für Kafkas *Prozess*," *Deutsche Vierteljahrsschrift für Literatur und Geistesgeschichte* 37 (1963): 50–70. Henel's article has been translated into English: Henel, "The Legend of the Doorkeeper and Its Significance," trans. James Rolleston, in *Twentieth-Century Interpretations of "The Trial,"* ed. Rolleston (Englewood Cliffs, N.J.: Prentice-Hall, 1976), pp. 40–55. On this point see also A. E. Dyson, "Trial by Enigma: Kafka's *The Trial*," in *Franz Kafka's "The Trial": Modern Critical Interpretations,* ed. Harold Bloom (New York: Chelsea House, 1987), pp. 69–70. For the interpretation of *The Trial* as a projection of K.'s mind, see also Meno Spann, *Franz Kafka* (Boston: Twayne Publishers, 1976), p. 97: "The mysterious Court is in his mind; it is a state of mind that K. never before allowed to gain dominance over his inner self."

130. Kafka, *Der Process*, pp. 157, 162–63 (*The Trial*, pp. 140, 144).

131. It is unclear why Wilk attributes to Politzer the belief that Kafka thought the Law was "nonexistent." When Politzer argues that the Law "has been lost to the world" he is saying not that it is nonexistent but only that it is inaccessible to Joseph K. See Politzer, *Franz Kafka*, p. 179; Melvin Wilk, *Jewish Presence in T. S. Eliot and Franz Kafka* (Atlanta: Scholars Press, 1986), p. 189. Wilk examines *The Trial* in terms of Job on pages 133–67. The study by Suter, *Kafkas "Prozess" im Lichte des "Buches Hiob,"* as Lasine points out ("Kafka's *The Trial*," p. 248 n.6), is more cautious in this type of analysis than that of Wilk.

132. Kafka, *Der Process*, p. 142 (*The Trial*, p. 128).

133. Ibid., pp. 196–97 (*The Trial*, pp. 168–69).

134. Ibid., p. 69 (*The Trial*, p. 62).

135. Ibid., p. 91 (*The Trial*, p. 79).

136. Ibid., p. 126 (*The Trial*, p. 116).

137. Ibid., pp. 201, 205 (*The Trial*, pp. 172, 175).

138. Ibid., pp. 250–69 (*The Trial*, pp. 195–210).

139. Ibid., p. 21 (*The Trial*, p. 27).

140. Ibid., p. 112 (*The Trial*, p. 105).

141. Ibid., p. 176 (*The Trial*, p. 154).

142. Ibid., p. 200 (*The Trial*, p. 171).

143. Suter, *Kafkas "Prozess" im Lichte des "Buches Hiob,"* pp. 65–66; Politzer, *Franz Kafka*, pp. 171–73.

144. Kafka, *Der Process*, pp. 40–43 (*The Trial*, pp. 42–43).

145. Politzer, *Franz Kafka*, p. 173.

146. Kafka, *Der Process*, p. 168 (*The Trial*, p. 148).

147. Ibid., p. 286 (*The Trial*, p. 234).

148. Ibid., p. 289 (*The Trial*, p. 236).

149. "'Ich bin aber nicht schuldig,' sagte K., 'Es ist ein Irrtum. Wie kann denn ein Mensch überhaupt schuldig sein. Wir sind hier doch alle Menschen, einer wie der andere.' 'Das ist richtig,' sagte der Geistliche, 'aber so pflegen die Schuldigen zu reden'" (ibid., p. 289 [*The Trial*, p. 236]).

150. "Du suchst zuviel fremde Hilfe" (ibid., p. 289 [*The Trial*, p. 237]).

151. Ibid., pp. 294–95 (*The Trial*, p. 240).

152. Politzer, *Franz Kafka*, p. 177. For an interpretation of Titorelli's painting as the "goddess of the Hunt," see Lida Kirchberger, *Franz Kafka's Use of the Law in Fiction: A New Interpretation of "In der Strafkolonie," "Der Prozess," and "Das Schloss"* (New York: Lang, 1986), p. 85; and H. H. Hiebel, *Die Zeichen des Gesetzes: Recht und Macht bei Franz Kafka* (Munich: Fink, 1983), pp. 214–15.

153. Erich Heller, *Kafka* (London: Fontana, 1974), p. 99.

154. Stuart Lasine, "Job and His Friends in the Modern World: Kafka's *The Trial*," in *The Voice from the Whirlwind*, ed. Gilpin and Perdue, pp. 144–56.

155. Henel, "The Legend of the Doorkeeper," p. 50.

156. Kafka, *Der Process*, p. 15 (*The Trial*, p. 23).

157. Robertson, *Kafka*, pp. 102, 110–11. It should be noted that Robertson does not compare *The Trial* to the Book of Job but to, among other works, Dostoevsky's *Crime and Punishment*. On Kafka and Dostoyevsky, see also Sissel Lägreid, *Ambivalenz als Gestaltungsprinzip: Eine Untersuchung der Querverbindungen zwischen Kafkas "Prozess" und Dostojewskis "Schuld und Sühne"* (Bergen: Tysk Institut, 1980).

158. Martin Buber, *Two Types of Faith* (New York: Macmillan, 1951), p. 165.

159. Martin Buber, *The Knowledge of Man*, trans. Maurice Friedman and Ronald Gregor Smith (New York: Harper and Row, 1956), pp. 141–43.

160. M. Walser, *Beschreibung einer Form: Versuch über Franz Kafka* (Frankfurt: Verlag Ullstein, 1972), p. 91. Cited by Stuart Lasine, "Kafka's 'Sacred Texts' and the Hebrew Bible," *Papers in Comparative Studies* 3 (1984): 132 n.5. The only edition of this work available to me was Walzer, *Beschreibung einer Form* (Munich: Carl Hanser, 1962), p. 120.

161. Sokel interprets the perspectival nature of the novel by arguing that the trial operates on two levels at once: the existential aspect of the Court policy,

and the lower Oedipal level. See Walter H. Sokel, "The Programme of K.'s Court: Oedipal and Existential Meanings of *The Trial*," in *On Kafka: Semi-Centenary Perspectives,* ed. Franz Kuna (New York: Barnes and Noble, 1976), pp. 1–21.

162. Kafka, *Der Process,* p. 14 (*The Trial,* p. 22). See also Henel, "The Legend of the Doorkeeper," p. 46.

163. Kafka, *Der Process,* pp. 21–22 (*The Trial,* p. 28).

164. Ibid., pp. 143 (*The Trial,* p. 129).

165. On the idea of K.'s concern with "motivations," see Henel, "The Legend of the Doorkeeper," p. 47; and Robertson, *Kafka,* pp. 111, 117–18. On K.'s "inner dishonesty," see Spann, *Franz Kafka,* pp. 97.

166. Sokel, "The Programme of K.'s Court: Oedipal and Existential Meanings of *The Trial*," p. 4. Sokel observes that "the trial should be considered a process of exploration and questioning. The double meaning of the German title, *Der Prozess,* meaning both trial and process, would lend support to the view that the trial is, or should be, the process of the discovery of K.'s guilt."

167. For an interesting comparison of *The Trial* with *Alice in Wonderland* and *Through the Looking Glass,* see Dyson, "Trial by Enigma: Kafka's *The Trial*," pp. 57–72. Compare Alvin J. Seltzer, "Waking into Nightmare: Dream as Reality in Kafka's *The Trial*," in *Chaos in the Novel* (New York: Schocken Books, 1974).

168. Henel, "The Legend of the Doorkeeper," p. 49.

169. Kafka, *Der Process,* pp. 289–90 (*The Trial,* p. 237).

170. Ibid., p. 290.

171. Politzer, *Franz Kafka,* pp. 182–84; Buber, *The Knowledge of Man,* p. 145. See also Josephine Donovan, *Gnosticism in Modern Literature: A Study of the Selected Works of Camus, Satre, Hesse, and Kafka* (New York: Garland Publishing, 1990).

172. Politzer, *Franz Kafka,* p. 184.

173. Kafka, *Der Process,* p. 304 (*The Trial,* p. 248).

174. Ibid., p. 312 (*The Trial,* p. 254).

175. Ibid., p. 304 (*The Trial,* p. 248).

176. Hans Jonas, "The Nobility of Sight: A Study in the Phenomenology of the Senses," in *The Phenomenon of Life: Toward a Philosophical Biology* (Chicago: University of Chicago Press, 1982), pp. 151–52.

INDEX

Albert the Great, 83
allegorical interpretation: Aquinas's
  use of, 149; Calvin rejects, 7, 91,
  141, 149; Gregory's use of, 25, 31–
  32, 39–40, 47, 53, 149; move from,
  to literal interpretation, 55, 154; of
  suffering, 39, 117
Ambrose: influence on Gregory 24;
  compares Job and David, 97–99;
  on suffering, 97, 99
angels, 106, 112–13
Aquinas, Thomas: use of Aristotle,
  57, 83, 87–88; on disputatious nature of Job, 73–74, 127; on evil, 5,
  58; Gregory's influence on, 57;
  hermeneutical method, 18, 20, 71–
  73; on history, 36, 77, 129; doctrine of personal immortality, 71,
  73, 74–76, 80–81, 153; limitation
  of human intellect, 82–84, 86; intellectual context, 5, 57; on Job's
  anger, 35; on Job's humility, 114;
  on Job's sinfulness, 107; on justice, 111; Maimonides's influence
  on, 57, 70; on nature, 83, 141; order concern of, 58, 74, 89; perceptual dimension of exegesis, 71–72,
  147, 149; on providence, 57, 72–
  76, 79–81, 88–90; on Satan, 48, 77;
  on suffering, 77–79, 87–88
—exegesis compared: to Calvin, 9–
  10, 74, 75, 122–24, 127–28, 131–
  32, 139–40, 142, 147, 149, 152–55;
  to Gregory, 70–72, 73, 76–78, 82,
  85–89; to Maimonides, 57–59, 71–
  72, 74, 79–83, 86–90; to modern
  commentators, 158–59, 165, 189
Aristotle: influence on Aquinas, 57;
  Aquinas's use of, 83; influence on
  twelfth- and thirteenth-century
  thought, 55; influence on Maimonides, 63; on suffering, 87–88
atonement, Gregory's view of, 50
Augustine, influence of on Gregory,
  24, 54

Barthes, Roland, 12
Behemoth: Aquinas's interpretation
  of, 85, 90; Calvin rejects allegorical
  interpretation of, 141, 142–44;
  identified with Satan, 48–50
Bellah, Robert N., 8
Besserman, Lawrence, 2, 156
Bildad, 43, 137–38; explanation of
  Job's lot, 63, 125. See also friends,
  Job's
Brenz, Johannes, 5, 228n.1
Brown, T. S., 3
Buber, Martin: critique of Jung, 167–
  68; critique of The Trial, 177, 186
Butler, Cuthbert, 22

Cajetan (Tommaso de Vio), 5, 228n.1
Calvin, John: on angels, 105, 112–13;
  compared to Aquinas, 122–23,
  126; on the church, 92; on creation, 92–93, 120, 135–38, 140–42,
  144–46, 149–50; on despair, 104–5;
  on divine power, 113–14, 147; doctrine of double justice, 105–6, 110–
  14, 116, 120, 147; on Elihu, 131–
  35; on the Epilogue, 147–52; on
  history, 8, 20, 36, 38, 92, 102, 120,
  135–36, 144, 151–52; doctrine of
  immortality, 91, 122, 147, 151; intellectual influences, 8–9; on Job's
  anger, 35, 121; on Job's sinfulness,
  144; ambivalence about Job, 45,
  100, 107–8, 114; compares Job and
  David, 96, 99–105, 117; on Job's
  friends, 99–100, 120, 122–25, 126,
  129–30, 132, 134, 147; on justice,
  19, 94, 109–13, 115–16, 118; literal
  interpretation of Leviathan and Behemoth of, 142–44; emphasis of
  on literal interpretation, 7, 20, 25,
  91, 141, 149; and modern interpreters, 160; on nature of God, 92,
  115, 117, 119–20, 121, 151; and
  noetic effect of sin, 94, 100, 125,
  150; and nominalism, 113; and

Calvin, John *(continued)*
   issue of perception, 19–20, 94–95,
   121, 122, 125, 130, 147, 149–50; on
   predestination, 92, 121; on providence, 5, 7–8, 91–93, 120, 121–22,
   126–28, 133–35, 138, 148, 151; on
   Satan, 40, 92–93, 105, 143–44; context of *Sermons on Job*, 5–8; and suffering, 34, 91, 99–100, 102, 117–
   18, 124, 148; on suffering of Old
   Testament figures, 96; and tension
   between revelation and hiddenness, 94, 102, 119–20, 122, 127–28,
   135–38, 141, 148, 153; theology
   summarized, 133; on whirlwind
   speech, 138–46
—exegesis compared: to Ambrose,
   99, 117; to Aquinas, 9–10, 74, 75,
   91, 94, 107, 108, 111–12, 114, 122–
   24, 127–28, 131–32, 139–40, 142,
   147, 149, 152–55; to Gregory, 9–10,
   91, 94, 99–104, 107, 108, 111–12,
   114, 117, 122, 131–32, 139–40,
   147, 149, 152–55; to Maimonides,
   9–10, 94, 143, 146, 150–55; to modern commentators, 158–62, 165–
   67, 189
Cassian, 24
Catry, Patrick, 25
church: adversities afflicting, 40, 42;
   Calvin and the suffering, 6–7; creation of demonstrates God's power,
   49
Cohen, Mark, 4
Courcelle, Pierre, 24

Dagens, Claude, 24
David, parallels with Job, 96–105, 117
deLubac, Henri, 3
Denis the Carthusian, 9, 205n.47
Derrida, Jacques, 12, 15
detachment, 53, 68, 108
Deuteronomy, 123–24
Dobbs-Weinstein, Idit, 83
Duns Scotus, 8
Dudden, F. Holmes, 22

Eco, Umberto, 12, 156
Elihu: Aquinas on, 131–33; Calvin
   on, 115, 131–35; on creation, 145;
   differs from other friends, 43, 74,
   131; Gregory on, 47, 131–33; on

justice, 139; angel of, in Maimonides's interpretation, 64–66;
   on providence, 133–35, 160
Eliphaz: Aquinas's interpretation of,
   74; Calvin's interpretation of, 112;
   and divine justice, 106, 123; explanation of Job's lot, 63, 125; quoted
   by Paul, 44; and perception, 45; discernment of providence, 75; identified with Satan, 180. *See also*
   friends, Job's
Epilogue: Calvin's interpretation of,
   148; commentators' difficulty with,
   89, 147
evil. *See* theodicy
exegesis: Aquinas's principles of, 20,
   71–73; Calvin's principles of, 5–9;
   Gregory's enduring influence on,
   91; Gregory's principles of, 20, 25–
   27; pedagogical purpose of, 4; perceptual implications of, 154; traditional presuppositions of, 18;
   principles of, compared, 20, 72,
   86, 106, 116
exegesis, history of: response to contemporary debates, 16–17; epistemological crisis and literary criticism, 10; philosophy of language,
   10, 12. *See also* Aquinas, Thomas;
   Calvin, John; Gregory the Great;
   Maimonides, Moses
Expositio super Iob ad litteram: context,
   5; dating, 70. *See also* Aquinas,
   Thomas

Fohrer, Georg, 156
Foucault, Michel, 13, 14, 18, 21
freedom, 29
friends, Job's: Aquinas's interpretation of, 73–75, 80–81; difference
   between Aquinas and Gregory concerning, 75; Calvin's interpretation
   of, 99–100, 120, 122–26, 129–30;
   Gregory's interpretation of, 20, 43–
   47; misperceive history, 134; rejected belief in immortality, 73, 75,
   122–23; Maimonides's interpretation of, 63; MacLeish's interpretation of, 174–75; on providence,
   123; exponents of retributive suffering, 44, 99, 123, 132, 171;
   Wells's interpretation of, 171–72.

See also Eliphaz; Bildad; Zophar; and Elihu
Frye, Northrop, 177

Gadamer, Hans-Georg, 10, 11, 16–18
Ganoczy, Alexandre, 8
Geertz, Clifford, 13, 190
Gerrish, Brian A., 93
Girard, René, critique of whirlwind speech, 48
Gillet, Robert, 24
gnosticism. *See* Jonas, Hans
Good, Edwin, 10, 157, 159–163
Gordis, Robert, 157, 159
Gregory the Great, 2–3; influence on Aquinas, 57; goal of detachment, 27–28, 35, 37, 39, 45, 53, 147; divine power resolves Book of Job, 48–52; exegetical methodology, 4, 18, 20, 25–27, 35–36, 44–47, 52–54, 91, 147; on freedom, 29; critique of Job's friends, 20, 43–47; on history, 26, 36–38; *Homilies on Ezekiel*, 41; praise of humility, 46, 114; perceives Job as patient, 35; and Job's sinfulness, 32, 51, 86, 107; and justice, 111; Neoplatonic metaphysics, 23–24, 26, 36–38, 52; theory of prophecy, 40–42, 53; on providence, 31, 38; understanding of Scripture, 25–26; centrality of suffering for, 23–24, 26–27, 153; meaning of suffering according to, 33–34, 45, 52, 117; mistrust of tranquillity, 29, 37; interpretation of whirlwind speech, 48–52, 111, 144
—exegesis compared: to Aquinas, 70–72, 73, 76–78, 82, 85–89; to Calvin, 9–10, 91, 94, 99–104, 107, 108, 111–12, 114, 117, 122, 131–32, 139–40, 147, 149, 152–55; to Maimonides, 35, 36; to modern commentators, 158, 165, 189. See also *Moralia in Job*
Guide of the Perplexed, intellectual context of, 55. *See also* Maimonides, Moses

Habel, Norman, 157–63
al-Ḥaziri, Judah, 57
Heller, Erich, 185

Henel, Ingeborg, 185, 187
historical-critical method, 156–57
history: Aquinas on, 36, 77, 129; Calvin on, 8, 20, 36, 38, 92, 102, 120, 135–36, 144, 151–52; realm of chaos, 88, 124, 127, 155; Deuteronomic view of, 75, 124, 134; Gregory on, 26, 36–38, 53–54; human exile in, 52–54; intelligibility of, 102; Job's understanding of, 36, 77–78, 122, 126, 127, 129–30, 135, 147, 148, 151–52, 155, 171; Job represents ambiguous nature of, 77–78, 126, 148; and perception, 20; relationship between nature and, 135–38, 141, 145–46, 150–52; and perception, 20; realm of providence, 88, 124; lowest level of reality, 24–26, 36; redemptive nature of, 42, 54, 144, 149; views of compared, 71, 88–90, 154
Homans, Peter, 163

immortality, doctrine of: Aquinas on, 71, 73, 74–76, 80–81, 153; Calvin on, 91, 122, 147, 151; modern interpretations of Job's belief in, 158–59; rejected, 171–72
Isidore, 83
Ivry, Alfred, 62, 65

Job: Book of, 31, 39, 157; and despair, 117; and detachment, 39, 122; faith of, 155; historical references to, 1, 156; understanding of history, 36, 77–78, 122, 126, 127, 129–30, 135, 147, 148, 151–52, 155, 171; and doctrine of immortality, 80, 130, 147; innocence of, 106–7; on justice, 109, 125–26, 155; inability to perceive God, 145; and perception, 67, 77; and sin of pride, 52, 140; progress of, 151; as prophet, 32, 39–41; protests meaninglessness, 172–73, 177; self-understanding of, 63, 68; sinfulness of, 32, 139–40, 144; and suffering, 31, 35, 174; as symbol, 153–54; temptation of, 103–4; themes in, 153; as type for Christ and church, 32, 39–40, 42; acquires wisdom through interiority, 38

John the Baptist, as righteous sufferer, 34
Jonas, Hans, 21, 189
Jung, Carl, 2, 18; compared to
Calvin's interpretation of Job, 166,
167; and dual nature of God, 164–
65, 166, 169; and the incarnation,
166–67; and Job's superior understanding, 166; and Satan, 167; and
transcendence, 167–68
justice, divine: and Job's arrogance,
140; Calvin and Job's quest for, 94–
95, 109–10, 113; Calvin's doctrine
of double justice, 105–6, 110–14,
116, 125–26, 147; God's will rule
of, 115; Gregory and, 48; Gregory's and Calvin's shared conclusion about, 51; human justice and,
110–11; and doctrine of immortality, 81, 90; and Job's innocence,
106; intelligibility of, 102; and justice of the Law, 112, 125–26; Maimonides and the question of, 67,
69; secret, 110, 111–12, 115–16,
125–26, 129; and modern interpretations of Job, 158–59; competing
views of, in Job, 116

Kafka, Franz, 2, 22; and absence of
God, 178; and question of innocence, 184–86; and issue of perception, 19, 186; *The Trial*, 177–78,
181–89
Kravitz, Leonard S., 64–65

LaCapra, Dominick, 13–16, 18
Lasine, Stuart, 185, 187
Leviathan: Aquinas's interpretation
of, 85, 90; Calvin rejects allegorical
interpretation of, 141, 142–44;
identified with Satan, 48–50
literal exegesis: Aquinas's view of 71–
72, 76–77; Calvin's view of, 72, 91,
116, 120, 141–43, 149; difficulties
in, 32; increasing importance of,
91, 154; Maimonides's, of Job's despair, 63
literary-critical interpretation, 157–63
Lombard, Peter, 8
Luther, Martin: parallels to Calvin,
119

McGrath, Alister E., 8
MacLeish, Archibald, 2, 18, 170, 173–
77
Maimonides, Moses: and the Active
Intellect, 64–68; influence on Aquinas, 57; critique of "Aristotelianism," 68, 128, 130; on authority, 63;
compared to Calvin, 151; cosmology of, 65; approves of Elihu, 132;
on nature of God, 61; historical
context of, 55–57; critical of imagination, 64; interpretation of Job,
59–70, 129; and Job's anger, 35; on
justice, 69; on perception, 18, 122,
153; and modern interpreters, 160;
on prophecy, 66; on providence,
20, 58, 61–63, 66–70, 88, 128; repentance as path to wisdom, 81;
view of Satan, 64, 70; understanding of Scripture, 59–61; on
suffering, 70; on wisdom, 63, 70
—exegesis compared: to Aquinas,
57–59, 71–72, 74, 79–83, 86–90; to
Calvin, 9–10, 94, 143, 146, 150–55;
to Gregory, 35–36; to modern commentators, 158–59, 165, 189
Mair, John, 8
Mann, Thomas, 181
Moralia in Job: internal coherency of,
23, 36; context of, 3; modern critiques of, 22; different than modern interpretations, 158; issue of
perception in, 23

nature: in modern interpretations of
Job, 161–62; fails to provide revela-
tion, 172
nature, divine, 165; remoteness of,
183
Neoplatonism: view of suffering, 117.
See also Gregory the Great
Nicholas of Lyra, 9
nominalism, 113, 118
Novick, Peter, 10

O'Brien, Patricia, 13
Oberman, Heiko A., 9
Oecolampadius, Johannes, 5, 228n.1

Paul, Saint, 44; view of history, 129–
31; as model sufferer, 28, 97

perception, 19–20; Calvin develops issue of, 94, 122, 124, 130, 146, 149–50; impact of Enlightenment, 21; as exegetical device, 38, 39; of friends and readers, 47; hiddenness of God, as temptation, 105, 128; limitation of human, 145, 149–50, 149, 189; human, and remoteness of God, 156, 181; issue structuring interpretations of Job, 24, 121, 152; as dilemma in modern interpretations, 159–60; Job's, 67, 88, 102, 125–27; Jung's critique of modern human, 169; levels of, 68; and metaphors of sight, 125–26, 189–90; distinction between nature and history as issue of, 138, 145–46, 152; of order key to Aquinas's interpretation, 74, 124; perceptual battle within Job, 128–31; and self-delusion, 187; and self-knowledge, 45; noetic effect of sin, 94, 100; and suffering, 30–31, 117, 171; traditional faith in, 18; as theme in *The Trial*, 182, 186–87; product of virtue, 46; in Western thought, 189

perspective: central to Calvin's exegesis, 121; limitation of human, 181; shift between human and divine, 34; structures Job, 20, 52, 94, 121, 152–53; Job's limitation of, 102; stressed by Maimonides, 67; changed by suffering, 45

Pliny, 83

Politzer, Heinz, 185, 188

Pope, Marvin, 157

power, divine, 113–15, 160–61, 165; Aquinas's emphasis on, 84–85; connection to resolves Book of Job, 48–52; Calvin's worry about absolute, 113; demonstrated, 49; and temptation of spiritual pride, 86

pride: danger of, 107; Gregory criticizes Job's, 51; Maimonides and Aquinas emphasize, 83, 84; sin of, 46, 52

providence: Aquinas's view of, 57, 74, 79, 88, 102; Aristotle's view of, 56, 63; error of "Aristotelianism," 68, 128; Calvin on, 91–93; contrast

between Aquinas and Maimonides concerning, 79; Elihu defends, 133–34; incomprehensibility of, 31, 38, 93, 94, 104, 120, 121–22, 126–28, 145; new emphasis on, in interpretation of Job, 4, 55; Job defends, 128–29; Job doubts, 108, 128; manifestation of, 92–93; in modern interpretations of Job, 161; evident in nature, 141–42; and perception, 146; tension between hiddenness and visibility of, in Calvin, 102, 119–20, 121–22, 128–29, 146; theme for all premodern exegetes, 4, 20–21. *See also* Aquinas, Thomas; Calvin, John; Gregory the Great; and Maimonides, Moses

Raffel, Charles, 61

Raguenier, M. Dennis, 5

Reines, Alvin J., 61

Reuter, Karl, 8

Riceour, Paul, 11–12

righteousness, human, 51; of God, 51

Robertson, Ritchie, 182, 185–86, 187

Rorty, Richard, 14

Rudavsky, Tamar, 61

Satan: contest between God and, 33, 77, 86; identified with Behemoth and Leviathan, 48–50, 85, 90; in Maimonides, 64; tempts Job, 104; in Weisel, 180

Sermons on Job, context, 5–8. *See also* Calvin, John

Smalley, Beryl, 22

Stadtland-Neumann, Hiltrud, 8

Steinmetz, David C., 17, 118

Straw, Carol, 24, 27–28

suffering: allegorical/tropological exegesis of, 117; Aquinas's understanding of, 76–79, 87–88; causes of, according to Gregory, 33; definitive of Christian life, 95; facilitates interiority, 24; Gregory's view of, 23; inexplicable, 102–3, 117–18; of the just, 34; Maimonides's view of, 70, 87, 88; meaninglessness of, 176–77; nonretributive, 33, 34, 91, 99, 121; of Old Testament figures,

suffering *(continued)*
96; pedagogical nature of, 148; positive effects of, 27, 28–31, 44, 45, 52, 97–98, 99, 100, 117; as punishment, 99–100, 123, 124; reasons for, according to Calvin, 103, 133; and sin, 44; shift away from therapeutic notion of, 55; as unjust, 171

Terrien, Samuel, 157, 158, 160
theodicy: not issue for Gregory, 48; Aquinas's explanation of, 5, 58
Thomas of Cantimpre, 83
ibn Tibbon, Samuel, 56
Torrance, T. F., 8
Tracy, David, 1
Tsevat, Matitiahu, 48
Typology, 25

Viguie, Ariste, 7

Weisheipl, James A., 5, 71
Wells, H. G., 2, 170–73
Wendel, Françoise, 8
whirlwind speech: Aquinas's exegesis of, 72, 81, 83; Calvin's interpretation of, 69, 138–46; Calvin's reading of, compared to Gregory and Aquinas, 139–40, 143–44, 149; Calvin's reading compared to Maimonides's, 146, 149; about creation, 143; divine deliverance expressed in, 34; Elihu echoes truth of, 132; Gregory's exegesis of, 48–52; demonstrates Job's limited understanding, 144–46; Kafka's representation of, 184; MacLeish's interpretation of, 175; Maimonides's interpretation of, 69–70, 82; modern critiques of, 48; in modern readings of Job, 162

White, Hayden, 13–15, 18
Wiesel, Elie, 2, 177; absence of God, 178–79; *The Trial of God,* 178–81
Wright, John H., 57

Yaffe, Martin D., 82–83

Zophar, 43, 122–23, 126; Aquinas's interpretation of, 74, 129; view of history, 129; explanation of Job's lot, 63, 123; mistaken, according to Calvin, 124. *See also* friends, Job's

DATE DUE

JUN 20 1997			
APR 1 9 2000			